Econometric Society Monographs No.

Mathematical economics

ECONOMETRIC SOCIETY MONOGRAPHS

Editors:
Jean-Michel Grandmont, *Centre d'Études Prospectives d'Économie Mathématique Appliquées à la Planification, Paris*
Charles F. Manski, *University of Wisconsin, Madison*

Editor for this volume:
Frank Hahn, *Cambridge University*

Editorial advisor for this volume:
Hugo Sonnenschein, *Princeton University*

The Econometric Society is an international society for the advancement of economic theory in relation to statistics and mathematics. The Econometric Society Monograph Series is designed to promote the publication of original research contributions of high quality in mathematical economics and theoretical and applied econometrics.

Other titles in the series:

Werner Hildenbrand, editor. *Advances in Economic Theory*
Werner Hildenbrand, editor. *Advances in Econometrics*
G. S. Maddala. *Limited-Dependent and Qualitative Variables in Econometrics*
Jean-Michel Grandmont. *Money and Value*
Franklin Fisher. *Disequilibrium Foundations of Equilibrium Economics*
Bezalel Peleg. *Game Theoretic Analysis of Voting in Committees*
Roger Bowden and Darrell Turkington. *Instrumental Variables*
Andreu Mas-Colell. *The Theory of General Economic Equilibrium*
James J. Heckman and Burton Singer. *Longitudinal Analysis of Labor Market Data*
Cheng Hsiao. *Analysis of Panel Data*

Gerard Debreu. (Photograph by G. Paul Bishop, Berkeley, California.)

Mathematical economics: Twenty papers of Gerard Debreu

GERARD DEBREU

University of California, Berkeley

INTRODUCTION BY WERNER HILDENBRAND

CAMBRIDGE
UNIVERSITY PRESS

Published by the Press Syndicate of the University of Cambridge
The Pitt Building, Trumpington Street, Cambridge CB2 1RP
40 West 20th Street, New York, NY 10011-4211, USA
10 Stamford Road, Oakleigh, Melbourne 3166, Australia

© Cambridge University Press 1983

First published 1983
Reprinted 1985
First paperback edition 1986
Reprinted 1989, 1993, 1995

Printed in the United States of America

Library of Congress Cataloging-in-Publication Data is available

A catalogue record for this book is available form the British Library

ISBN 0-521-23736-X hardback
ISBN 0-521-33561-2 paperback

Contents

Contents

Acknowledgments for reprinted articles

The Coefficient of Resource Utilization, *Econometrica*, **19**, 273–92 (1951). Reprinted by permission of the Econometric Society.

A Social Equilibrium Existence Theorem, *Proceedings of the National Academy of Sciences*, **38**, 886–93 (1952).

A Classical Tax-Subsidy Problem, *Econometrica*, **22**, 14–22 (1954). Reprinted by permission of the Econometric Society.

Existence of an Equilibrium for a Competitive Economy (with K. J. Arrow), *Econometrica*, **22**, 265–90 (1954). Reprinted by permission of the Econometric Society.

Valuation Equilibrium and Pareto Optimum, *Proceedings of the National Academy of Sciences*, **40**, 588–92 (1954).

Representation of a Preference Ordering by a Numerical Function, in *Decision Processes*, R. M. Thrall, C. H. Coombs, and R. L. Davis, eds., Wiley, New York, 159–65 (1954). Reprinted by permission of the editor R. M. Thrall.

Market Equilibrium, *Proceedings of the National Academy of Sciences*, **42**, 876–8 (1956).

Une Economique de l'incertain, *Economie Appliquée*, **13**, 111–16 (1960), translated as Economics under Uncertainty, by Shantayanan Devarajan. Reprinted by permission of Shantayanan Devarajan.

Topological Methods in Cardinal Utility Theory, reprinted from *Mathematical Methods in the Social Sciences, 1959*, edited by Kenneth J. Arrow, Samuel Karlin, and Patrick Suppes, pp. 16–26. Reprinted with the permission of the publisher, Stanford University Press, © 1960 by the Board of Trustees of the Leland Stanford Junior University.

New Concepts and Techniques for Equilibrium Analysis, *International Economic Review*, **3**, 257–73 (1962). Reprinted by permission of the International Economic Review.

A Limit Theorem on the Core of an Economy (with H. Scarf), *International Economic Review*, **4**, 235–46 (1963). Reprinted by permission of the International Economic Review.

Continuity Properties of Paretian Utility, *International Economic Review*, **5**, 285–93 (1964). Reprinted by permission of the International Economic Review.

Neighboring Economic Agents, *La Décision*, Colloques Internationaux du Centre National de la Recherche Scientifique no. 171, Paris, 85–90 (1969). Reprinted by permission of the Centre National de la Recherche Scientifique.

Economies with a Finite Set of Equilibria, *Econometrica*, **38**, 387–92 (1970). Reprinted by permission of the Econometric Society.

Smooth Preferences, *Econometrica*, **40**, 603–15 (1972). Reprinted by permission of the Econometric Society.

Smooth Preferences: A Corrigendum, *Econometrica*, **44**, 831–2 (1976). Reprinted by permission of the Econometric Society.

Excess Demand Functions, *Journal of Mathematical Economics*, **1**, 15–21 (1974). Reprinted by permission of North-Holland Publishing Company.

The Rate of Convergence of the Core of an Economy, *Journal of Mathematical Economics*, **2**, 1–7 (1975). Reprinted by permission of North-Holland Publishing Company.

Four Aspects of the Mathematical Theory of Economic Equilibrium, *Proceedings of the International Congress of Mathematicians*, Vancouver, Vol. 1, 65–77 (1974). Reprinted by permission of the Canadian Mathematical Society.

Regular Differentiable Economies, *American Economic Review*, **66**, 280–87 (1976). Reprinted by permission of the American Economic Association.

Least Concave Utility Functions, *Journal of Mathematical Economics*, **3**, 121–9 (1976). Reprinted by permission of North-Holland Publishing Company.

Introduction

by Werner Hildenbrand

Alles, was Gegenstand des wissenschaftlichen Denkens überhaupt sein kann, verfällt, sobald es zur Bildung einer Theorie reif ist, der axiomatischen Methode und damit mittelbar der Mathematik.[1]

David Hilbert

The opening address on the occasion of an important retrospective of a great artist is not expected to include a detailed analysis of all exhibits. Rather, the artist and his work are set in their context in the history of art; those features that characterize his work are highlighted and related to earlier and contemporary contributions. This is what I shall try to do on the present occasion; the reprinting of twenty scientific papers of Gerard Debreu.

The striking feature that characterizes Debreu's scientific contributions is that they are both *general* and *simple* – general in the sense of universal, in contrast to ad hoc specific or particular, simple certainly not in the sense of elementary, facile, or effortless, but in the sense of pure in contrast to compound and complex. To sense the depth of Debreu's contributions, one has to understand them in full generality. An appreciation of the simplicity of his contributions requires, alas, a certain familiarity with some elementary but basic concepts of modern mathematics. Some knowledge of set theory, linear spaces and convex analysis, general topology, measure theory, differential topology ... is, indeed, a prerequisite. I assume that only

---

[1] Everything, which may possibly be subject to scientific thought, as soon as it is ready for the development of a theory, comes within the scope of the axiomatic method and thus becomes treatable by means of mathematics. From D. Hilbert, Axiomatisches Denken, *Mathematische Annalen*, **78** (1918): 415.

1

a few will object to my claim that to read Debreu's contributions requires a substantial intellectual effort from every reader. Nevertheless, the formulation of the economic problem that motivated the work and the statement of the main results can always be grasped quite easily.

To a traditionally educated economist, who does not have a training in modern mathematics, Debreu's contributions might appear, at first glance, incomprehensibly "abstract." There is, then, a great temptation to dismiss the work as "too abstract" (with the implication of "unrealistic" whatever this term may mean) rather than to invest the required intellectual effort.[2] In this respect Debreu has never compromised just as he has never followed fashions in economic research. I have often heard him say that every economic problem requires its own appropriate mathematical treatment. The economic problem determines the mathematical tool that is applied to obtain a precise formulation of the problem and to analyze it; one does not take a mathematical tool and then look for applications.

In this context one may think of Debreu's statement in the Preface of *Theory of Value*, "Outstanding among these influences has been the work ... which freed mathematical economics from its traditions of differential calculus and compromises with logic."[3] It seems to me that this statement has often been misunderstood. It definitely does not imply the unqualified statement that the use of calculus is a compromise with logic. Rather, it emphasizes the fact that fixed-point theory and convex analysis, and not differential calculus, are the appropriate mathematical tools for studying the existence of competitive equilibrium and the basic welfare propositions in a general framework – and this is after all the subject of *Theory of Value*.

Debreu's aim – presenting his analysis of an economic problem in as general and simple a form as possible, even if a substantial intellectual effort from the reader is required – is not exclusively motivated by purely aesthetical considerations, although no doubt aesthetics play an important role in Debreu's thinking. I am convinced that Debreu profoundly distrusts any conclusions that are only based on examples or specific ad hoc

---

[2] I cannot refrain from repeating here the quotation from Bertrand Russell cited by F. Hahn in his inaugural lecture in Cambridge: "Many people have a passionate hatred of abstraction, chiefly, I think, because of its intellectual difficulty; but as they do not wish to give this reason they invent all sorts of others that sound grand. They say that all abstraction is falsification, and that as soon as you have left out any aspect of something actual you have exposed yourself to the risk of fallacy in arguing from its remaining aspects alone. Those who argue in this way are in fact concerned with matters quite other than those that concern science." F. H. Hahn, *On the Notion of Equilibrium in Economics*, Cambridge University Press (1973), p. 7.

[3] G. Debreu, *Theory of Value. An Axiomatic Analysis of Economic Equilibrium*, New York: Wiley (1959), p. viii.

assumptions. There are numerous examples in economic theory where the conclusions of an analysis – sometimes even the conceptual formulation – depend crucially on the specific structure of the example and are not at all robust.

Yet there is another characteristic feature of Debreu's scientific contributions. The generality and simplicity are accompanied by a certain austerity. Debreu's style of writing can hardly be called exuberant. This is mainly due to the axiomatic method that he applies in all his writings and, also, to a certain extent, to a trait of his character. Debreu does not like to speculate in public. Whatever he writes is definitive. This is what F. Hahn probably had in mind when he wrote the following lines in reviewing Debreu's *Theory of Value*:

> It is clear that it was Debreu's intention to provide a definitive statement of the theory of competitive equilibrium where possible and to eschew all those problems which have not yet been solved in an equally satisfactory manner. In this he certainly succeeds, but I believe that he was perhaps not well-advised to deny the reader the benefit of his reflections on a number of problems directly arising from his work.[4]

1 The axiomatic method

Debreu presents his scientific contributions in the most honest way possible by explicitly stating all underlying assumptions and refraining at any stage of the analysis from flowery interpretations that might divert attention from the restrictiveness of the assumptions and lead the reader to draw false conclusions. More than anybody else he has contributed to and pursued the axiomatization of economic theory.

The axiomatic method is of course old. Indeed there had already been a few axiomatic treatments in economic theory prior to Debreu. The contributions of A. Wald (1933–6),[5] *Theory of Games and Economic Behavior* (1944) of von Neumann and Morgenstern,[6] T. Koopmans's *Activity Analysis of Production and Allocation* (1951),[7] and Arrow's *Social Choice and Individual Value* (1951)[8] are outstanding examples. The axiomatic method, however, has never been applied in economics as

---

[4] F. H. Hahn, Review of Theory of Value, *Journal of Political Economy*, **69** (1961): 204.

[5] A. Wald, Über die eindeutige positive Lösbarkeit der neuen Produktionsgleichungen, *Ergebnisse eines mathematischen Kolloquiums*, No. 6 (1933/4): 1220; Über die Produktionsgleichungen der ökonomischen "Wertlehre," *Ergebnisse eines mathematischen Kolloquiums*, No. 7 (1934/5): 1–6; Über einige Gleichungssysteme der mathematischen Ökonomie, *Zeitschrift für Nationalökonomie*, No. 7 (1936): 637–70.

[6] J. von Neumann and O. Morgenstern, *Theory of Games and Economic Behavior*, Princeton: Princeton University Press (1944).

[7] T. Koopmans, *Activity Analysis of Production and Allocation*, New York: Wiley (1951).

[8] K. Arrow, *Social Choice and Individual Value*. New York: Wiley (1951).

forcefully as by Debreu in his classic monograph *Theory of Value, An Axiomatic Analysis of Economic Equilibrium* (1959).

Let me briefly recall the main characteristics of an axiomatic theory of a certain economic phenomenon as formulated by Debreu.

> First, the primitive concepts of the economic analysis are selected, and then, each one of these primitive concepts is represented by a mathematical object.

In *Theory of Value* the primitive concepts are the commodity space, the price system, consumption units (characterized by individual preferences, individual initial endowments, and profit shares), and production units (characterized by their set of feasible production plans). The commodity space is represented mathematically by a linear space; the price system is represented by a linear functional on the commodity space; and preferences are represented by binary relations. . . . Given the representations of these primitive concepts, derived concepts can now be defined, for example, demand, supply, attainable state or equilibrium.

> Second, assumptions on the mathematical representations of the primitive concepts are made explicit and are fully specified. Mathematical analysis then establishes the consequences of these assumptions in the form of theorems.

In *Theory of Value*, for example, the existence theorem is obtained from the assumptions that the commodity space is a finite-dimensional real vector space; that there is a given finite number of consumption and production units; furthermore, that preferences are continuous, transitive, complete, convex, and so on.

I would like to emphasize the qualitative difference of the first and second step in forming an axiomatic theory. The first step is more fundamental than the second because it defines the conceptual framework in which the model receives a specific mathematical structure. It is likely that during the development of a theory certain assumptions will be modified or weakened. This, indeed, has happened to a large extent in Walrasian equilibrium theory. The primitive concepts, however, did not change. For example, Arrow and Debreu (1954),[9] in their existence theorem for competitive equilibria, assume that preferences are complete, transitive, and convex. Later it was shown that completeness and transitivity of preferences can be dropped if one keeps convexity, and completeness and convexity can be dropped if the finite set of consumption units is replaced by a continuum of consumption units with transitive preferences. Similarly,

---

[9] K. Arrow and G. Debreu, Existence of an Equilibrium for a Competitive Economy, *Econometrica*, **22** (1954): 265–90. [Chapter 4 in this book.]

on the production side, the assumptions of free disposal and irreversibility for the production set also turned out to be unnecessarily strong.

According to Debreu, any axiomatic economic theory has to pass the severe test of removing all the economic interpretations interspersed throughout the model and of checking whether its bare mathematical structure stands by itself. When Debreu received the doctorate *honoris causa* from the Rheinische Friedrich-Wilhelm-Universität at Bonn (1977), he gave an address on "The Axiomatization of Economic Theory," in which he said:

Among the many consequences of the transformation in methodology that the field of economic theory underwent in the recent past, the clarity of expression that it made possible is perhaps one of the greatest gains that it has yielded. The very definition of an economic concept is usually subject to a substantial margin of ambiguity. An axiomatized theory substitutes for an ambiguous economic concept a mathematical object that is subject to entirely definite rules of reasoning. No doubt the economic interpretation of the primitive mathematical objects of the theory is free, and this is indeed one of the sources of the power of the axiomatic method. As an illustration of this freedom of interpretation, consider the concept of an economic commodity which was at first understood to be a good or a service with well defined physical characteristics, such as steel of a certain type. It was later perceived that by including in the definition of a commodity the date and the location at which it is available, one could introduce time and space in economic theory without any change in its formal structure by a simple reinterpretation of a primitive concept. A still richer interpretation was proposed in 1953 by Kenneth Arrow in his study of an economy whose agents are faced with uncertainty about their future environment. In the language of the statistician, we say that this uncertainty is due to the unknown choice that nature will make from the set of possible states of the world. The definition of an economic commodity now specifies in addition to its physical characteristics, its date and its location, the state of the world in which it will be available. Here again the unaltered formal theory is extended to cover a wide new range of economic phenomena by a novel interpretation of the same primitive concept.

But while a primitive concept of an axiomatic theory·admits different interpretations a theorist who has chosen one of them succeeds in communicating his intended meaning with little ambiguity because of the completely specified formal context in which he operates. Indeed the more developed this context is, the richer it is in theorems and in other primitive concepts, the smaller the margin of ambiguity in the intended interpretation of the theory will be.

The axiomatization of a certain part of economic theory also requires a full specification of the assumptions under which any one of its conclusions is asserted. Thereby it protects its practitioners against one of the common dangers of informal economic theory where conclusions that are valid under a set of assumptions that is not made entirely explicit, are sometimes applied to situations in which some of those assumptions are violated. More positively, the complete specification of assumptions, the exact statement of conclusions, and the rigor of the deductions of an axiomatized study provide a secure foundation on which the construction of economic theory can proceed. Moreover the possibility for research workers to be able to use directly the results of their predecessors is a decisive factor in the rapid development of a scientific field. The reasons I have listed alone would explain why the proponents of a particular economic theory welcome its axiomatization. Several of these reasons also explain why the opponents of the same economic theory may welcome its axiomatic form since this brings out more sharply the aspects of that theory to which they object. A good illustration is provided by the criticism of the theory of general equilibrium in recent years. Thus axiomatization facilitates the detection of logical errors within the model, and perhaps more importantly it facilitates the detection of conceptual errors in the formulation of the theory and in its interpretations. The recent effort toward the axiomatization of economic theory therefore seems to be fully supported by Francis Bacon's assertion in the *Novum Organum*: "citius emergit veritas ex errore quam ex confusione" (truth emerges sooner from error than from confusion).

In this spirit let us look at Debreu's *Theory of Value, An Axiomatic Analysis of Economic Equilibrium*, and recall the main limitations of this theory. These have been recognized from the outset, in particular, by the founders of the theory. I mention them here in order to demonstrate that one sees only one aspect of the analysis if one's attention is confined to the fact that a certain proposition holds under specified assumptions; sometimes it is more important to understand why the proposition no longer holds if some of the assumptions are not satisfied. This insight then paves the way for new inquiries and the development of richer models. In this sense Debreu's fundamental work is the benchmark for the most important recent developments in economic theory.

First, by definition, all commodities are "private" and external effects among consumption and production units are excluded. Indeed, the individual characteristics of an economic agent are defined independently of the actions taken by the other agents. Thus the theory restricts the interdependence among economic agents to a bare minimum; namely, the interdependence through markets. We know today that the existence of a "competitive equilibrium" can still be established if various kinds of externalities prevail. But in this generality the concept of equilibrium loses some of its much warranted properties. Typically it is not Pareto optimal. Furthermore, the price system at equilibrium does not decentralize individual decisions in the sense that individual decisions are determined only by the price system and individual characteristics. One might mention here that, strictly speaking, even in *Theory of Value* the price system does not convey sufficient information for perfect decentralization. Indeed, if positive profits are possible at equilibrium, the consumer has to know the profits of those firms of which he holds a share. On the other hand, if this problem is avoided by assuming constant returns to scale in production, which implies zero profit in equilibrium, then the level of the optimal production plan is not determined by the price system.

Second, the concept of equilibrium is built on the hypothesis that a *complete* set of prices is "quoted" and regarded by all economic agents as exogenously given. Debreu did not present *Theory of Value* as an equilibrium theory for a "perfectly competitive" economy. Actually the term "perfect competition" does not even appear in *Theory of Value*. (In Arrow–Debreu (1954) this concept is defined as follows: "perfect competition prevails, in the sense, that each producer and consumer regards the prices paid and received as independent of his own choices"[10]). *Theory of Value* shows the consequences of this hypothesis, which really consists of two parts. The first is the assumption of a *complete* price system – for every commodity there is a price that specifies the amount (in accounting units) that has to be paid *now* in order to obtain one unit of that commodity at a specified location, time period, and event. With such a complete price system and no transaction costs there is, of course, no need for money. The second part is the assumption that prices are quoted and regarded as given. A partial theoretical explanation of the second part of the hypothesis was given later by the theory of the core (see Section 4), and more recently, by the noncooperative approach to the theory of perfect competition. I hardly have to stress the heroic nature of the first part of the hypothesis. An important part of recent research has been devoted to weakening this assumption.

Third, there is a conceptual difficulty with the time horizon, which is assumed to extend over finitely many periods. If the horizon is short, one has to specify what happens afterward. To avoid this problem, one might consider a very long horizon (possibly infinitely many periods). Since all contracts are made at the beginning of time, one not only increases the number of future markets but also encounters the generation problem. Human life is finite and to envisage contracts with unborn agents is somewhat ambitious. These conceptual difficulties, together with others, show that equilibrium theory should reflect the sequential character of real markets. This consideration led to the development of the theory of temporary equilibria and of overlapping generation models.

Fourth, "perfect competition" and the assumption of a given finite number of production units is, in a sense, a conceptual contradiction. The problem of "entry" has recently attracted great attention. Also, increasing returns to scale and fixed costs in production are not covered by the analysis.

No doubt there are other problems that are not satisfactorily treated in *Theory of Value* – uncertainty and incomplete information, transaction costs, various kinds of market imperfections, just to mention some key words – but in every case it becomes clear that Debreu's fundamental work is, as claimed above, the benchmark for all these new investigations.

[10] Ibid., p. 265.

Before discussing in detail some of Debreu's contributions that are reprinted in this volume, I would like to give a biographical sketch.

In 1948 two young French mathematicians, both keen to learn modern economic theory, tossed a coin to let fortune decide which of them should be proposed by Maurice Allais – the leading French theoretical economist at that time – for a Rockefeller Fellowship. Debreu won the toss, and thus fortune may have played a decisive role in his personal and professional life and in the development of mathematical economics.

Gerard Debreu was born on July 4, 1921 in Calais, France. In 1941 he was admitted to the Ecole Normale Supérieure where he studied mathematics and physics. Having served in the French army during the last year of World War II, he then passed the *concours d'agrégation de Mathématiques* in 1946 and became a Research Associate of the Centre National de la Recherche Scientifique in Paris. As a Rockefeller Fellow, Debreu first spent six months at Harvard in 1949, went to Berkeley during the summer, and spent part of the fall at the Cowles Commission in Chicago. In the winter of 1950 he studied the work of the Swedish School at Uppsala, and then spent the spring with Ragnar Frisch in Oslo.

After these *Wanderjahre* he joined the Cowles Commission and moved with it to Yale University in 1955, where it became the Cowles Foundation and Debreu was made Associate Professor of Economics. In 1954 he was elected a Fellow of the Econometric Society. A first version of *Theory of Value* was presented as a Doctor of Science thesis at the University of Paris in 1956.

During the academic year 1960–1 Debreu was a Fellow of the Center for Advanced Study in the Behavioral Sciences at Stanford. It was there in "sunny California," that Debreu, like other Frenchmen before him, began to doubt the popular fairy tale, that God on earth could only choose to live in France. In 1962 Debreu became Professor of Economics and in 1975, also of Mathematics, at the University of California in Berkeley – positions he still holds today. From 1969 to 1971 he was Vice-President and President of the Econometric Society. Since 1970 he has been Fellow of the American Academy of Arts and Sciences, became Chevalier de la Légion d'Honneur in 1976, and was made a Member of the National Academy of Sciences (U.S.) in 1977. Debreu holds honorary degrees, Doctor *honoris causa* of Economics from the Universities of Bonn, Germany (1977), Lausanne, Switzerland (1980), and Northwestern University, U.S.A. (1981). He is a Distinguished Fellow of The American Economic Association (1982).

2   Contributions to welfare economics

One of the first pieces of economics that Debreu studied was the book by M. Allais, *A la Recherche d'une Discipline Economique* (1943), better known today under the title *Traité d'Economie Pure* (1953).[11] In this treatise Allais presented and substantially extended the thoughts of the Lausanne school, that is, Walrasian general equilibrium analysis and Paretian optimality theory. The latter theory was considered particularly relevant by some economists for the postwar economy in France. At that time France was faced with an exceptional variety of economic problems, postwar reconstruction, overseas wars and difficulties with colonial territories, a series of nationalizations (electricity, gas, coal mining, public transportation), and the launching of nationwide planning. In this economic situation the analysis of efficient allocation of scarce economic resources was considered, with good reason, as a most important and relevant task for a theorist who wanted to understand the economic difficulties that had to be faced.

Therefore it is not surprising that one of Debreu's first publications in economics, "The Coefficient of Resource Utilization" in 1951[12] dealt with Paretian welfare economics.

Before summarizing Debreu's main contributions to this subject, I would like to give some historical background.

The belief that perfect competition leads to an "optimal" state of the economy goes back at least to the time of the physiocrats and Adam Smith. The exact contents of this belief, nevertheless, did not become clear until the notion of an "optimal state" was precisely formulated. As long as the notion of "optimum" was connected with the concept of an "appropriate" distribution of income and wealth – a view shared by many nineteenth century economists, among them Marshall and Wicksell – there is clearly no reason why a competitive equilibrium of any economy should be optimal in this sense.

For the first time the problem was adequately formulated by V. Pareto in his *Cours d'Economie Politique* (1896–7)[13] and, more extensively, in his *Manuel d'Economie Politique* (1906),[14] where he wrote,

Consider any position, and assume that we move away from it by a very small amount, consistent with the restrictions. If in so doing the welfare of the individuals of the collectivity is increased, it is obvious that the new position is more advantageous to each one of them . . . Moreover, the welfare of some of them can remain the same, without changing these conclusions. . . . These considerations lead

---

[11] M. Allais, *A la Recherche d'une Discipline Economique*, Vol. 1, Paris: Ateliers Industria (1943); deuxième édition, *Traité d'Economie Pure*. Paris: Imprimerie Nationale et Centre National de la Recherche Scientifique (1953).

[12] G. Debreu, The Coefficient of Resource Utilization, *Econometrica*, **19** (1951): 273–91. [Chapter 1 in this book.]

[13] V. Pareto, *Cours d'Economie Politique*, Vol. 1 (1896) and Vol. 2 (1897), Paris: Pichon, here: Vol. 2, notes 720–30 (1896/1897).

[14] V. Pareto, *Manuel d'Economie Politique*, Paris: V. Giard and E. Brière (1909), Chapter VI, Sections 33–64 and Appendix 89.

to defining the position of maximum ophelimity to be one from which it is impossible to move a very small distance, in such a way that the ophelimities of the individuals, except for some which remain constant, all increase.[15]

If one drops the qualification "very small" for a move, then one obtains the standard definition of optimum that is referred to in the literature as *Pareto optimum*. This definition of relative maximum welfare for a society had, in fact, been given earlier in 1881 by Edgeworth in his *Mathematical Psychics*[16] as part of his definition of the contract curve (see Section 4).[17]

Pareto showed graphically in an "Edgeworth box" that every competitive equilibrium is optimal. He represented the box (Figure 1) in a way in which we are used to draw it and not in Edgeworth's original version (see Figure 1, p. 28) in *Mathematical Psychics*. Pareto's argument (Chapter VI, Section 35) is well known: He first observes that at an equilibrium the two indifference curves *t* and *s* are tangent and then shows that this implies optimality.

There are obviously two interpretations of Pareto's Figure 50: a *local* one – at an equilibrium as well as at an optimum, the marginal rate of substitution is equal for both agents – or a *global* interpretation – the tangent (the straight line) through an equilibrium as well as through an optimum, say, the point *c*, separates the two indifference curves *t* and *s*. The latter interpretation, which is deeper and captures the essence of the problem, is, as I shall show, Debreu's starting point.

As a matter of fact, Pareto failed in the Appendix (Sections 89–92) of his *Manuel* . . . to treat the problem by means of differential calculus. If I am not mistaken, a great part of the literature after Pareto and up to the early fifties just filled this gap by using the Lagrangean multiplier method. But whenever this method is applicable, then it is not really required because a pure geometrical argument leads to the same result,[18] namely, at a competitive equilibrium as well as at an optimum there is equality of marginal rates of substitution between any given pair of commodities for all economic agents.

O. Lange wrote in his famous article, "The Foundation of Welfare Economics" of 1942 that "The equations . . . [the above conditions] . . . contain *in nuce* most theorems of welfare economics, e.g., all the propositions in Pigou's *Economics of Welfare*. The only theorems not contained

---

[15] V. Pareto, *Manual of Political Economy*, translated by A. Schweir, London: Macmillan (1971), pp. 451–2.

[16] F. Y. Edgeworth, *Mathematical Psychics*, London: P. Kegan (1881), pp. 23, 27.

[17] In a letter of January 1892 (see Lettere a Maffeo Pantaleoni 1890–1923, edited by Gabriele de Rosa, Rome, 1962) Pareto refers to Edgeworth's *Mathematical Psychics*. In the relevant parts of his *Cours* . . . and his *Manuel*. . . . Pareto, however, does not give credit to Edgeworth. We may note in passing that even Walras was not given full credit by Pareto.

[18] For example, Allais (1943), Chapter IV, note 266.

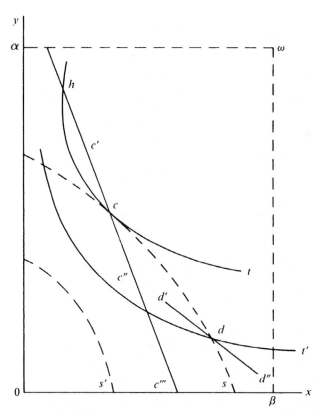

Figure 1   Figure 50 in Pareto's *Manuel d'Economie Politique*, Paris, V. Giard and E. Brière, 1909, p. 355.

in these equations are those which relate to the optimum distribution of incomes."[19] If this is so, not much progress had been made in Paretian welfare economics in half a century!

The limitations of all contributions prior to the fifties consist in the fact that they use marginal rates of substitution in characterizing an optimum. However, the marginal rate of substitution is not a primitive concept of the theory; it is a derived concept and may not be defined by lack of differentiability, of either the utility functions or, more important, the production relationships – the latter became particularly apparent with the development of linear activity analysis by T. Koopmans in the late forties. Further, and the most fundamental limitation, if one takes into account that the quantities of certain commodities for some economic agents at an

[19] O. Lange, The Foundations of Welfare Economics, *Econometrica*, **10** (1942): 215–28, here p. 218.

optimum may be zero, then the equality of the marginal rates of substitution is no longer a necessary condition for optimality.

Obviously, the analysis of efficient allocation of economic resources would be of little relevance to the actual world if it were not applicable to situations where the commodities are sharply defined, that is to say, in which a commodity is defined by its physical characteristics as well as by the time, location, and possibly the state of the world of its availability. As a consequence, in this case, the individual consumption and production plans will typically have some zero coordinates. Thus one is forced to consider as the typical case those situations that are excluded in the traditional analysis. In this situation the economic problem definitely required a new mathematical tool, which allowed an extension of the preceding global interpretation of Pareto's Figure 50.

Inspired by the recent development in linear programming and duality theory, and in particular by T. Koopmans's linear activity analysis Debreu and K. Arrow independently and simultaneously used convex analysis (essentially the separation theorem for convex sets) in order to extend the classical welfare propositions. Debreu presented his results in the summer of 1950 at the Meeting of the Econometric Society at Harvard, while at the same time K. Arrow presented his results at the Second Berkeley Symposium on Mathematical Statistics and Probability.[20]

Their models do not differ essentially. Debreu allows for a finite number of independent production units (firms) with closed and convex production sets and assumes free disposal of all commodities, whereas Arrow treats production as a choice from one aggregate, compact, and convex production set. Debreu requires convex preferences without satiation, whereas Arrow allows satiation but assumes strongly convex preferences.

The essential arguments of Debreu are easily explained because they are geometric, which is also a characteristic feature of his way of thinking. Debreu shows that the original geometric argument of Pareto (see Figure 1), if suitably formulated, can be extended to a general proof. Indeed, let an economic system be defined by individual preferences $\succcurlyeq_i (i = 1, \ldots, m)$, production sets $Y_j (j = 1, \ldots, n)$, and total initial endowments z^0, as in Debreu (1951). Thus no externalities in consumption and production are allowed. If (x_i^0, y_j^0, p^0) denotes a competitive equilibrium (where individual income is given by $p^0 \cdot x_i^0$), then the hyperplane $\{x \in R^l | p^0 \cdot x = p^0 \cdot x_i^0\}$ with normal p^0 through x_i^0 supports the set $X_i(x_i^0) = \{x \in R^l | x \succcurlyeq_i x_i^0\}$; that is, $p^0 \cdot x \geq p^0 \cdot x_i^0$ for every $x \in X_i(x_i^0)$, and the hyperplane $\{y \in R^l | p^0 \cdot y = p^0 \cdot y_j^0\}$ with normal p^0 through y_j^0 supports the production set Y_j; that

[20] K. Arrow, An Extension of the Basic Theorems of Classical Welfare Economics. J. Neyman, ed., *Proceedings of the Second Berkeley Symposium on Mathematical Statistics and Probability*, Berkeley: University of California Press (1952), pp. 507–32.

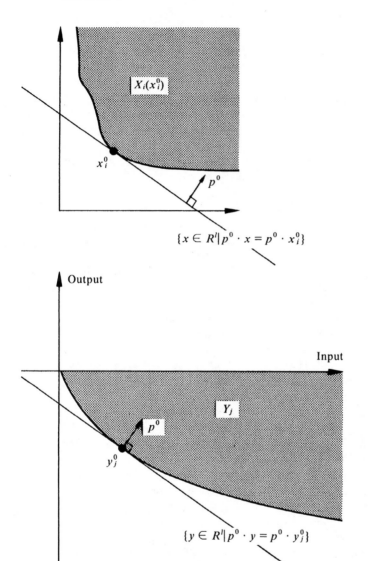

Figure 2

is, $p^0 \cdot y \geq p^0 \cdot y_j^0$ for every $y \in Y_j$. [Note the sign convention for input and output in Debreu (1951), which differs from that in *Theory of Value*.] This in turn implies Pareto optimality of the state (x_i^0, y_j^0) (see Figure 2).

This argument is perfectly general; no assumptions on the primitive concepts of the economy are needed other than that preferences are locally nonsatiated ("thin indifference curves"); in particular, no convexity of preferences is required. The first welfare proposition thus turns out to be a direct consequence of the definitions of competitive equilibria and Pareto optima, provided no externalities in consumption or production prevail. In this case, individual decisions, decentralized by the price system, lead to an optimum allocation of economic resources. This is a remarkable result. It turned out to be mathematically trivial but conceptually most important.

With this geometric insight, Debreu proceeded to prove the second welfare proposition. Let (x_i^0, y_j^0) be a Pareto optimum of the economy defined by $(\preccurlyeq_i, Y_j, z^0)$. Then the vector z^0 of initial total resources of the economy lies on the boundary of the set

$$ Z = \sum_{i=1}^{m} X_i(x_i^0) + \sum_{j=1}^{n} Y_j. $$

Therefore if the set Z is convex, which will be the case if preferences and the total production set are convex, then there exists a hyperplane through z^0 supporting the set Z. The normal to this hyperplane defines a price system $p^0 \in R^l$, which decentralizes the given optimum (x_i^0, y_j^0) in the following sense; if every consumer receives the "income" $w_i = p^0 \cdot x_i^0$, and if this income is not at the minimum subsistence level, then the state (x_i^0, y_j^0) with the price vector p^0 forms a competitive equilibrium.

Debreu's profound geometric insight revealed the relationship between competitive equilibria and Pareto optima in a surprisingly simple way. His analysis led to a deeper understanding of the role of prices for economies where externalities can be neglected.

The geometrical approach – that is, the use of separating hyperplanes for convex sets – led to an important further extension of the welfare propositions. In his 1954 paper, "Valuation Equilibrium and Pareto Optimum,"[21] Debreu extends the propositions from finite-dimensional to general linear topological spaces. This generality is needed if one wants to consider economies extending over an infinite time horizon or, in the case of uncertainty, economies with infinitely many states of nature. A price system now becomes a continuous linear functional. Here the topology of the commodity space – that is to say, the concept of nearness (similarity) of consumption or production plans – has to be introduced explicitly and justified economically according to the situation under discussion. It seems to me that this point has not yet received its full recognition and attention in the literature. Debreu proves the welfare proposition under the same general assumptions as in the case of a finite-dimensional commodity space with one exception, the total production set Y has to have an interior point. Again, we see that the topology chosen plays a crucial role.

---

[21] G. Debreu, Valuation Equilibrium and Pareto Optimum, *Proceedings of the National Academy of Sciences of USA*, **40** (1954): 588–92. [Chapter 5 in this book.]

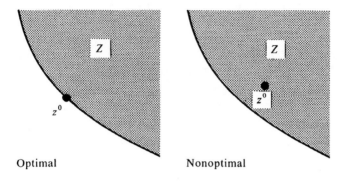

Optimal · Nonoptimal

Figure 3

The second part of Debreu's paper, "The Coefficient of Resource Utilization," contains – as the title expresses – a numerical evaluation of the "dead loss" associated with a nonoptimal state of an economy.

As explained above, with every state (x_i^0, y_j^0) of an economy (described by preferences $\preccurlyeq_i$, production sets Y_j and total initial resources z^0), one can associate the set Z. The relative position of the total initial resource vector z^0 to the set Z then determines whether the state (x_i^0, y_j^0) is optimal (see Figure 3). Debreu's coefficient of resource utilization $\rho(x_i^0, y_j^0, z^0)$ is defined as the smallest fraction $\rho \cdot z^0$ of the available resources z^0 that would permit the achievement of the level of utilities as given by x_i^0. Since the coefficient $\rho(x_i^0, y_j^0, z^0)$ summarizes a complex situation by a single numerical value, it has to be interpreted with care. Clearly, $\rho(x_i^0, y_j^0, z^0) = 1$ expresses Pareto optimality, but what conclusion can one draw if for two states, say, (x_i^1, y_j^1) and (x_i^2, y_j^2), one has

$$0 < \rho(x_i^1, y_j^1, z^1) < \rho(x_i^2, y_j^2, z^2)?$$

Despite this difficulty, a decisive advantage of Debreu's coefficient is that it is compatible with the partial Pareto ordering of states of an economy.

A detailed study of Debreu's coefficient of resource utilization, including a comparison with other measures of economic loss (Hotelling, Allais, Boiteux), was made by W. E. Diewert (1982),[22] and an axiomatic characterization was recently given by J. Weinberg (1980).[23]

Debreu's coefficient ρ and variants of it have been used in applied studies on the measurement of productive efficiency, starting with M. J.

[22] W. E. Diewert, The Measurement of Deadweight Loss Revisited, *Econometrica*, **49** (1982): 1225–44.

[23] J. Weinberg, A Note on Debreu's Coefficient of Resource Utilization, University of Bonn, Discussion Paper No. 71, Sonderforschungsbereich 21, Projektgruppe "Theoretische Modelle" (1980).

Farrell (1957).[24] Debreu himself applied the coefficient ρ in his paper, "A
Classical Tax-Subsidy Problem" (1954), which is reprinted in this volume.
J. Whalley (1976)[25] used Debreu's coefficient of resource utilization to
obtain numerical measures of the resources that could be saved by
changing the tax system of some European countries.

3   Existence of competitive equilibria

General competitive equilibrium theory was conceived in 1874 when Léon
Walras formulated a multimarket theory of exchange in the first part of his
Eléments d'Economie Politique Pure[26] (the second part dealing with
production was published in 1877). However, it was actually born eighty
years later with the publication of the paper, "Existence of an Equilibrium
for a Competitive Economy," by Kenneth Arrow and Gerard Debreu in
1954.

It is not surprising that it took so long to establish the consistency of the
general Walrasian system. Today we know that a proof of the existence of
a competitive equilibrium is equivalent to the existence of a fixed point of a
continuous mapping of the simplex into itself; a mathematical result that
was first proved by Brouwer around 1910. Yet one has to agree with
Koopmans, who writes,

It is, however, surprising that the fundamental importance of the [existence]
problem to the entire edifice of the theory of competitive markets does not seem to
have been commented on or even recognized by economists generally, other than
the small group of European economists writing in German whose penetrating
observations and searching questions originally started Abraham Wald off on his
investigations.[27] It is true that there is ample precedent in physics for the bypassing
of questions on the mathematical existence of analytical constructs by investigators
anxious to explore the useful properties these constructs can be shown to have,
provided they exist at all. But the fruits of such studies are like predated checks until
the non-contradictory character of their premises has been established.[28]

Indeed, neither in Samuelson's *Foundations of Economic Analysis*
(1947)[29] nor in Hicks's *Value and Capital* (1946),[30] to cite two classic

[24] M. J. Farrel, The Measurement of Productive Efficiency, *Journal of the Royal Statistical Society*, **120** (1957): 253–91.
[25] J. Whalley, Some General Equilibrium Analysis Applied to Fiscal Harmonization in the European Community, *European Economic Review*, **8** (1976): 290–312.
[26] L. Walras, *Eléments d'Economie Politique Pure*, Lausanne: L. Corbaz (1874).
[27] For a detailed discussion of Wald's contributions and the work of Neisser, von Stackelberg, Zeuthen, and Schlesinger on which Wald's work is based, we refer to section 6, historical note, in Arrow–Debreu (1954), Existence of an Equilibrium....
[28] T. Koopmans, *Three Essays on the State of Economic Science*, New York: McGraw-Hill (1957), p. 58.
[29] P. A. Samuelson, *Foundations of Economic Analysis*, Cambridge, Mass.: Havard University Press (1947).
[30] J. R. Hicks, *Value and Capital*, 2nd ed., Oxford: Clarendon Press (1946).

monographs, was the problem of existence of competitive equilibria seriously questioned. They rushed to analyze the comparative statics behavior of the system before the problem of existence, let alone uniqueness, was settled. For example, Samuelson (1947) writes, "In every problem of economic theory certain variables (quantities, prices, etc.) are designated as unknowns, in whose determination we are interested. Their values emerge as a solution of a specified set of relationships imposed upon the unknowns by assumption or hypothesis" (p. 7). "It was an achievement of the first magnitude for the older mathematical economists to have shown that the number of independent and consistent economic relations was in a wide variety of cases sufficient to determine the equilibrium values of unknown economic prices and quantities" (p. 257).

The first contribution to the existence of competitive equilibria is due to A. Wald in a series of papers in 1933–6.[31] Wald's work is based on the inquiries of Neisser, Stackelberg, Zeuthen, and Schlesinger, which are discussed in Arrow–Debreu (1954, section 6). Wald solves the existence problem for two models: One includes production (constant returns to scale) and the consumption sector is described directly by demand functions, which among other assumptions are assumed to fulfill the weak axiom of revealed preference. Thus he is near to a situation in which there is only one consumer; a case where no fixed-point argument is actually needed to prove the existence of competitive equilibria. There is, however, another paper [cited in Wald (1936)[32] which was "to appear in No. 8 of *Ergebnisse eines Mathematischen Kolloquiums* 1937," but which was actually never published] on pure exchange where the individual demand functions are derived from utility maximization. The fundamental contributions of Wald were not recognized by the profession at that time. For example, Samuelson in his *Foundations* gives reference to Wald but not in connection with the existence problem. The situation changed drastically in the early fifties.

Stimulated by the contributions of Wald and von Neumann, the development of linear programming and activity analysis, and in particular, the work of John F. Nash (1950)[33] in game theory, "it was perceived independently by a number of scholars that existence theorems of greater simplicity and generality than Wald's were now possible."[34]

At the meeting of the Econometric Society in December 1952 in Chicago, two path-breaking contributions were presented: "Existence of an Equilibrium for a Competitive Economy" by K. Arrow and G. Debreu and

[31] See footnote 5.
[32] Ibid.
[33] J. F. Nash, Equilibrium Points in N-Person Games, *Proceedings of the National Academy of Sciences of USA*, **36** (1950): 48–9.
[34] K. Arrow and F. H. Hahn, *General Competitive Analysis*, San Francisco: Holden Day (1971), p. 11.

"On Equilibrium in Graham's Model of World Trade and other Competitive Systems" by L. McKenzie. Their results had been obtained independently and their methods of proof were different. Both papers were published in *Econometrica* in 1954.[35]

Arrow and Debreu presented a general model of Walrasian equilibrium theory in their paper of 1954. This model of a "private ownership economy" is today the standard reference in general competitive equilibrium analysis. The primitive concepts of their general model are the following:

> *Commodity space R^l.* Commodities (including all kinds of services) are defined by their physical characteristics as well as by the location and time of their availability. No a priori classification into primary, intermediate, or desired commodities is made.

> *Characteristics of consumption units.* A consumption unit (household) i $(i = 1, \ldots, m)$ is described by a *consumption set* $X_i \subset R^l$, a *utility* function $u_1 : X_i \to R$, an initial *endowment* vector $e_i \in R^l$ and the *share* α_{ij} of the profit of the jth production unit. This individualistic description of a consumption unit excludes all kinds of externalities in consumption. The demand of the ith consumption unit is derived from utility maximization (supply of labor is treated within this maximization) under budget constraints, where the income, given the price system $p \in R^l$, is defined by the value of the initial endowments plus the shares in profits.

> *Characteristics of production units.* A production unit j $(j = 1, \ldots, n)$ is described by a production set $Y_j \subset R^l$, describing all technologically possible production plans for the jth unit. Again, this description excludes all externalities in production.

Under certain *assumptions on these primitive concepts* – it is not necessary to list these assumptions (see Arrow and Debreu, 1954, pp. 267–70); some of them have since been considerably weakened – Arrow and Debreu showed that there exists a competitive equilibrium for a "private ownership economy." Their method of proof consists in introducing a "fictitious agent" whose role is to choose the price system and thereby reducing the problem of existence of a competitive equilibrium for the given economy to

[35] L. McKenzie, On Equilibrium in Graham's Model of World Trade and other Competitive Systems, *Econometrica*, **22** (1954): 147–61, and K. Arrow and G. Debreu (1954), Existence of an Equilibrium....

the problem of the existence of a Nash-equilibrium for a "generalized game." The existence of Nash-equilibrium for such generalized games, where the set of strategies of a player depends on the actions taken by the other players, was previously shown by Debreu in his paper "A Social Equilibrium Existence Theorem" (1952).[36] Thus the proof of Arrow–Debreu had its roots in game theory. Indeed, Debreu's "A Social Equilibrium Existence Theorem" is a generalization of the work of Nash (1950), whose result is based on Kakutani's fixed-point theorem (1941).[37] This, in turn, is a reformulation of a topological lemma due to J. von Neumann (1937).[38]

McKenzie presented his result in a more restricted model, Graham's model of world trade; yet he showed at the end of the paper that his method of proof covers a more general situation. He assumes constant returns to scale in production and the consumption sector is described by a demand function for final goods that satisfies a certain boundary condition that, however, does not follow from individual utility maximization under budget contraints. For this reason the models of Arrow–Debreu and McKenzie are not directly comparable. McKenzie's proof is motivated by the work of Wald and Koopmans. He constructs a correspondence of the price simplex into itself and shows that a fixed point of this correspondence, whose existence is assured by Kakutani (1941), implies the existence of a competitive equilibrium.

After 1954 competitive equilibrium analysis developed rapidly; Gale (1955)[39] and Nikaido (1956)[40] gave existence proofs, which were developed independently of Arrow–Debreu and McKenzie. Further contributions were made by Kuhn (1956),[41] McKenzie (1959),[42] and Debreu (1959, 1962).[43]

---

[36] G. Debreu, A Social Equilibrium Existence Theorem, *Proceedings of the National Academy of Sciences of USA*, **38** (1952): 886–93. [Chapter 2 in this book.]

[37] S. Kakutani, A Generalisation of Brouwer's Fixed Point Theorem, *Duke Mathematical Journal*, **8** (1941): 457–9.

[38] J. von Neumann, Über ein ökonomisches Gleichungssystem und eine Verallgemeinerung des Brouwerschen Fixpunktsatzes, *Ergebnisse eines mathematischen Kolloquiums*, No. 8 (1937): 73–83. Translated in *Review of Economic Studies*, **13** (1945): 1–9.

[39] D. Gale, The Law of Supply and Demand, *Mathematica Scandinavica*, **3** (1955): 155–69.

[40] H. Nikaido, On the Classical Multilateral Exchange Problem *Metroeconomica*, **8** (1956): 135–45.

[41] H. W. Kuhn, A Note on "The Law of Supply and Demand," *Mathematica Scandinavica*, **4** (1956): 143–6.

[42] L. W. McKenzie, On the Existence of General Equilibrium for a Competitive Market, *Econometrica*, **27** (1959): 54–71.

[43] G. Debreu (1959), *Theory of Value*, and G. Debreu, New Concepts and Techniques for Equilibrium Analysis, *International Economic Review*, **3** (1962): 257–73. [Chapter 10 in this book.]

It is interesting that Debreu used another method of proof in his further work on competitive equilibrium analysis. Indeed, in his monograph *Theory of Value* (1959) and paper, "New Concepts and Techniques for Equilibrium Analysis" (1962), Debreu uses the "excess demand approach" because he thought that this method of proving existence is more in the line of traditional economic thinking.[44]

However, I would like to emphasize that Debreu's fundamental insight when writing the short but profound paper, "A Social Equilibrium Existence Theorem" (1952), turned out much later to be extremely fruitful. In fact, the excess demand approach fails to work if preferences are not necessarily transitive and complete because then the demand correspondence need not be convex-valued. The remarkable existence theorem of A. Mas-Colell (1974)[45] and extensions of it to the case where externalities in comsumption and production are allowed can most easily be obtained by a generalization of Debreu's "Social Equilibrium Existence Theorem" (1952) due to W. Shafer and H. Sonnenschein.[46] I refer to Debreu's chapter in the *Handbook of Mathematical Economics*[47] for an up-to-date and complete survey of the literature.

As already mentioned, when Debreu began to write his *Theory of Value* in 1954 he based the existence proof on a result that today is called the "fundamental lemma" [*Theory of Value*, Chapter 5, section 6, (1)]. This result is a version of Kakutani's fixed-point theorem, which is particularly well suited to the excess demand approach. It was proved independently of Debreu by D. Gale (1955) and H. Nikaido (1956). An important and very useful generalization, in which the domain of definition of the excess demand correspondence need not be the whole price simplex, was published by Debreu in 1956 in his paper, "Market Equilibrium."[48] The 'market equilibrium' theorem is used extensively in Debreu's paper "New Concepts and Techniques for Equilibrium Analysis." In this paper Debreu presents an existence theorem that contains all previously published results of the fifties.

Let me recall that all existence theorems for competitive equilibria for economies, where demand is derived from individual utility (preference)

[44] It is also more general in the sense that the consumer demand and producer supply correspondences need not be derived from utility and profit maximization.

[45] A. Mas-Colell, An Equilibrium Existence Theorem Without Complete or Transitive Preferences, *Journal of Mathematical Economics*, 1 (1974): 237–46.

[46] W. J. Shafer and H. F. Sonnenschein, Some Theorems on the Existence of Competitive Equilibrium, *Journal of Economic Theory*, 11 (1975): 83–93.

[47] G. Debreu, Existence of Competitive Equilibrium, *Handbook of Mathematical Economics*, K. J. Arrow and H. D. Intriligator, eds., Amsterdam: North Holland (1982), pp. 697–743.

[48] G. Debreu, Market Equilibrium, *Proceedings of the National Academy of Sciences of USA*, **42** (1956): 876–8. [Chapter 7 in this book.]

maximization, have to face a basic mathematical difficulty, namely, the demand correspondence of a consumer may not be upper hemi-continuous when his wealth is equal to the minimum compatible with his consumption set. To overcome this unavoidable technical difficulty, Debreu introduces the concept of a "quasi-equilibrium." The only difference between this concept and a competitive equilibrium is that agents, whose wealth is equal to the minimum compatible with their consumption set, receive a consumption bundle that is consistent with their budget but is not necessarily maximal in utility. Under very general assumptions on the primitive concepts of a private ownership economy, Debreu then shows the existence of a quasi-equilibrium [see the theorem on p. 254 in Debreu (1962)]. One has to admit that Debreu's proof is quite complex, but this is the price that must be paid if one strives for full generality. To go from here to a full equilibrium there are essentially two possibilities. Either assumptions are made on the primitive concepts of the economy that exclude the "minimum existence level" from ever occurring. [This approach was chosen, for simplicity, in Arrow–Debreu (1954) and Debreu (1959).] However, in general, these assumptions are very restrictive and far from realistic. Or assumptions are made on the economic system as a whole rather than on the individual primitive concepts. These assumptions imply that a quasi-equilibrium is actually an equilibrium. An example is the concept of "irreducibility," due to Gale and McKenzie.

4 Large economies and the core

Competitive equilibrium analysis is based – as is repeatedly emphasized – on the assumption that prices are "quoted" and taken as given by every economic agent. For an economy consisting of relatively few agents, this assumption – and hence the Walrasian equilibrium state of the economy derived from it – is, however, hardly plausible. Therefore let us consider an economy with many agents. Yet even in this case, why is the "plausible" final state of the economy of the Walrasian type? It seems clear that a satisfactory theoretical foundation of competitive equilibrium theory requires another more fundamental equilibrium concept that should be defined without reference to quoted prices and which is plausible even for small economies. The circumstances in which these equilibria become Walrasian have then to be specified.

The first contribution to the foundation of competitive equilibrium analysis along these lines was made by F. Edgeworth in his book *Mathematical Psychics* in 1881. Edgeworth introduced the "contract curve," which was later called the core, and studied for exchange economies with two commodities and two types of agents the limit of the core as the number of agents of each type grows.[49] His famous conclusions that "(α) Contract without competition is indeterminate, (β) Contract with perfect competition is perfectly determinate," and in particular that "(γ) Contract with more or less perfect competition is less or more indeterminate" (Edgeworth 1881, p. 20) have been paraphrased by saying that the contract curve shrinks to the set of competitive equilibria as the number of agents becomes arbitrarily large.

Edgeworth's fundamental contribution received little attention and was not further developed for almost eighty years, without any doubt, mainly because of the manner in which Edgeworth presented his ideas.[50]

The subject was taken up again in the late fifties and in a surprisingly short time tremendous progress was made. In 1963 Debreu and Scarf published the paper, "A Limit Theorem on the Core of an Economy," which gives a rigorous, fully satisfactory, and definitive treatment of Edgeworth's analysis and is an example of lucidity, simplicity, and elegance. It would be presumptuous to summarize the results instead of referring to the original. Accordingly, I shall content myself with explaining the historical development that led to this outstanding contribution.

Again, the decisive stimulus came from game theory. As an outgrowth of an analysis of von Neumann – Morgenstern solutions for games in characteristic function forms with transferable utility, L. S. Shapley and D. B. Gillies[51] formulated a new solution concept for such games in 1953, which they called the *core*. The connection between Edgeworth's contract curve and the core of a game was recognized by M. Shubik (1959)[52] who presented and partly extended Edgeworth's ideas in the framework of game theory with transferable utility.

---

[49] F. Y. Edgeworth, *Mathematical Psychics*, p. 31: "The advantage of this general method [here Edgeworth refers to this contract curve] is that it is applicable to the particular cases of imperfect competition; where the conceptions of *demand and supply at a price* are no longer appropriate," and on p. 34 he writes "But it is not the purpose of the present study . . . , but rather to inquire how far contract is determinate in cases of imperfect competition. It is not necessary for this purpose to attack the general problems of *Contract qualified by Competition* [in our language, an equivalence theorem for a perfectly competitive economy] which is much more difficult. . . . It will suffice to proceed synthetically, observing in a simple typical case the effect of continually introducing into the field additional competitors" [in our language, limit theorem].

[50] For an explanation of Edgeworth's ideas on the core in modern terminology, we refer to Debreu and Scarf, The Limit of the Core of an Economy, in *Decision and Organization*, C. B. McGuire and R. Radner, eds. Amsterdam: North Holland (1972), a paper not included in this volume.

[51] D B. Gillies, Some Theorems on *N*-person Games, Ph.D. thesis, Princeton University (1953).

[52] M. Shubik, Edgeworth Market Games, *Contributions to the Theory of Games, IV*, R. D. Luce and A. W. Tucker, eds. *Annals of Mathematical Studies*, **40**, Princeton, N. J.: Princeton University Press (1959), 267–78.

Inspired by these contributions, H. Scarf,[53] in 1962, presented a stimulating analysis of the core and Walrasian equilibria for general exchange economies (i.e., any finite number of commodities and types of agents) without the assumption of transferable utilities. Scarf's paper contains a limit theorem on the core for a sequence of replica economies and an equivalence theorem of the core and the set of Walrasian equilibria for an economy with countably many agents of each type. Actually Scarf (1962, p. 23) states his limit theorem for "that part of the core consisting of those allocations which assign identical commodities to identical consumers"; the equal treatment property for core allocations, Theorem 2 in Debreu–Scarf (1963)[54] had yet to be proved.

In 1963 Debreu gave a different and much simpler proof of Scarf's equivalence theorem.[55] This paper "On a Theorem of Scarf" is not contained in this volume because the definition of an attainable allocation that they used in a model with countably many agents of each type is not fully satisfactory.[56] However, this paper played a decisive role in the further development, because as is often the case, the simpler proof revealed the essential structure of the problem and could therefore be applied to more general situations.

Indeed, Debreu showed that a price system $p \in R^l$, which decentralizes the core allocation (x_i), can be obtained as the normal of a supporting hyperplane for the set $\bigcup_i \Gamma_i$, where $\Gamma_i = \{z \in R^l | z + \omega_i \succ_i x_i\}$ is the set of preferred net trades of agent i. Thus the central argument of the proof was to show that the origin is not an interior point of the convex hull of $\bigcup_i \Gamma_i$.

It was precisely at this point that R. Aumann became aware of the possibility of replacing the model with countably many agents by one with a continuum of agents (i.e., an atomless measure space), which is the appropriate mathematical model of a perfectly competitive economy. Thus Debreu's proof led Aumann to his outstanding contribution, the equivalence theorem for the core and the set of competitive equilibria of an economy with a continuum of agents.[57]

On the other hand, Debreu's proof in his paper of 1963 could easily be adapted to obtain the well-known simple proof for "A Limit Theorem on

[53] H. Scarf, An Analysis of Markets with a Large Number of Participants, *Recent Advances in Game Theory*, The Princeton University Conference, (1962), 127–55.

[54] G. Debreu and H. Scarf, A Limit Theorem on the Core of an Economy, *International Economic Review*, **4** (1963): 235–46. [Chapter 11 in this book.]

[55] Scarf's proof is most original but quite complex. It is worth mentioning that in his analysis of characterizing the core he used a variant of Debreu's "coefficient of resource utilization," Debreu (1951), The Coefficient of Resource Utilization.

[56] In order to define an *attainable allocation* (i.e., to give meaning to the statement, "total demand equals total supply") in an economy with countably many agents, one has to rely on integration theory for finitely (not countably) additive measures.

[57] R. J. Aumann, Markets with a Continuum of Traders, *Econometrica*, **32** (1964): 39–50.

the Core of an Economy" for a sequence of replica economies. We refer to Debreu–Scarf (1963).[58]

The limit theorem of Debreu and Scarf and Aumann's equivalence theorem initiated an enormous research activity. But this is not the place to survey these contributions.[59]

5   Utility and demand theory

In the microeconomic theory of consumer behavior one can describe the preferences of an individual by either a utility function or a binary relation. The strict equivalence of these two primitive concepts – ordinal utility functions and preference relations – was established rigorously by Debreu in a series of papers. In his paper "Topological Methods in Cardinal Utility Theory"[60] he also characterized certain traditional properties of utility functions (e.g., additive utility) in terms of properties of the underlying preference relations. These contributions clarified to a great extent the previously rather nebulous discussions on the concept of utility. As a particular case of Debreu's results in "Representation of a Preference Ordering by a Numerical Function" (1954)[61] and "Continuity Properties of Paretian Utility" (1964),[62] it follows that for every continuous complete and transitive binary relation $\lesssim$ defined on an arbitrary subset X of the commodity space R^l, there is a continuous utility representation; that is, there is a continuous function u of X into R such that $u(x) \leq u(y)$ if and only if $x \lesssim y$.

In many cases it is simpler to work with the more basic concept of preferences instead of utilities, because the latter is only determined up to strictly increasing transformations. As an important example, consider the formalization of the intuitive concept of "similar tastes" by means of a topology or a metric on the space of preferences. To study continuity properties of the core, Y. Kannai (1970)[63] introduced for the first time a

[58] G. Debreu and H. Scarf (1963), Limit Theorem., in particular, pp. 242, 243.

[59] Most of the material is surveyed in my book *Core and Equilibria of a Large Economy*, Princeton, N.J.: Princeton University Press (1974), and more recently, in Core of an Economy, Chapter 18 of *Handbook of Mathematical Economics*, Vol. 2, K. J. Arrow and M. Intriligator, eds., Amsterdam: North Holland (1982), pp. 831–75.

[60] G. Debreu, Topological Methods in Cardinal Utility Theory, *Mathematical Methods in Social Sciences*, K. J. Arrow, S. Karlin, and P. Suppes, eds., Stanford, Calif.: Stanford University Press (1960), pp. 16–26. [Chapter 9 in this book.]

[61] G. Debreu, Representation of a Preference Ordering by a Numerical Function, *Decision Processes*, Thrall, Coombs, and Davis, eds.; New York: Wiley (1954), pp. 159–65.

[62] G. Debreu, Continuity Properties of Paretian Utility, *International Economic Review*, **5** (1964): 285–93. [Chapter 12 in this book.]

[63] Y. Kannai, Continuity Properties of the Core of a Market, *Econometrica*, **38** (1970): 791–815.

metric on the space of monotonic preferences. In this case one can choose a canonical utility representation and use these uniquely determined functions to define a distance between two preference relations. In the general case, however, it is simpler to define the distance between two preference relations directly in terms of the preference relation. This was done by Debreu in his paper "Neighboring Economic Agents" (1968)[64] in which he defines the distances between two preference relations by the Hausdorff distance between their graphs. He then proves an important theorem that contains, as a special case, the result that the demand correspondence $\varphi(\preccurlyeq, w, p)$ is upper hemicontinuous in preferences $\preccurlyeq$, wealth w, and prices p if preferences are defined on the positive orthant R^l_+, $w > 0$ and $p \gg 0$. In particular, if preferences are strictly convex, the demand correspondence is a continuous function in preferences, wealth, and prices. This result justifies the choice of the metric on the space of preferences because it says that the demand of neighboring preferences is similar in similar wealth–price situations.

The topological structure on the space of preferences turned out to be very fruitful. For example, in my own work I used the topological structure on the space of preferences (the topology I actually used is slightly different from the one introduced by Debreu but it is in the same spirit) to describe an exchange economy by its distribution of agents' characteristics: preferences and endowments. This concept of a distribution of agents' characteristics together with the notion of weak convergence of distributions made it possible to extend the limit theorem on the core for a sequence of replica economies to much more general sequences.

The microeconomic foundations of competitive analysis – in particular, those of the consumption sector – seem to be solid. Individual demand and hence market demand are derived from the primitive concepts of the model. Moreover, the corresponding market excess demand system possesses the required properties to prove the existence of competitive equilibria. But does this microeconomic foundation put sufficient structure on the market excess demand system to enable us to go beyond the existence problem? Many economists expect much more from general equilibrium analysis. Here are two famous quotations:

If no more than this could be said, the economist would be truly vulnerable to the gibe that he is only a parrot taught to say 'supply and demand.' . . . In order for the analysis to be useful it must provide information concerning the way in which our equilibrium quantities will change as a result of changes in the parameters taken as independent data. [Samuelson (1947)][65]

[64] G. Debreu, Neighboring Economic Agents, *La Décision*, Colloques Internationaux du C.N.R.S. No. 171, Paris (1968), pp. 85–90. [Chapter 13 in this book.]
[65] P. A. Samuelson (1947), p. 257.

Now the reason for this sterility of the Walrasian system is largely, I believe, that he (Walras) did not go on to work out the laws of change for his system of General Equilibrium. He could tell what conditions must be satisfied by the prices established with given resources and given preferences, but he did not explain what would happen if tastes or resources changed. [Hicks (1946)][66]

As a matter of fact, in *Theory of Value* the problem of uniqueness and stability is only referred to in a note,[67] and comparative statics are not mentioned at all. From my first conversation with Debreu (when, quite naively, I expressed the intention of working on these problems), I remember that he was always convinced that the microeconomic foundations do not imply sufficient structure for total excess demand to allow a satisfactory treatment of these problems. Of course, by specific more or less ad hoc assumptions, imposed directly on the excess demand system, certain comparative statics properties, for example, can be obtained. But what is the relevance of such results? The challenging and audacious question, first raised and partially answered by H. Sonnenschein, is whether – under reasonably general assumptions – the excess demand, say, of an exchange economy, has any structure other than the trivial restrictions of continuity, homogeneity, and Walras identity. As Debreu has shown in his paper, "Excess Demand Functions" (1974),[68] the answer is negative. Any continuous function f from $S = \{p \in R^l | p \gg 0, |p| = 1\}$ to R^l, which satisfies the Walras identity, that is, $p \cdot f(p) = 0$, is identical up to boundary behavior with the excess demand function of an exchange economy consisting of l economic agents with continuous strictly convex and monotonic preference relations. This result, indeed, is rather negative. Does it imply that general equilibrium analysis has come to a dead end? The results[69] of Sonnenschein (1972),[70] Mantel (1974),[71] Debreu (1974), Mas-Colell (1977),[72] and others show, in my opinion, that an exchange economy can no longer serve as an appropriate prototype example for an economy if one wants to go beyond the existence and optimality problem. This is an extremely important insight that must have an impact on future research projects since until recently the pure exchange model played such a

---

[66] J. R. Hicks (1946), p. 61.

[67] Ibid., p. 89.

[68] G. Debreu, Excess Demand Functions, *Journal of Mathematical Economics*, 1 (1974): 15–21. [Chapter 16 in this book.]

[69] For a complete survey of these results see W. Shafer and H. Sonnenschein, Market Demand and Excess Demand Functions, *Handbook of Mathematical Economics*, K. Arrow and M. Intriligator, eds, Amsterdam: North Holland (1982), pp. 671–93.

[70] H. Sonnenschein, Market Excess Demand Functions, *Econometrica*, **40** (1972): 549–63.

[71] R. Mantel, On the Characterization of Aggregate Excess Demand, *Journal of Economic Theory*, 7 (1974): 348–53.

[72] A. Mas-Colell, On the Equilibrium Price Set of an Exchange Economy, *Journal of Mathematical Economics*, 4 (1977): 117–26.

dominant role in mathematical economics. One might object to this conclusion on the grounds that the above mentioned constructions of an economy are not subject to any restriction of the distribution of agents' characteristics. Yet, in general, what are reasonable restrictions on the distribution of agents' characteristics in a pure exchange economy other than a restriction on the fixed total supply? Clearly, if f is an excess demand function, then the total resources $\bar{e}_h$ of commodity h for any exchange economy that generates the function f must be larger than $b_h = \sup_p \left(-f_h(p)\right)$. It is true that in Debreu's construction the economy has total endowments that are much larger than this bound, namely, $3l^2 \cdot b_h$. Debreu did not take this point into account, and it is very likely that one can find alternative constructions of an economy where the required total endowments are much nearer to the bound. But this kind of weak restriction on the distribution of agents' characteristics will not lead very far. Perhaps I should remark here that the above mentioned results are concerned with *excess* demand of an exchange economy and not with demand functions of a consumption sector. After all, the consumers of a community are not just a collection of points picked arbitrarily in the universe of agents' characteristics, such as preferences and income! If, for example, one describes the consumption sector of an economy by a joint distribution μ of preferences and income, which moreover is independent of prices – this, indeed, leads us quite far away from a general equilibrium model – then one can show that the mean demand function for such a distribution μ is a continuous function in prices such that the value of mean demand equals mean income. It is known that not every function with these properties can be generated (up to boundary behavior) by a preference-income distribution. Moreover, in this case it seems reasonable to restrict the distributions of income to those that are supported by empirical studies. This restriction in itself, without restricting the universe and/or the distribution of preferences, however, is unlikely to lead to interesting properties of the mean demand functions. Whether the requirement that distributions of agents' characteristics should explicitly be taken into account will lead out of the dilemma has yet to be shown. I am looking forward to interesting investigations along these lines.

6   Regular differential economies

It should be clear from the discussion in Section 5 that the uniqueness of competitive equilibria can only be obtained by imposing strong assumptions on the excess demand system of the economy.[73] Four years

[73] For an excellent survey on the uniqueness problem we refer to Arrow–Hahn (1971), *General Competitive Analysis*, Chapter 9.

before the results on the structure of excess demand were published Debreu (1970) in his paper, "Economies with a Finite Set of Equilibria,"[74] made the following statement:

> ... economies with multiple equilibria must be allowed for. Such economies still seem to provide a satisfactory explanation of equilibrium as well as a satisfactory foundation for the study of stability provided that all the equilibria of the economy are locally unique. But if the set of equilibria is compact (a common situation), local uniqueness is equivalent to finiteness.

As we can see by simple examples in the Edgeworth box, the possibility of infinitely many equilibria cannot be excluded by making assumptions exclusively on the characteristics of the individual agents. There is nothing pathological in the individual preferences and endowments of these examples, yet "the pathology [of infinite equilibria] is due to the manner in which the agents are matched, a situation entirely different from that of existence theory where it was possible to give general conditions on the behaviour of each agent separately. . . ."[75]

The pathbreaking contribution of Debreu consists in showing that under differentiability assumptions on the individual demand functions, the pathological situations are, in a specified sense, exceptions; they are not typical cases. This way of analyzing a problem, that is to say, formulating a statement that does not hold universally but only "generically," was entirely new in economic theory. This point of view has its tradition in differential topology and was subsequently applied to many economic problems other than the question of local uniqueness of equilibria.

To make this approach precise Debreu considers exchange economies with m agents; every agent is described by a fixed continuously differentiable demand function. Every distribution $\omega = (\omega_1, \ldots, \omega_m)$ of initial endowments is described by a vector in $R^{l \cdot m}$ and specifies an exchange economy. With the usual boundary conditions on the demand functions, expressing the idea that every commodity is desired, Debreu then shows by standard arguments that the set $W(\omega)$ of equilibrium prices for the economy defined by ω is nonempty.[76] He next proves that the set of vectors $\omega = (\omega_1, \ldots, \omega_m)$ in $R^{l \cdot m}$ for which the set $W(\omega)$ is infinite is closed and of Lebesgue measure zero.

[74] G. Debreu, Economies with a Finite Set of Equilibria, *Econometrica*, **38** (1970): 387–92. [Chapter 14 in this book.]

[75] G. Debreu, The Application to Economics of Differential Topology and Global Analysis, *The American Economic Review*, **66** (1976): 280–7, p. 281. [Chapter 19 in this book.]

[76] In an addendum to his paper of 1970 Debreu states that his result is contained in McKenzie (1954). Strictly speaking, this is incorrect because McKenzie's boundary condition is stronger than the one assumed by Debreu. The addendum is therefore not included in this volume.

This fundamental and stimulating contribution initiated considerable research activity in the seventies. The basic ideas and results as well as the required mathematical theorems are explained in Debreu's (1976) expository paper, "The Application to Economics of Differential Topology and Global Analysis; Regular Differentiable Economies." For a complete survey of this area the reader is referred to E. Dierker "Regular Economies."[77]

To define the concept of regular economies one has to assume that the demand functions are continuously differentiable. Therefore the problem of characterizing the class of preference relations that lead to continuously differentiable demand functions remained. This and related problems have been settled in Debreu's presidential address, "Smooth Preferences," given at the meeting of the Econometric Society in Barcelona in 1971.[78]

The edifice of General Equilibrium Theory has been compared to the great gothic cathedrals. These cathedrals were designed by inspired architects and constructed by great master builders who quite often extended and improved on the original design. If Walras and Pareto are generally credited with being the architects of the General Equilibrium Theory, it becomes apparent from the reprinted contributions in this volume that Debreu is the great master builder of that edifice.

[77] E. Dierker, Regular Economies, *Handbook of Mathematical Economics*, K. Arrow and M. Intriligator, eds., Amsterdam: North Holland (1982), pp. 795–830.

[78] G. Debreu, Smooth Preferences, *Econometrica*, **40** (1972): 603–15. [Chapter 15 in this book.]

CHAPTER 1

The coefficient of resource utilization[1]

A numerical evaluation of the "dead loss" associated with a nonoptimal situation (in the Pareto sense) of an economic system is sought. Use is made of the intrinsic price systems associated with optimal situations of whose existence a noncalculus proof is given. A coefficient of resource utilization yielding measures of the efficiency of the economy is introduced. The treatment is based on vector-set properties in the commodity space.

1   Introduction

The activity of the economic system we study can be viewed as the transformation by n production units and the consumption by m consumption units of l commodities (the quantities of which may or may not be perfectly divisible). Each consumption unit, say the ith one, is assumed to have a preference ordering of its possible consumptions, and therefore an index of its satisfaction, s_i. Each production unit has a set of possibilities (depending, for example, on technological knowledge) defined independently of the limitation of physical resources and of conditions in the

[1] Based on a Cowles Commission Discussion Paper, Economics No. 284 (hectographed), June 1950, and a paper presented at the Harvard Meeting of the Econometric Society, August 1950. The research on which this paper reports was undertaken at the Cowles Commission for Research in Economics as part of the project on the theory of allocation of resources conducted by the Commission under contract with The RAND Corporation. This article will be reprinted as Cowles Commission Paper, New Series, No. 45.

Acknowledgement is due to R. Solow of the Massachusetts Institute of Technology, and to staff members and guests of the Cowles Commission. To nobody is my debt more specific than to T. C. Koopmans and M. Slater, and perhaps to nobody greater than to M. Allais, whose interest in this kind of question has been the origin of mine.

30

consumption sector. Finally, the total *net* consumption of all consumption units and all production units for each commodity must be at most equal to the available quantity of this commodity.

If we impose on the economic system the constraints defined by (1) the set of possibilities of each production unit and (2) the limitation of physical resources, we cannot indefinitely increase the m satisfactions. In trying to do so we would find situations where it is impossible to increase any satisfaction without making at least one other one decrease. In any one of these situations all the resources are fully exploited, and it can be considered optimal. When a situation is nonoptimal is it possible to find some measure of the loss involved, indicating how far it is from being optimal? The basic difficulty comes from the fact that no meaningful metrics exists in the satisfaction space.

For this reason we take up the following dual problem. We impose on the economic system the constraints defined by (1) the set of possibilities of each production unit and (2) the condition that for each consumption unit the satisfaction s_i is at least equal to a given value s_i^0. We cannot decrease indefinitely the l quantities of available physical resources. In trying to do so we would find situations where it is impossible to decrease one of them without making at least one other one increase. In any one of these situations the prescribed levels of satisfaction have been attained with as small an amount of physical resources as possible, and it can be considered optimal. The loss associated with a nonoptimal situation is now a measure of the distance from the actually available complex of resources to the set of optimal complexes; this concept is far simpler than the former one because we are dealing now with *quantities of commodities*. The two definitions of optimality are equivalent if the saturation cases are excluded.

Using the second definition of optimality we proceed to a noncalculus proof of the intrinsic existence of price systems associated with the optimal complexes of physical resources – the basic theorem of the new welfare economics. This proof is more general than the usual ones since it does not require the existence of derivatives which, indeed, do not exist in simple and realistic cases; more complete, since it deals with global instead of local properties of maxima or minima; more concise, as the synthetic nature of the problem requires it to be; it gives a deeper explanation of the intrinsic existence of prices by its geometric interpretation in the commodity space. These reasons seem to justify the higher level of abstraction on which it is placed.

This proof is based on convexity properties which imply continuity of quantities of commodities; if this assumption of continuity is dropped, the same technique shows that to achieve an optimal situation the use of a (real or virtual) price system is still sufficient but no longer necessary.

We are now prepared to measure the distance from the actually given complex of physical resources to the set of optimal complexes, i.e., the minimum of the distance from the given complex to a varying optimal complex. To evaluate such a distance we multiply, for each commodity, the difference between the available quantity and the optimal quantity by the price derived from the intrinsic price system whose existence has been previously proved. We take the sum of all such expressions for all commodities, and we divide by a price index in order to eliminate the arbitrary multiplicative factor affecting all the prices. It is then proved that the distance function so defined reaches its minimum for an optimal complex resulting from a reduction of all quantities of the nonoptimal complex by a ratio ρ, the coefficient of resource utilization of the economic system. This number, equal to 1 if the situation is optimal, smaller than 1 if it is nonoptimal, measures the efficiency of the economy and summarizes (1) the underemployment of physical resources, (2) the technical inefficiency of production units, and (3) the inefficiency of economic organization (due, for example, to monopolies or a system of indirect taxes or tariffs).

The money value of the "dead loss" associated with a nonoptimal situation can be derived from ρ, and the inefficiency of the economy is now described by a certain number of dollars representing the value of the physical resources which could be thrown away without preventing the achievement of the prescribed levels of satisfaction. This definition seems to obviate the shortcomings of the older ones.

The theory which led to the introduction of ρ can be imbedded in a more general one. Let us consider the ratio of the money value of any complex of resources that allows one to achieve for each consumption unit at least s_i^0 to the money value of actually available resources, the price system being arbitrary. The antagonistic activities of a central agency, which chooses the prices so as to make this ratio as large as possible, and of the economic units, which behave in such a way as to make it as small as possible, eventually give the value ρ to it.

This minimax interpretation of ρ points out a rather striking isomorphism with the theory of statistical decision functions.

The end of Section 9 might be useful as a supplement to this introduction by its more detailed exposition of the significance of the coefficient of resource utilization. The two most important sections are 6, where the noncalculus proof of the basic theorem of the new welfare economics is given, and 9, where ρ is introduced. Section 11, which gives the minimax interpretation of ρ, is a natural complement of 9. Section 12, which brings out the isomorphism with the theory of statistical decision functions, includes an elementary and self-contained exposition of the latter.

2   Basic mathematical concepts

Vectors are denoted by bold face lower case roman or Greek types; their components, by corresponding ordinary lower case types with a subscript characterizing the coordinate axis. We use the following notations for inequalities among vectors:

$$\mathbf{u} \geqq \mathbf{v} \quad \text{if} \quad u_i \geqq v_i \quad \text{for every } i,$$
$$\mathbf{u} > \mathbf{v} \quad \text{if} \quad u_i > v_i \quad \text{for every } i,$$
$$\mathbf{u} \geqslant \mathbf{v} \quad \text{if} \quad \mathbf{u} \geqq \mathbf{v} \quad \text{and} \quad \mathbf{u} \neq \mathbf{v}.$$

A function $w(\mathbf{u})$ is increasing (resp. nondecreasing) if "$\mathbf{u}^2 \geqslant \mathbf{u}^1$" implies "$w(\mathbf{u}^2) \geqslant w(\mathbf{u}^1)$ [resp. $w(\mathbf{u}^2) \geqq w(\mathbf{u}^1)$]."

Sets are denoted by German letters. According to the usual terminology, $\mathbf{v}$ is a *maximal* (resp. *minimal*) element of $\mathfrak{U}$ if (1) $\mathbf{v} \in \mathfrak{U}$ and (2) there is no $\mathbf{u}$ such that $\mathbf{u} \in \mathfrak{U}$ and $\mathbf{v} \leqslant \mathbf{u}$ (resp. $\mathbf{v} \geqslant \mathbf{u}$). The set of maximal (resp. minimal) elements of $\mathfrak{U}$ is denoted by $\mathfrak{U}^{\max}$ (resp. $\mathfrak{U}^{\min}$).

The vector sum of a finite number of sets $\mathfrak{U}_i$, $\mathfrak{B} = \sum_i \mathfrak{U}_i$, is the set of $\mathbf{v} = \sum_i \mathbf{u}_i, \mathbf{u}_i \in \mathfrak{U}_i$.

A set $\mathfrak{U}$ is convex if "$\mathbf{u} \in \mathfrak{U}, \mathbf{v} \in \mathfrak{U}, 0 \leqq t \leqq 1$" implies "$t\mathbf{u} + (1 - t) \mathbf{v} \in \mathfrak{U}$."

A set $\mathfrak{U}$ is closed if it contains every point at a zero distance from $\mathfrak{U}$.

$\mathbf{u}$ is an interior point of $\mathfrak{U}$ if there exists a sphere of nonzero radius, centered at $\mathbf{u}$ and entirely contained in $\mathfrak{U}$.

A set $\mathfrak{U}^2$ is greater than (more strictly speaking, at least as great as) a set $\mathfrak{U}^1$ if it includes $\mathfrak{U}^1$; i.e., $\mathfrak{U}^2 \supset \mathfrak{U}^1$.

3   Description of the economic system

A *commodity* of the economic system is characterized by a subscript $h(h = 1, \ldots, l)$. This concept can be given various contents: it can be a good or a service, direct or indirect, playing a role in any production or consumption process (for example, the training of pilots by some Air Force agency). The quantity of the hth commodity can either vary continuously or be an integral multiple of a given unit. The discontinuous case, which is indeed very widespread, can easily be included in the frame we present, as will be shown.

A *consumption unit* is characterized by a subscript $i(i = 1, \ldots, m)$; its activity is represented by a *consumption vector* $\mathbf{x}_i$ of the l-dimensional Euclidean commodity space $\mathfrak{R}_l$; the components x_{hi} are quantities of commodities actually consumed or negatives of quantities of commodities produced (for a consumer of the classical type the only negative components correspond to the different kinds of labor he can produce). We assume that, if x_i^1 and x_i^2 are two arbitrary consumption vectors of the ith consumption unit, it either "prefers x_i^1 to x_i^2," "think x_i^1 equivalent to x_i^2," or "prefers x_i^2 to x_i^1" ($x_i^2 \geqslant x_i^1$ excluding x_i^1 preferred to x_i^2) with the usual transitivity property. One can therefore construct equivalence classes (an equivalence class may happen to contain only one vector), which will be denoted by s_i; a given x_i belongs to one and only one such class, $s_i(x_i)$. The preference ordering on the x_i induces *complete* ordering on the s_i which will be denoted by $s_i^2 \geqq s_i^1$ (an element of s_i^1 is *not* preferred to an element of s_i^2). The usual procedure is to assume that a one-to-one, order preserving correspondence can be established between the set of s_i and the set of real numbers so that a satisfaction function $s_i(x_i)$ is obtained. First of all, such a correspondence need not exist, but even more important is the fact that the numerical value of this function has never any role to play, that only the ordering itself matters. The advisability of introducing such a function (always accompanied by the mention "defined but for an arbitrary monotonically increasing transformation"), which is useless and which moreover might not exist at all, may be questionable. However, one's intuition is likely to be helped if one views the ordering of the s_i as the ordering of real numbers; we will draw Figures 1a and 3a in that spirit. The m s_i are considered as the components of the element $s = (s_1, \ldots, s_m)$ of the product space $\mathfrak{E}$. s_i could conveniently be called the satisfaction or standard of living of the ith consumption unit and s the satisfaction or standard of living of the economic system. A partial ordering on the satisfaction space $\mathfrak{E}$ is defined in the following way: $s^2 \geqslant s^1$ if $s_i^2 \geqq s_i^2$ for every i and $s^2 \neq s^1$. The basic features of this reasoning are well known; our purpose is only to reformulate it in a language applicable to more general cases, including the discontinuous case. Here again the content of the concept of the *consumption unit* is left indeterminate: it can be a consumer, a household unit, a governmental agency, etc. In an economy provided with a central planning board incarnating a social welfare function there is only one consumption unit. The whole economic system can be divided into nations among which consumption units are distributed. The theory to be developed applies to all such cases.

The production activity of the system is represented by the *total input vector* $y \in \mathfrak{R}_l$; the conponents of y are inputs (*net* quantities of commodities consumed by the *whole* production sector during the period considered) or negatives of outputs (defined in a symmetrical way). Constraints such as the limitation of technological knowledge determine the set $\mathfrak{Y}$ of possible y. $\mathfrak{Y}$ is defined independently of the limitation of physical resources (which will be dealt with later) and of conditions in the consumption sector. The set of efficient vectors in production is $\mathfrak{Y}^{\min}$. (This concept is studied in great detail in [14] for the case where $\mathfrak{Y}$ is a convex polyhedral cone.)

A family of sets $\mathfrak{Y}_j (j = 1, \ldots, n)$ is a *decomposition*[2] of $\mathfrak{Y}$ if $\mathfrak{Y} = \sum_j \mathfrak{Y}_j$; in other words $\mathbf{y} = \sum_j \mathbf{y}_j, \mathbf{y}_j \in \mathfrak{Y}_j$. The *input vector* $\mathbf{y}_j$ characterizes the activity of the jth *production unit*. The concept of *production unit* may coincide with that of industry, firm, plant, etc. This formulation allows for production and consumption of intermediate commodities, even in a circular way, with as many intermediate steps as one wants. It allows, of course, for discontinuities of variables, or, if they are continuous, for nonsmooth surfaces $\mathfrak{Y}_j^{\min}$, for the existence of fixed ratios between some variables, etc. The more usual exposition, which amounts to starting from the $\mathfrak{Y}_j$ to obtain $\mathfrak{Y}$, is valid only if the assumption that $\mathfrak{Y}$ is nothing more than $\sum_j \mathfrak{Y}_j$ is explicitly made. In order that $\mathbf{y} \in \mathfrak{Y}^{\min}$ it is necessary but not sufficient that $\mathbf{y}_j \in \mathfrak{Y}_j^{\min} (j = 1, \ldots, n)$.

The vector $\mathbf{x} = \sum_i \mathbf{x}_i$ is the total *consumption vector*, and $\mathbf{z} = \mathbf{x} + \mathbf{y}$ is the total *net* consumption of the *whole* economy (all consumption units and all production units) which can come only from the available physical resources: we call it the *utilized physical resources vector* as opposed to $\mathbf{z}^0$, a vector of $\mathfrak{R}_l$, whose components are the available quantities of each commodity (natural resources and services of existing capital, for example; the different kinds of labor would give rise to zero components[3]). We call $\mathbf{z}^0$ the *utilizable physical resources vector*. We thus have $\mathbf{z} \leqq \mathbf{z}^0$.

4 Optimum and loss defined in the satisfaction space

The constraints imposed on the economic system are[4]

$$\mathbf{y} \in \mathfrak{Y}, \qquad \mathbf{z} \leqq \mathbf{z}^0;$$

this determines in $\mathfrak{E}$ the set $\mathfrak{S}$ of attainable $\mathfrak{s}$. According to the Paretian criterion, if the goal of the economic system is to make the $\mathfrak{s}_i$, which cannot be compared to each other, as great as possible, $\mathfrak{s}^2$ is better than $\mathfrak{s}^1$ if, and only if, $\mathfrak{s}^2 \geqslant \mathfrak{s}^1$, and $\mathfrak{s}$ is *optimal* if, and only if, it is maximal: $\mathfrak{s} \in \mathfrak{S}^{\max}$. Any economic system, anxious to satisfy the needs of the consumption units as well as possible, and confronted with the problem of selecting one $\mathfrak{s}$ in $\mathfrak{S}$, would in fact restrict its choice to $\mathfrak{S}^{\max}$.

---

[2] This decomposition is not meant to be unique. If $0 \in \mathfrak{Y}_j$ for every j, $\mathfrak{Y}_j \subset \mathfrak{Y}$. A study of decentralization of economic decisions is concerned with the extent to which decisions can be made with respect to $\mathfrak{Y}_j$ instead with respect to $\mathfrak{Y}$.

[3] The quantity of a certain kind of labor can be treated in two different ways: either as a component of the $\mathbf{x}_i$, if one wishes to emphasize the possibility of varying it, or as a nonzero component of $\mathbf{z}^0$ if the opposite assumption is made.

[4] Supplementary constraints such as the existence of some minimum standard of living $\mathfrak{s} \geqq \mathfrak{s}^0$, would involve no essential change in the following analysis.

If $s^0 \notin \mathfrak{S}^{max}$ (Figure 3a)[5] a *dead loss* is associated with s^0; its magnitude is, intuitively, the distance from s^0 to the set $\mathfrak{S}^{max}$ (i.e., the minimum of the distance from s^0 to a variable s belonging to $\mathfrak{S}^{max}$). The very nature of the space $\mathfrak{E}$ prevents us from finding a meaningful content for that definition.

5   Optimum and loss defined in the commodity space

Let us therefore study the following *dual* problem and consider in $\mathfrak{R}_l$ the set $\mathfrak{Z}(s^0)$ of vectors z defined by the constraints

$$y \in \mathfrak{Y}, \quad s \geq s^0.$$

$\mathfrak{Z}$ is the set of utilized physical resources vectors which, taking into account the production possibilities $\mathfrak{Y}$, enable the economy to achieve at least s^0. Let $\mathfrak{X}_i(s_i^0)$ be the set of x_i defined by $s_i(x_i) \geq s_i^0$, and $\mathfrak{X}(s^0) = \sum_i \mathfrak{X}_i$; then, since $z = x + y$, $\mathfrak{Z}$ is nothing else than $\mathfrak{Z} = \mathfrak{X} + \mathfrak{Y}$.

$\mathfrak{Z}^{min}(s^0)$ is a natural concept: it describes the minimal physical resources required to achieve at least s^0. One sees that z^0 can be defined as optimal with respect to $\mathfrak{Y}$ and s^0 if, and only if, $z^0 \in \mathfrak{Z}^{min}$, and that, if $z^0 \notin \mathfrak{Z}^{min}$ (Figure 3b), the dead loss can be defined as the distance from z^0 to the set $\mathfrak{Z}^{min}$ This distance can now be meaningful since the coordinates of the commodity space $\mathfrak{R}_l$ are *quantities of commodities*.

The definitions of optimum and loss given in Sections 4 and 5 are not necessarily equivalent but, under conditions which amount essentially to excluding the saturation cases,[6] "$s^0 \in \mathfrak{S}^{max}$" is equivalent to "$z^0 \in \mathfrak{Z}^{min}$." (See Figures 1a and 1d.)

6   The optimum theorem

Let us now assume that the sets $\mathfrak{X}_i$, $\mathfrak{Y}_j$ are all *convex* and closed (convexity implies, of course, that the quantities of all commodities can be varied

[5] Occasional references will be made to figures. They are all drawn in the two-dimensional case and, with one exception, contain only smooth curves, while the reasoning deals with a greater number of dimensions, nonsmooth surfaces, and even discrete sets of points. They are therefore mere illustrations, loosely connected with the text but likely to be found useful.

[6] This can be done by a few additional simple postulates which we do not discuss in detail for they would lead to very formal developments without throwing more light on the heart of our problem. The saturation case has been considered by K. J. Arrow in the paper, "A Generalization of the Basic Theorem of Classical Welfare Economics" (to be published in the *Proceedings of the Second Berkeley Symposium*), given in the summer of 1950 at the Berkeley meeting of the Econometric Society independently of the present paper, which was given at the same time at the Harvard meeting of the Society.

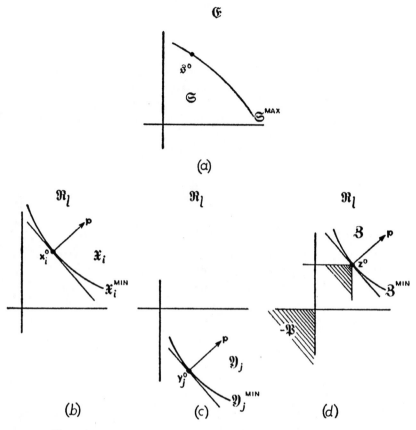

Figure 1

continuously); it follows that $\mathfrak{Z} = \sum_i \mathfrak{X}_i + \sum_j \mathfrak{Y}_j$ is convex.[7] As for the $\mathfrak{X}_i$, the assumption is a classical one and needs no particular comment; as for the $\mathfrak{Y}_j$, it may be worth noticing that if one added the two postulates,

1 $\mathbf{y}_1 \in \mathfrak{Y}_j$, $\mathbf{y}_2 \in \mathfrak{Y}_j$ implies $\mathbf{y}_1 + \mathbf{y}_2 \in \mathfrak{Y}_j$ (additivity postulate),
2 $\mathbf{0} \in \mathfrak{Y}_j$,

then $\mathfrak{Y}_j$ would be a cone.

We now concentrate our attention on a vector $\mathbf{z}^0 = \sum_i \mathbf{x}_i^0 + \sum_j \mathbf{y}_j^0$ ($\mathbf{x}_i^0 \in \mathfrak{X}_i$, $\mathbf{y}_j^0 \in \mathfrak{Y}_j$) (Figure 1). If $\mathfrak{P}$ denotes the positive orthant of $\mathfrak{R}_l$ (the

---

[7] The sum of a finite number of closed sets is not necessarily closed when those sets are unbounded. However, it is sufficient that they are all contained in some closed, convex, pointed cone for their sum to be closed. We will assume that such is the case so that $\mathfrak{Z}$ is closed.

set of vectors of $\Re_l \geqq 0$), we have the following chain of *equivalent propositions:*

1 $z^0 \in \mathfrak{Z}^{\min}$.
2 The convex sets $\mathfrak{Z}$ and $z^0 - \mathfrak{P}$ have no other point in common than z^0 (this is just another way of expressing proposition 1).[8]
3 There is a plane through z^0 separating these two sets. (When two closed convex sets with interior points have only one point in common there is at least one plane through that point separating them [6].)
4 There is a vector $\mathbf{p} > 0$ (normal to the separating plane) such that $z \in \mathfrak{Z}$ implies $\mathbf{p} \cdot (z - z^0) \geqq 0$.
5 There is a vector $\mathbf{p} > 0$ such that

$$x_i \in \mathfrak{X}_i \quad \text{implies} \quad \mathbf{p} \cdot (x_i - x_i^0) \geqq \text{for every } i, \tag{1}$$

$$y_j \in \mathfrak{Y}_j \quad \text{implies} \quad \mathbf{p} \cdot (y_j - y_j^0) \geqq 0 \quad \text{for every } j.[9] \tag{2}$$

Proof of the equivalence of propositions 4 and 5: $\mathbf{p} \cdot (z - z^0) = \sum_i \mathbf{p} \cdot (x_i - x_i^0) + \sum_j \mathbf{p} \cdot (y_j - y_j^0)$; the condition is therefore sufficient. It is necessary, for if one term of the right-hand member could be made < 0, as all the others can be made $= 0$, the left-hand member could be made < 0.[10]

Finally, (1) is equivalent to

$$\mathbf{p} \cdot (x_i - x_i^0) < 0 \quad \text{implies} \quad x_i \notin \mathfrak{X}_i \quad [\text{i.e., } \mathfrak{s}_i(x_i) < \mathfrak{s}_i(x_i^0) \quad \text{for every } i] \tag{1'}$$

or

$$\mathbf{p} \cdot (x_i - x_i^0) \leqq 0 \quad \text{implies} \quad \mathfrak{s}_i(x_i) \leqq \mathfrak{s}_i(x_i^0) \quad \text{for every } i. \tag{1''}$$

Interpreting $\mathbf{p}$ as a price vector and, defining $a_i = \mathbf{p} \cdot x_i^0 (i = 1, \ldots, m)$, we have the statement:

The necessary and sufficient condition for $\mathfrak{s}^0$ to be maximal, or for $z^0 = \sum_i x_i^0 + \sum_j y_j^0$ to be minimal, is the existence of a price vector $\mathbf{p} > 0$ and of a set of numbers $a_i (i = 1, \ldots, m)$ such that
(α) x_i being constrained by $\mathbf{p} \cdot x_i \leqq a_i$, $\mathfrak{s}_i(x_i)$ reaches its maximum at x_i^0, for every i,
(β) y_j being constrained by $y_j \in \mathfrak{Y}_j$, $\mathbf{p} \cdot y_j$ reaches its minimum at y_j^0 for every j.

---

[8] No distinction is made between a vector such as z^0 and the set containing only this vector. $z^0 - \mathfrak{P}$ is written in short for $z^0 + (-\mathfrak{P})$.

[9] Therefore $x_i^0 \in \mathfrak{X}_i^{\min}$, $y_j^0 \in \mathfrak{Y}_i^{\min}$ (this could be seen directly).

[10] The geometric interpretation of this is the following: The necessary and sufficient condition for the existence of a supporting plane through z^0 for $\mathfrak{Z}$ is the existence of a family of parallel supporting planes through the x_i^0 (resp. y_j^0) for the $\mathfrak{X}_i$ (resp. $\mathfrak{Y}_j$). Such is the deeper meaning of the optimum theorem to be enunciated in a moment.

This is a formalization of well-known rules of behavior of consumption units and production units: each consumption unit, subject to a budgetary constraint, maximizes its satisfaction and each production unit, subject to technological constraints, maximizes its profit.

Given z^0, $\mathfrak{Y}$, and $s^0 \in \mathfrak{S}^{max}$, the direction of $\mathbf{p}$ is not always uniquely determined.[11] It is only constrained to belong to the set of directions normal to supporting planes for $\mathcal{3}$ through z^0, which we call briefly the cone of normals. Even if its direction is known, $\mathbf{p}$ is determined only up to a multiplication by a positive scalar. Once $\mathbf{p}$ is known, the set of m numbers (a_i) is determined.

Given z^0 and $\mathfrak{Y}$, the different s^0 belonging to $\mathfrak{S}^{max}$ determine all possible pairs $\mathbf{p}$, (a_i). To attain an arbitrary maximal s^0 one can imagine the following procedure: choose (a_i) among its possible values; then find a $\mathbf{p} > \mathbf{0}$ such that, when

(α') every consumption unit maximizes $s_i(\mathbf{x}_i)$ subject to $\mathbf{p} \cdot \mathbf{x}_i \leqq a_i$,
(β) every production unit minimizes $\mathbf{p} \cdot \mathbf{y}_j$ subject to $\mathbf{y}_j \in \mathfrak{Y}_j$,
the $\mathbf{x}_i^0$ and $\mathbf{y}_j^0$ thus determined satisfy $\sum_i \mathbf{x}_i^0 + \sum_j \mathbf{y}_j^0 = z^0$.

A proper choice of (a_i) can lead to any given point $s^0 \in \mathfrak{S}^{max}$ that one wishes to attain.[12]

If the activity of the economic system extends over t successive time intervals of equal length, the subscript h can be made to characterize the time interval as well. Nothing is changed in the preceding analysis; $\mathbf{p}$ now need only be interpreted as a set of actual prices for present and future commodities.

7   Historical note

Proofs of this basic theorem of the new welfare economics published so far were based on the use of the calculus.[13] They required unnecessary restrictive assumptions on the existence of derivatives, assumptions which cannot be made, for example, in the very simple and realistic case of linear

[11] Unless, of course, $\mathcal{3}^{min}$ is a smooth surface having only one normal direction at each point.
[12] If the conditions of differentiability are fulfilled, (β') coincides with the well-known rule that "every production unit produces its output at the smallest possible total cost and sells it at marginal cost."
  If $\mathfrak{Y}_j$ is a cone, the minimum of $\mathbf{p} \cdot \mathbf{y}_j$ is zero and (β') coincides with the rule of perfect competition within the jth industry.
[13] K. J. Arrow's paper quoted in footnote 6 contains a noncalculus proof of the basic theorem. Unfortunately, I had his manuscript in my hands for too short a time to appraise it fully here.

programming in which $\mathfrak{Y}$ is a polyhedral cone [14]; moreover, they could at best establish the existence of a *local* maximal. Indeed, they generally limited themselves to the study of first-order conditions.

Pareto himself, who defined [18, 19] an optimal $\mathfrak{s}$ as a maximal $\mathfrak{s}$ and conceived the set[14] $\mathfrak{S}^{max}$ [20], did not establish those conditions satisfactorily in spite of lengthy developments [19]. The gradual improvements brought by Barone [3], Bergson [4, 5], Hotelling [12, 13], Hicks [8], Lange [15], Lerner [16], Allais [1, 2], Samuelson [21], and Tintner [25] clarified, made more rigorous, and extended the content of his writings.

The long and piecemeal treatment, which consisted of proving that the rates of substitution between any two commodities are independent of the individual, of the industry, etc., failed to comply with the *synthetic* nature of the problem; moreover, it put the emphasis on the equality of rates of substitution, which disappear in the simplest cases (polyhedral cones), instead of putting it on the necessary and sufficient existence of a price system (real or virtual), which is the actually meaningful operational concept. For these reasons the proofs given independently by O. Lange [15] and M. Allais [1, 2] were of particular interest: they were essentially synthetic and some of their Lagrange multipliers could be interpreted immediately as prices, which was done forcefully by M. Allais. However, they used an asymmetrical exposition (one individual or one commodity played a particular role) to obtain symmetrical results from symmetrical assumptions. Their Lagrange multipliers were a mathematical trick obscuring the more fundamental facts; they had the weaknesses of calculus proofs already mentioned.

8   The discontinuous case

If the quantities of some commodities vary discontinuously, we can, in an attempt to preserve certain properties of convexity, define a *quasi-convex* set (Figure 2) as a set which has at least one supporting plane through each minimal point. But the assumption that all the $\mathfrak{X}_i$ and $\mathfrak{Y}_j$ are quasi-convex does not imply that $\mathfrak{Z} = \sum_i \mathfrak{X}_i + \sum_j \mathfrak{Y}_j$ is quasi-convex.[15] In other words, the theorem proved in Section 6 was based on the additivity property of convexity. Quasi-convexity is not additive and the theorem cannot be extended; that is, the existence of a price vector $\mathbf{p} > \mathbf{0}$ used according to the rules (α) and (β) is still sufficient but no longer necessary for $\mathfrak{s}^0$ to be maximal.

---

[14] Here, as in similar cases, the author quoted did not use the language we use; however, the translations should not raise any difficulty.

[15] It is easy to build a two-dimensional counterexample.

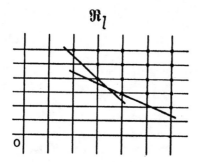

Figure 2

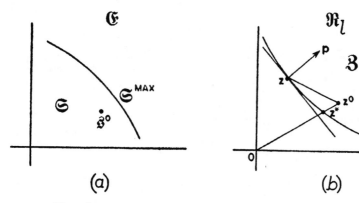

(a)   (b)

Figure 3

9   The coefficient of resource utilization ρ

We therefore go back to the convexity case and concern ourselves with the measurement of the dead loss associated with a vector $z^0 \notin \mathfrak{Z}^{min}(s^0)$ (Figure 3). This loss is depicted entirely by, and only by, the relative positions of z^0 and the set $\mathfrak{Z}^{min}$. However, if we want, instead of this complex picture, a simple representation by a number, we define the magnitude of the loss as the distance from z^0 to $\mathfrak{Z}^{min}$, i.e., the minimum of the distance from the fixed point z^0 to the point z varying in $\mathfrak{Z}^{min}$. To have a distance with an economic meaning we evaluate the vector $z^0 - z$, which represents the nonutilized resources, by the *intrinsic* price vector p associated with z, whose existence we proved in Section 6. We thus obtain $p \cdot (z^0 - z)$. In fact, there can be several p associated with z; it is easy to see that, whatever the p chosen in the cone of normals, the result to be obtained below is the *same*. No other price vector can be taken for this evaluation, for (1) it is quite possible that no price vector exists at all in the concrete economic situation observed (if, for example, there is no uniqueness of price for one commodity) and (2) even if there were one, let us say $\mathbf{p}^0$, it would have no intrinsic significance.

Before we engage in a minimization process we must not forget that $\mathbf{p}$ is affected by an arbitrary positive multiplicative scalar whose influence we eliminate by dividng by a price index for which we may take either $\mathbf{p} \cdot \mathbf{z}$ or $\mathbf{p} \cdot \mathbf{z}^0$. It must be pointed out that the result to be obtained is again independent of this choice. Indeed, the use of $\mathbf{p} \cdot \mathbf{z}$ has a very intuitive justification: all the points $\mathbf{z}$ of $\mathfrak{Z}^{\min}$ then have the same "value."

We are thus led to look for

$$\underset{\mathbf{z} \in \mathfrak{Z}\min}{\mathrm{Min}} \frac{\mathbf{p} \cdot (\mathbf{z}^0 - \mathbf{z})}{\mathbf{p} \cdot \mathbf{z}}, \quad \text{i.e., for} \quad \underset{\mathbf{z} \in \mathfrak{Z}\min}{\mathrm{Max}} \frac{\mathbf{p} \cdot \mathbf{z}}{\mathbf{p} \cdot \mathbf{z}^0}.$$

Let $\mathbf{z}^*$ be the vector collinear with $\mathbf{z}^0$ and belonging to $\mathfrak{Z}^{\min}$:

$$\mathbf{z}^* = \rho \mathbf{z}^0, \quad \mathbf{z}^* \in \mathfrak{Z}^{\min},$$

$$\underset{\mathbf{z} \in \mathfrak{Z}\min}{\mathrm{Max}} \frac{\mathbf{p} \cdot \mathbf{z}}{\mathbf{p} \cdot \mathbf{z}^0} = \rho \underset{\mathbf{z} \in \mathfrak{Z}\min}{\mathrm{Max}} \frac{\mathbf{p} \cdot \mathbf{z}}{\mathbf{p} \cdot \mathbf{z}^*}.$$

But the convexity of $\mathfrak{Z}$ insures that

$$\mathbf{p} \cdot (\mathbf{z}^* - \mathbf{z}) \geqq 0, \quad \text{i.e.,} \quad \frac{\mathbf{p} \cdot \mathbf{z}}{\mathbf{p} \cdot \mathbf{z}^*} \leqq 1;$$

since this ratio is equal to 1 when $\mathbf{z} = \mathbf{z}^*$, we have

$$\underset{\mathbf{z} \in \mathfrak{Z}\min}{\mathrm{Max}} \frac{\mathbf{p} \cdot \mathbf{z}}{\mathbf{p} \cdot \mathbf{z}^0} = \rho;$$

the maximum is reached at every point $\mathbf{z} \in \mathfrak{Z}^{\min}$ such that a supporting plane through $\mathbf{z}$ contains $\mathbf{z}^*$ (i.e., at every point $\mathbf{z}$ contained in a supporting plane through $\mathbf{z}^*$).

We call ρ defined in the preceding way *the coefficient of resource utilization* of the economic system; it is a function $\rho(\mathfrak{s}^0, \mathbf{z}^0, \mathfrak{Y})$ describing the efficiency of the economy. To be precise, it is the smallest fraction of the actually available physical resources that would permit the achievement of $\mathfrak{s}^0$. $\rho = 1$ if and only if $\mathfrak{s}^0$ is maximal (i.e., $\mathbf{z}^0$ minimal). $\rho < 1$ if and only if $\mathfrak{s}^0$ is attainable but not maximal. ρ decreases if $\mathfrak{s}^0$ decreases or if $\mathfrak{Y}$ increases, for in both cases $\mathfrak{Z}$ increases; it is hardly more difficult to see that ρ decreases if $\mathbf{z}^0$ increases ("decreases" has been used for short to mean "does not increase" and vice versa).

The appellation suggested for ρ has a general content which must be clearly brought out. An economic system has three kinds of *resources*: (1) its physical resources z^0, (2) its production possibilities $\mathfrak{Y}$, and (3) its economic organization possibilities. If s^0 is not maximal there is a loss originating from one or several of the following sources:

1 underemployment of physical resources, such as unemployment of labor, idle machinery, lands uncultivated by agreement, etc. This is the most obvious source of loss. In a very narrow sense a coefficient of resource utilization would describe only this phenomenon; this is by no means our only purpose.

2 inefficiency in production; $y_j \in \mathfrak{Y}_j^{min}$. This kind of loss is already much less obvious but is not, by its very nature, the main concern of the economist.

3 imperfection of economic organization; if the physical resources are fully utilized, if the production is perfectly efficient, it is still possible that s^0 is not maximal if the conditions of the basic theorem are not satisfied. As is well known, such a case arises, for example, with monopolies or indirect taxation or a system of tariffs. This kind of loss is the most subtle (in fact, perhaps hardly conceivable to the layman) and therefore the one for which a numerical evaluation is the most necessary.

The coefficient ρ takes into account the three kinds of loss.

The definition of the coefficient of resource utilization as the ratio of a vector collinear with z^0 to z^0 can be legitimized in cases more general than the convexity case, and defined in still further general cases, but this would lead to a certain amount of undesirable sophistication.

10   Definitions of the economic loss

In summary, the loss is $z^0 - z^* = z^0(1 - \rho)$; its *value* is $p^* \cdot z^0(1 - \rho)$, p^* being the price vector associated with z^*. However, p^* has no immediate concrete significance and, if a price vector p^0 exists in the economic situation actually observed, a more interesting evaluation is probably $p^0 \cdot z^0(1 - \rho)$. p^0, which was inacceptable in the minimization process leading to z^0, is, of course, acceptable now that an approximate numerical evaluation is sought. Whether one wants the magnitude of the loss due to monopolies (in the absence of other distortions, the total degree of monopoly could be taken as $1 - \rho$), or to a taxation system, or to tariffs,[16] the above expression gives the answer under the form of a certain number of billions of dollars. ρ itself, a percentage describing the degree of efficiency of the economy, can be found more useful in some cases.

Since J. Dupuit [7] several definitions of the loss described have been

[16] The loss thus measured is the loss for the set of nations trading with each other as a whole.

more or less explicitly suggested. A very simple one is the variation of real national income[17] [9, 22] [according to our notation,[18] $\mathbf{p} \cdot (\mathbf{x}^2 - \mathbf{x}^1)$]; other definitions were directly based on the various notions of consumers' surplus as presented in their modern forms by J. R. Hicks [10, 11]. All of them derived the value of the loss from the comparison of two sets of individual consumptions $(\mathbf{x}_1^1, \ldots, \mathbf{x}_m^1)$ and $(\mathbf{x}_1^2, \ldots, \mathbf{x}_m^2)$, and, if those two sets varied in such a way that $\mathfrak{s}^1$ and $\mathfrak{s}^2$ did not change, the value of the loss *did vary*. This was inconsistent with the Paretian philosophy which considers two situations which yield the same point $\mathfrak{s}$ to be equivalent.[19] Even if this were overcome by the construction of a plausible numerical index of comparison of $\mathfrak{s}^1$ and $\mathfrak{s}^2$, it would still be unsatisfactory for finding the loss associated with $\mathfrak{s}^1$ to compare it with an $\mathfrak{s}^2$ *arbitrarily* selected in $\mathfrak{S}^{max}$ instead of comparing it with the set $\mathfrak{S}^{max}$.

The treatment of this question by M. Allais [1] overcomes this difficulty, but its exposition *and its results* rely entirely on the asymmetrical role played by a particular commodity.

11   Minimax interpretation of ρ

In Section 9 we were led to consider the expression $(\mathbf{p} \cdot \mathbf{z}/\mathbf{p} \cdot \mathbf{z}^0)$, where $\mathbf{z} \in \mathfrak{Z}^{min}(\mathfrak{s}^0)$ and $\mathbf{p}$ is one of the normals to $\mathfrak{Z}^{min}$ at $\mathbf{z}$. It was proved that its maximum is reached at $\mathbf{z}^*$ (and possibly at other points) collinear with $\mathbf{z}^0$, and that its value is ρ, the ratio of $\mathbf{z}^*$ to $\mathbf{z}^0$. This is but a part of a more complete theory that we present now.

We still assume that the quantity of every commodity varies continuously, but we drop for a moment the convexity hypothesis and look for

$$\underset{\mathbf{z} \in \mathfrak{Z}}{\text{Min}} \ \underset{\mathbf{p} \in \mathfrak{P}'}{\text{Max}} \ \frac{\mathbf{p} \cdot \mathbf{z}}{\mathbf{p} \cdot \mathbf{z}^0},$$

where $\mathfrak{P}'$ is the closed positive orthant, origin excluded. $\mathbf{z}$ being given,

$$\underset{\mathbf{p} \in \mathfrak{P}'}{\text{Max}} \ \frac{\mathbf{p} \cdot \mathbf{z}}{\mathbf{p} \cdot \mathbf{z}^0} = \underset{h}{\text{Max}} \ \frac{z_h}{z_h^0},$$

which may be infinite.[20]

If $\mathbf{z} \in \mathfrak{Z}, (z_h/z_h^0) \geq \rho$ for at least one h; otherwise one would have $\mathbf{z} < \mathbf{z}^*$, contradicting the fact that $\mathbf{z}^* \in \mathfrak{Z}^{min}$. Therefore, $\text{Max}_{\mathbf{p} \in \mathfrak{P}'} \ (\mathbf{p} \cdot \mathbf{z}/\mathbf{p} \cdot \mathbf{z}^0) \geq \rho$

[17] But it can be defined only if a price vector with some intrinsic meaning exists at all.

[18] The superscripts 1 and 2 will denote the two economic situations compared.

[19] Moreover, the roles played by situations (1) and (2) were generally asymmetrical in such a way that inconsistencies pointed out by T. de Scitovsky [23, 24] arose.

[20] Some ratios (z_h/z_h^0) might be of the form (0/0); they would be disregarded in the operation described by the right-hand member.

whatever be z in $\mathfrak{Z}$; it is equal to ρ if, and only if, $z = z^*$ (again an immediate consequence of "$z^* \in \mathfrak{Z}^{min}$"). In other words, $Min_{z \in \mathfrak{Z}} Max_{p \in \mathfrak{P}'}(p \cdot z/p \cdot z^0) = \rho$; it is reached for z^* and p arbitrary in $\mathfrak{P}'$. If p is chosen (say by some central agency) in $\mathfrak{P}'$ so as to make $(p \cdot z/p \cdot z^0)$ as great as possible, and if z is chosen in $\mathfrak{Z}$ so as to make this expression as small as possible [this amounts to choosing y_j in $\mathfrak{Y}_j$ (resp. x_i in $\mathfrak{X}_i$) so as to make $p \cdot y_j$ (resp. $p \cdot x_i$) as small as possible for every j (resp. i)], the economic system is led to z^* and the final value of the expression is ρ. The order in which the operations Max and Min are carried out is of utmost importance.

If the set $\mathfrak{Z}$ is convex (this property of $\mathfrak{Z}$ has been studied in Sections 6 and 9), this order becomes *indifferent*. In effect, let us look for

$$Max_{p \in \mathfrak{P}'} Min_{z \in \mathfrak{Z}} \frac{p \cdot z}{p \cdot z^0}.$$

p being given, $Min_{z \in \mathfrak{Z}}(p \cdot z/p \cdot z^0)$ is reached for a point of $\mathfrak{Z}^{min}$ (and possibly other points of $\mathfrak{Z}$). We can therefore restrict ourselves to the case where $z \in \mathfrak{Z}^{min}$ and p is a normal to $\mathfrak{Z}^{min}$ at z. The problem of finding the maximum of $(p \cdot z/p \cdot z^0)$ under these conditions is precisely the problem we solved in Section 9. The maximum ρ is reached at z^* (and possibly at other points of $\mathfrak{Z}^{min}$), the corresponding p^* being any one of the normals to $\mathfrak{Z}^{min}$ at z^*.

To sum up,

$$\rho = Min_{z \in \mathfrak{Z}} Max_{p \in \mathfrak{P}'} \frac{p \cdot z}{p \cdot z^0} = Max_{p \in \mathfrak{P}'} Min_{z \in \mathfrak{Z}} \frac{p \cdot z}{p \cdot z^0},$$

the set of saddle points of the function $(p \cdot z/p \cdot z^0)$ is the product [17, Section 13] of:

the set of z where $Min_z Max_p (p \cdot z/p \cdot z^0)$ is reached; it is composed of z^* only;

the set of p where $Max_p Min_z (p \cdot z/p \cdot z^0)$ is reached; it is composed of the normals p^* to $\mathfrak{Z}^{min}$ at z^*.[21]

If s^0 is maximal, the value of the minimax is, of course, 1.

12 Isomorphism with the theory of statistical decision functions

If none of the components of z^0 is null, we can, by an appropriate choice of the units, make them all equal to 1. The expression $(p \cdot z/p \cdot z^0)$ then takes the form $(p/\sum_h p_h) \cdot z$; we put $\bar{p} = (p/\sum_h p_h)$, normalizing the price vector in such a way that the sum of its components is 1, and we have, finally, the very

---

[21] If we were interested only in the fact that the operations Min and Max can be inverted, we could give the very short following proof: choose z^* and one of the p^* and show that this is a saddle point [17, Section 13]. This is indeed immediate but hardly enlightening.

simple form $\bar{\mathbf{p}} \cdot \mathbf{z}$, where $\mathbf{z} \in \mathfrak{Z}$, $\bar{\mathbf{p}} \in \bar{\mathfrak{P}}$, the simplex defined by $\sum_h \bar{p}_h = 1$ and $\bar{p}_h \geq 0$.

We have proved that, $\mathfrak{Z}$ being convex,

$$\rho = \underset{\mathbf{z} \in \mathfrak{Z}}{\text{Min}} \ \underset{\bar{\mathbf{p}} \in \bar{\mathfrak{P}}}{\text{Max}} \ \bar{\mathbf{p}} \cdot \mathbf{z} = \underset{\bar{\mathbf{p}} \in \bar{\mathfrak{P}}}{\text{Max}} \ \underset{\mathbf{z} \in \mathfrak{Z}}{\text{Min}} \ \bar{\mathbf{p}} \cdot \mathbf{z}.$$

The saddle points are $\mathbf{z}^*$, all of whose components are equal to ρ, associated with any normal $\bar{\mathbf{p}}^*$ to $\mathfrak{Z}^{\min}$ at $\mathbf{z}^*$. They appear to be the result of the antagonistic activities of a central agency which chooses $\bar{\mathbf{p}}$ in $\bar{\mathfrak{P}}$ so as to *maximize* $\bar{\mathbf{p}} \cdot \mathbf{z}$ and of production units (resp. consumption units) which choose $\mathbf{y}_j$ (resp. $\mathbf{x}_i$) in $\mathfrak{Y}_j$ (resp. $\mathfrak{X}_i$) so as to *minimize* $\bar{\mathbf{p}} \cdot \mathbf{z}$.[22]

On the other hand, a simple case of the theory of statistical decision functions can be presented in the following way.[23] Let $F(\mathbf{x})$ be the cumulative distribution function of a random variable ξ, a vector with possibly a denumerable infinity of components (probability that $\xi < \mathbf{x}$); F is merely known to be an element of a finite set $(F_1, \ldots, F_i, \ldots, F_v)$. The statistician is faced with the choice of a decision d in a set $\mathfrak{D}$. With every pair F_i, d is associated a number $r \geq 0$ called risk, expressing what it costs to use d when F_i is true.

The expression $r(F_i, d)$ can be more conveniently written $r_i(d)$; it is thus clear that to each d corresponds a risk vector $\mathbf{r}(d) = (r_1, \ldots, r_i, \ldots, r_v)$ of the space $\mathfrak{R}_v$. The image of the set $\mathfrak{D}$ by the function $\mathbf{r}(d)$ is a set $\mathfrak{R}$ of $\mathfrak{R}_v$, and the initial problem of choice of d in $\mathfrak{D}$ can be replaced by the problem of choosing a point $\mathbf{r}$ in $\mathfrak{R}$. In the usual framework of the theory (including the use of randomized decisions; i.e., d_1 and d_2 being two decisions, one can choose d_1 with the probability α and d_2 with the probability $1 - \alpha$), $\mathfrak{R}$ is closed and convex. If $\mathbf{r}^1 \leq \mathbf{r}^2$, $\mathbf{r}^1$ is better than $\mathbf{r}^2$ [whatever be the true F_i, $r(F_i, d_1) \leq r(F_i, d_2)$, the strict inequality holding for at least one i], and the choice of $\mathbf{r}$ is therefore restricted to $\mathfrak{R}^{\min}$. Let us make the further assumption that the straight line whose equations are $r_1 = r_2 = \cdots = r_v$ meets $\mathfrak{R}$ and meets it for the first time (when one is moving away from the origin) at a point $\mathbf{r}^*$ of $\mathfrak{R}^{\min}$ (Figure 4); this assumption is not significant for the theory of statistical decision functions, but the isomorphism can be brought out in this case.

The principle of minimizing the maximum risk amounts to taking $\text{Min}_r \text{Max}_i (r_1, \ldots, r_v)$; it leads to the selection of $\mathbf{r}^*$. Indeed, if $\bar{\mathbf{p}}$ is a vector whose

[22] The structure of the set $\mathfrak{Z}$ makes these antagonistic activities formally different from a zero-sum two-person game in the von Neumann–Morgenstern [**17**, Section 17] sense.

[23] The theory of which this paragraph and the three following ones give a summary is developed in greater detail and generality in the basic work of A. Wald [**26**]. Its geometric interpretation was pointed out by J. Wolfowitz at the Chicago meeting of the Econometric Society in December 1950, in a paper, "Some Recent Advances in the Theory of Decision Functions," which is unfortunately not available in printed form.

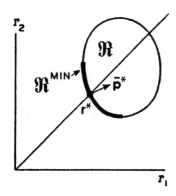

Figure 4

v components p_t satisfy $\bar{p}_t \geqq 0$ and $\sum \bar{p}_t = 1$, the Min Max operation mentioned is equivalent to $\mathrm{Min}_r \, \mathrm{Max}_{\bar{p}} \, \bar{p} \cdot r$. The formal analogy with our former concepts is obvious: z and $\mathfrak{Z}$ have been replaced by r and $\mathfrak{R}$; the normalized price vector $\bar{p}$, by the vector $\bar{p}$ whose interpretation will be given in a moment. We proved in Section 11 that the operation $\mathrm{Min}_r \, \mathrm{Max}_{\bar{p}} \, \bar{p} \cdot r$ leads to r^*.

We proved also that the operations Min and Max can be inverted. $\mathrm{Max}_{\bar{p}} \, \mathrm{Min}_r \, \bar{p} \cdot r$ now has the following interpretation: $\bar{p}$ is a probability vector, $\bar{p}_t$ being the a priori probability that F_t is true. The statistician minimizes the expected risk and $\mathrm{Min}_r \, \bar{p} \cdot r$ gives the Bayes solution relative to the a priori distribution $\bar{p}$. It is a point of $\mathfrak{R}^{\min}$. (Conversely, every point of $\mathfrak{R}^{\min}$ is a Bayes solution for a properly chosen $\bar{p}$.) Therefore r^* is the Bayes solution relative to $\bar{p}^*$ (one of the normals to $\mathfrak{R}^{\min}$ at r^*); $\bar{p}^*$ is the a priori distribution which gives the greatest value to the minimum expected risk, i.e., the least favorable a priori distribution.

In the same way that prices were historically first considered as primary data and later only as an indirect theoretical construction with optimal properties, the controversial concept of an a priori distribution, at first taken at its face value, is here considered as an indirect construction with intrinsic optimal properties.

The formal analogies between the theories of zero-sum two-person games, statistical decision functions, and resource allocation are valuable since a result obtained in any one of them can have an interesting counterpart in the two others; the differences between their philosophies should, however, by no means be overlooked. In a game we have a clear-cut case of naturally antagonistic interests: one player tries to make his gain as great as possible, the other tries to make his loss as small as possible. In a statistical decision problem, according to A. Wald's words [26, Section 1.6],

Whereas the experimenter wishes to minimize the risk $r(F, d)$ we can hardly say that Nature wishes to maximize $r(F, d)$. Nevertheless, since Nature's choice is unknown to the experimenter, it is perhaps not unreasonable for the experimenter to behave as if Nature wanted to maximize the risk. But, even if one is not willing to take this attitude, the theory of games remains of fundamental importance for the problem of statistical decisions, since ... it leads to basic results concerning admissible decision functions and complete classes of decision functions.

In the resource allocation problem the central agency determining $\bar{p}$ is not inert and its behavior can be chosen precisely to conflict fully with the behavior of the various economic units.

References

[1] Allais, M., *A la Recherche d'une discipline économique*, Tome I, Paris: Ateliers Industria, 1943, Chapter IV, Section E.

[2] Allais, M., *Economie pure et rendement social*, Paris: Sirey, 1945, 72 pp.

[3] Barone, E., The Ministry of Production in the Collectivist State, in *Collectivist Economic Planning*, F. A. Hayek, ed., London: Routledge, 1935, pp. 245–290 (reprinted from *Giornale degli Economisti*, 1908).

[4] Bergson (Burk), A., A Reformulation of Certain Aspects of Welfare Economics, *Quarterly Journal of Economics*, Vol. 52, February 1938, pp. 310–334.

[5] Bergson (Burk), A., Socialist Economics, Chapter XII in *A Survey of Contemporary Economics*, H. S. Ellis, ed., Philadelphia: Blakiston., 1948, pp. 412–448.

[6] Bonnesen, T., and W. Fenchel, *Theorie der Konvexen Körper*, New York: Chelsea., 1948, p. 5.

[7] Dupuit, J., *De l'Utilité et de sa mesure*, Turin: La Riforma Sociale, 1933 (reprints of works published in 1844 and the following years).

[8] Hicks, J. R., The Foundations of Welfare Economics, *Economic Journal*, Vol. 49, December 1939, pp. 696-712.

[9] Hicks, J. R., The Valuation of the Social Income, *Economica*, Vol. 7, May 1940, pp. 105–124.

[10] Hicks, J. R., Consumers' Surplus and Index-Numbers, *Review of Economic Studies*, Vol. 9, Summer 1942, pp. 126–137.

[11] Hicks, J. R., The Generalised Theory of Consumer's Surplus, *Review of Economic Studies*, Vol. 13 (1), No. 34, 1945–46, pp. 68–74.

[12] Hotelling, H., The General Welfare in Relation to Problems of Taxation and of Railway and Utility Rates, *Econometrica*, Vol. 6, July 1938, pp. 242–269.

[13] Hotelling, H., and R. Frisch, Papers on the Dupuit Taxation Theorem, *Econometrica*, Vol. 7, April 1939, pp. 145–160.

[14] Koopmans, T. C., Analysis of Production as an Efficient Combination of Activities, Chapter III in *Activity Analysis of Production and Allocation*, Cowles Commission Monograph 13, T. C. Koopmans, ed., New York: Wiley, 1951, pp. 33–97.

[15] Lange, O. The Foundations of Welfare Economics, *Econometrica*, Vol. 10, July–October, 1942, pp. 215–228.

[16] Lerner, A. P., *The Economics of Control*, New York: Macmillan., 1944, 428 pp.

[17] Neumann, J. von, and O. Morgenstern, *Theory of Games and Economic Behavior*, Princeton: Princeton University Press, 1947, 641 pp.

[18] Pareto, V., *Cours d'économie politique*, Lausanne, 1897, Vol. II, Paragraphs 720–735, 1.013–1.023.

[19] Pareto, V., *Cours d'économie politique*, Paris: M. Giard, 1909, Chapter VI, Paragraphs 32–64; Chapter IX, Paragraph 35; and Appendix 89 to the end.

[20] Pareto, V., *Traité de sociologie générale*, Paris, 1917–1919, Paragraphs 2.128–2.130.

[21] Samuelson, P. A., *Foundations of Economic Analysis*, Cambridge, Mass.: Harvard University Press, 1947, Chapter VIII.

[22] Samuelson, P. A., Evaluation of Real National Income, *Oxford Economic Papers*, Vol. 2, January 1950, pp. 1–29.

[23] Scitovsky, T. de, A Note on Welfare Propositions in Economics, *Review of Economic Studies*, Vol. 9, November 1941, pp. 77–88.

[24] Scitovsky, T. de, A Reconsideration of the Theory of Tariffs, *Review of Economic Studies*, Vol. 9, Summer 1942, pp. 89–110.

[25] Tintner, G., A Note on Welfare Economics, *Econometrica*, Vol. 14, January 1946, pp. 69–78.

[26] Wald, A., *Statistical Decision Functions*, New York: Wiley, 1950, 179 pp.

CHAPTER 2

A social equilibrium existence theorem*

In a wide class of social systems each agent has a range of actions among which he selects one. His choice is not, however, entirely free and the actions of all the other agents determine the subset to which his selection is restricted. Once the action of every agent is given, the outcome of the social activity is known. The preferences of each agent yield *his* complete ordering of the outcomes and each one of them tries by choosing his action in his restricting subset to bring about the best outcome according to his own preferences. The existence theorem presented here gives general conditions under which there is for such a social system an equilibrium, i.e., a situation where the action of every agent belongs to his restricting subset and no agent has incentive to choose another action.

This theorem has been used by Arrow and Debreu [2] to prove the existence of an equilibrium for a classical competitive economic system, it contains the existence of an equilibrium point for an N-person game (see Nash [8] and Section 4) and, naturally, as a still more particular case the

* Based on two Cowles Commission Discussion Papers, Mathematics 412 (Nov. 1, 1951) and Economics 2032 (Feb. 11, 1952). This paper has been undertaken as part of the project on the theory of allocation of resources conducted by the Cowles Commission for Research in Economics under contract with The RAND Corporation. To be reprinted as Cowles Commission Paper, New Series, No. 64.

One of the main motivations for this article has been to lay the mathematical foundations for the paper by Arrow and Debreu [2]; in this respect I am greatly indebted to K. J. Arrow. Acknowledgment is also due to staff members and guests of the Cowles Commission and very particularly to I. N. Herstein and J. Milnor. I owe to J. L. Koszul and D. Montgomery references 6 and 3. Finally, I had the privilege of consulting with S. MacLane and A. Weil on the contents of Ref. [6].

existence of a solution for a zero-sum two-person game (see von Neumann and Morgenstern, Ref. [11], Section 17.6).

In Section 1 the topological concepts to be used are defined. In Section 2 an abstract definition of equilibrium is presented with a proof of the theorem. In Section 3 saddle points are presented as particular cases of equilibrium points and in connection with the closely related MinMax operator. Section 4 concludes with a short historical survey of results about saddle points, fixed points for multi-valued transformations and equilibrium points.

Only subsets of finite Euclidean spaces will be considered here.

1 Topological concepts

Two sets in R^n are said to be *homeomorphic* when it is possible to set up between them a one-to-one bicontinuous (h and h^{-1} continuous) correspondence h (called a homeomorphism).

A *convex cell* C in R^n is determined by r points z^k ($k = 1, \ldots, r$); it is the set

$$ C = \left\{ z \mid z = \sum_{k=1}^{r} \zeta_k z^k, \ \zeta_k \geq 0 \quad \text{for } k = 1, \ldots, r, \ \sum_{k=1}^{r} \zeta_k = 1 \right\}. $$

Such a set is closed.

The product of two convex cells $A \subset R^l$ and $B \subset R^m$ is a convex cell $C \subset R^{l+m}$. Let A be generated by the p points x^i ($i = 1, \ldots, p$) and B by the q points y^j ($j = 1, \ldots, q$). Denote by C the convex cell in R^{l+m} generated by the pq points (x^i, y^j). Obviously $A \times B \supset C$, and one shows easily that $A \times B \subset C$.

A *geometric polyhedron* is the union of a finite number of convex cells in R^n. It is clearly closed.

The product of two geometric polyhedra P, Q is a geometric polyhedron. Let $P = \bigcup_{i=1}^{p} A_i (Q = \bigcup_{j=1}^{q} B_j)$ where the A_i (the B_j) are convex cells in R^l (in R^m). The relation $P \times Q = (\bigcup_i A_i) \times (\bigcup_j B_j) = \bigcup_{ij}(A_i \times B_j)$ proves the result.

A *polyhedron* is a set in R^n homeomorphic to a geometric polyhedron (called geometric antecedent of the first one).

The product of two polyhedra is a polyhedron (since it is homeomorphic to the product of the two geometric antecedents).

Let $I = \{t \mid 0 \leq t \leq 1\}$ denote the closed interval $[0, 1]$ on the real line. A nonempty set Z of R^n is said to be *contractible*, or more precisely, deformable into a point $z^0 \in Z$, if there exists a continuous function

$H(t, z)$ (called a deformation) taking $I \times Z$ into Z such that for all $z \in Z$, $H(0, z) = z$ and $H(1, z) = z^0$.

The product of two sets $X \subset R^l$, $Y \subset R^m$ deformable into the two points $x^0 \in X$, $y^0 \in Y$, respectively, is clearly deformable into the point (x^0, y^0).

Finally the real function $t = (e^\theta - 1)/(e^\theta + 1)$ of the real variable θ is monotonically increasing from -1 to $+1$ when θ increases from $-\infty$ to $+\infty$. It establishes a one-to-one correspondence between the closed interval $[-1, +1]$ and the set $\bar{R}$ of all real numbers to which are added two elements $-\infty$ and $+\infty$. Open sets in $\bar{R}$ are defined as images of the usual open sets in $[-1, +1]$, an order is defined in $\bar{R}$ as an image of the usual order in $[-1, +1]$. $\bar{R}$ endowed with this topology and this order is called the *completed real line* (which can naturally be defined directly [5]).

2   Equilibrium points

Let there be v agents characterized by a subscript $\iota = 1, \ldots, v$.

The ιth agent chooses an action a_ι in a set $\mathfrak{A}_\iota$. The v-tuple of actions $(a_1, \ldots, a_v)$, denoted by a, is an element of $\mathfrak{A} = \mathfrak{A}_1 \times \cdots \times \mathfrak{A}_v$. The payoff to the ιth agent is a function $f_\iota(a)$ from $\mathfrak{A}$ to the completed real line.

Denote further by $\bar{a}_\iota$ the $(v - 1)$-tuple $(a_1, \ldots, a_{\iota-1}, a_{\iota+1}, \ldots, a_v)$ and by $\bar{\mathfrak{A}}_\iota$ the product $\mathfrak{A}_1 \times \cdots \times \mathfrak{A}_{\iota-1} \times \mathfrak{A}_{\iota+1} \times \cdots \times \mathfrak{A}_v$. Given $\bar{a}_\iota$ (the actions of all the others), the choice of the ιth agent is restricted to a *non-empty, compact* set $A_\iota(\bar{a}_\iota) \subset \mathfrak{A}_\iota$; the ιth agent chooses a_ι in $A_\iota(\bar{a}_\iota)$ so as to maximize $f_\iota(\bar{a}_\iota, a_\iota)$, assumed to be continuous in a_ι on $A_\iota(\bar{a}_\iota)$.

This background makes the following formal definition intuitive:

> *Definition:* a^* is an equilibrium point if for all $\iota = 1, \ldots, v$, $a_\iota^* \in A_\iota(\bar{a}_\iota^*)$ and $f_\iota(a^*) = \text{Max}_{a_\iota \in A_\iota(\bar{a}_\iota^*)} f_\iota(\bar{a}_\iota^*, a_\iota)$.

The *graph* of the function $A_\iota(\bar{a}_\iota)$ is defined as the subset of $\bar{\mathfrak{A}}_\iota \times \mathfrak{A}_\iota$, $G_\iota = \{(\bar{a}_\iota, a_\iota) | a_\iota \in A_\iota(\bar{a}_\iota)\}$. For any $\bar{a}_\iota$, $A_\iota(\bar{a}_\iota)$ is always understood to be non-void.

Theorem

For all $\iota = 1, \ldots, v$, let $\mathfrak{A}_\iota$ be a contractible polyhedron, $A_\iota(\bar{a}_\iota)$ a multi-valued function from $\bar{\mathfrak{A}}_\iota$ to $\mathfrak{A}_\iota$ whose graph G_ι is closed, f_ι a continuous function from G_ι to the completed real line such that $\varphi_\iota(\bar{a}_\iota) = \text{Max}_{a_\iota \in A_\iota(\bar{a}_\iota)} f_\iota(\bar{a}_\iota, a_\iota)$ is continuous. If for very ι and $\bar{a}_\iota$, the set $M_{\bar{a}_i} = \{a_i \in A_i(\bar{a}_i) | f_i(\bar{a}_i, a_i) = \varphi_i(\bar{a}_i)\}$ is contractible, then there exists an equilibrium point.

The proof uses as a lemma a particular case of the fixed point theorem of S. Eilenberg and D. Montgomery [6] or of the even more general result of E. G. Begle [3].

Let Z be a set and ϕ a function associating with each $z \in Z$ a subset $\phi(z)$ of Z. We have defined above the graph of ϕ as the subset of $Z \times Z$, $\{(z, z') | z' \in \phi(z)\}$. ϕ is said to be *semicontinuous* if its graph is closed. A *fixed point* of ϕ is a point z^* such that $z^* \in \phi(z^*)$.

Lemma

Let Z be a contractible polyhedron and $\phi: Z \to Z$ a semi-continuous multi-valued function such that for every $z \in Z$ the set $\phi(z)$ is contractible. Then ϕ has a fixed point.[†]

$\mathfrak{A}$, the product of ν contractible polyhedra, is a contractible polyhedron (Section 1). Define on $\mathfrak{A}$ the multi-valued function ϕ as follows:

$$\phi(a) = M_{\bar{a}_1} \times \cdots \times M_{\bar{a}_\nu}.$$

Since $M_{\bar{a}_i}$ is contractible for all i and $\bar{a}_i$, $\phi(a)$ is contractible for all $a \in \mathfrak{A}$ (Section 1). To be able to apply the lemma it remains only to show that ϕ is semicontinuous.

For this first define in $\mathfrak{A}_i \times \mathfrak{A}_i$ the set

$$M_i = \{(\bar{a}_i, a_i) | a_i \in M_{\bar{a}_i}\}.$$

The equivalent definition

$$M_i = \{(\bar{a}_i, a_i) \in G_i | f_i(\bar{a}_i, a_i) = \varphi_i(\bar{a}_i)\}$$

shows that M_i is closed since G_i is closed and f_i and φ_i are continuous.

The graph Γ of ϕ is the subset of $\mathfrak{A} \times \mathfrak{A}$

$$\Gamma = \{(a, a') | a' \in \phi(a)\} = \{(a, a') | a'_i \in M_{\bar{a}_i} \text{ for all } i\}$$
$$= \{(a, a') | (\bar{a}_i, a'_i) \in M_i \text{ for all } i\}.$$

[†] The statement of E. G. Begle [Ref. 3, p. 546] is indeed much more general and the existence theorem can accordingly be generalized. Instead of a contractible polyhedron one might take for example an Absolute Retract (as defined in [Ref. 4, p. 222]) using the fact that the product of two A.R. is an A.R. [Ref. 1, p. 197]. For finite dimensions "Absolute Retract" is equivalent to "contractible and locally contractible (Ref. 4, pp. 235–236) compact metric space" [Ref. 4, p. 240].

Consider the subset of $\mathfrak{A} \times \mathfrak{A}$

$$\mathfrak{M}_\iota = \{(a, a')|(\bar{a}_\iota, a'_\iota) \in M_\iota\};$$

$\mathfrak{M}_\iota$ is closed since M_ι is. As $\Gamma = \bigcap_\iota \mathfrak{M}_\iota$, Γ is closed.

The conclusion of the lemma is then that there exists $a^* \in \mathfrak{A}$ such that $a^* \in \phi(a^*)$, i.e., for all ι, $a^*_\iota \in M_{\bar{a}^*_\iota}$; this is the definition of an equilibrium point a^*.

The requirement that $\varphi_\iota(\bar{a}_\iota)$ be continuous is a *joint* requirement on the two functions f_ι and $A_\iota(\bar{a}_\iota)$; it is therefore not well adapted to applications. The following *Remark* tries to overcome this.

The function $A_\iota(\bar{a}_\iota)$ is said to be *continuous* at $\bar{a}^0_\iota$ if for any $a^0_\iota \in A_\iota(\bar{a}^0_\iota)$ and any sequence $(\bar{a}^n_\iota)$ converging to $\bar{a}^0_\iota$, there exists a sequence (a^n_ι) converging to a^0_ι such that for all n, $a^n_\iota \in A_\iota(\bar{a}^n_\iota)$.

> *Remark:* If $A_\iota(\bar{a}_\iota)$ has a compact graph G_ι and is continuous at $\bar{a}^0_\iota$, if f_ι is a continuous function from G_ι to the completed real line, then $\varphi_\iota(\bar{a}_\iota)$ is continuous at $\bar{a}^0_\iota$.

We drop subscripts ι everywhere and reason as if f took its values in the real line (the isomorphism $(e^f - 1)/(e^f + 1)$ between the completed real line and the closed interval $[-1, +1]$ immediately extends the results to the general case).

> (α)   *Using only the compactness of G and the continuity of f we first prove:* For any sequence $(\bar{a}^n)$ converging to $\bar{a}^0$ and any $\varepsilon > 0$, there is an N such that $n > N$ implies $\varphi(\bar{a}^n) < \varphi(\bar{a}^0) + \varepsilon$ (in other words, $\varphi(\bar{a})$ is upper semicontinuous at $\bar{a}^0$).

For every n, choose $a^n \in A(\bar{a}^n)$ such that $f(\bar{a}^n, a^n) = \varphi(\bar{a}^n)$. Since G is compact it is possible to extract from the sequence $(\bar{a}^n, a^n)$ a subsequence $(\bar{a}^{n'}, a^{n'})$ converging to $(\bar{a}^0, a^0)$.

By the continuity of f, $f(\bar{a}^{n'}, a^{n'})$ [which is $= \varphi(\bar{a}^{n'})$] tends to $f(\bar{a}^0, a^0)$ [which is $\leq \varphi(\bar{a}^0)$]. Therefore there exists N' such that $n' > N'$ implies $\varphi(\bar{a}^{n'}) < \varphi(\bar{a}^0) + \varepsilon$. Since from any sequence $(\bar{a}^n)$ converging to $\bar{a}^0$ it is possible to extract a subsequence $(\bar{a}^{n'})$ having the desired property, any sequence $(\bar{a}^n)$ converging to $\bar{a}^0$ has the property.

> (β)   *Using in addition the continuity of $A(\bar{a})$ at $\bar{a}^0$ we prove:* For any sequence $(\bar{a}^n)$ converging to $\bar{a}^0$ and any $\varepsilon > 0$, there is an N such that $n > N$ implies $\varphi(\bar{a}^n) > \varphi(\bar{a}^0) - \varepsilon$ (in other words, $\varphi(\bar{a})$ is lower semicontinuous at $\bar{a}^0$).

Choose $a^0 \in A(\bar{a}^0)$ such that $f(\bar{a}^0, a^0) = \varphi(a^0)$. By continuity of $A(\bar{a})$ at $\bar{a}^0$, there is a sequence (a^n) converging to a^0 such that for all n, $a^n \in A(\bar{a}^n)$. By the continuity of f, $f(\bar{a}^n, a^n)$ [which is $\leq \varphi(\bar{a}^n)$] tends to $f(\bar{a}^0, a^0)$ [which is $= \varphi(\bar{a}^0)$]. Therefore there exists N such that $n > N$ implies $\varphi(\bar{a}^n) > \varphi(\bar{a}^0) - \varepsilon$.

(α) and (β) together naturally prove that $\varphi(\bar{a})$ is continuous at $\bar{a}^0$.

3   Saddle points and MinMax operator

In this section $x \in X \subset R^l$, $y \in Y \subset R^m$ and $f(x, y)$ is a function from $X \times Y$ to the completed real line. A *saddle point* of f is a point (x^0, y^0) such that

$$\text{Min}_y \; f(x^0, y) = f(x^0, y^0) = \text{Max}_x \; f(x, y^0) \tag{1}$$

It is a very particular case of an equilibrium point for two agents:

$$a_1 = x, \quad \mathfrak{A}_1 = X, \quad A_1(\bar{a}_1) \equiv X, \quad f_1(a) = f(x, y)$$
$$a_2 = y, \quad \mathfrak{A}_2 = Y, \quad A_2(\bar{a}_2) \equiv Y, \quad f_2(a) = -f(x, y)$$

One obtains therefore by using the remark:

Corollary

Let X, Y be two contractible polyhedra, and $f(x, y)$ a continuous function from $X \times Y$ to the completed real line. If for every $x^0 \in X$, $U_{x^0} = \{y \in Y | f(x^0, y) = \text{Min}_{y \in Y} f(x^0, y)\}$ is contractible and for every $y^0 \in Y$, $V_{y^0} = \{x \in X | f(x, y^0) = \text{Max}_{x \in X} f(x, y^0)\}$ is contractible, then f has a saddle point.

This corollary contains as more and more particular cases the saddle point theorems of Kakutani [7], von Neumann [Ref. 9, p. 307, and 10], and von Neumann and Morgenstern [Ref. 11, Section 17.6].

The special interest of saddle points comes from their intimate relation with the MinMax operator.

From now on X, Y are assumed to be compact and $f(x, y)$ to be continuous.

We know from the Remark that $\text{Min}_y f(x, y)$ [resp., $\text{Max}_x f(x, y)$] *is a continuous function of* x [resp., y]. The following results, already given in Ref. 11, Section 13, are proved here for completeness.

(a) $\operatorname*{Max}_{x} \operatorname*{Min}_{y} f(x, y) \leqq \operatorname*{Min}_{y} \operatorname*{Max}_{x} f(x, y).$

Let

$$A = \{x' | \operatorname*{Min}_{y} f(x', y) = \operatorname*{Max}_{x} \operatorname*{Min}_{y} f(x, y)\},$$

$$B = \{y' | \operatorname*{Max}_{x} f(x, y') = \operatorname*{Min}_{y} \operatorname*{Max}_{x} f(x, y)\}.$$

If $x' \in A$ and $y' \in B$,

$$\operatorname*{Max}_{x} \operatorname*{Min}_{y} f(x, y) = \operatorname*{Min}_{y} f(x', y) \leqq f(x', y') \leqq \operatorname*{Max}_{x} f(x, y')$$

$$= \operatorname*{Min}_{y} \operatorname*{Max}_{x} f(x, y). \tag{2}$$

The result follows from a comparison of the first and last terms.

(b)   The existence of a saddle point (x^0, y^0) implies the equality

$$\operatorname*{Max}_{x} \operatorname*{Min}_{y} f = \operatorname*{Min}_{y} \operatorname*{Max}_{x} f [= f(x^0, y^0)].$$

From the definition (1) it follows that

$$\operatorname*{Max}_{x} \operatorname*{Min}_{y} f(x, y) \geqq \operatorname*{Min}_{y} f(x^0, y) = f(x^0, y^0) = \operatorname*{Max}_{x} f(x, y^0)$$

$$\geqq \operatorname*{Min}_{y} \operatorname*{Max}_{x} f(x, y), \tag{3}$$

which together with (a) gives the result. It also gives $\operatorname*{Max}_{x} f(x, y^0) = \operatorname*{Min}_{y}\operatorname*{Max}_{x} f(x, y)$, i.e., $y^0 \in B$, and similarly $x^0 \in A$.

(c)   The equality $\operatorname*{Max}_{x}\operatorname*{Min}_{y} f = \operatorname*{Min}_{y}\operatorname*{Max}_{x} f$ implies the existence of a saddle point.

Assume that the equality holds and take $x^0 \in A$, $y^0 \in B$, Eq. (2) gives $\operatorname*{Min}_{y} f(x^0 y) = f(x^0, y^0) = \operatorname*{Max}_{x} f(x, y^0)$, which is the definition Eq. (1) of a saddle point (x^0, y^0). We have, incidentally, proved

(d)   the set of saddle points is either empty or equal to $A \times B$.

4   Historical note

A function $f(z)$ from a set Z to the completed real line $\bar{R}$ is said to be *quasi-convex* (resp., *quasi-concave*) if for any $\alpha \in \bar{R}$, the set of $z \in Z$ such that $f(z) \leqq \alpha$ (resp., $f(z) \geqq \alpha$) is convex.

Let

$$S_n = \left\{ z \in R^n | z_k \geqq 0 \quad \text{for } k = 1, \ldots, n \quad \text{and} \quad \sum_{k=1}^{n} z_k = 1 \right\}.$$

In his first study on the theory of games, J. von Neumann [9] proved:

(I)   Let $f(x, y)$ be a continuous real-valued function for $x \in S_l$ and $y \in S_m$. If for every $x^0 \in S_l$ the function $f(x^0, y)$ is quasi-convex, and if for every $y^0 \in S_m$ the function $f(x, y^0)$ is quasi-concave, then f has a saddle point.

In another paper on economics [10] he later proved a closely related lemma which S. Kakutani [7] restated in the more convenient form of the following (equivalent) fixed point theorem:

(II) Let Z be a compact convex set in R^n and $\phi: Z \to Z$ a semi-continuous multi-valued function such that for every $z \in Z$ the set $\phi(z)$ is non-empty and convex. Then ϕ has a fixed point.

The convexity assumptions were, however, irrelevant and S. Eilenberg and D. Montgomery [6] gave a fixed point theorem where convexity was replaced by acyclicity. Their result was further generalized by E. G. Begle [3].

These last two theorems deserve particular attention as valuable contributions to topology whose origin can be traced directly to economics.

The notion of an equilibrium point was first formalized by J. F. Nash [8] in the following game context. There are v players; the lth player chooses a strategy s_l in S_{n_l}; his payoff is $f_l(s)$, a polylinear function of $s_1, \ldots, s_v$. An equilibrium point is a v-tuple s^* such that for all l, $f_l(s^*) = \text{Max}_{s_l \in S_l} f_l(s_l^*, s_l)$. Nash proved the existence of such an equilibrium point.

References

[1] Aronszajn, N., and Borsuk, K., Sur la somme et le produit combinatoire des rétractes absolus, *Fundamenta Mathematicae*, 18, 193–197 (1932).

[2] Arrow, K. J., and Debreu, G., Existence of an Equilibrium for a Competitive Economy, *Econometrica*, in press (1954).

[3] Begle, E. G., A Fixed Point Theorem, *Ann. Math.*, 51, No. 3, 544–550 (May 1950).

[4] Borsuk, K., Uber eine Klasse von lokal zusammenhängenden Räumen, *Fundamenta Mathematicae*, 19, p. 220–242 (1932).

[5] Bourbaki, N., *Eléments de Mathématique*, Première partie, Livre III, Chap. IV Sec. 4, Hermann, Paris, 1942.

[6] Eilenberg, S., and Montgomery, D., Fixed Point Theorems for Multi-valued Transformations, *Am. J. Math.*, 68, 214–222 (1946).

[7] Kakutani, S., A Generalization of Brouwer's Fixed Point Theorem, *Duke Math. J.*, 8, No. 3, 457–459 (September 1941).

[8] Nash, John F., Equilibrium Points in *N*-Person Games, *Proc. Natl. Acad. Sci.* 36, 48–49 (1950).

[9] Neumann, J. von, Zur Theorie der Gesellschaftsspiele, *Math. Ann.*, 100, 295–320 (1928).

[10] Neumann, J. von, Uber ein ökonomisches Gleichungssystem und eine Verallgemeinerung des Brouwerschen Fixpunktsatzes, *Ergebnisse eines Mathematischen Kolloquiums*, 8, 73–83 (1937), translated in *Rev. Economic Studies*, *XIII*, No. 33, 1–9 (1945–46).

[11] Neumann, J. von, and Morgenstern, O., *Theory of Games and Economic Behavior*, 2nd ed., Princeton University Press, Princeton, N.J. 1947 (1st ed., 1944).

CHAPTER 3

A classical tax-subsidy problem[1]

Summary

Of Section 1: In the economic system l commodities (given quantities of which are initially available) are transformed into each other by n production-units (the technological knowledge of which is limited) and consumed by m consumption-units (the preferences of which are represented by m satisfaction functions).

Of Section 2: Given a set of values $(s_1, \ldots, s_i, \ldots, s_m)$ of the individual satisfactions, the economic efficiency of this situation is defined as follows: the quantities of all the available resources are multiplied by a number such that using these new resources and the same technological knowledge as before it is still possible to achieve for the ith individual ($i = 1, \ldots, m$) a satisfaction at least equal to s_i. The smallest of the numbers satisfying this condition is ρ, the coefficient of resource utilization of the economy in this situation[2] [3]; ρ equals one for a Pareto optimal situation, is smaller than one for a nonoptimal situation. In the last case the loss of efficiency is $1 - \rho$; a more interesting quantity (immediately derived from $1 - \rho$) is the money value of the resources which might be thrown away while still permitting the achievement of the same individual satisfactions. This latter quantity will be referred to *as the economic loss associated* with the situation $(s_1, \ldots, s_i, \ldots, s_m)$.

[1] This paper (based on Cowles Commission Discussion Paper, Economics No. 2020, July 1951) was presented at the Minneapolis Meeting of the Econometric Society, September 1951. It was prepared as part of a research project on the theory of allocation of resources conducted by the Cowles Commission for Research in Economics under contract with the RAND Corporation. It will be reprinted as Cowles Commission Paper, New Series, No. 80.

The conception of this study goes back to my reading correspondence of 1946 between M. Allais and H. Hotelling. I am very grateful to both of them for having made it available to me. I have also benefited greatly from the comments of M. Boiteux, T. C. Koopmans, and other Cowles Commission staff members and guests.

[2] The number ρ is clearly independent of the arbitrary monotonic increasing transformations affecting the satisfaction functions.

59

This definition of the loss has been critically compared in [3] with other definitions. We will only recall here that these took as a reference an *arbitrarily selected* optimal state (which was, in the problems of Sections 4–5, the initial state); moreover they could associate with two states of the system, where *all* satisfactions were the *same*, two different values of the economic loss.[3] The one exception to which these criticisms do not apply is the definition given by M. Allais [1] p. 638, but the latter rests on the *arbitrary choice* of a particular commodity.

The tastes, the technology, and the available resources are fixed in this paper and ρ is thus a function $\rho(s_1, \ldots, s_m)$ of the individual levels of satisfaction.

Of Section 3: The first and second differentials of this function play an essential role later on; they are calculated in this section.

Of Section 4: We consider now as an initial state of the economic system a Pareto optimal situation observed in a competitive market economy. In the final state, which is in the neighborhood of the initial state, all consumption-units maximize their satisfactions according to a certain price system but the behavior of production-units is entirely unspecified. Under these conditions one obtains from the results of Section 3 the general approximation formula (14) for the economic loss.

Of Section 5: As an application we consider the case where a system of indirect taxes and subsidies is introduced in a Pareto optimal state of the economy and we obtain the approximation formula (17) for the resulting economic loss.

The problem of the evaluation of this loss was first considered by J. Dupuit. His work stimulated a large number of further studies which have been reviewed by H. Hotelling in [5]. H. Hotelling himself bases his study on the assumption that in the economic change which takes place the first differential of every satisfaction vanishes, in other words that there are no (first order) income redistribution effects. Formula (17) then reduces to the much more simple formula (18); the choice among the various definitions of the loss also becomes irrelevant for these definitions practically all lead to the same result in this particular case. Only in exceptional circumstances, however, will the income redistribution effects of a system of indirect taxes and subsidies be of the second order.

The recent article [2] of M. Boiteux starts from a definition of the loss to which several of the criticisms listed at the end of the summary of section 2 apply.

1   The economic system

The activity of the economic system extends over a finite number of consecutive time-intervals and takes place in a finite number of locations. A commodity is characterized by its physical properties, the time-interval during which it is available and the place at which it is available. There are altogether l commodities (goods or services,[4] direct or indirect, etc.).

A consumption-unit is characterized by a subscript i $(i = 1, \ldots, m)$. Its activity is represented by a consumption vector x_i of the l-dimensional

---

[3] The other definitions could also yield a *positive* loss for an optimal state and/or a *negative* loss for a nonoptimal state.

[4] Including transportation services.

commodity space R_l; the components of x_i are quantities of commodities actually consumed or negatives of quantities of commodities produced (for example, different kinds of labor). The tastes of the consumption-unit are represented by a satisfaction function $s_i(x_i)$, defined but for an arbitrary monotonically increasing transformation. The *total* consumption-vector is $x = \sum_i x_i$.

A production-unit is characterized by a subscript j ($j = 1, \ldots, n$). Its activity is represented by an input-vector y_j of R_l; the components of y_j are inputs (net quantities of commodities consumed) or negatives of outputs (net quantities of commodities produced). The limitation of technological knowledge constrains y_j to satisfy the equation $e_j(y_j) = 0$ of the production surface. (We are not concerned in this paper with technological inefficiencies, i.e., with points that are above the production surfaces.) The *total* input-vector is $y = \sum_j y_j$.

Finally, if z^0 is the utilizable physical resources vector (whose components are the available quantities of each commodity), the total *net* consumption of the whole economic system must equal z^0: $x + y = z^0$. (We are not concerned with free commodities for which the total net consumption would be smaller than the available quantity.)

In a given state of the economy some components of x_i are null (commodities neither consumed nor produced by the ith consumption unit); throughout this paper we shall assume that, in the neighboring states of the economy considered, the set of null components of x_i is *the same* as in the initial state. This assumption is made for all $i = 1, \ldots, m$ and similarly for all $y_j, j = 1, \ldots, n$. $R_l^i(R_l^j)$ denotes the subspace of R_l corresponding to the nonzero components of $x_i(y_j)$; the projection of a vector such as p on $R_l^i(R_l^j)$ is denoted by $p^i(p^j)$, $x^i(y^j)$ stands for $x_i^i(y_j^j)$.

Functions are supposed to be continuous and differentiable whenever necessary.

2   The coefficient of resource utilization ρ

An economic situation is defined by the values $(s_1, \ldots, s_m)$ of the m satisfactions. The efficiency of this situation is measured by ρ, the coefficient of resource utilization of the economic system [3], the smallest number by which the quantities of all the available resources can be multiplied while still permitting for every consumption unit a satisfaction $s_i(x_i)$ at least equal to s_i. Thus, for an economic system whose technology is described by the n functions $e_j(y_j)$ and whose available resources vector is ρz^0, the situation $(s_1, \ldots, s_m)$ is optimal (in Pareto's sense). Therefore, under suitable convexity assumptions, there exists [3] an intrinsic price vector $\bar{p}$ to which consumption units and production units are adapted according to the familiar pattern (satisfaction maximization and profit maximization). In mathematical terms, there exist a vector $\bar{p}$, m vectors $\bar{x}_i$, n vectors $\bar{y}_j$, m numbers $\bar{\sigma}_i$ and n numbers $\bar{\varepsilon}_j$ such that

$$\begin{cases} s_i(\bar{x}^i) = s_i, \qquad e_j(\bar{y}^j) = 0, \\ \dfrac{ds_i}{d\bar{x}^i} = \bar{\sigma}_i \bar{p}^i, \qquad \dfrac{de_j}{d\bar{y}^j} = \bar{\varepsilon}_j \bar{p}^j, \\ \displaystyle\sum_i \bar{x}_i + \sum_j \bar{y}_j = \rho z^0. \end{cases} \qquad (1)$$

The first and the third equations hold for all i, the second and the fourth for all j. The same convention will be made for all equations of this form.

The tastes (the m functions $s_i(x_i)$), the technology (the n functions $e_j(y_j)$), and the available resources (z^0) are fixed throughout this paper. ρ is thus a function $\rho(s_1, \ldots, s_m)$ implicitly defined by (1).

The loss of efficiency associated with the situation $(s_1, \ldots, s_m)$ is $1 - \rho$.

3   First and second differentials of ρ

Let S^i be the hessian[5] matrix of $s_i(x^i)$, and similarly let E^j be that of $e_j(y^j)$. Differentiate[6] all equations of (1)

$$\begin{cases} \dfrac{ds_i}{d\bar{x}^i} \cdot d\bar{x}^i = ds_i, \qquad \dfrac{de_j}{d\bar{y}^j} \cdot d\bar{y}^j = 0, \\ S^i d\bar{x}^i = \bar{\sigma}_i \, d\bar{p}^i + \bar{p}^i \, d\bar{\sigma}_i, \qquad E^j d\bar{y}^j = \bar{\varepsilon}_j \, d\bar{p}^j + \bar{p}^j \, d\bar{\varepsilon}_j, \\ \displaystyle\sum_i d\bar{x}_i + \sum_j d\bar{y}_j = z^0 \, d\rho. \end{cases} \qquad (2)$$

From the third and fourth equations of (1), designated (1_3) and (1_4), the first and second equations of (2), designated (2_1) and (2_2), become

$$\bar{\sigma}_i(\bar{p}^i)' \, d\bar{x}^i = ds_i, \qquad \bar{\varepsilon}_j(\bar{p}^j)' \, d\bar{y}^j = 0. \qquad (3)$$

Premultiplication of (2_5) by $\bar{p}'$ yields

$$\bar{p}' \sum_i d\bar{x}_i + \bar{p}' \sum_j d\bar{y}_j = \bar{p}' z^0 \, d\rho. \qquad (4)$$

---

[5] $S^i = \left[\dfrac{\partial^2 s_i}{\partial x_h^i \partial x_k^i} \right]$ where x_h^i, x_k^i are coordinates of x^i.

[6] Primed letters indicate transposes of matrices and for the inner product of two (column) vectors, u, v we use indifferently the notations $u \cdot v$ and $u'v$. For a presentation of differentials see, for example, [7].

Since $(\bar{p}^i)' d\bar{x}^i = \bar{p}' d\bar{x}_i$ and $(\bar{p}^j)' d\bar{y}^j = \bar{p}' d\bar{y}_j$, (3) and (4) give

$$\bar{p}' z^0 \, d\rho = \sum_i \frac{ds_i}{\bar{\sigma}_i}. \tag{5}$$

The first differential of ρ is thus known. To obtain the second differential of ρ we differentiate (5) to obtain

$$\bar{p}' z^0 \, d^2\rho + d\bar{p}' z_0 \, d\rho = \sum_i \left(\frac{d^2 s_i}{\bar{\sigma}_i} - \frac{ds_i \, d\bar{\sigma}_i}{\bar{\sigma}_i^2} \right). \tag{6}$$

However, $d\bar{p}$ and $d\bar{\sigma}_i$ are not known and the rest of the present section is devoted to the solution of this difficulty.

Rewrite (2_3) and (3_1) as follows:

$$\begin{cases} \dfrac{1}{\bar{\sigma}_i} S^i \, d\bar{x}^i - \bar{p}^i \dfrac{d\bar{\sigma}_i}{\bar{\sigma}_i} = d\bar{p}^i \\[2ex] (\bar{p}^i)' \, d\bar{x}^i = \dfrac{ds_i}{\bar{\sigma}_i}. \end{cases}$$

If $\sum^i = \begin{bmatrix} \dfrac{1}{\bar{\sigma}_i} S^i & \bar{p}^i \\[1.5ex] (\bar{p}^i)' & 0 \end{bmatrix}$, the above system can be written

$$\sum^i \begin{bmatrix} d\bar{x}^i \\[1ex] -\dfrac{d\bar{\sigma}_i}{\bar{\sigma}_i} \end{bmatrix} = \begin{bmatrix} d\bar{p}^i \\[1ex] \dfrac{ds_i}{\bar{\sigma}_i} \end{bmatrix}, \quad \text{i.e.,} \quad \begin{bmatrix} d\bar{x}^i \\[1ex] -\dfrac{d\bar{\sigma}_i}{\bar{\sigma}_i} \end{bmatrix} = \left(\sum^i \right)^{-1} \begin{bmatrix} d\bar{p}^i \\[1ex] \dfrac{ds_i}{\bar{\sigma}_i} \end{bmatrix}. \tag{7}$$

$\left(\sum^i \right)^{-1}$ has the form $\left(\sum^i \right)^{-1} = \begin{bmatrix} X^i & \gamma^i \\ (\gamma^i)' & c^i \end{bmatrix}$ where γ^i is a column vector, c^i a number.[7] Therefore (7_2) is equivalent to

$$\begin{cases} d\bar{x}^i = X^i \, d\bar{p}^i + \gamma^i \dfrac{ds_i}{\bar{\sigma}_i} \\[2ex] -\dfrac{d\bar{\sigma}_i}{\bar{\sigma}_i} = (\gamma^i)' \, d\bar{p}^i + c^i \dfrac{ds_i}{\bar{\sigma}_i}. \end{cases} \tag{8}$$

[7] The elements of $\left(\sum^i\right)^{-1}$ are familiar concepts: γ^i is the derivative $\partial x^i/\partial r$ of demanded quantities x^i with respect to income r when prices are constant; the elements of X^i are the classical substitution terms; the equations of Slutsky amount to the remark that the matrix X^i is symmetric, an immediate consequence of the fact that S^i is symmetric; c^i is the only term of $\left(\sum^i\right)^{-1}$ which depends on the arbitrary monotonically increasing transformation affecting $s_i(x^i)$.

The convexity assumptions [3] underlying this study imply that X^i, Y^j and therefore X, Y, Z are semi-definite negative matrices.

Strict convexity must in fact be assumed here so that matrices such as $\left(\sum^i\right)^{-1}$ may exist.

Let X_i be the $l \cdot l$ matrix obtained by inserting in X^i rows and columns of zeros corresponding to the zero components of x_i. Let γ_i be the $l \cdot 1$ matrix obtained by inserting similarly zeros in γ^i. It is clear that in (8), $\bar{x}^i, X^i, \bar{p}^i, \gamma^i$ can be replaced by $\bar{x}_i, X_i, \bar{p}, \gamma_i$.

We add then all the equations (8_1) denoting by $X = \sum_i X_i$ the aggregate consumption substitution matrix.

$$d\bar{x} = X d\bar{p} + \sum_i \gamma_i \frac{ds_i}{\bar{\sigma}_i}. \tag{9}$$

Since (2_3) and (3_1) are identical in form to (2_4) and (3_2) one obtains without any calculation.

$$d\bar{y} = Y d\bar{p} \tag{10}$$

where the aggregate production substitution matrix Y is derived from the E^j exactly as X is derived from the S^i.

Let finally $Z = X + Y$ be the aggregate substitution matrix; one obtains by addition of (9) and (10). (See (2_5).)

$$Z d\bar{p} = z^0 d\rho - \sum_i \gamma_i \frac{ds_i}{\bar{\sigma}_i}. \tag{11}$$

All the terms of the right-hand member are known; however, the matrix Z is singular and $d\bar{p}$ is not uniquely determined (this was obvious a priori since $\bar{p}$ is determined but for a multiplication by a positive number). Still two distinct solutions $(d\bar{p})^1$ and $(d\bar{p})^2$ of (11) give the same value for $d^2\rho$ in (6). (The value of $-(d\bar{\sigma}_i/\bar{\sigma}_i)$ is obtained from (8_2).)

4   A general expression of the economic loss

We consider as an initial state of the system a Pareto optimal situation $(s_1^0, \ldots, s_m^0)$ observed in a competitive market economy (the superscript 0 shall refer to the initial point); equations (1) are therefore satisfied by the actually observed values $p^0, x_i^0, y_j^0, \sigma_i^0, \varepsilon_j^0$ and by the value $\rho^0 = 1$ [3].

A new observed state of the system is characterized by the values of the observed quantities (denoted by non-barred letters). The new values $(s_1, \ldots, s_m)$ of the satisfactions determine, by means of equations (1), the values of the quantities (denoted by barred letters) characterizing a certain hypothetical state of the system. We must consider this hypothetical state in order to determine the value of ρ associated with the new observed state. At the initial point the values of barred and non-barred letters are equal.

If ρ is the value of the coefficient of resource utilization for the new observed state, the change $\Delta\rho = \rho - \rho^0$ is given by the development

$$\Delta\rho = d\rho + \tfrac{1}{2}d^2\rho + \cdots.$$

Since $\rho^0 = 1$ is the maximum [3] of the function $\rho(s_1, \ldots, s_m)$ under the constraints $e_j(y_j) = 0$ and $x + y = z^0$, $d\rho = 0$ at the initial point. An approximation formula for $\Delta\rho$, based on the lowest order term of the above development, is thus $\frac{1}{2}d^2\rho$, and the money value of the economic loss admits the approximation $-\frac{1}{2}p^0 \cdot z^0 d^2\rho$.

We assume that in every observed state of the economy, there is a price vector p according to which every consumption-unit maximizes its satisfaction. Then, as in (3), $ds_i/\sigma_i = p' dx_i$ which yields after differentiation and summation over i

$$dp' \, dx + p' \, d^2x = \sum_i \left(\frac{d^2 s_i}{\sigma_i} - \frac{ds_i \, d\sigma_i}{\sigma_i^2} \right). \tag{12}$$

Subtract (12) from (6) (remembering that at the initial point $d\rho = 0$ and barred letters coincide with non-barred letters).

$$p^0 \cdot z^0 d^2\rho - [dp \cdot dx + p^0 \cdot d^2x] = \sum_i \frac{ds_i}{\sigma_i^0} \left(\frac{d\sigma_i}{\sigma_i^0} - \frac{d\bar{\sigma}_i}{\sigma_i^0} \right). \tag{13}$$

(8) holds for non-barred as well as for barred letters, so (8_2) gives

$$\sum_i \frac{ds_i}{\sigma_i^0} \left(\frac{d\sigma_i}{\sigma_i^0} - \frac{d\bar{\sigma}_i}{\sigma_i^0} \right) = \sum_i \frac{ds_i}{\sigma_i^0} \gamma_i'(d\bar{p} - dp).$$

(8_1) gives in turn $ds_i/\sigma_i^0 \, \gamma_i' = (dx_i - X_i dp)'$. Denoting $d\xi = dx - X dp$, we finally obtain from (13)

$$-\tfrac{1}{2}p^0 \cdot z^0 d^2\rho = -\tfrac{1}{2}[dp \cdot dx + p^0 \cdot d^2x + d\xi \cdot (d\bar{p} - dp)]. \tag{14}$$

The right-hand member is the general expression of the economic loss that we sought. Every vector therein is an *observed* vector with the exception of $d\bar{p}$ which is obtained (see (11) and (8_1)) as a solution of the equation

$$Z d\bar{p} = -d\xi.$$

(We emphasized at the end of Section 4 that any solution may be chosen.)

$d\xi$ is the excess of dx, the actual variation of total consumption, over $X dp$, the variation which would take place if consumption-units were confronted with the actual price change dp, while their satisfactions were all held constant. If one assumes, as Hotelling does in [5], that in the actual change the first differential of every satisfaction vanishes ($ds_i = 0$, i.e., $p \cdot dx_i = 0$ for all $i = 1, \ldots, m$),[8] then $d\xi = 0$, and (14) takes a notably more simple form, already given by Allais [1] p. 616.

---

[8] In general it can only be said that $p \cdot dx = \sum_i p \cdot dx_i = 0$ since $d\rho = 0$.

$Zd\bar{p}$ is the variation in the net consumption of the whole economy corresponding to the price change $d\bar{p}$ when all satisfactions are held constant and all production-units maximize their profits on the basis of $\bar{p}$.

5   Application to the tax-subsidy case

The initial state of the economy is the same as in section 4[9] and a system of indirect taxes and subsidies is introduced.[10] Since in every observed state of the economy every consumption-unit is adapted to the price system p, we can apply formula (14) to the present particular case.

In a precise way, the amount t_h^+ is paid by every production-unit for every unit of the hth commodity ($h = 1, \ldots, l$) which is an input and the amount t_h^- for every unit which is an output. t_h^+ or t_h^- is positive for a tax, negative for a subsidy.[11] The tax-subsidy system is thus represented by two vectors t^+ and t^- in R_l. Its net return is redistributed to consumption-units in a way which is left unspecified.

The production function of the jth production-unit can be written in the form $e_j(y_j^+, y_j^-) = 0$ where the components of y_j^+ (y_j^-) coincide with those of y_j when they are positive (negative) and are null otherwise. Let p be the price system prevailing throughout the economy. The jth production-unit behaves as if the prices of its inputs were actually $(p + t^+)^j$ and the prices of its outputs $(p - t^-)^j$; since it maximizes its profit on the basis of the price system p and the tax-subsidy system t^+, t^-, the relation

$$(p + t^+)^j \cdot d(y_j^+)^j + (p - t^-)^j \cdot d(y_j^-)^j = 0 \tag{15}$$

holds in every observed state of the economy. Denoting[12] $q^+ = \sum_j y_j^+$, $q^- = \sum_j y_j^-$ and summing the equations (15) over j we obtain

$$(p + t^+)^j \cdot d(y_j^+)^j + (p - t^-)^j \cdot d(y_j^-)^j = 0$$

Differentiating, and noting that at the initial point $t^+ = 0 = t^-$, we obtain

$$(dp + dt^+) \cdot dq^+ + (dp - dt^-) \cdot dq^- + p^0 \cdot d^2q^+ + p^0 \cdot d^2q^- = 0.$$

[9] Thus there may exist direct taxes of the following kind: a given (positive or negative) amount θ_i is paid by the ith consumption-unit and $\sum_i \theta_i = 0$.

[10] We might also consider the economy as partitioned into nations and introduce further a system of tariffs (which is formally identical with a system of taxes on transportation services). Formula (17) would then give an approximation of the economic loss for the set of trading nations as a whole; however a tariff on a commodity is not, in general, a small enough fraction of the price for that approximation to be satisfactory.

[11] These taxes and subsidies might as well be given in the form of percentages of the prices.

It must also be remarked that proportional taxes paid by consumption-units for the commodities that they buy (or sell like labor) are *equivalent* to the same taxes paid by production-units when they sell (or buy) those commodities.

[12] Note that q^+ (q^-) is different from y^+ (y^-) formed from y as y_j^+ (y_j^-) was formed from y_i.

Since $q^+ + q^- + x = z^0$,

$$dt^+ \cdot dq^+ - dt^- \cdot dq^- = dp \cdot dx + p^0 \cdot d^2x. \qquad (16)$$

(14) and (16) finally yield the approximation formula for the money value of the economic loss due to the tax-subsidy system:

$$-\tfrac{1}{2}[dt^+ \cdot dq^+ - dt^- \cdot dq^- + d\xi \cdot (d\bar{p} - dp)]. \qquad (17)$$

Its interpretation is as follows:

Select any commodity, say the hth; dt_h^+ is the amount of the tax (or subsidy) on a unit of the hth commodity when it is an input; dq_h^+ is the variation of the *gross* input of the hth commodity for the whole production sector due to the introduction of the tax-subsidy system. The products $dt_h^+ \times dq_h^+$ are formed and added for all commodities. One proceeds similarly to obtain $dt^- \cdot dq^-$ and so to obtain the first term

$$-\tfrac{1}{2}[dt^+ \cdot dq^+ - dt^- \cdot dq^-] \qquad (18)$$

to which (17) reduces when $ds_i = 0$ for all $i = 1, \ldots, m$. The interpretation of all the elements of the second term

$$-\tfrac{1}{2}d\xi \cdot (d\bar{p} - dp) \qquad (19)$$

has been given at the end of section 4.[13]

References[14]

[1] Allais, M., *A la Recherche d'une Discipline Economique*, Tome I, Paris: Ateliers Industria, 1943, Ch. IV, Section E.
[2] Boiteux, M., Le "Revenu Distribuable" et les Pertes Economiques, *Econometrica*, Vol. 19, April 1951, pp. 112–133.
[3] Debreu, G., The Coefficient of Resource Utilization, *Econometrica*, Vol. 19, July 1951, pp. 273–292.
[4] Friedman, M., The "Welfare" Effects of an Income Tax and an Excise Tax, *Journal of Political Economy*, Vol. 60, February 1952, pp. 25–33.
[5] Hotelling, H., The General Welfare in Relation to Problems of Taxation and of Railway and Utility Rates, *Econometrica*, Vol. 6, July 1938, pp. 242–269.
[6] Hotelling, H., and R. Frisch, Papers on the Dupuit Taxation Theorem, *Econometrica*, Vol. 7, April 1939, pp. 145–160.
[7] La Vallée Poussin, Ch.-J. de, *Cours d'Analyse Infinitésimale*, Vol. 1, 8th ed., New York: Dover, 1946, Chs. I to IV.

[13] The net return of the tax-subsidy system is $q^+ \cdot dt^+ - q^- \cdot dt^-$.

[14] A good survey of the literature up to 1938 has been made by H. Hotelling in [5]. To my knowledge, [2] is the only study published since then dealing with the specific problem of evaluating the economic loss associated with a system of indirect taxes and subsidies. However, a score of articles have studied other efficiency aspects of taxation during the same period (see for example the bibliography of M. Friedman [4]). The closely related work of M. Allais [1] must also be added.

References concerning Pareto optimal states and the general problem of definition of the economic loss will be found in [3].

CHAPTER 4

Existence of an equilibrium for a competitive economy

by Kenneth J. Arrow and Gerard Debreu[1]

A. Wald has presented a model of production and a model of exchange and proofs of the existence of an equilibrium for each of them. Here proofs of the existence of an equilibrium are given for an *integrated* model of production, exchange and consumption. In addition the assumptions made on the technologies of producers and the tastes of consumers are significantly weaker than Wald's. Finally a simplification of the structure of the proofs has been made possible through use of the concept of an abstract economy, a generalization of that of a game.

Introduction

L. Walras [24] first formulated the state of the economic system at any point of time as the solution of a system of simultaneous equations representing the demand for goods by consumers, the supply of goods by producers, and the equilibrium condition that supply equal demand on every market. It was assumed that each consumer acts so as to maximize his utility, each producer acts so as to maximize his profit, and perfect competition prevails, in the sense that each producer and consumer regards the prices paid and received as independent of his own choices. Walras did not, however, give any conclusive arguments to show that the equations, as given, have a solution.

The investigation of the existence of solutions is of interest both for descriptive and for normative economics. Descriptively, the view that the

[1] This paper was read at a meeting of the Econometric Society, Chicago, December 27, 1952. The work of the authors was prepared for the Office of Naval Research under contracts N6onr-25133 (NR-047-004) and Nonr-358(01) (NR-047-006), respectively.

competitive model is a reasonably accurate description of reality, at least for certain purposes, presupposes that the equations describing the model are consistent with each other. Hence, one check on the empirical usefulness of the model is the prescription of the conditions under which the equations of competitive equilibrium have a solution.

Perhaps as important is the relation between the existence of solutions to a competitive equilibrium and the problems of normative or welfare economics. It is well known that, under suitable assumptions on the preferences of consumers and the production possibilities of producers, the allocation of resources in a competitive equilibrium is optimal in the sense of Pareto (no redistribution of goods or productive resources can improve the position of one individual without making at least one other individual worse off), and conversely every Pareto-optimal allocation of resources can be realized by a competitive equilibrium (see for example, Arrow [1], Debreu [4], and the references given there). From the point of view of normative economics the problem of existence of an equilibrium for a competitive system is therefore also basic.

To study this question, it is first necessary to specify more carefully than is generally done the precise assumptions of a competitive economy.The main results of this paper are two theorems stating very general conditions under which a competitive equilibrium will exist. Loosely speaking, the first theorem asserts that if every individual has initially some positive quantity of every commodity available for sale, then a competitive equilibrium will exist. The second theorem asserts the existence of competitive equilibrium if there are some types of labor with the following two properties: (1) each individual can supply some positive amount of at least one such type of labor; and (2) each such type of labor has a positive usefulness in the production of desired commodities. The conditions of the second theorem, particularly, may be expected to be satisfied in a wide variety of actual situations, though not, for example, if there is insufficient substitutability in the structure of production.

The assumptions made below are, in several respects, weaker and closer to economic reality than A. Wald's [23]. Unlike his models, ours presents an integrated system of production and consumption which takes account of the circular flow of income. The proof of existence is also simpler than his. Neither the uniqueness nor the stability of the competitive solution is investigated in this paper. The latter study would require specification of the dynamics of a competitive market as well as the definition of equilibrium.

Mathematical techniques are set-theoretical. A central concept is that of an abstract economy, a generalization of the concept of a game.

The last section contains a detailed historical note.

1   Statement of the first existence theorem for a competitive equilibrium

1.0 In this section, a model of a competitive economy will be described, and certain assumptions will be made concerning the production and consumption units in the economy. The notion of equilibrium for such an economy will be defined, and a theorem stated about the existence of this equilibrium.

1.1 We suppose there are a finite number of distinct commodities (including all kinds of services). Each commodity may be bought or sold for delivery at one of a finite number of distinct locations and one of a finite number of future time points. For the present purposes, the same commodity at two different locations or two different points of time will be regarded as two different commodities. Hence, there are altogether a finite number of commodities (when the concept is used in the extended sense of including spatial and temporal specifications). Let the number of commodities be l; the letter h, which runs from 1 to l, will designate different commodities.

1.2.0 The commodities, or at least some of them, are produced in *production units* (e.g., firms). The number of production units will be assumed to be a finite number n; different production units will be designated by the letter j. Certain basic assumptions will be made about the technological nature of the production process; before stating them, a few elements of vector and set notation will be given.

1.2.1

$x \geqq y$ means $x_h \geqq y_h$ for each component h;

$x \geq y$ means $x \geqq y$ but not $x = y$;

$x > y$ means $x_h > y_h$ for each component h.

R^l is the Euclidean space of l dimensions, i.e., the set of all vectors with l components.

0 is the vector all of whose components are 0.

$\{x| \quad \}$, where the blank is filled in by some statement involving x, means the set of all x's for which that statement is true.

$\Omega = \{x | x \in R^l, x \geqq 0\}$.

For any set of vectors A, let $-A = \{x | -x \in A\}$.

For any sets of vectors A_ι $(\iota = 1, \ldots, v)$, let

$$\sum_{\iota=1}^{v} A_\iota = \left\{ x | x = \sum_{\iota=1}^{v} x_\iota \text{ for some } x_1, \ldots, x_v, \text{ where } x_\iota \in A_\iota \right\}.$$

1.2.2 For each production unit j, there is a set Y_j of possible production plans. An element y_j of Y_j is a vector in R^l, the hth component of which, y_{hj}, designates the output of commodity h according to that plan. Inputs are treated as negative components. Let $Y = \sum_{j=1}^{n} Y_j$; then the elements of Y represent all possible input – output schedules for the production sector as a whole. The following assumptions about the sets Y_j will be made:

I.a Y_j is a closed convex subset of R^l containing 0 $(j = 1,\ldots,n)$.
I.b $Y \cap \Omega = 0$.
I.c $Y \cap (-Y) = 0$.

Assumption I.a. implies non-increasing returns to scale, for if $y_j \in Y_j$ and $0 \leq \lambda \leq 1$, then $\lambda y_j = \lambda y_j + (1 - \lambda)0 \in Y_j$, since $0 \in Y_j$ and Y_j is convex. If we assumed in addition the additivity of production possibility vectors, Y_j would be a convex cone, i.e., constant returns to scale would prevail. If, however, we assume that among the factors used by a firm are some which are not transferable in the market and so do not appear in the list of commodities, the production possibility vectors, if we consider only the components which correspond to marketable commodities, will not satisfy the additivity axiom.[2] The closure of Y_j merely says that if vectors arbitrarily close to y_j are in Y_j, then so is y_j. Naturally, $0 \in Y_j$, since a production unit can always go out of existence. It is to be noted that the list of production units should include not only actually existing ones but those that might enter the market under suitable price conditions.

I.b says that one cannot have an aggregate production possibility vector with a positive component unless at least one component is negative; i.e., it is impossible to have any output unless there is some input.

I.c asserts the impossibility of two production possibility vectors which exactly cancel each other, in the sense that the outputs of one are exactly the inputs of the other. The simplest justification for I.c. is to note that some type of labor is necessary for any production activity, while labor cannot be produced by production units. If $y \in Y$, and $y \neq 0$, then $y_h < 0$ for some h corresponding to a type of labor, so that $-y_h > 0$, (here, y_h is the hth component of the vector y). Since labor cannot be produced, $-y$ cannot belong to Y.[3]

Since commodities are differentiated according to time as well as physical characteristics, investment plans which involve future planned purchases and sales are included in the model of production used here.

[2] The existence of factors private to the firm is the standard justification in economic theory for diminishing returns to scale. See, e.g., the discussion of "free rationed goods" by Professor Hart [9], pp. 4, 38; also, Hicks [10], pp. 82–83; Samuelson [18], pp. 84.

[3] The assumptions about production used here are a generalization of the "linear programming" assumptions. The present set is closely related to that given by Professor Koopmans [12]. In particular, I.b. is Koopmans' "Impossibility of the Land of Cockaigne," I.c. is "Irreversibility" (see [12], pp. 48–50).

1.2.3 The preceding assumptions have related to the *technological* aspects of production. Under the usual assumptions of perfect competition, the *economic* motivation for production is the maximization of profits taking prices as given. One property of the competitive equilibrium must certainly be

1   y_j^* maximizes $p^* \cdot y_j$ over the set Y_j, for each j.

Here, the asterisks denote equilibrium values, and p^* denotes the equilibrium price vector.[4] The above condition is the first of a series which, taken together, define the notion of *competitive equilibrium*.

1.3.0 Analogously to production, we assume the existence of a number of *consumption units*, typically families or individuals but including also institutional consumers. The number of consumption units is m; different consumption units will be designated by the letter i. For any consumption unit i, the vector in R^l representing its consumption will be designated by x_i. The hth component, x_{hi}, represents the quantity of the hth commodity consumed by the ith individual. For any commodity, other than a labor service supplied by the individual, the rate of consumption is necessarily non-negative. For labor services, the amount supplied may be regarded as the negative of the rate of "consumption," so that $x_{hi} \leq 0$ if h denotes a labor service. Let $\mathscr{L}$ denote the set of commodities which are labor services. For any $h \in \mathscr{L}$, we may suppose there is some upper limit to the amount supplied, i.e., a lower limit to x_{hi}, since, for example, he cannot supply more than 24 hours of labor in a day.

II   The set of consumption vectors X_i available to individual i $(= 1, \ldots, m)$ is a closed convex subset of R^l which is bounded from below; i.e., there is a vector ξ_i such that $\xi_i \leq x_i$ for all $x_i \in X_i$.

The set X_i includes all consumption vectors among which the individual could conceivably choose if there were no budgetary restraints. Impossible combinations of commodities, such as the supplying of several types of labor to a total amount of more than 24 hours a day or the consumption of a bundle of commodities insufficient to maintain life, are regarded as excluded from X_i.

1.3.1 As is standard in economic theory, the choice by the consumer from a given set of alternative consumption vectors is supposed to be made in accordance with a preference scale for which there is a utility indicator function $u_i(x_i)$ such that $u_i(x_i) \geq u_i(x_i')$ if and only if x_i is preferred or indifferent to x_i' according to individual i.

---

[4]   For any two vectors u, v, the notation $u \cdot v$ denotes their inner product, i.e., $\sum_h u_h v_h$. Since y_{hj} is positive for outputs, negative for inputs, $p^* \cdot y_j$ denotes the profit from the production plan y_j at prices p^*.

III.a $u_i(x_i)$ is a continuous function on X_i.

III.b   For any $x_i \in X_i$, there is an $x_i' \in X_i$ such that $u_i(x_i') > u_i(x_i)$.

III.c   If $u_i(x_i) > u_i(x_i')$ and $0 < t < 1$, then $u_i[tx_i + (1-t)x_i'] > u_i(x_i')$.

III.a is, of course, a standard assumption in consumers' demand theory. It is usually regarded as a self-evident corollary of the assumption that choices are made in accordance with an ordering, but this is not accurate. Actually, for X_i a subset of a Euclidean space (as is ordinarily taken for granted), the existence of a continuous utility indicator is equivalent to the following assumption: for all x_i', the sets $\{x_i | x_i \in X_i \text{ and } x_i' \text{ preferred or indifferent to } x_i\}$ and $\{x_i | x_i \in X_i \text{ and } x_i \text{ preferred or indifferent to } x_i'\}$ are closed (in X_i); see Debreu [6]. The assumption amounts to a continuity assumption on the preference relation.

III.b assumes that there is no point of saturation, no consumption vector which the individual would prefer to all others. It should be noted that this assumption can be weakened to state merely that no consumption vector attainable with the present technological and resource limitations is a point of saturation. Formally, the revised assumption would read,

III'.b   For any $x_i \in \hat{X}_i$, there is an $x_i' \in X_i$ such that $u_i(x_i') > u_i(x_i)$, where $\hat{X}_i$ has the meaning given it in 3.3.0 below.

III.c corresponds to the usual assumption that the indifference surfaces are convex in the sense that the set $\{x_i | x_i \in X_i \text{ and } u_i(x_i) \geq \alpha\}$ is a convex set for any fixed real number α.

The last statement, which asserts the *quasi-concavity* of the function $u_i(x_i)$ is indeed implied by III.c (but is obviously weaker). For suppose x^1 and x^2 are such that $u_i(x^n) \geq \alpha$ $(n = 1, 2)$ and $0 < t < 1$. Let $x^3 = tx^1 + (1-t)x^2$. Without loss of generality, we may suppose that $u_i(x^1) \geq u_i(x^2)$. If the strict inequality holds, then $u_i(x^3) > u_i(x^2) \geq \alpha$, by III.c. Suppose now $u_i(x^1) = u_i(x^2)$, and suppose $u_i(x^3) < u_i(x^2)$. Then, from III.a, we can find x^4, a strict convex combination of x^3 and x^1, such that $u_i(x^3) < u_i(x^4) < u_i(x^1) = u_i(x^2)$. The point x^3 can be expressed as a strict convex combination of x^4 and x^2; since $u_i(x^4) < u_i(x^2)$, it follows from III.c that $u_i(x^3) > u_i(x^4)$, which contradicts the inequality just stated. Hence, the supposition that $u_i(x^3) < u_i(x^2)$ is false, so that $u_i(x^3) \geq u_i(x^2) \geq \alpha$.

Actually, it is customary in consumers' demand theory to make a slightly stronger assumption than the quasi-concavity of $u_i(x_i)$, namely, that $u_i(x_i)$ is *strictly* quasi-concave, by which is meant that if $u_i(x_i) \geq u_i(x_i')$ and $0 < t < 1$, then $u_i[tx_i + (1-t)x_i'] > u_i(x_i')$. This is equivalent to saying that the indifference surfaces do not contain any line segments, which again is equivalent to the assumption that for all sets of prices and incomes, the demand functions, which give the coordinates of the consumption vector which maximizes utility for a given set of prices and income, are single-valued. Clearly, strict quasi-concavity is a *stronger* assumption than III.c.[5]

1.3.2 We also assume that the ith consumption unit is endowed with a vector ζ_i of initial holdings of the different types of commodities available and a contractual claim to the share α_{ij} of the profit of the jth production unit for each j.

IV.a $\zeta_i \in R^l$; for some $x_i \in X_i$, $x_i < \zeta_i$;
IV.b   For all i, j, $\alpha_{ij} \geqq 0$; for all j, $\sum_{i=1}^{m} \alpha_{ij} = 1$.

The component ζ_{hi} denotes the amount of commodity h held initially by individual i. We may extend this to include all debts payable in terms of commodity h, debts owed to individual i being added to ζ_{hi} and debts owed by him being deducted. Thus, for $h \in \mathscr{L}$, ζ_{hi} would differ from 0 only by the amount of debts payable in terms of that particular labor service. (It is not necessary that the debts cancel out for the economy as a whole; thus debts to or from foreigners may be included, provided they are payable in some commodity.)

The second half of IV.a asserts in effect that every individual could consume out of his initial stock in some feasible way and still have a positive amount of *each* commodity available for trading in the market.[6] This assumption is clearly unrealistic. However, the necessity of this assumption or some parallel one for the validity of the existence theorem points up an important principle; to have equilibrium, it is necessary that each individual possess some asset or be capable of supplying some labor service which commands a positive price at equilibrium. In IV.a, this is guaranteed by insisting that an individual be capable of supplying something of each commodity; at least one will be valuable (in the sense of having a price greater than zero) at equilibrium since there will be at least one positive price at equilibrium, as guaranteed by the assumptions about the nature of the price system made in 1.4 below. A much weaker assumption of the same type is made in Theorem II.

1.3.3 The basic economic motivation in the choice of a consumption vector is that of maximizing utility among all consumption vectors which satisfy the budget restraint, i.e., whose cost at market prices does not exceed the individual's income. His income, in turn, can be regarded as having

[5] The remarks in the text show that strict quasi-concavity implies III.c, while III.c implies quasi-concavity. To show that strict quasi-concavity is actually a stronger assumption than III.c, we need only exhibit a utility function satisfying III.c but not strictly quasi-concave. The function $u_i(x_i) = \sum_{h=1}^{l} x_{hi}$ has these properties.

[6] This assumption plays the same role as the one made by Professor von Neumann in his study of a dynamic model of production [16] that each commodity enters into every production process either as an input or as an output.

three components: wages, receipts from sales of initially held stocks of commodities and claims expressible in terms of them, and dividends from the profits of production units. This economic principle must certainly hold for equilibrium values of prices and of the profits of the production units.

2   x_i^* maximizes $u_i(x_i)$ over the set $\{x_i | x_i \in X_i, \ p^* \cdot x_i \leq p^* \cdot \zeta_i + \sum_{j=1}^{n} \alpha_{ij} p^* \cdot y_j^* \}$.

This, like Condition 1 in 1.2.3, is a condition of a competitive equilibrium. Because of the definition of labor services supplied as negative components of x_i, $p^* \cdot x_i$ represents the excess of expenditures on commodities over wage income. The term $p^* \cdot \zeta_i$ represents the receipts from the sale of initially held commodities. The term $\sum_{j=1}^{n} \alpha_{ij} p^* \cdot y_j^*$ denotes the revenue of consumption unit i from dividends.

1.4.0 It remains to discuss the system of prices and the meaning of an equilibrium on any market.

3   $p^* \in P = \left\{ p \mid p \in R^l, \ p \geq 0, \ \sum_{h=1}^{l} p_h = 1 \right\}$.

Condition 3 basically expresses the requirement that prices be non-negative and not all zero. Without any loss of generality, we may normalize the vector p by requiring that the sum of its coordinates be 1, since all relations are homogeneous (of the first order) in p.

1.4.1 Conditions 1 and 2 are the conditions for the equilibrium of the production and consumption units, respectively, for given p^*. Hence, the supply and demand for all commodities is determined as a function of p (not necessarily single-valued) if we vary p and at the same time instruct each production and consumption unit to behave as if the announced value of p were the equilibrium value. The market for any commodity is usually considered to be in equilibrium when the supply for that commodity equals the demand; however, we have to consider the possibility that at a zero price, supply will exceed demand. This is the classical case of a free good.

Let

$$x = \sum_i x_i, \ y = \sum_j y_j, \ \zeta = \sum_i \zeta_i, \ z = x - y - \zeta.$$

The vector z has as its components the excess of demand over supply (including both produced and initially available supply) for the various commodities.

4   $z^* \leq 0, \ p^* \cdot z^* = 0$.

Condition 4 expresses the discussion of the preceding paragraph. We have broadly the dynamic picture of the classical "law of supply and demand" (see, e.g., [18], p. 263). That is, the price of a commodity rises if demand exceeds supply, falls if supply exceeds demand. Equilibrium is therefore incompatible with excess demand on any market, since price would simply rise; hence the first part of Condition 4 for equilibrium is justified. An excess of supply over demand drives price down, but, in view of Condition 3, no price can be driven below 0. Hence, $z_h^* < 0$ for some commodity h is possible, but only if $p_h^* = 0$. Since $p_h^* \geqq 0$ for all h and $z_h^* \leqq 0$ for all h, $p^* \cdot z^* = \sum_h p_h^* z_h^*$ is a sum of nonpositive terms. This sum can be zero if and only if $p_h^* z_h^* = 0$ for all h, i.e., either $z_h^* = 0$ or $z_h^* < 0$ and $p_h^* = 0$. Condition 4, therefore, sums up precisely the equilibrium conditions that are desired.[7]

1.4.2 In the preceding paragraph, it was implicitly assumed that for a commodity with a positive price the entire initial stock held by a consumption unit was available as a supply on the market along with amounts supplied by production and consumption units as a result of profit- and utility-maximization respectively (in this context, consumption by a consumption unit out of his own stocks counts both as supply on the market and as demand to the same numerical amount).

This becomes evident upon noting that each individual spends his entire *potential* income because of the absence of saturation (and since the model covers his entire economic life). More precisely, III.b. shows that there exists an x_i' such that

$$u_i(x_i') > u_i(x_i^*),$$

where x_i^* is the equilibrium value of x_i. Let t be an arbitrarily small positive number; by III.c, $u_i[tx_i' + (1 - t)x_i^*] > u_i(x_i^*)$. That is, in every neighborhood of x_i^*, there is a point of X_i preferred to x_i^*. From Condition 2,

$$p^* \cdot x_i^* \leqq p^* \cdot \zeta_i + \sum_j \alpha_{ij} p^* \cdot y_j^*.$$

Suppose the strict inequality held. Then we could choose a point of X_i for which the inequality still held and which was preferred to x_i^*, a contradiction of Condition 2.

$$p^* \cdot x_i^* = p^* \cdot \zeta_i + \sum_j \alpha_{ij} p^* \cdot y_j^*. \tag{1}$$

To achieve his equilibrium consumption plan, x_i^*, individual i must actually receive the total income given on the right-hand side. He cannot

---

[7] The view that some commodities might be free goods because supply always exceeded demand goes back to the origins of marginal utility theory (see Menger [13], pp. 98–100). The critical importance of rephrasing the equilibrium condition for prices in the form of Condition 4 for the problem of the existence of a solution to the Walrasian equilibrium equations was first perceived by Schlesinger [19].

therefore withhold any initial holdings of commodity h from the market if $p_h^* > 0$.

1.5.0 *Definition:* A set of vectors $(x_1^*, \ldots, x_m^*, y_1^*, \ldots, y_n^*, p^*)$ is said to be a competitive equilibrium if it satisfies Conditions 1–4.

1.5.1 *Theorem I*

For any economic system satisfying *Assumptions* I–IV, there is a competitive equilibrium.

2 A lemma on abstract economies

2.0 In this section, the concept of an *abstract economy*, a generalization of that of a *game*, will be introduced, and a definition of equilibrium given. A lemma giving conditions for the existence of equilibrium of an abstract economy will be stated. The lemma is central in the proofs of the theorems stated in this paper.

2.1 Let there be v subsets of R^l, $\mathfrak{A}_i (i = 1, \ldots, v)$. Let $\mathfrak{A} = \mathfrak{A}_1 \times \mathfrak{A}_2 \times \cdots \times \mathfrak{A}_v$, i.e., $\mathfrak{A}$ is the set of ordered v-tuples $a = (a_1, \ldots, a_v)$, where $a_i \in \mathfrak{A}_i$ for $i = 1, \ldots, v$. For each i, suppose there is a real function f_i defined over $\mathfrak{A}$. Let $\bar{\mathfrak{A}}_i = \mathfrak{A}_1 \times \mathfrak{A}_2 \times \cdots \times \mathfrak{A}_{i-1} \times \mathfrak{A}_{i+1} \times \cdots \times \mathfrak{A}_v$, i.e., the set of ordered $(v - 1)$-tuples $\bar{a}_i = (a_1, \ldots, a_{i-1}, a_{i+1}, \ldots, a_v)$, where $a_{i'} \in \mathfrak{A}_{i'}$ for each $i' \neq i$. Let $A_i(\bar{a}_i)$ be a function defining for each point $\bar{a}_i \in \bar{\mathfrak{A}}_i$ a subset of $\mathfrak{A}_i$. Then the sequence $[\mathfrak{A}_1, \ldots, \mathfrak{A}_v, f_1, \ldots, f_v, A_1(\bar{a}_1), \ldots, A_v(\bar{a}_v)]$ will be termed an *abstract economy*.

2.2 To motivate the preceding definition, consider first the special case where the functions $A_i(\bar{a}_i)$ are in fact constants, i.e., $A_i(\bar{a}_i)$ is a fixed subset of $\mathfrak{A}_i$, independent of $\bar{a}_i$; for simplicity, suppose that $A_i(\bar{a}_i) = \mathfrak{A}_i$. Then the following interpretation may be given: there are v individuals; the ith can choose any element $a_i \in \mathfrak{A}_i$; after the choices are made, the ith individual receives an amount $f_i(a)$, where $a = (a_1, \ldots, a_v)$. In this case, obviously, the abstract economy reduces to a game.

In a game, the pay-off to each player depends upon the strategies chosen by all, but the domain from which strategies are to be chosen is given to each player independently of the strategies chosen by other players. An abstract economy, then, may be characterized as a generalization of a game in which the choice of an action by one agent affects both the pay-off and the domain of actions of other agents.

The need for this generalization in the development of an abstract model of the economic system arises from the special position of the consumer. His "actions" can be regarded as alternative consumption vectors; but these are restricted by the budget restraint that the cost of the goods chosen at current prices not exceed his income. But the prices and possibly some or all of the components of his income are determined by choices made by other agents. Hence, for a consumer, who is one agent in the economic system, the function $A_\iota(\bar{a}_\iota)$ must not be regarded as a constant.

2.3 In [14], Professor Nash has formally introduced the notion of an *equilibrium point* for a game.[8] The definition can easily be extended to an abstract economy (see Debreu [5], p. 888.)

> *Definition:* a^* is an equilibrium point of $[\mathfrak{A}_1, \ldots, \mathfrak{A}_v, f_1, \ldots, f_v, A_1(\bar{a}_1), \ldots, A_v(\bar{a}_v)]$ if, for all $\iota = 1, \ldots, v$, $a_\iota^* \in A_\iota(\bar{a}_\iota^*)$ and $f_\iota(\bar{a}_\iota^*, a_\iota^*) = \max_{a_\iota \in A_\iota(a_\iota^*)} f_\iota(\bar{a}_\iota^*, a_\iota)$.

Thus an equilibrium point is characterized by the property that each individual is maximizing the pay-off to him, given the actions of the other agents, over the set of actions permitted him in view of the other agents' actions.

2.4 We repeat here some definitions from [5], pp. 888–889.

The *graph* of $A_\iota(\bar{a}_\iota)$ is the set $\{a | a_\iota \in A_\iota(\bar{a}_\iota)\}$. This clearly generalizes to the multi-valued functions $A_\iota(\bar{a}_\iota)$ the ordinary definition of the graph of a function. The function $A_\iota(\bar{a}_\iota)$ is said to be *continuous* at $\bar{a}_\iota^0$, if for every $a_\iota^0 \in A_\iota(\bar{a}_\iota^0)$ and every sequence $\{\bar{a}_\iota^n\}$ converging to $\bar{a}_\iota^0$, there is a sequence $\{a_\iota^n\}$ converging to a_ι^0 such that $a_\iota^n \in A_\iota(\bar{a}_\iota^n)$ for all n. Again, if $A_\iota(\bar{a}_\iota)$ were a single-valued function, this definition would coincide with the ordinary definition of continuity.

2.5   Lemma

> If, for each ι, $\mathfrak{A}_\iota$ is compact and convex, $f_\iota(\bar{a}_\iota, a_\iota)$ is continuous on $\mathfrak{A}$ and quasi-concave[9] in a_ι for every $\bar{a}_\iota$, $A_\iota(\bar{a}_\iota)$ is a continuous function whose graph is a closed set, and, for every $\bar{a}_\iota$, the set $A_\iota(\bar{a}_\iota)$ is convex and non-empty, then the abstract economy $[\mathfrak{A}_1, \ldots, \mathfrak{A}_v, f_1, \ldots, f_v, A_1(\bar{a}_1), \ldots, A_v(\bar{a}_v)]$ has an equilibrium point.

This lemma generalizes Nash's theorem on the existence of equilibrium points for games [14]. It is a special case of the Theorem in [5], when taken in conjunction with the Remark on p. 889.[10]

[8] Actually, the concept had been formulated by Cournot [3] in the special case of an oligopolistic economy (see pp. 80–81).

[9] For the definition of a quasi-concave function, see 1.3.1 above.

[10] To see this, we need only remark that a compact convex set is necessarily a contractible polyhedron (the definition of a contractible polyhedron is given in [5] pp. 887–888), that the compactness of the graph of $A_\iota(\bar{a}_\iota)$ follows from its closure, as assumed here, and the

3   Proof of Theorem I

3.1.0 We will here define an abstract economy whose equilibrium points will have all the properties of a competitive equilibrium. There will be $m + n + 1$ participants, the m consumption units, the n production units, and a fictitious participant who chooses prices, and who may be termed the *market participant*.

For any consumption unit i, let $\bar{x}_i$ denote a point in $X_1 \times \cdots \times X_{i-1} \times X_{i+1} \times \cdots \times X_m \times Y_1 \times \cdots \times Y_n \times P$, i.e., $\bar{x}_i$ has as components $x_{i'}(i' \neq i)$, $y_j(j = 1, \ldots, n)$, p. Define

$$A_i(\bar{x}_i) = \left\{ x_i | x_i \in X_i, p \cdot x_i \leqq p \cdot \zeta_i + \max\left[0, \sum_{j=1}^{n} \alpha_{ij} p \cdot y_j \right] \right\}.$$

We will then study the abstract economy $E = [X_1, \ldots, X_m, Y_1, \ldots, Y_n, P,$ $u_1(x_1), \ldots, u_m(x_m), p \cdot y_1, \ldots, p \cdot y_n, p \cdot z, A_1(\bar{x}_1), \ldots, A_m(\bar{x}_m), Y_1, \ldots, Y_n,$ $P]$. That is, each of the first m participants, the consumption units, chooses a vector x_i from X_i, subject to the restriction that $x_i \in A_i(\bar{x}_i)$, and receives a pay-off $u_i(x_i)$; the jth out of the next n participants, the production units, chooses a vector y_j from Y_j (unrestricted by the actions of other participants), and receives a pay-off $p \cdot y_j$; and the last agent, the market participant, chooses p from P (again the choice is unaffected by the choices of other participants), and receives $p \cdot z$. Here, z is defined as in 1.4.1. in terms of $x_i(i = 1, \ldots, m)$ and $y_j(j = 1, \ldots, n)$. The domains X_i, Y_j, P have been defined in 1.3.0., 1.2.2, 1.4.0., respectively.

3.1.1 Only two of the component elements of the abstract economy E call for special comment. One is the pay-off function of the market participant. Note that z is determined by x_i and y_j. Suppose the market participant does not maximize instantaneously but, taking other participants' choices as given, adjusts his choice of prices so as to increase his pay-off. For given z, $p \cdot z$ is a linear function of p; it can be increased by increasing p_h for those commodities for which $z_h > 0$, decreasing p_h if $z_h < 0$ (provided p_h is not already 0). But this is precisely the classical "law of supply and demand" (see 1.4.1 above), and so the motivation of the market participant corresponds to one of the elements of a competitive equilibrium. This intuitive comment is not, however, the justification for this *particular* choice of a market pay-off, that justification will be found in 3.2.[11]

---

compactness and hence boundedness of $\mathfrak{A}$ which contains the graph of $A_i(\bar{a}_i)$, and that the set $\{a_i | a_i \in A_i(\bar{a}_i), f_i(\bar{a}_i, a_i) = \max_{a_i' \in A(\bar{a}_i)}, f_i(\bar{a}_i, a_i')\}$ is, for any given $\bar{a}_i$, a convex and therefore contractible set when $f_i(\bar{a}_i, a_i)$ is quasi-concave in a_i.

[11] A concept similar to that of the present market pay-off is found in Debreu [4] sections 11, 12.

3.1.2 In the definition of $A_i(\bar{x}_i)$, the expression $\sum_{j=1}^{n} \alpha_{ij} p \cdot y_j$ is replaced by max $[0, \sum_{j=1}^{n} \alpha_{ij} p \cdot y_j]$. For arbitrary choices of p and y_j (within their respective domains, P and Y_j), it is possible that $\{x_i | x_i \in X_i, px_i \leqq p \cdot \zeta_i + \sum_{j=1}^{n} \alpha_{ij} p \cdot y_j\}$ is empty. To avoid this difficulty, we make the replacement indicated. Since, for some $x_i' \in X_i$, $\zeta_i \geqq x_i'$ (by Assumption IV.a, 1.3.2 above), $p \cdot \zeta_i \geqq p \cdot x_i'$, and

$$ p \cdot \zeta_i + \max\left[0, \sum_{j=1}^{n} \alpha_{ij} p \cdot y_j \right] \geqq p \cdot \zeta_i \geqq p \cdot x_i', $$

so that $A_i(\bar{x}_i)$ is non-empty.

Of course, it is necessary to show that the substitution makes no difference *at equilibrium*. By definition of E-equilibrium (see 2.3 above), y_j^* maximizes $p^* \cdot y_j$ subject to the condition that $y_j \in Y_j$ (here asterisks denote E-equilibrium values). By Assumption I.a (see 1.2.2 above), $0 \in Y_j$; hence, in particular

$$ p^* \cdot y_j^* \geqq p^* \cdot 0 = 0. \tag{1} $$

By Assumption IV.b; $\sum_{j=1}^{n} \alpha_{ij} p^* \cdot y_j^* \geqq 0$, and max$[0, \sum_{j=1}^{n} \alpha_{ij} p^* \cdot y_i^*] = \sum_{j=1}^{n} \alpha_{ij} p^* \cdot y_i^*$. Therefore,

$$ A_i(\bar{x}_i^*) = \left\{ x_i | x_i \in X_i, p^* \cdot x_i \leqq p^* \cdot \zeta_i + \sum_{j=1}^{n} \alpha_{ij} p^* \cdot y_j^* \right\}. $$

From the definition of an equilibrium point for an abstract economy and the pay-off for a consumption unit,

> Condition 2 is satisfied at an equilibrium point of the abstract economy E. (2)

3.2 Before establishing the existence of an equilibrium point for E, it will be shown that such an equilibrium point is also a competitive equilibrium in the sense of 1.5.0. It has already been shown that Condition 2 is satisfied, while Conditions 1 and 3 follow immediately from the definition of an equilibrium point and the pay-offs specified.

In 1.4.2, it was shown that equation (1) of that section followed from Condition 2, which we have already shown to hold here, and Assumptions III.b and III.c. Sum over i, and recall that, from IV.b. $\sum_{i=1}^{m} \alpha_{ij} = 1$. Then, from the definition of z

$$ p^* \cdot z^* = 0. \tag{1} $$

Let δ^h be the vector in which every component is 0, except the hth, which is 1. Then $\delta^h \in P$ (see Condition 3, 1.4.0). Hence, by definition of an equilibrium point,

$$0 = p^* \cdot z^* \geqq \delta^h \cdot z^* = z_h^*,$$

or,

$$z^* \leqq 0. \tag{2}$$

(1) and (2) together assert Condition 4. It has been shown that any equilibrium point of E satisfies Conditions 1–4 and hence is a competitive equilibrium. The converse is obviously also true.

3.3.0 Unfortunately, the Lemma stated in 2.5 is not directly applicable to E, since the action spaces are not compact.

Let

$$\hat{X}_i = \{x_i | x_i \in X_i, \text{ there exist } x_{i'} \in X_{i'} \text{ for each } i' \neq i \text{ and}$$
$$y_j \in Y_j \text{ for each } j \text{ such that } z \leqq 0\},$$

$$\hat{Y}_j = \{y_j | y_j \in Y_j, \text{ there exist } x_i \in X_i \text{ for each } i, y_{j'} \in Y_{j'}$$
$$\text{for each } j' \neq j \text{ such that } z \leqq 0\}.$$

$\hat{X}_i$ is the set of consumption vectors available to individual i if he had complete control of the economy but had to take account of resource limitations. $\hat{Y}_j$ has a similar interpretation. We wish to prove that these sets are all bounded. It is clear that an E equilibrium x_i^* must belong to $\hat{X}_i$ and that an E equilibrium y_j^* must belong to $\hat{Y}_j$.

3.3.1 Suppose $\hat{Y}_1$ is unbounded. Then there exist sequences y_j^k, x_i^k such that

$$\lim_{k \to \infty} |y_1^k| = \infty, \quad \sum_{j=1}^n y_j^k \geqq \sum_{i=1}^m x_i^k - \zeta, \quad y_j^k \in Y_j, \quad x_i^k \in X_i. \tag{1}$$

Let

$$\xi = \sum_{i=1}^m \xi_i.$$

Then, from Assumption II, $\sum_{i=1}^m x_i^k \geqq \xi$, so that

$$\sum_{j=1}^n y_j^k \geqq \xi - \zeta. \tag{2}$$

Let $\mu^k = \max_j |y_j^k|$; for k sufficiently large, $\mu^k \geqq 1$. From Assumption I.a., $(1/\mu^k)y_j^k + (1 - 1/\mu^k)0 \in Y_j$. From (1) and (2),

$$\sum_{j=1}^n (y_j^k/\mu^k) \geqq (\xi - \zeta)/\mu^k; \qquad y_j^k/\mu^k \in Y_j \text{ for } k \text{ sufficiently large;}$$

$$\lim_{k \to \infty} \mu^k = \infty; \qquad |y_j^k/\mu^k| \leqq 1. \tag{3}$$

From the last statement, a subsequence $\{k_q\}$ can be chosen so that for every j

$$\lim_{q \to \infty} y_j^{k_q}/\mu^{k_q} = y_j^0. \tag{4}$$

From (3), (4), and the closure of Y_j (see Assumption I.a.),

$$\sum_{j=1}^{n} y_j^0 \geq 0, \quad \text{and} \quad y_j^0 \in Y_j. \tag{5}$$

From (5), $\sum_{j=1}^{n} y_j^0 \in Y$. From Assumption I.b., $\sum_{j=1}^{n} y_j^0 = 0$, or, for any given j',

$$\sum_{j \neq j'} y_j^0 = -y_{j'}^0. \tag{6}$$

Since $0 \in Y_j$ for all j, both the left-hand side and $y_{j'}^0$ belong to Y. The right-hand side therefore belongs to both Y and $-Y$; by I.c., $y_{j'}^0 = 0$ for any j'. From (4) then, the equality $|y_j^{k_q}| = \mu^{k_q}$, can hold for at most finitely many q for fixed j. But this is a contradiction since, from the definition of μ^{k_q}, the equality must hold for at least one j for each q, and hence for infinitely many q for some j. It has therefore been shown that $\hat{Y}_1$ is bounded, and, by the same argument,

$$\hat{Y}_j \text{ is bounded for all } j. \tag{7}$$

3.3.2 Let $x_i \in \hat{X}_i$. By definition,

$$\xi_i \leq x_i \leq \sum_{j=1}^{n} y_j - \sum_{i' \neq i} x_{i'} + \zeta, \qquad (x_{i'} \in X_{i'}, y_j \in Y_j) \tag{1}$$

By definition, again, it follows that $y_j \in \hat{Y}_j$ for all j; also $x_{i'} \geq \xi_{i'}$.

$$\xi_i \leq x_i \leq \sum_{j=1}^{n} y_j - \sum_{i'=i} \xi_{i'} + \zeta, \qquad (y_j \in \hat{Y}_j).$$

From (7) in 3.3.1, the right-hand side is bounded.

$$\hat{X}_i \text{ is bounded for all } i. \tag{2}$$

3.3.3 We can therefore choose a positive real number c so that the cube $C = \{x | |x_h| \leq c \text{ for all } h\}$ contains in its *interior* all $\hat{X}_i$ and all $\hat{Y}_j$. Let $\tilde{X}_i = X_i \cap C$, $\tilde{Y}_j = Y_j \cap C$.

3.3.4 Now introduce a new abstract economy $\tilde{E}$, identical with E in 3.1, except that X_i is replaced by $\tilde{X}_i$ and Y_j by $\tilde{Y}_j$ everywhere. Let $\tilde{A}_i(\bar{x}_i)$ be the resultant modification of $A_i(\bar{x}_i)$ (see 3.1.0). It will now be verified that all the conditions of the Lemma are satisfied for this new abstract economy.

From II and I.a, X_i and Y_j are closed convex sets; the set C is a compact convex set; therefore, $\tilde{X}_i$ and $\tilde{Y}_j$ are compact convex sets. P is obviously compact and convex.

For a consumption unit, the continuity and quasi-concavity of $u_i(x_i)$ are assured by III.a and III.c (see the discussion in 1.3.1). For a production unit or the market participant, the continuity is trivial, and the quasi-concavity holds for any linear function.

For a production unit or the market participant, Y_j or P is a constant and therefore trivially continuous; the closure of the graph is simply the closure of $\mathfrak{A} = \tilde{X}_1 \times \cdots \times \tilde{X}_m \times \tilde{Y}_1 \times \cdots \times \tilde{Y}_n \times P$. The sets Y_j, P are certainly convex and non-empty.

For a consumption unit, the set $\tilde{A}_i(\bar{x}_i)$ is defined by a linear inequality in x_i (3.1.0) and hence is certainly convex. For each i, let x_i' have the property $x_i' \leq \zeta_i$, $x_i' \in X_i$ (see Assumption IV.a.); set $y_j' = 0$. Since $\sum_{i=1}^{m} x_i' - \sum_{j=1}^{n} y_j' - \zeta \leq 0$, $x_i' \in \hat{X}_i$ for each i, by definition, and hence $x_i' \in C$. It was shown in 3.1.2 that $x_i' \in A_i(\bar{x}_i)$ for all $\bar{x}_i$; since $\tilde{A}_i(\bar{x}_i) = [A_i(\bar{x}_i)] \cap C$, $\tilde{A}_i(\bar{x}_i)$ contains x_i' and therefore is non-null.

Since the budget restraint is a weak inequality between two continuous functions of a, it is obvious that the graph of $\tilde{A}_i(\bar{x}_i)$ is closed.

3.3.5 It remains only to show that $\tilde{A}_i(\bar{x}_i)$ is continuous.

Remark: If $p \cdot \zeta_i > \min_{x_i \in \tilde{X}_i} p \cdot x_i$, then $\tilde{A}_i(\bar{x}_i)$ is continuous at the point $\bar{x}_i = (x_1, \ldots, x_{i-1}, x_{i+1}, \ldots, x_m, y_1, \ldots, y_n, p)$.

Proof: Let $r_i = p \cdot \zeta_i + \max [0, \sum_{j=1}^{n} \alpha_{ij} p \cdot y_j]$. When $\bar{x}_i^k$ converges to $\bar{x}_i$, $\lim_{k \to \infty} p^k = p$, $\lim_{k \to \infty} r_i^k = r_i$. Consider a point $x_i \in \tilde{A}_i(\bar{x}_i)$; then,

$$x_i \in \tilde{X}_i, \qquad p \cdot x_i \leq r_i. \tag{1}$$

(a) If $p \cdot x_i < r_i$, then $p^k \cdot x_i < r_i^k$ for all k sufficiently large, and $x_i \in \tilde{A}_i(\bar{x}_i^k)$. Then we need only choose $x_i^k = x_i$ for all k sufficiently large. (See the definition of continuity in 2.4.)

(b) If $p \cdot x_i = r_i$, choose x_i', by hypothesis, so that $x_i' \in \tilde{X}_i$, $p \cdot x_i' < p \cdot \zeta_i \leq r_i$. For k sufficiently large, $p^k \cdot x_i' < r_i^k$. Define $x_i(\lambda) = \lambda x_i + (1 - \lambda)x_i'$, and consider the set of values of λ for which $0 \leq \lambda \leq 1$, $x_i(\lambda) \in \tilde{A}_i(\bar{x}_i^k)$. Since $\tilde{X}_i$ is convex, $x_i(\lambda) \in \tilde{X}_i$. Then one must have

$$p^k \cdot [\lambda x_i + (1 - \lambda)x_i'] \leq r_i^k,$$

or

$$\lambda \leq (r_i^k - p^k \cdot x_i')/(p^k \cdot x_i - p^k \cdot x_i'),$$

if we note that the denominator is positive for k sufficiently large, since $p \cdot x_i = r_i > p \cdot x_i'$. The largest value of λ satisfying the above conditions is, then

$$\lambda^k = \min[1, (r_i^k - p^k \cdot x_i')/(p^k \cdot x_i - p^k \cdot x_i')].$$

For k sufficiently large, $\lambda^k > 0$. Then $x_i(\lambda^k) \in \tilde{A}_i(\bar{x}_i^k)$ for all k sufficiently large. But also

$$\lim_{k \to \infty} r_i^k = r_i = \lim_{k \to \infty} p^k \cdot x_i,$$

so that

$$\lim_{k \to \infty} \lambda^k = 1, \quad \text{and} \quad \lim_{k \to \infty} x_i(\lambda^k) = x_i.$$

The continuity of $\tilde{A}_i(\bar{x}_i)$ is therefore established.

If Assumption IV.a holds, then the condition of the Remark is trivially satisfied for any $p \in P$, and $y_j \in \tilde{Y}_j (j = 1, \ldots, n)$.

3.4.0 The existence of an equilibrium point $(x_1^*, \ldots, x_m^*, y_1^*, \ldots, y_n^*, p^*)$ for the abstract economy $\tilde{E}$ has, therefore, been demonstrated. It will now be shown that this point is also an equilibrium point for the abstract economy E described in 3.1. The converse is obvious; therefore a competitive equilibrium is *equivalent* to an $\tilde{E}$ equilibrium. (See end of 3.2.)

3.4.1 From Asssumption I.a. and the definition of C (3.3.3) it follows that $0 \in \tilde{Y}_j$ for each j. So that, as in 3.1.2,

$$\max\left[0, \sum_{j=1}^{n} \alpha_{ij} p^* \cdot y_j^*\right] = \sum_{j=1}^{n} \alpha_{ij} p^* \cdot y_j^*.$$

From the definition of $\tilde{A}_i(\bar{x}_i)$,

$$p^* \cdot x_i^* \leq p^* \cdot \zeta_i + \sum_{j=1}^{n} \alpha_{ij} p^* \cdot y_j^*.$$

Sum over i; then $p^* \cdot x^* \leq p^* \cdot \zeta + p^* \cdot y^*$, or $p^* \cdot z^* \leq 0$. For fixed z^*, p^* maximizes $p \cdot z^*$ for $p \in P$; by an argument similar to that used in 3.2, this implies that

$$z^* \leq 0. \tag{1}$$

From (1) and the definitions in 3.3.0, $x_i^* \in \hat{X}_i$, $y_j^* \in \hat{Y}_j$ for all i and j, and, by 3.3.3, x_i^* and y_j^* are *interior* points of C.

Suppose, for some $x_i' \in A_i(\bar{x}_i^*)$, $u_i(x_i') > u_i(x_i^*)$. By III.c, $u_i[tx_i' + (1 - t)x_i^*] > u_i(x_i^*)$ if $0 < t < 1$. But for t sufficiently small, $tx_i' + (1 - t)x_i^*$ belongs to C. Since $tx_i' + (1 - t)x_i^* \in A_i(\bar{x}_i^*)$, by the convexity of the latter set, $tx_i' + (1 - t)x_i^* \in \tilde{A}_i(\bar{x}_i^*)$, for t small enough, which contradicts the definition of x_i^* as an equilibrium value for $\tilde{E}$.

$$x_i^* \text{ maximizes } u_i(x_i) \text{ for } x_i \in A_i(\bar{x}_i^*). \tag{2}$$

Suppose, for some $y_j' \in Y_j$, $p^* \cdot y_j' > p^* \cdot y_j^*$. Then, $p^* \cdot [t y_j' + (1 - t) y_j^*] > p^* \cdot y_j^*$ for $0 < t < 1$. As in the preceding paragraph, the convex combination belongs to $\tilde{Y}_j$ for t sufficiently small, a contradiction to the equilibrium character of y_j^* for $\tilde{E}$.

$$y_j^* \text{ maximizes } p^* \cdot y_j \text{ for } y_j \in Y_j. \tag{3}$$

That p^* maximizes $p \cdot z^*$ for $p \in P$ is directly implied by the definition of equilibrium point for $\tilde{E}$, since the domain of p is the same in both abstract economies.

It has been shown, therefore, that the point $(x_1^*, \ldots, x_m^*, y_1^*, \ldots, y_n^*, p^*)$ is also an equilibrium point for E; as shown in 3.2, it is, therefore, a competitive equilibrium. Theorem I has thus been proved.

4   Statement of the second existence theorem for a competitive equilibrium

4.0 As noted in 1.3.2, Assumption IVa, which states in effect that a consumption unit has initially a positive amount of every commodity available for trading, is clearly unrealistic, and a weakening is very desirable. Theorem II accomplishes this goal, though at the cost of making certain additional assumptions in different directions and complicating the proof. Assumptions I–III are retained. The remaining assumptions for Theorem II are given in the following paragraphs of this section.

4.1 Assumption IV.a is replaced by the following:

IV'.a $\zeta_i \in R^l$; for some $x_i \in X_i$, $x_i \leqq \zeta_i$ and, for at least one $h \in \mathscr{P}$, $x_{hi} < \zeta_{hi}$.

The set $\mathscr{P}$ is defined more closely in 4.4 below; briefly, it consists of all types of labor that are always productive. IV'.a is a weakening of IV.a; it is now only supposed that the individual is capable of supplying at least one type of productive labor. IV'.a and IV.b together will be denoted by IV'.

4.2   Let $X = \sum_{i=1}^{m} X_i$.

V   There exist $x \in X$ and $y \in Y$ such that $x + \zeta$.

V asserts that it is possible to arrange the economic system by choice of production and consumption vectors so that an excess supply of all commodities can be achieved.

4.3 As in 3.2, δ^h will be the positive unit vector of the hth axis in R^l. For any $\lambda > 0$, $x_i + \lambda \delta^h$ represents an increase λ in the amount of the hth commodity over x_i, with all other commodities remaining unchanged in consumption.

Definition: Let $\mathscr{D}$ be the set of commodities such that if $i = 1, \ldots, m$, $x_i \in X_i$, $h \in \mathscr{D}$, then there exists $\lambda > 0$ such that $x_i + \lambda \delta^h \in X_i$ and

$$u_i(x_i + \lambda \delta^h) > u_i(x_i).$$

$\mathscr{D}$ is the set of commodities which are always desired by every consumer.

VI   The set $\mathscr{D}$ is not empty.

Assumption VI is a stronger form of III.b as given in 1.3.1. In the same manner as noted there, VI can be weakened to assert that the set $\mathscr{D}'$ of commodities desired for all consumption vectors compatible with existing resource and technological conditions is not empty. Formally we could introduce the

Definition: Let $\mathscr{D}'$ be the set of commodities such that if $i = 1, \ldots, m$, $x_i \in \hat{X}_i$, $h \in \mathscr{D}'$, then there exists $\lambda > 0$ such that $x_i + \lambda \delta^h \in X_i$ and

$$u_i(x_i + \lambda \delta^h) > u_i(x_i).$$

VI can then be replaced by:

VI′   The set $\mathscr{D}'$ is not empty.

4.4   *Definition:* Let $\mathscr{P}$ be the set of commodities such that if $y \in Y$, $h \in \mathscr{P}$, then (a) $y_h \leqq 0$ and (b) for some $y' \in Y$ and all $h' \neq h$, $y'_h \geqq y_{h'}$, while for at least one $h'' \in \mathscr{D}$, $y'_{h''} > y_{h''}$.

VII   The set $\mathscr{P}$ is not empty.

Assumption VII plays a key role in the following proof. We interpret the set $\mathscr{P}$ as consisting of some types of labor. Part (a) simply asserts that no labor service, at least of those included in $\mathscr{P}$, can be produced by a production unit. Part (b) asserts that, if no restriction is imposed on the amount (consumed) of some one type of "productive" labor, then it is possible to increase the output of at least one "desired" commodity (a commodity in $\mathscr{D}$) without decreasing the output or increasing the input of any commodity other than the type of productive labor under consideration.

A case where VII might not hold is an economic system with fixed technological coefficients where production requiring a given type of labor also requires, directly or indirectly, some complementary factors. It is easy to see intuitively in this case how an equilibrium may be impossible. Given the amount of complementary resources initially available,[12] there will be a maximum to the quantity of labor that can be employed in the sense that no further increase in the labor force will increase the output of any commodity. Now, as is well known, the supply of labor may vary either way as real wages vary (see Robbins [17]) and broadly speaking is rather inelastic with respect to real wages. In particular, as real wages tend to zero, the supply will not necessarily become zero; on the contrary, as real incomes decrease, the necessity of satisfying more and more pressing needs may even work in the direction of increasing the willingness to work despite the increasingly less favorable terms offered. It is, therefore, quite possible that for any positive level of real wages, the supply of labor will exceed the maximum employable and hence *a fortiori* the demand by firms. Thus, there can be no equilibrium at positive levels of real wages. At zero real wages, on the contrary, demand will indeed be positive but of course supply of labor will be zero, so that again there will be no equilibrium. The critical point in the argument is the discontinuity of the supply curve for labor as real wages go to zero.

Assumption VII rules out any situation of limitational factors in which the marginal productivity of all types of labor in terms of desired commodities is zero. In conjunction with IV'.a, on the one hand, and VI, on the other, it insures that any individual possesses the ability to supply a commodity which has at least derived value.

It may be remarked that Assumption VII is satisfied if there is a productive process turning a form of labor into a desired commodity without the need of complementary commodities. Domestic service or other personal services may fall in this category.[13]

Let $\hat{Y} = \{y \mid y \in Y,$ there exists $x_i \in X_i$ for all i such that $z \leq 0\}$. It may be remarked that VII can be effectively weakened (in the same way that VI could be weakened to VI') to

VII'   The set $\mathscr{P}'$ is not empty, where

> *Definition:* Let $\mathscr{P}'$ be the set of commodities such that if $h \in \mathscr{P}'$ and
> (a) $y \in Y$, then $y_h \leq 0$,
> (b) $y \in \hat{Y}$, then for some $y' \in Y$ and all $h' \neq h$, $y'_{h'} \geq y_{h'}$, while for at least one $h'' \in \mathscr{D}$, $y'_{h''} > y_{h''}$.

Note that III.b, VI and VII can simultaneously be weakened to III'.b, VI', and VII'.

---

[12] These complementary resources may be land, raw materials critical in certain industrial processes, or initial capital equipment.

[13] The possibility of disequilibrium and therefore unemployment through failure of Assumption VII to hold corresponds to so-called "structural unemployment."

4.5   *Theorem II*

For an economic system satisfying Assumptions I–III, IV', and V–VII, there is a competitive equilibrium.

5   Proof of Theorem II

5.0 Let π be the number of elements of $\mathscr{P}$. For any ε, $0 < \varepsilon \leqq \frac{1}{2}\pi$, define

$$P^\varepsilon = \{p | p \in P, p_h \geqq \varepsilon \quad \text{for all } h \in \mathscr{P}\}.$$

From IV'a, we can choose $x_i \in X_i$ so that $x_{hi} \leqq \zeta_{hi}$ for all h, $x_{h'i} < \zeta_{h'i}$ for some $h' \in \mathscr{P}$. For any $p \in P^\varepsilon$,

$$p \cdot (\zeta_i - x_i) = \sum_h p_h(\zeta_{hi} - x_{hi}) \geqq p_{h'}(\xi_{h'i} - x_{h'i}) > 0$$

or

$$\text{for some } x_i \in X_i, \ p \cdot x_i < p \cdot \zeta_i. \tag{1}$$

5.1.0 The basic method of proof of Theorem II will be similar to that of Theorem I. We seek to show that an equilibrium point for the abstract economy E, defined in 3.1.0, exists. As already shown in 3.2, such an equilibrium point would define a competitive equilibrium. First, the economy E is replaced by the economy E^ε [$X_1, \ldots, X_m, Y_1, \ldots, Y_n, P^\varepsilon$, $u_1(x_1), \ldots, u_m(x_m), p \cdot y_1, \ldots, p \cdot y_n, p \cdot z, A_1(\bar{x}_1), \ldots, A_m(\bar{x}_m), Y_1, \ldots, Y_m, P^\varepsilon$]. Clearly, E^ε is the same as E, except that the price domain has been contracted to P^ε. The existence of an equilibrium point for E^ε for each ε will first be shown; then, it will be shown that for some ε, an equilibrium point of E^ε is also an equilibrium point of E.[14]

To show the existence of an equilibrium point for E^ε, the same technique will be used as in proving the existence of an equilibrium point for E in Theorem I. The argument is that the equilibrium point, if it exists at all, must lie in a certain bounded domain. Hence, if we alter the abstract economy E^ε by intersecting the action domains with a suitably chosen hypercube, we will not disturb the equilibrium points, if any; but the Lemma of 2.5 will now be applicable, and the existence of an equilibrium point shown (see 3.3 above).

5.1.1 This section will be purely heuristic, designed to motivate the choice of the hypercube mentioned in the previous paragraph. Suppose an equilibrium point [$x_1^*, \ldots, x_m^*, y_1^*, \ldots, y_n^*, p^*$] exists for the abstract economy E^ε. Since $x_i^* \in A_i(\bar{x}_i^*)$ for all i, by definition (see 3.1.0),

---

[14] The introduction of E^ε is made necessary by the following fact: (1) of 5.0 may not hold for all $p \in P$ and the condition of the Remark in 3.3.5, may not be satisfied for all $p \in P$.

$$p^* \cdot x_i^* \leq p^* \cdot \zeta_i + \sum_{j=1}^{n} \alpha_{ij} p^* \cdot y_j^*,$$

(see also 3.1.2) If we sum over i and recall that $\sum_{i=1}^{m} \alpha_{ij} = 1$,

$$p^* \cdot \left(\sum_{i=1}^{m} x_i^* - \sum_{i=1}^{m} \zeta_i - \sum_{j=1}^{n} y_j^* \right) \leq 0,$$

or

$$p^* \cdot z^* \leq 0.$$

Since p^* maximizes $p \cdot z^*$ for $p \in P^\varepsilon$, by definition of equilibrium, $p \cdot z^* \leq 0$ for all $p \in P^\varepsilon$, or,

$$p_{h'} z_{h'}^* \leq \sum_{h \neq h'} p_h(\zeta_h - x_h^* + y_h^*), \quad \text{for any } h'. \tag{1}$$

Note that since $y_h^* \leq 0$ for $h \in \mathscr{P}$, by (a) of the first Definition in 4.4

$$x_h^* - y_h^* \geq x_h^* \geq \zeta_h, \quad \text{for } h \in \mathscr{P}, \tag{2}$$

by II. ζ and ξ are defined in 1.4.1 and 3.3.1, respectively.

For any given h', define p as follows: $p_h = \varepsilon$ for $h \in \mathscr{P}$ and $h \neq h'$; $p_h = 0$ for $h \notin \mathscr{P}$ and $h \neq h'$; $p_{h'} = 1 - \sum_{h \neq h'} p_h$. Then, if $h' \in \mathscr{P}$, $p_{h'} = 1 - (\pi - 1)\varepsilon$ (which is indeed $\geq \varepsilon$ if $\varepsilon \leq \frac{1}{2}\pi$; if $h' \notin \mathscr{P}$, $p_{h'} = 1 - \pi\varepsilon$. From (1) and (2),

$$\begin{cases} \text{if } h' \in \mathscr{P}, [1 - (\pi - 1)\varepsilon]z_{h'}^* \leq \varepsilon \sum_{\substack{h \in \mathscr{P} \\ h \neq h'}} (\zeta_h - \xi_h), \\ \\ \text{if } h' \notin \mathscr{P}, (1 - \pi\varepsilon)z_{h'}^* \leq \varepsilon \sum_{h \in \mathscr{P}} (\zeta_h - \xi_h). \end{cases} \tag{3}$$

If $0 < \varepsilon \leq (\frac{1}{2}\pi)$, then certainly $1 - \pi\varepsilon > 0$, $1 - (\pi - 1)\varepsilon > 0$, and necessarily

$$\varepsilon/[1 - (\pi - 1)\varepsilon] < \varepsilon/(1 - \pi\varepsilon).$$

Finally, for any h, $\zeta_h - \xi_h \geq 0$ from IV'a and II. If we divide through the first inequality in (3) by $[1 - (\pi - 1)\varepsilon]$,

$$z_{h'}^* \leq \{\varepsilon/[1 - (\pi - 1)\varepsilon]\} \sum_{\substack{h \in \mathscr{P} \\ h \neq h'}} (\zeta_h - \xi_h)$$

$$\leq [\varepsilon/(1 - \pi\varepsilon)] \sum_{h \in \mathscr{P}} (\zeta_h - \xi_h), \text{ for } h' \in \mathscr{P}. \tag{4}$$

The same inequality between the extreme items holds for $h' \notin \mathscr{P}$, as can be seen by dividing through in the second inequality in (3) by $(1 - \pi\varepsilon)$. But if $\varepsilon \leq (\frac{1}{2}\pi)$, then we see in turn that $2\pi\varepsilon \leq 1$, $\pi\varepsilon \leq 1 - \pi\varepsilon$, and, by division by $\pi(1 - \pi\varepsilon)$, $\varepsilon/(1 - \pi\varepsilon) \leq 1/\pi$. From (4),

$$z_h^* \le (1/\pi) \sum_{h \in \mathscr{P}} (\zeta_h - \xi_h).$$

Let $\zeta'_h = \zeta_h + (1/\pi) \sum_{h \in \mathscr{P}} (\zeta_h - \xi_h)$, with ζ' being the vector whose components are $\zeta'_1, \ldots, \zeta'_l$; then

$$x^* - y^* \le \zeta'. \tag{5}$$

The equilibrium point then will lie in a region defined by (5) and the conditions $x_i^* \in X_i$, $y_j^* \in Y_j$, $p^* \in P^\varepsilon$. These are exactly the same as the requirements for E in the proof of Theorem I, except that ζ has been replaced by ζ', and P by P^ε.

5.2.0 The proof proper will now be resumed. Define

$$\hat{X}'_i = \{x_i | x_i \in X_i, \text{ and there exist } x_{i'} \in X_{i'} \text{ for all } i' \ne i,$$
$$y_j \in Y_j \text{ for all } j \text{ such that } x - y \le \zeta'\},$$

$$\hat{Y}'_j = \{y_j | y_j \in Y_j, \text{ and there exist } x_i \in X_i \text{ for all } i, y_{j'} \in Y_{j'}$$
$$\text{for all } j' \ne j \text{ such that } x - y \le \zeta'\}.$$

These definitions are identical with those of $\hat{X}_i$, $\hat{Y}_j$ in 3.3.0, except that ζ has been replaced by ζ'. The arguments of 3.3.0–.3 may therefore be repeated exactly. We can choose a positive real number c' so that the cube

$$C' = \{x | |x_h| \le c' \text{ for all } h\}$$

contains in its *interior* all $\hat{X}'_i$ and all $\hat{Y}'_j$. Let $\tilde{X}'_i = X_i \cap C'$, $\tilde{Y}'_j = Y_j \cap C'$.

5.2.1 Let $\tilde{E}^\varepsilon$ be an abstract economy identical with E^ε in 5.1.0, except that X_i is replaced by $\tilde{X}'_i$ and Y_j by $\tilde{Y}'_j$ everywhere. Let $\tilde{A}'_i(\bar{x}_i)$ be the resultant modification of $A_i(\bar{x}_i)$. It is easy to see that the argument of 3.3.4 remains completely applicable in showing that all the requirements of the Lemma are satisfied other than the continuity of $\tilde{A}'_i(\bar{x}_i)$. The last follows immediately from the Remark of 3.3.5, and (1) in 5.0, since $x_i \in \hat{X}'_i$ and hence to $\tilde{X}'_i$. Hence, $\tilde{E}^\varepsilon$ has an equilibrium point $[x_1^*, \ldots, x_m^*, y_1^*, \ldots, y_n^*, p^*]$ for each ε, $0 < \varepsilon \le (\frac{1}{2}\pi)$. We show now that an equilibrium point of $\tilde{E}^\varepsilon$ is an equilibrium point of E^ε (the converse is obvious).

5.2.2 Since $0 \in \tilde{Y}'_j$,

$$p^* \cdot y_j^* \ge p^* \cdot 0 = 0, \tag{1}$$

so that $\sum_{j=1}^{m} \alpha_{ij} p^* \cdot y_j^* \ge 0$, and, as in 5.1.1, $p^* \cdot z^* \le 0$, from which it can be concluded that, as in equation (5), section 5.1.1, $x^* - y^* \le \zeta'$. From the definitions of $\hat{X}'_i$, $\hat{Y}'_j$ in 5.2.0, $x_i^* \in \hat{X}'_i$, $y_j^* \in \hat{Y}'_j$ for all i and j; hence, as shown in that section,

$$x_i^*, y_j^* \text{ are interior points of } C'. \tag{2}$$

From the definition of an equilibrium point, x_i^* maximizes $u_i(x_i)$ for $x_i \in \tilde{A}_i'(\bar{x}_i^*)$. From (2), it follows exactly as in 3.4.1, that

$$x_i^* \text{ maximizes } u_i(x_i) \qquad \text{for } x_i \in A_i(\bar{x}_i^*). \tag{3}$$

In the same way,

$$y_j^* \text{ maximizes } p^* \cdot y_j \qquad \text{for } y_j \in Y_j. \tag{4}$$

From the definition of equilibrium for $\tilde{E}^\varepsilon$,

$$p^* \text{ maximizes } p \cdot z^* \qquad \text{for } p \in P^\varepsilon. \tag{5}$$

5.3.0 Suppose that, for some ε, $0 < \varepsilon \leq \frac{1}{2}\pi$,

$$p_h^* > \varepsilon \qquad \text{for all } h \in \mathscr{P}. \tag{1}$$

Let p be any element of P, $p' = tp + (1 - t)p^*$, where $0 < t \leq 1$. Suppose $p \cdot z^* > p^* \cdot z^*$; then $p' \cdot z^* > p^* \cdot z^*$. But, from (1), $p' \in P^\varepsilon$ for t sufficiently small, which contradicts (5) of the preceding paragraph. Thus, if (1) holds for some ε, $p \cdot z^* \leq p^* \cdot z^*$ for all $p \in P$, i.e., p^* maximizes $p \cdot z^*$ for $p \in P$ (and not merely $p \in P^\varepsilon$). In conjunction with (3) and (4) of the preceding paragraph, this shows that the abstract economy E has an equilibrium point and therefore, as shown in 3.2,

$$\text{If (1) holds, there is a competitive equilibrium.} \tag{2}$$

5.3.1 It will therefore now be assumed that (1) of 5.3.0 does not hold for any $\varepsilon > 0$. Then, for each ε, $0 < \varepsilon \leq \frac{1}{2}\pi$,

$$p_h^* = \varepsilon \text{ for at least one } h \in \mathscr{P}. \tag{1}$$

For all ε, $p^* \in P$, $x_i^* \in C'$, $y_j^* \in C'$ (see 5.2.2(2)). P and C' are compact sets; a set of converging sequences can therefore be chosen so that

$$\lim_{k \to \infty} \varepsilon_k = 0, (x_1^k, \ldots, x_m^k, y_1^k, \ldots, y_n^k, p^k) \text{ is an equilibrium}$$

point for $E^{\varepsilon k}$, $\lim_{k \to \infty} x_i^k = x_i^0$, $\lim_{k \to \infty} y_j^k = y_j^0$, $\lim_{k \to \infty} p^k = p^0$.
$$\tag{2}$$

Since the sets X_i, Y_j, P are closed, $x_i^0 \in X_i$, $y_j^0 \in Y_j$, $p^0 \in P$. From (1), there must be at least one $h \in \mathscr{P}$ for which $p_h^k = \varepsilon_k$ for infinitely many k, and hence by (2) $p_h^0 = 0$ for that h. For convenience, let $h = 1$.

$$p_1^0 = 0, 1 \in \mathscr{P}. \tag{3}$$

As shown in 3.2, statement (3) of 5.2.2, which is Condition 2, implies equation (1) of 3.2, namely, $p^k \cdot z^k = 0$. Let k approach ∞; by (2),

$$p^0 \cdot z^0 = 0. \tag{4}$$

For any fixed y_j, statement (4) of 5.2.2 tells us that $p^k \cdot y_j^k \geqq p^k \cdot y_j$. Let k approach ∞; then $p^0 \cdot y_j^0 \geqq p^0 \cdot y_j$.

$$y_j^0 \text{ maximizes } p^0 \cdot y_j \quad \text{for } y_j \in Y_j. \tag{5}$$

5.3.2 Choose any $x_i \in X_i$ such that $u_i(x_i) > u_i(x_i^0)$. For k sufficiently large, $u_i(x_i) > u_i(x_i^k)$, from 5.31 (2) and the continuity of u_i. This is not compatible with the statement that $x_i \in A_i(\bar{x}_i^k)$, by 5.2.2 (3), so that $p^k \cdot x_i > p^k \cdot x_i^k$. Let k approach ∞.

$$\text{If } x_i \in X_i \text{ and } u_i(x_i) > u_i(x_i^0), \text{ then } p^0 \cdot x_i \geqq p^0 \cdot x_i^0. \tag{1}$$

5.3.3 This section is a digression which may be of some interest for general techniques in the theory of the consumer. It can easily be shown that from 5.3.2(1)

$$x_i^0 \text{ minimizes } p^0 \cdot x_i \text{ on } \{x_i | x_i \in X_i, u_i(x_i) \geqq u_i(x_i^0)\} \tag{1}$$

and that p^0 maximizes $p \cdot z^0$ for $p \in P$. In conjunction with 5.3.1(5), it is then shown that all the conditions for a competitive equilibrium are satisfied, except that utility-maximization by a consumption unit under a budget restraint has been replaced by minimization of cost for a given utility level (compare (1) with Condition 2). The duality between cost-minimization and utility-maximization is indeed valid almost everywhere, i.e., in the interior of P, where all prices are positive, but not everywhere.

From the viewpoint of welfare economics, it is the principle that the consumption vector chosen should be the one which achieves the given utility at least cost which is primary, and the principle of maximizing utility at a given cost only relevant when the two give identical results.[15] For a descriptive theory of behavior under perfect competition, on the other hand, it is, of course, the concept of utility maximization which is primary. To the extent that the duality is valid, the principle of cost minimization leads to much simpler derivations, for example, of Slutzky's relations. Actually, minimization of cost for a given utility is essentially minimization of a linear function when the argument is limited to a convex set; mathematically, the problem is identical with that of maximizing profits subject to the transformation conditions, so that the theories of the consumer and the firm become identical.[16] However, the failure of the duality to hold in all cases shows that there are delicate questions for which the principle of utility maximization cannot be replaced by that of cost minimization.

5.3.4 From 5.3.1(3), $1 \in \mathscr{P}$. By (b) of the first Definition in 4.4, there exists $y' \in Y$ such that

$$y_h' \geqq y_h^0 \quad \text{for all } h \neq 1; \quad y_{h'}' > y_{h'}^0 \quad \text{for some } h' \in \mathscr{D}. \tag{1}$$

---

[15] See Arrow [1], Lemma 4, p. 513; a brief discussion of the conditions for the duality to be valid is given in Lemma 5, pp. 513–4. See also Debreu [4], Friedman [8].

[16] Professors Knight [11] and Friedman [7] (esp. pp. 469–474) have therefore gone so far as to argue that it is always better to draw up demand functions as of a given real income (i.e., utility) instead of a given money income.

Here, $y^0 = \sum_{j=1}^n y_j^0$. From 5.3.1(5), $p^0 \cdot y_j' \leq p^0 \cdot y_j^0$ for all j. Summing over j then gives

$$p^0 \cdot y' \leq p^0 \cdot y^0. \tag{2}$$

With the aid of (1) and 5.3.1(3),

$$p^0 \cdot (y' - y^0) = \sum_h p_h^0(y_h' - y_h^0)$$

$$= \sum_{h \neq 1} p_h^0(y_h' - y_h^0) \geq p_{h'}^0(y_{h'}' - y_{h'}^0).$$

Since $y_{h'}' - y_{h'}^0 > 0$, (2) requires that $p_{h'}^0 = 0$.

$$p_{h'}^0 = 0 \qquad \text{for at least one } h' \in \mathcal{D}. \tag{3}$$

Let $x_i \in X_i$, $x_i(t) = tx_i + (1 - t)x_i^0$, where $0 < t \leq 1$. From the first Definition in 4.3, there exists

$$\lambda > 0, u_i(x_i^0 + \lambda\delta^{h'}) > u_i(x_i^0). \tag{4}$$

Since $x_i(t) + \lambda\delta^{h'}$ approaches $x_i^0 + \lambda\delta^{h'}$ as t approaches 0, it follows from (4) that,

$$u_i[x_i(t) + \lambda\delta^{h'}] > u_i(x_i^0) \qquad \text{for } t \text{ sufficiently small.} \tag{5}$$

From (5) and 5.3.2(1), $p^0 \cdot [x_i(t) + \lambda\delta^{h'}] \geq p^0 \cdot x_i^0$. But, from (3),

$$p^0 \cdot (\lambda\delta^{h'}) = \lambda p_{h'}^0 = 0.$$

Since $p^0 \cdot [x_i(t) + \lambda\delta^{h'}] = tp^0 \cdot x_i + (1 - t)p^0 \cdot x_i^0 + p^0 \cdot (\lambda\delta^{h'})$, it follows easily that $p^0 \cdot x_i \geq p^0 \cdot x_i^0$.

$$x_i^0 \quad \text{minimizes} \quad p^0 \cdot x_i \quad \text{over} \quad X_i. \tag{6}$$

Let X be defined as in 4.2. Since $p^0 \cdot x = \sum_{i=1}^m p^0 \cdot x_i$, it follows immediately from (6) that,

$$x^0 \quad \text{minimizes} \quad p^0 \cdot x \quad \text{over} \quad X. \tag{7}$$

5.3.5 In accordance with Assumption V, choose $x \in X$, $y \in Y$ so that $x < y + \zeta$. Then, with the aid of 5.3.4(7), $p^0 \cdot (y + \zeta) > p^0 \cdot x^0$, or

$$p^0 \cdot y > p^0 \cdot (x^0 - \zeta). \tag{1}$$

From 5.3.1(4),

$$p^0 \cdot (x^0 - y^0 - \zeta) = 0. \tag{2}$$

This, combined with (1), gives

$$p^0 \cdot y > p^0 \cdot y^0. \tag{3}$$

But this implies that, for some j, $p^0 \cdot y_j > p^0 \cdot y_j^0$, while $y_j \in Y_j$, a contradiction to 5.3.1(5). Thus, the assumption made at the beginning of 5.3.1, that for every $\varepsilon > 0$, $p_h^* = \varepsilon$ for at least one $h \in \mathscr{P}$, has led to a contradiction and must be false. Statement 5.3.0(1) must then be valid, and by statement (2) in the same paragraph, Theorem II has been proved.

5.3.6 The following theorem, slightly more general than theorem II, can easily be proved in a way practically identical to the above.

Assumption IV'a is replaced by

IV"a $\zeta_i \in R^l$; for some $x_i \in X_i$, $x_i \leq \zeta_i$ and, for at least one $h \in \mathscr{D} \cup \mathscr{P}$, $x_{hi} < \zeta_{hi}$. IV"a and IVb together are denoted by IV".

Theorem II'

For an economic system satisfying Assumptions I–III, IV", V, and VI there is a competitive equilibrium.

6   Historical note

The earliest discussion of the existence of competitive equilibrium centered around the version presented by Cassel [2]. There are four basic principles of his system: (1) demand for each final good is a function of the prices of all final goods; (2) zero profits for all producers; (3) fixed technical coefficients relating use of primary resources to output of final commodities; and (4) equality of supply and demand on each market. Let x_i be the demand for final commodity i, p_i the price of final commodity i, a_{ij} the amount of primary resource j used in the production of one unit of commodity i, q_j the price of resource j and r_j the amount of resource j available initially. Then Cassel's system may be written,

$$x_i = f_i(p_1, \ldots, p_m) \tag{1}$$

$$\sum_j a_{ij}q_j = p_i \quad \text{for all } i, \tag{2}$$

$$\sum_i a_{ij}x_i = r_j \quad \text{for all } j. \tag{3}$$

Professor Neisser [15] remarked that the Casselian system might have negative values of prices or quantities as solutions, ([15], pp. 424–425). Negative quantities are clearly meaningless and, at least, in the case of labor and capital, negative prices cannot be regarded as acceptable solutions since the supply at those prices will be zero. Neisser also observed that even some variability in the technical coefficients might not be sufficient to remove the inconsistency. (pp. 448–453).

Stackelberg [20] pointed out that if there were fewer commodities than resources, the equations (3) would constitute a set of linear equations with more equations than unknowns and therefore possess, in general, no solution. He correctly noted that the economic meaning of this inconsistency was that some of the equations in (3) would become inequalities, with the corresponding resources becoming free goods. He argued that this meant the loss of a certain number of equations and hence the indeterminacy of the rest of the system. For this reason, he held that the assumption of fixed coefficients could not be maintained and the possibility of substitution in production must be admitted. This reasoning is incorrect; the loss of the equations (3) which are replaced by inequalities is exactly balanced by the addition of an equal number of equations stating that the prices of the corresponding resources must be zero.

Indeed, this suggestion had already been made by Professor Zeuthen [25] (see pp. 2–3, 6), though not in connection with the existence of solutions. He argued that the resources which appeared in the Casselian system were properly only the scarce resources; but it could not be regarded as known a priori which resources are free and which are not. Hence equations (3) should be rewritten as inequalities,

$$\sum_i a_{ij} x_i \leqq r_j,$$

with the additional statement that if the strict inequality holds for any j, then the corresponding price $q_j = 0$.

Schlesinger [19] took up Zeuthen's modification and suggested that it might resolve the difficulties found by Neisser and Stackelberg. It was in this form that the problem was investigated by Wald [21, 22] under various specialized assumptions. These studies are summarized and commented on in [23].

From a strictly mathematical point of view the first theorem proved by Wald [23] pp. 372–373 neither contains nor is contained in our results. In the assumptions concerning the productive system, the present paper is much more general since Wald assumes fixed proportions among the inputs and the single output of every process. On the demand side, he makes assumptions concerning the demand functions instead of deriving them, as we do, from a utility maximization assumption. It is on this point that no direct comparison is possible. The assumptions made by Wald are somewhat specialized ([23], pp. 373, assumptions 4, 5 and 6). One of them, interestingly enough, is the same as Samuelson's postulate ([18], pp. 108–111), but applied to the collective demand functions rather than to individual ones. Wald gives a heuristic argument for this assumption which is based essentially on utility-maximization grounds. In the same model, he also assumes that the demand functions are independent of the distribution of income, depending solely on the total. In effect, then, he assumes a single consumption unit.

In his second theorem, [23], pp. 382–383, about the pure exchange case, he assumes utility maximization but postulates that the marginal utility of each commodity depends on that commodity alone and is a strictly decreasing non-negative function of the amount of that commodity. The last clause implies both the convexity of the indifference map and nonsaturation with respect to every commodity. This theorem is a special case of our Theorem II′, when $\mathscr{P}$ is the null set and $\mathscr{D}$ contains all commodities (See 5.3.6).

Wald gives an example, under the pure exchange case, where competitive equilibrium does not exist ([23], pp. 389–391). In this case, each individual has an initial stock of only one commodity, so that Theorem I is not applicable.

At the same time only one commodity is always desired by all, but two of the three consumers have a null initial stock of that commodity. Hence Theorem II′ is not applicable.

It may be added that Wald has also investigated the uniqueness of the solutions; this has not been done here.

References

[1] Arrow, K. J., An Extension of the Basic Theorems of Classical Welfare Economics, in *Proceedings of the Second Berkeley Symposium on Mathematical Statistics and Probability*, J. Neyman (ed.), Berkeley and Los Angeles: University of California Press, 1951, pp. 507–532.

[2] Cassel, G., *The Theory of Social Economy*, New York: Harcourt, Brace, 1924.

[3] Cournot, A. A., *Researches into the Mathematical Principles of the Theory of Wealth*, New York and London: Macmillan, 1897, 213 pp.

[4] Debreu, G., The Coefficient of Resource Utilization, *Econometrica*, Vol. 19, July 1951, pp. 273–292.

[5] Debreu, G., A Social Equilibrium Existence Theorem, *Proceedings of the National Academy of Sciences*, Vol. 38, No. 10, 1952, pp. 886–893.

[6] Debreu, G., Representation of a Preference Ordering by a Numerical Function, in *Decision Processes*, R. M. Thrall, C. H. Coombs, and R. L. Davis, eds., New York: Wiley, forthcoming.

[7] Friedman, M., The Marshallian Demand Curve, *Journal of Political Economy*, Vol. 57, 1949, pp. 463–495.

[8] Friedman, M., The "Welfare" Effects of an Income Tax and an Excise Tax, *Journal of Political Economy*, Vol. 60, February 1952, pp. 25–33.

[9] Hart, A. G., *Anticipations, Uncertainty, and Dynamic Planning*, Chicago: The University of Chicago Press, 1940, 98 pp.

[10] Hicks, J. R., *Value and Capital*, Oxford: Clarendon Press, 1939, 331 pp.

[11] Knight, F. H., Realism and Relevance in the Theory of Demand, *Journal of Political Economy*, Vol. 52, 1944, pp. 289–318.

[12] Koopmans, T. C., Analysis of Production as an Efficient Combination of

Activities, in *Activity Analysis of Production and Allocation*, Cowles Commission Monograph No. 13, T. C. Koopmans, ed., New York: Wiley, 1951, Chapter III, pp. 33–97.

[13] Menger, C., *Principles of Economics*, (tr.), Glencoe, Illinois: Free Press, 1950, 328 pp.

[14] Nash, J. F., Jr., Equilibrium Points in N-Person Games, *Proceedings of the National Academy of Sciences*, Vol. 36, 1950, pp. 48–49.

[15] Neisser, H., Lohnhöhe und Beschäftigungsgrad im Marktgleichgewicht, *Weltwirtschaftliches Archiv*, Vol. 36, 1932, pp. 415–455.

[16] von Neumann, J., Über ein ökonomisches Gleichungssystem und eine Verallgemeinerung des Brouwerschen Fixpunktsatzes, *Ergebnisse eines mathematischen Kolloquiums*, No. 8, 1937, pp. 73–83, translated as, A Model of General Economic Equilibrium, *Review of Economic Studies*, Vol. 13 No. 33, 1945–6, pp. 1–9.

[17] Robbins, L., On the Elasticity of Demand for Income in Terms of Effort, *Economica*, Vol. 10, 1930, pp. 123–129.

[18] Samuelson, P. A., *Foundations of Economic Analysis*, Cambridge, Massa.: Harvard University Press, 1947, 477 pp.

[19] Schlesinger, K., Über die Produktionsgleichungen der ökonomischen Wertlehre, *Ergebnisse eines mathematischen Kolloquiums*, No. 6, 1933–4, pp. 10–11.

[20] Stackelberg, H., Zwei Kritische Bemerkungen zur Preistheorie Gustav Cassels, *Zeitschrift für Nationalökonomie*, Vol. 4, 1933, pp. 456–472.

[21] Wald, A., Über die eindeutige positive Lösbarkeit der neuen Produktionsgleichungen, *Ergebnisse eines mathematischen Kolloquiums*, No. 6, 1933–4, pp. 12–20.

[22] Wald, A., Über die Produktionsgleichungen der ökonomischen Wertlehre, *Ergebnisse eines mathematischen Kolloquiums*, No. 7, 1934–5, pp. 1–6.

[23] Wald, A., Über einige Gleichungssysteme der mathematischen Ökonomie, *Zeitschrift für Nationalökonomie*, Vol. 7, 1936, pp. 637–670, translated as On Some Systems of Equations of Mathematical Economics, *Econometrica*, Vol. 19, October 1951, pp. 368–403.

[24] Walras, L., *Eléments d'économie politique pure*, 4ème édition, Lausanne, Paris, 1900, 20 + 491 pp.

[25] Zeuthen, F., Das Prinzip der Knappheit, technische Kombination, und Oekonomische Qualität, *Zeitschrift für Nationalökonomie*, Vol. 4, 1933, pp. 1–24.

CHAPTER 5

Valuation equilibrium and Pareto optimum*

For an economic system with given technological and resource limitations, individual needs and tastes, a valuation equilibrium with respect to a set of prices is a state where no consumer can make himself better off without spending more, and no producer can make a larger profit; a Pareto optimum is a state where no consumer can be made better off without making another consumer worse off. Theorem 1 gives conditions under which a valuation equilibrium is a Pareto optimum. Theorem 2, in conjunction with the Remark, gives conditions under which a Pareto optimum is a valuation equilibrium. The contents of both theorems (in particular that of the first one) are old beliefs in economics. Arrow[1] and Debreu[2] have recently treated this question with techniques permitting proofs. A synthesis of their papers is made here. Their assumptions are weakened in several respects; in particular, their results are extended from finite dimensional to general linear spaces. This extension yields as a possible immediate application a solution of the problem of infinite time horizon (see sec. 6). Its main interest, however, may be that by forcing one to a greater generality it brings out with greater clarity and simplicity the basic concepts of the analysis and its logical structure. Not a single simplification

* Based on Cowles Commission Discussion Paper, Economics, No. 2067 (January, 1953). This article has been prepared under contract Nonr-358(01), NR 047-006 between the Office of Naval Research and the Cowles Commission for Research in Economics.
  I am grateful to E. Malinvaud, staff members and guests of the Cowles Commission, in particular I. N. Herstein, L. Hurwicz, T. C. Koopmans, and R. Radner for their comments.
[1] K. J. Arrow, An Extension of the Basic Theorems of Classical Welfare Economics, *Proceedings of the Second Berkeley Symposium* (Berkeley: University of California Press, 1951), pp. 507–532.
[2] G. Debreu, The Coefficient of Resource Utilization, *Econometrica*, **19**, 273–292, 1951.

of the proofs would indeed be brought about by restriction to the finite dimensional case.

As far as possible the mathematical structure of the theory has been dissociated from the economic interpretation, to be found in brackets.

1 The economic system

Let L be a linear space (on the reals R).[3] The economic system can be described as follows:

The ith consumer $(i = 1, \ldots, m)$ chooses a point x_i [his consumption] in a given subset X_i [his consumption-set] of L. [x_i completely describes the quantities of commodities he actually consumes, to be thought of as positive, and the quantities of the various types of labor he produces, to be thought of as negative. X_i is determined by constraints of the following types: quantities of commodities consumed (labor produced) must be nonnegative (nonpositive), and, moreover, they must enable the individual to survive.] There is on X_i a complete ordering, denoted by $\leqq_i$ [corresponding to the preferences of that consumer].[4] x_i^0 is a saturation point of X_i, if, for all $x_i \in X_i$, one has $x_i \leqq_i x_i^0$.

The jth producer $(j = 1, \ldots, n)$ chooses a point y_j [his production] in a given subset Y_j [his production-set] of L. [y_j is a complete description of all his outputs, to be thought of as positive, and his inputs, to be thought of as negative. Y_j is determined by technological limitations.]

Denote $x = \sum_i x_i, y = \sum_j y_j$; they are constrained to satisfy the equality $x - y = \zeta$, where ζ is a given point of L. [ζ corresponds to the exogenous resources avaliable (including all capital existing at the initial

---

[3] A real linear space L is a set where the addition of two elements $(x + y)$ and the multiplication of a real number by an element (tx) are defined and satisfy the eight axioms:
1   For all x, y, z in $L, (x + y) + z = x + (y + z)$.
2   There is an element $0 \in L$ such that for every $x \in L, x + 0 = x$.
3   For every $x \in L$, there is an $x' \in L$ such that $x + x' = 0$.
4   For all x, y in $L, x + y = y + x$. For all x, y in L, t, t' in R,
5   $t(x + y) = tx + ty$,
6   $(t + t')x = tx + t'x$,
7   $t(t'x) = (tt')x$,
8   $1x = x$.

[4] An order is a reflexive and transitive binary relation (generally denoted by $\leqq$). $x \sim x'$ means $x \leqq x'$ and $x' \leqq x$, while $x < x'$ means $x \leqq x'$ and not $x' \leqq x$. The order is complete (as opposed to partial) if for any x, x' one has $x \leqq x'$ and/or $x' \leqq x$.

One may object to completeness of the preference ordering as well as to its transitivity. The reader must therefore note that, with slight modifications of the definitions and the assumptions. Theorems 1 and 2 can easily be proved for *arbitrary* binary relations on the X.

date). $x - y$ is the *net* consumption of all consumers and all producers together. It must clearly equal ζ.][5]

A $(m + n)$-tuple $[(x_i), (y_j)]$, one x_i for each i, one y_j for each j, is called a state of the economy. [It is a complete description of the activity of every consumer and every producer.] A state $[(x_i), (y_j)]$ is called attainable if $x_i \in X_i$ for all i, $y_j \in Y_j$ for all j, $x - y = \zeta$.

2　　　Valuation equilibrium

$v(z)$ will denote a (real-valued) linear form on L.[6] [It gives the value of the commodity-point z. When L is suitably specialized, this value can be represented by the linear product $p \cdot z$, where p is the price system.] A state $[(x_i^0), (y_j^0)]$ is a valuation equilibrium with respect to $v(z)$ if:

(2.1) $[(x_i^0), (y_j^0)]$ is attainable.

(2.2) For every i "$x_i \in X_i, v(x_i) \leqq v(x_i^0)$" implies "$x_i \leqq_i x_i^0$". [Best satisfaction of preferences subject to a budget constraint.]

(2.3) For every j "$y_j \in Y_j$" implies "$v(y_j) \leqq v(y_j^0)$". [Maximization of profit subject to technological constraints.]

3　　　Pareto optimum

The set $X_1 \times \cdots \times X_m$ of m-tuples (x_i), one x_i for each i, is (partially) ordered as follows: $(x_i') \geqq (x_i)$ if and only if $x_i' \geqq_i x_i$ for all i.

A state $[(x_i^0), (y_j^0)]$ is a Pareto optimum if:

(3.1) $[(x_i^0), (y_j^0)]$ is attainable.

(3.2) There is no attainable state $[(x_i), (y_j)]$ for which $(x_i) > (x_i^0)$. (It is impossible to make one consumer better off without making another worse off.)

4　　　A valuation equilibrium is a Pareto optimum

The following assumptions will be made:

I　For every i, X_i is convex.

II　For every i, "$x_i' \in X_i$, $x_i'' \in X_i$, $x_i' <_i x_i'''$" implies "$x_i' <_i (1 - t)$ $x_i' + t x_i''$ for all t, $0 < t < 1$".

---

[5] Usually the net consumption is only constrained to be at most equal to the available resources. But this implies that any surplus can be freely disposed of. Such an assumption on the technology should be made explicit (see sec. 6) while requiring at the same time $x - y = \zeta$.

[6] For all x, y, $v(x + y) = v(x) + v(y)$. For all t, x, $v(tx) = tv(x)$. $v(z)$ is said to be trivial if it vanishes everywhere.

These two axioms on the convexity of the consumption-sets and the convexity of preferences have been used by Arrow and Debreu[7] in a different context.

Theorem 1

Under assumptions I and II, every valuation equilibrium $[(x_i^0),$ $(y_j^0)]$, where no x_i^0 is a saturation point, is a Pareto optimum.

Proof

(4.1) "$x_i \in X_i$ and $x_i >_i x_i^0$" implies "$v(x_i) > v(x_i^0)$."
This is a trivial consequence of definition (2.2).

(4.2) "$x_i \in X_i$ and $x_i \sim_i x_i^0$" implies "$v(x_i) \geq v(x_i^0)$."

Since x_i^0 is not a saturation point, there is $x_i' \in X_i$, such that $x_i' >_i x_i^0$, hence $x_i' >_i x_i$. Consider $x_i(t) = (1 - t) x_i + t x_i'$. By assumption II, for all $t, 0 < t < 1, x_i(t) >_i x_i$, hence $x_i(t) >_i x_i^0$, so (by [4.1]) $v(x_i^0) < v(x_i(t)) = (1 - t) v(x_i) + t v(x_i')$. Let t tend to zero; in the limit $v(x_i^0) \leq v(x_i)$.

To complete the proof we consider a state $[(x_i), (y_j)]$, where $x_i \in X_i$ for all i, $y_j \in Y_j$ for all j, and show that if $(x_i) > (x_i^0)$, the state is not attainable, i.e., $x - y \neq \zeta$.

$(x_i) > (x_i^0)$ means that for all i, $x_i \geq_i x_i^0$, and for some i', $x_{i'} >_{i'} x_{i'}^0$; so by (4.1) and (4.2) $\sum_i v(x_i) > \sum_i v(x_i^0)$, i.e., $v(x) > v(x^0)$. On the other hand, (2.3) implies $v(y) \leq v(y^0)$, so $v(x) - v(y) > v(x^0) - v(y^0)$. Since $x^0 - y^0 = \zeta, v(x - y) > v(\zeta)$, which rules out $x - y = \zeta$.

5   A Pareto optimum is a valuation equilibrium

In this section L is a topological linear space.[8] Let x_i', x_i'' be points of X_i; we define $I(x_i', x_i'') = \{t | [(1 - t)x_i' + t x_i''] \in X_i\}$. When X_i is convex, $I(x_i', x_i'')$ is a real interval with possibly one or two end-points excluded. In addition to assumptions I and II, three further assumptions are needed here.

[7] K. J. Arrow, and G. Debreu, Existence of an Equilibrium for a Competitive Economy, *Econometrica*, 22, 265–290, 1954.

[8] A topological linear space is a linear space with a topology such that the functions $(x, y) \to x + y$ from $L \times L$ to L and $(t, x) \to tx$ from $R \times L$ to L are continuous. For definition of a topology, of the topology on a product, of a continuous function see N. Bourbaki, *Eléments de mathématique* (Paris: Hermann et Cie, 1940), Part I, Book 3, Chap. i. For the representation of continuous linear forms on L see S. Banach, *Théorie des opérations linéaires* (Warsaw, 1932), in particular, Chap. iv, sec. 4.

III For every i, x_i, x_i', x_i'' in X_i the sets $\{t \in I(x_i', x_i'')|(1 - t)x_i' + tx_i'' \geq_i x_i\}$ and $\{t \in I(x_i', x_i'')|(1 - t)x_i' + tx_i'' \leq_i x_i\}$ are closed in $I(x_i', x_i'')$.

This weak axiom of continuity for preferences has been introduced by Herstein and Milnor[9] in another context. We define $Y = \sum_j Y_j$ (the set of all $y = \sum_j y_j$, where $y_j \in Y_j$ for all j).

IV *Y is convex.* [The assumption that the aggregate production-set is convex is strictly weaker than the assumption that the individual production-sets Y_j are all convex.]
V *L is finite dimensional and/or Y has an interior point.* [The assumption that Y has an interior point will be shown in section 6 to be implied by free disposal of commodities.]

Theorem 2

Under assumptions I–V, with every Pareto optimum $[(x_i^0), (y_j^0)]$, where some x_i^0 is not a saturation point, is associated a (nontrivial) continuous linear form $v(z)$ on L such that:
   (5.1) For every i "$x_i \in X_i$, $x_i \geq_i x_i^0$" implies "$v(x_i) \geq v(x_i^0)$."
   (5.2) For every j "$y_j \in Y_j$" implies "$v(y_j) \leq v(y_j^0)$."

Proof: From assumptions I, II, and III follows:
   (a) "x_i', x_i'' in X_i, $x_i' \leq_i x_i''$" implies "for all t, $0 \leq t \leq 1$, $x_i' \leq_i [(1 - t)x_i' + tx_i''] \in X_i$."

By assumption III, the set $\{t \in I(x_i', x_i'')|(1 - t)x_i' + tx_i'' <_i x_i'\}$ is open in $I(x_i', x_i'')$. Its intersection with the interval $]0, 1[$ (end points excluded) is open. We wish to show that this intersection is empty. If it were not, it would contain two numbers $t_1 < t_2$. Take the corresponding points x_i^1, x_i^2. Then $x_i^1 <_i x_i' \leq_i x_i''$. By assumption II, $x_i^1 <_i x_i''$ gives $x_i^1 <_i x_i^2$.

$$\overline{x_i'} \cdot \overline{x_i^1} \cdot \overline{x_i^2} \cdot \overline{x_i''}$$

Similarly, $x_i^2 <_i x_i'$ gives $x_i^2 <_i x_i^1$, a contradiction.
   As an immediate consequence of (a), for all i, the sets $X_{i(x_i^0)} = \{x_i \in X_i | x_i \geq_i x_i^0\}$ and $\mathring{X}_{i(x_i^0)} = \{x_i \in \mathring{X}_i | x_i > x_i^0\}$ are convex.

9 I. N. Herstein and J. Milnor, An Axiomatic Approach to Measurable Utility, *Econometrica*, **21**, 291–297, 1953.

Let i' be a value of i for which $x_{i'}^0$ is not a saturation point, and consider the set

$$Z = \mathring{X}_{i'(x_{i'}^0)} + \sum_{i \neq i'} X_{i(x_i^0)} - \sum_j Y_j.$$

$\zeta \notin Z$, this is the definition of a Pareto optimum $[(x_i^0), (y_j^0)]$. Z is convex as it is the sum of convex sets. If $Y = \sum_j Y_j$ has an interior point, Z also has one. The Hahn–Banach theorem[10] can therefore be applied to Z and ζ. There is a (non-trivial) continuous linear form $v(z)$ on L such that $v(z) \geqq v(\zeta)$ for all $z \in Z$, i.e., since

$$\zeta = \sum_i x_i^0 - \sum_j y_j^0, \qquad v\left[\sum_i (x_i - x_i^0) - \sum_j (y_j - y_j^0)\right] \geqq 0$$

for all $x_{i'} \in \mathring{X}_{i'(x_{i'}^0)}$, $x_i \in X_{i(x_i^0)}$ (for $i \neq i'$), $y_j \in Y_j$ (for all j).

In this statement $\mathring{X}_{i'(x_{i'}^0)}$ can be replaced by $X_{i'(x_{i'}^0)}$, for every $x_{i'} \in X_{i'}$, $x_{i'} \sim_{i'} x_{i'}^0$, can be exhibited, as in the proof of (4.2), as a limit of points belonging to $\mathring{X}_{i'(x_{i'}^0)}$. Therefore,

(b) $\sum_i v(x_i - x_i^0) + \sum_j v(y_j^0 - y_j) \geqq 0$ for all $x_i \in X_i(x_i^0)$, $y_j \in Y_j$.

By making all but one of the x_i, y_j equal to the corresponding x_i^0, y_j^0, one proves that for the remaining term in (b) $v(x_i - x_i^0) \geqq 0$ for all $x_i \in X_i(x_i^0)$ (or $v(y_j^0 - y_j) \geqq 0$ for all $y_j \in Y_j$) which is precisely the statement of Theorem 2.

(5.2) is identical to (2.3), but (5.1) does not necessarily imply (2.2), and Theorem 2 does not quite correspond to the title of this section. The following Remark, due to Arrow[11] in its essence, tries to fill this gap:

Remark. Under assumptions I and III, if there is, for every i, an $x_i' \in X_i$ such that $v(x_i') < v(x_i^0)$, then (5.1) implies (2.2).

Consider an $x_i \in X_i, v(x_i) \leqq v(x_i^0)$. Let $x_i(t) = (1 - t) x_i + t x_i'$. For all t, $0 < t < 1, v(x_i(t)) < v(x_i^0)$ and thus, by (5.1), $x_i(t) < x_i^0$. The set $\{t \in I (x_i, x_i')|(1 - t) x_i + t x_i' \leqq_i x_i^0\}$ contains the interval $]0, 1[$; since it is closed in $I(x_i, x_i')$ (by assumption III), it contains 0, i.e., $x_i \leqq_i x_i^0$.

[The condition that there is $x_i' \in X_i$ such that $v(x_i') < v(x_i^0)$ means that the consumer does not have such a low $v(x_i^0)$ that with any lower value he could not survive.]

[10] In a real topological linear space, if Z is a convex set with interior points, ζ a point which does not belong to Z, there is a closed hyperplane through ζ, bounding for Z. (See, for example, N. Bourbaki, *Eléments de mathématique* [Paris: Hermann et Cie, 1953], Part I, Book 5, Chap. ii, in particular, sec. 3.)

[11] Arrow, Extension of the Basic Theorems, Lemma 5.

6   The free disposal assumption

An example will show the economic justification of assumption V when L is not finite dimensional. Suppose that there is an infinite sequence of commodities [because, for example, economic activity takes place at an infinite sequence of dates, a case studied by Malinvaud[12] with different techniques]. The space L will be the set of infinite sequences of real numbers (z_h) such that $\text{Sup } |z_h| < +\infty$. L is normed by $\|z\| = \text{Sup } |z_h|$.

The assumption of free disposal for the technology means that if $y \in Y$ and $y'_h \leq y_h$ for all h, then $y' \in Y$ [if an input-output combination is possible, so is one where some outputs are smaller or some inputs larger; it is implied that a surplus can be freely disposed of]. With this assumption, if Y is not empty, it clearly has an interior point: select a number $\rho > 0$ and a point $y \in Y$; consider y' defined by $y'_h = y_h - \rho$ for all h. The sphere of center y', radius ρ, is contained in Y.

Other examples of linear spaces in economics are provided by the case where there is a finite number l of commodities, and time and/or location is a continuous variable. The activity of an economic agent is then described by the l rates of flow of the commodities as functions of time and/or location. The space L is the set of l-tuples of functions of the continuous variable.

In any case, if L is properly chosen, the existence of an interior point for Y will follow from the free disposal assumption. Then application of Theorem 2 will give a continuous linear form $v(z)$.

---

[12] E. Malinvaud, Capital Accumulation and Efficient Allocation of Resources, *Econometrica*, **21**, 233–268, 1953.

CHAPTER 6

Representation of a preference ordering by a numerical function

1   Introduction

It has often been assumed in economics that if a set X (usually in the finite Euclidean space of commodity bundles) is completely ordered by the preferences of some agent, it is always possible to define on that set a real-valued order-preserving function (utility, satisfaction). This is easily seen to be false.[1]

The particular case where there exists on X (the set of *prospects*) a certain algebra of combining (corresponding to the combination of probabilities) has been rigorously and extensively studied by J. von Neumann and O. Morgenstern [7], J. Marschak [6], I. N. Herstein and J. Milnor [5].

But, rather paradoxically, the general case, which is more basic and simpler, has received little attention from economists. H. Wold's study [8]

Based on Cowles Commission Discussion Paper, Economics 2040 (April 1952). This article has been prepared under contract Nonr-358(01), NR 047-006 between the Office of Naval Research and the Cowles Commission for Research in Economics, to be reprinted as a Cowles Commission Paper.

I am grateful to staff members and guests of the Cowles Commission and very particularly to I. N. Herstein for their comments. I owe to P. R. Halmos reference [4]. My greatest debt is to L. J. Savage who suggested in the course of a valuable discussion that Cantor's postulate $x < z_i < y$ (see Lemma II) might be weakened to $x \leqq z_i \leqq y$.

[1] Consider the lexicographic ordering of the plane: a point of coordinates (a', b') is better than the point (a, b) if "$a' > a$" or if "$a' = a$ and $b' > b$." Suppose that there exists a real order-preserving function $\alpha(a, b)$. Take two fixed numbers $b_1 < b_2$ and with a number a associate the two numbers $\alpha_1(a) = \alpha(a, b_1)$ and $\alpha_2(a) = \alpha(a, b_2)$. To two different numbers a, a' correspond two disjoint intervals $[\alpha_1(a), \alpha_2(a)]$ and $[\alpha_1(a'), \alpha_2(a')]$. One obtains therefore a one-to-one correspondence between the set of real numbers (*non-countable*) and a set of *non-degenerate disjoint* intervals (*countable*).

indeed seems to be the only rigorous one; its assumptions are however restrictive.

This note gives conditions under which a complete order (denoted by $\leqq$) can be represented by a numerical function. The most common preference ordering in economics is that of bundles of n commodities, i.e., of points of an n-dimensional Euclidean space. We shall however treat the problem in a more general frame since this involves no additional mathematical cost.

The familiar case of a set in a finite Euclidean space is covered by the following proposition which is a very special application of theorem II below:

> Let X be a completely ordered subset of a finite Euclidean space. If for every $x' \in X$ the sets $\{x \in X | x \leqq x'\}, \{x \in X | x' \leqq x\}$ are closed (in X), there exists on X a continuous, real, order-preserving function.

The assumption that the set $\{x \in X | x' \leqq x\}$ is closed (in X) is equivalent to the more intuitive assumption: let (x^k) be any sequence of points in X having a limit $x^0 \in X$, if for all k, x^k is at least as good as x', then x^0 is at least as good as x'.

2   Two representation lemmas

A *complete ordering* on X is, to be precise, a binary relation, denoted $\leqq$, satisfying

(1)   Given any two elements x, y of X; $x \leqq y$ and/or $y \leqq x$
(2)   Given three elements of X such that $x \leqq y$, $y \leqq z$ then $x \leqq z$.

From this relation can be derived two new ones:

$$x \sim y \,(x \text{ indifferent to } y) \quad \text{if} \quad x \leqq y \quad \text{and} \quad y \leqq x$$
$$x < y \,(y \text{ better than } x) \quad \text{if} \quad x \leqq y \quad \text{and not} \quad y \leqq x.$$

The *quotient* set $X/\sim$, i.e., the set of indifference classes in X, will be denoted by A.[2] The trivial case where all elements of X are indifferent (i.e., where A has just one element) will always be excluded.

The *interval* $[x', y']$ is the set $\{x \in X | x' \leqq x \leqq y'\}$.
The *interval* $]x', y'[$ is the set $\{x \in X | x' < x < y'\}$.

A real-valued function $\phi(x)$ defined on X is said to be *order-preserving* if $x \leqq y$ is equivalent to $\phi(x) \leqq \phi(y)$.

---

[2] For definitions relating to an equivalence relation see [1].

A *natural topology* on X is a topology[3] for which the sets $\{x \in X | x \leqq x'\}$, $\{x \in X | x' \leqq x\}$ are closed for all $x' \in X$.

Lemma I

Let X be a completely ordered set whose quotient A is countable. There exists on X a real, order-preserving function, continuous[3] in any natural topology.

Rank the elements of A; it is clearly possible to construct by induction on the rank an order-preserving function ψ taking A into some finite real interval. Let $\lambda = \text{Inf}_{a \in A} \psi(a)$, $\mu = \text{Sup}_{a \in A} \psi(a)$. If α' satisfies $\lambda < \alpha' < \mu$ and $\alpha' \notin \psi(A)$, four cases may occur: the set $\{\alpha \in \psi(A) | \alpha < \alpha'\}$ (1) may, or (2) may not, have a largest element; and the set $\{\alpha \in \psi(A) | \alpha' < \alpha\}$ (1') may, or (2') may not, have a smallest element. We wish to eliminate the gaps of type (1–2'), (2–1') and (2–2'); this can easily be done by means of a non-decreasing step function $\Theta(\alpha)$, the height of each step being equal to the length of the corresponding gap. The new function $\phi^*(a) = \psi(a) - \Theta[\psi(a)]$ is still order-preserving and $\phi^*(A)$ has no gaps of the unwanted types. Denote by $a(x)$ the indifference class a to which x belongs; we finally define $\phi(x) = \phi^*[a(x)]$. To show that ϕ is continuous in any *natural* topology on X consider a number $\alpha', \lambda < \alpha' < \mu$ and the set $X_{\alpha'} = \{x \in X | \phi(x) \leqq \alpha'\}$.

(1) If $\alpha' \in \phi(X)$, let $x' \in X$ be such that $\alpha' = \phi(x')$. $X_{\alpha'} = \{x \in X | x \leqq x'\}$ and is therefore closed.

(2) If $\alpha' \notin \phi(X)$ and if the set $R_{\alpha'} = \{\alpha \in \phi(X) | \alpha < \alpha'\}$ has a largest element α'', $X_{\alpha'} = X_{\alpha''}$ which is closed by 1).

(3) If $\alpha' \notin \phi(X)$ and if the set $R_{\alpha'}$ has no largest element, then the set $R^{\alpha'} = \{\alpha \in \phi(X) | \alpha' < \alpha\}$ has no smallest element since $\phi(X)$ has no gap of type (2–1'). Thus $X_{\alpha'} = \bigcap_{\alpha \in R^{\alpha'}} X_\alpha$ and $X_{\alpha'}$ is closed as an intersection of closed sets.

Similarly one proves that for any number α' the set $X^{\alpha'} = \{x \in X | \alpha' \leqq \phi(x)\}$ is closed. It follows that the inverse image by ϕ of any closed set of the real line R is a closed set of X.

Lemma II

Let X be a completely ordered set, $Z = (z_0, z_1, \ldots)$ a countable subset of X. If for every pair x, y of elements of X such that $x < y$,

---

[3] For definitions of a topology and of a continuous function see [2, Sec. 1] and [2, Sec. 4] respectively.

there is an element z_i of Z such that $x \leq z_i \leq y$, then there exists on X a real, order-preserving function, continuous in any natural topology.

The assumption made is a weakening of the postulate $(x < z_i < y)$ used by G. Cantor in [3].

Take first the quotient sets $X/\sim = A$ and $Z/\sim = C$. C is clearly countable and plays for A the role that Z played for X. If A has a smallest and/or a largest element, we can assume, without any loss of generality, that they are contained in C.

Define a new equivalence relation[4] among elements of A by: aFb if and only if between a and b there is a finite number of elements of A. The binary relation F is indeed reflexive, symmetric and transitive. Equivalence classes for F are denoted by $[a]_F$, $[b]_F$, ...

Every equivalence class is clearly countable. Moreover an equivalence class $[c]_F$ containing more than one element of A contains an element of C and thus the equivalence classes $[c]_F$ form a countable set. Summing up, C' the union over these classes $[c]_F$, is countable and so is $D = C \cup C'$.

Construct now on D the function ϕ^* as in the proof of Lemma I. ϕ^* is extended from D to A as follows. Let $a \in A$ and $a \notin D$; the set $D_a = \{d \in D | d < a\}$ has no largest element. To see this consider any $d' \in D_a$. Since $a \notin D$, $a \notin C'$ and there is an infinity of elements of A between d' and a, there is therefore an infinity of elements of C, i.e., of D, between d' and a. Similarly the set $D^a = \{d \in D | a < d\}$ has no smallest element. As a consequence the values $\text{Sup}_{d \in D_a} \phi^*(d)$ and $\text{Inf}_{d \in D^a} \phi^*(d)$ are not taken on. Moreover these two values are equal since $\phi^*(D)$ has no gap of the (2–2') type; they define $\phi^*(a)$. The function $\phi^*(a)$, and therefore the function $\phi(x) = \phi^*[a(x)]$, are clearly order-preserving and, since $\phi(X) = \phi^*(A)$ has no gaps of types (1–2') or (2–1'), $\phi(x)$ is continuous in any natural topology on X (the proof is the same as for Lemma I).

3   Two representation theorems

Before stating Theorem I we recall two definitions. A (topological) space X is *separable* if it contains a countable subset whose closure is X. A (topological) space X is *connected* if there is no partition of X into two disjoint, non-empty, closed sets.

Theorem I

Let X be a completely ordered, separable, and connected space. If for every $x' \in X$ the sets $\{x \in X | x \leq x'\}$ and $\{x \in X | x' \leq x\}$ are

---

[4] See footnote 2.

closed, there exists on X a continuous, real, order-preserving function.[5]

This theorem can easily be derived from the results of S. Eilenberg [4]. It will be proved here as an immediate consequence of Lemma II. A much more direct proof could assuredly be given: the motivation for the two lemmas is Theorem II.

Call Z the countable set dense in X and consider a pair x', y' of elements of X such that $x' < y'$. The sets $\{x \in X | x \leq x'\}$ and $\{x \in X | y' \leq x\}$ are disjoint, non-empty and closed, they cannot exhaust X which is connected, therefore the open interval $]x', y'[$ is not empty, and it must contain an element $z_i \in Z$. The theorem is proved since the topology on X is a *natural* topology.

The assumption of connectedness is however very strong. We give a second theorem where it is removed at the cost of a slightly stronger separability assumption.

A topological space X is *perfectly separable* if there is a countable class (S) of open sets such that every open set in X is the union of sets of the class (S).

We remark that a separable metric space is perfectly separable, that a subspace of a perfectly separable space is perfectly separable.

Theorem II

Let X be a completely ordered, perfectly separable space. If for every $x' \in X$ the sets $\{x \in X | x \leq x'\}$ and $\{x \in X | x' \leq x\}$ are closed, there exists on X a continuous, real, order-preserving function.

Choose an element in each non-empty set S; they form a countable set Z''.

Consider then the pairs a', b' of elements of A such that $a' < b'$ and the interval $]a', b'[$ is empty. The set of those pairs is countable. To see this, associate with each such pair a set $S_{b'}$ as follows: take two elements x', y' in the indifference classes a', b', respectively. The set $\{x \in X | x < y'\}$ is open and therefore there exists a set $S_{b'}$ in the class (S) such that $x' \in S_{b'} \subset \{x \in X | x < y'\}$. If a'', b'' is another pair with the same properties, $S_{b''}$ is different from $S_{b'}$ for one has $a' < b' \leq a'' < b''$, in which case $x'' \in S_{b''}$ and $x'' \notin S_{b'}$ or $a'' < b'' \leq a' < b'$, in which case $x' \in S_{b'}$ and $x' \notin S_{b''}$. The pairs a', b' are thus in one-to-one correspondence with a subclass of the countable class (S). Choose then an element x' in each class a' and an element y' in each class b'. All those x' and y' form a countable set Z'.

---

[5] The closedness assumptions have already been used in a similar context by I. N. Herstein in an earlier unpublished version of [5].

Consider finally the countable set $Z = Z' \cup Z''$; it has all the properties required by Lemma II. Let x, y be a pair of elements of X such that $x < y$. If the open set $]x, y[$ is not empty, it contains a non-empty set S and therefore an element of Z''. If the set $]x, y[$ is empty, $x \sim x' \in Z'$ and $y \sim y' \in Z'$. So that in any case $[x, y]$ contains an element of Z.

References

[1] Bourbaki, N., *Eléments de Mathématique* Première partie, Livre I (Fascicule de résultats) Sec. 5. Paris, Hermann, 1939.

[2] Bourbaki, N., *Eléments de Mathématique* Première partie, Livre III Chap. I. Paris, Hermann, 1940.

[3] Cantor, G., Beiträge zur Begründung der transfiniten Mengenlehre, Sec. 11 *Mathematische Annalen* Vol. 46, 1895, pp. 481–512.

[4] Eilenberg, S., Ordered Topological Spaces, *American Journal of Mathematics*, Vol. 63, January 1941, pp. 39–45.

[5] Herstein, I. N. and Milnor, J., An Axiomatic Approach to Measurable Utility, *Econometrica*, Vol. 21, April 1953, pp. 291–297.

[6] Marschak, J., Rational Behavior, Uncertain Prospects, and Measurable Utility, *Econometrica*, Vol. 18, April 1950, pp. 111–141.

[7] von Neumann, J. and Morgenstern, O., *Theory of Games and Economic Behavior*, Chap. 1, Section 3 and Appendix. Princeton, N.J., Princeton University Press, 1947.

[8] Wold, H., A Synthesis of Pure Demand Analysis, Part II *Skandinavisk Aktuarietidskrift*, Vol. 26, 1943, pp. 220–263.

CHAPTER 7

Market equilibrium*

Let there be l commodities in the economy. When the price system is $p \in R^l$, the excess of demand over supply is $z \in R^l$. Generally, p does not uniquely determine z; it determines a set $\zeta(p)$ of which z can be any element. The problem of market equilibrium has the natural formulation: Is there a p compatible with $z = 0$, i.e., is there a p such that $0 \in \zeta(p)$?

In usual contexts, two price systems derived from each other by multiplication by a positive number are equivalent, and all prices do not vanish simultaneously. Thus the domain of p is a cone C with vertex 0, but with 0 excluded.

Since no agent spends more than he receives, the value of total demand does not exceed the value of total supply; hence $p \cdot z \leqq 0$ for every z in $\zeta(p)$. This can also be written $p \cdot \zeta(p) \leqq 0$, i.e., the set $\zeta(p)$ is below (with possibly points in) the hyperplane through 0 orthogonal to p (see Fig. 1).

It is intuitive that, under proper regularity assumptions, there is in C a p, different from 0, for which $\zeta(p)$ intersects Γ, the polar of C (whose definition is recalled in the Appendix). The theorem gives a precise statement of this result. Its interest lies in the fact that, for a wide class of economies, $\Gamma \cap \zeta(p) \neq \varnothing$ implies $0 \in \zeta(p)$ [1].

It is convenient to normalize p by restricting it to the unit sphere $S = \{p \in R^l | |p| = 1\}$.

* A technical report of research undertaken by the Cowles Foundation for Research in Economics under contract with the Office of Naval Research. Based on Cowles Foundation Discussion Paper No. 10 (February, 1956). Reproduction in whole or in part is permitted for any purpose of the United States Government.

I thank Shizuo Kakutani for the valuable discussion of this question I had with him, and Lionel McKenzie for his comments on an earlier draft.

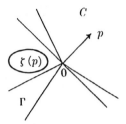

Figure 1

Theorem

Let C be a closed, convex cone with vertex 0 in R^l, which is not a linear manifold; let Γ be its polar. If the multivalued function ζ from $C \cap S$ to R^l is upper semicontinuous and bounded, and if for every p in $C \cap S$ the set $\zeta(p)$ is nonempty, convex, and satisfies $p \cdot \zeta(p) \leqq 0$, then there is a p in $C \cap S$ such that $\Gamma \cap \zeta(p) \neq \varnothing$.

Proof: Throughout, Z denotes a compact, convex subset of R^l in which ζ takes its values; such a subset exists, since ζ is bounded.

1. The theorem is first proved in the case where Γ has an interior point z^0. It is more convenient here to normalize p by restricting it to the set $P = \{p \in C | p \cdot z^0 = -1\}$, which is easily seen to be nonempty, compact, and convex.

Given z in Z, let $\pi(z)$ be the set of maximizers of $p \cdot z$ in P. The set $\pi(z)$ is clearly nonempty and convex; and the multivalued function π from Z to P is easily seen to be upper semicontinuous.

Consider, then, the set $P \times Z$ and the multivalued transformation φ of this set into itself defined by $\varphi(p, z) = \pi(z) \times \zeta(p)$. Since φ satisfies the conditions of the Kakutani [2] fixed-point theorem, there is a pair (p^*, z^*) which belongs to $\varphi(p^*, z^*)$, i.e., $p^* \in \pi(z^*)$ and $z^* \in \zeta(p^*)$.

The first relation implies that $p \cdot z^* \leqq p^* \cdot z^*$ for every p in P; the second implies that $p^* \cdot z^* \leqq 0$; therefore, $p \cdot z^* \leqq 0$ for every p in P; hence $z^* \in \Gamma$. This, with $z^* \in \zeta(p^*)$, proves that $\Gamma \cap \zeta(p^*) \neq \varnothing$.

2. In the general case, Γ is considered as the limit of an infinite sequence of cones Γ^m with vertex 0, having *nonempty* interiors. These cones are constrained to be closed, convex, different from R^l, and to contain Γ.

Let C^m be the polar of Γ^m; it is contained in C, which is the polar of Γ. Apply, then, the result of paragraph 1 to the pair C^m, Γ^m: there is a pair (p^m, z^m) such that $p^m \in C^m \cap S$, $z^m \in \Gamma^m$, and $z^m \in \zeta(p^m)$.

Since $S \times Z$ is compact, one can extract from the sequence (p^m, z^m) a subsequence converging to (p^*, z^*). Clearly, $p^* \in C \cap S$, $z^* \in \Gamma$, and $z^* \in \zeta(p^*)$ (the last relation by upper semicontinuity of ζ).

Remarks: The central idea of the proof is taken from Arrow–Debreu [3, 4]. It consists, given an excess z of demand over supply, in choosing p so as to maximize $p \cdot z$. It has a simple economic interpretation: in order to reduce the excess demand, the weight of the price system is brought to bear on those commodities for which the excess demand is the largest.

Since the convexity assumptions in Kakutani's theorem can be weakened (see Eilenberg-Montgomery [5] and Begle [6]), the assumption that $\zeta(p)$ is convex is inessential.

Gale [7] and Debreu [1] have, independently, stated (and Kuhn [8] has proved in a third way) the theorem in the particular case where C is the set of points in R^l all of whose co-ordinates are non-negative. The underlying economic assumption is that commodities can be freely disposed of. As McKenzie [9] emphasizes, it is very desirable to relax that assumption. The purpose of this note was to give a general market equilibrium theorem with a simple and economically meaningful proof.

Appendix

Let C be a cone with vertex 0 in R^l; its polar Γ is the set $\{z \in R^l | p \cdot z \leqq 0$ for every p in $C\}$. This set is a closed, convex cone with vertex 0. It can also be described as the intersection of the closed half-spaces below the hyperplanes through 0 with normals p in C.

It is immediate that "C^1 contains C^2" implies "Γ^2 contains Γ^1." One can prove that if C is closed, and convex, then C is the polar of Γ, i.e., the relation "is the polar of" becomes symmetric.

Let ψ be a multivalued function from a subset E of R^n to R^n; it is said to be upper semicontinuous if "$x^q \to x^0$, $y^q \in \psi(x^q)$, $y^q \to y^0$" implies "$y^0 \in \psi(x^0)$."

References

[1] G. Debreu, *Value Theory* (forthcoming), Chap. 5.
[2] S. Kakutani, A Generalization of Brouwer's Fixed Point Theorem, *Duke Math. J.*, 8, 457–459, 1941.

[3] K. J. Arrow and G. Debreu, Existence of an Equilibrium for a Competitive Economy, *Econometrica*, 22, 265–290, 1954, secs. 3.1, 3.2.

[4] G. Debreu, The Coefficient of Resource Utilization, *Econometrica*, 19, 273–292, 1951, secs. 11, 12.

[5] S. Eilenberg and D. Montgomery, Fixed Point Theorems for Multi-valued Transformations, *Am. J. Math.*, 68, 214–222, 1946.

[6] E. G. Begle, A Fixed Point Theorem, *Ann. Math.*, 51, 544–550, 1950.

[7] D. Gale. The Law of Supply and Demand, *Math. Scand.*, 3, 155–169, 1955, secs. 2, 3.

[8] H. W. Kuhn, A Note on "The Law of Supply and Demand," *Math Scand.*, 4, 1956.

[9] L. W. McKenzie, Competitive Equilibrium with Dependent Consumer Preferences, *Second Symposium in Linear Programming* (U.S. National Bureau of Standards, 1955), 1, 277–294.

CHAPTER 8

Economics under uncertainty[1,2]

By a simple reinterpretation of the concept of a commodity, the classical economic theories of equilibrium and optimality can be extended, without change of form, to the case where uncertain events determine the consumption sets, the production sets, and the resources of the economy. According to the usual definition, a commodity is a good or service whose physical characteristics and date and place of delivery, are specified; in this article, the definition of a commodity also specifies an exogenous event (which will be known to have, or not to have, occurred by the delivery date). By agreement of the contracting parties, delivery of the commodity is conditional upon the occurrence of this event. This extended definition, which originated in the paper by K. J. Arrow at the May 1952 CNRS Colloquium on Risk, permits an immediate transposition of the results of economics under certainty to those of economics under uncertainty, thanks to the identity of forms already mentioned; it also has the advantage of leading to a theory of uncertainty that makes no reference to the notion of probability. Admittedly, there are no markets for the commodities as defined here, but economists are familiar with the fruitful hypothesis that

[1] Translated from the French by Shantayanan Devarajan.

[2] This article is based on the mimeographed manuscript, "Une Economie de l'Incertain," written at Electricité de France during the summer of 1953, and the contents of which were the subject of a seminar at the Service des Etudes et Recherches of E.D.F., on September 4 of the same year. I wish to thank M. Boiteux, G. Dessus, T. C. Koopmans, E. Malinvaud, J. Marschak, P. Massé and R. M. Solow variously for both their comments and assistance in facilitating my work at Electricité de France during my stay there.

This paper, parts of which were presented in greater detail and in a more technical form in Chapter VII of my *Theory of Value*, was prepared under a contract between the Cowles Commission for Research in Economics and the Office of Naval Research.

there exist futures markets for all commodities, although only an insignificant number of such markets are observed. The analysis we will present takes this idea one step further. It appears justified by its explanatory power, perhaps also by its implicit invitation to consider a larger class of problems of economic decision making in terms of choices of Nature.

A similar analysis has been published by E. Baudier in *Les Cahiers Economiques* in December 1954. In addition, at the CNRS colloquium of May 1952, M. Allais independently presented an extension of the theories of the Lausanne school to the case of uncertainty, but his model does not appear to lend itself to satisfactory generalization.

Consider an economy whose activity takes place over T consecutive elementary time intervals, each interval being small enough that all its points are indistinguishable for the purposes of this analysis. The uncertain environment of this economy can be described in the language of statisticians by a choice made by Nature from a finite number of possibilities. We call these possibilities *events at time* T and denote them by an index e_T, going from 1_T to k_T. Once e_T is given, atmospheric conditions, technological knowledge, natural disasters, . . . are determined for the entire period under consideration.

At a time t before T, economic agents have some information about the event at T which will occur, since they have been making observations from the beginning of the period until t. This information can be described by a partition of the set of events at T into sets called *events at* t and denoted by an index e_t going from 1_t to k_t: At date t, each economic agent knows to which event at t the event at T that will occur belongs. We assume that the information about the choices of Nature becomes more and more complete with time; that is, the partition at $t + 1$ is finer than the partition at t. Therefore these events can be conveniently represented by a tree whose vertex 1_0 corresponds to the absence of information which prevails at the beginning of the period. Figure 1 illustrates the case where $T = 3$.

A commodity is defined, as we said earlier, by its physical characteristics, its place of delivery, and an event (that is to say, a vertex of the event tree, which vertex implicitly determines the delivery date). A contract between a buyer and a seller, then, takes the following form: The seller shall deliver to the buyer, who shall accept delivery, a specified quantity of a certain good or service in a specified place in a specified event e_t. If the event e_t does not occur, delivery does not take place. To have a plan of action for the whole period under consideration, an agent specifies the amount of each good and service he will consume or produce in each place, for each event. In other words, he specifies the quantity of each commodity he will consume or produce.

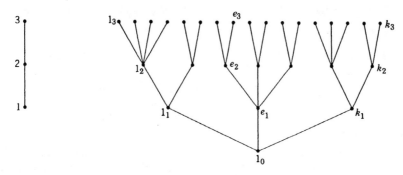

Figure 1

The price of a commodity is the total amount debited from (respectively, credited to) the account of the buyer (respectively, seller) for each unit of this commodity of which he agrees to take (respectively, to make) delivery. This debit or credit is naturally irrevocable, although delivery is uncertain. When an agent buys on the Chicago grain futures market 5,000 bushels of No. 2 Red Winter Wheat to be delivered in Chicago at date t, it is understood that delivery will take place whatever the event at t. We can interpret this transaction as a purchase of as many commodities as there are events at t. The "price" observed on the futures market is thus the *sum* of the prices in the preceding sense (with a minor difference: The price, as we have defined it, is payable at the beginning of the period, i.e., at the date when the contract is signed; the "price" observed on the futures market is payable at the date of delivery. A discount factor reconciles these two notions.)

The agents of the economy we are studying are divided into two classes: producers and consumers. The role of a producer consists of choosing and carrying out a production plan. Let us, then, specify the set of plans from which he can choose, and the criterion that he uses in making his choice. Consider an event e_t and the ascending path in the event tree going from 1_0 to e_T. On this path, no uncertainty due to the exogenous events remains, and the set of technologically feasible production plans of each producer is well determined. A production plan covering all eventualities is thus possible if, and only if, for every event e_T at T, the components of the plan associated with the path $(1_0, e_T)$ form a restricted plan that is feasible with the certain technology associated with that path.

The producer chooses from the feasible set a plan whose net value, calculated with respect to a price system that he considers as given, is maximized. It should be emphasized that this behavior requires of the producer neither the estimation of probabilities of different events nor an attitude toward risk. It corresponds for a firm in an economy with a perfect stock market to choosing a production plan so as to maximize the total value of its outstanding shares where the latter is determined in the stock market.

In a similar fashion, the role of a consumer consists of choosing and executing a consumption plan, and the set of his possible plans is characterized as before. This set is completely preordered by the preferences of the consumer which reflect his tastes for the goods and services (and their dates and places of delivery), his personal estimation of the likelihoods of the different events, and his attitude towards risk. On this last point, it should be noted that the hypotheses of convexity of preferences which have been made in the theories of equilibrium and optimality imply an attitude of aversion to risk on the part of the consumer (see K. J. Arrow, 1952). The behavior of the consumer is described in the usual terms: Given a price system and his wealth, he satisfies his preferences in choosing a consumption plan whose net value does not exceed his wealth.

To complete the description of the economy, it only remains to specify its resources, that is, the quantity of each commodity given a priori that is at the disposal of the agents in the economy. To define a private ownership economy, we must also specify the resources of each consumer (the sum of which should equal the resources of the economy) and the portion of each producer's profit that each consumer receives.

The formal identity of economics under uncertainty with economics under certainty which we asserted above is thus established, and the equilibrium problem in this new context can be posed in the usual fashion. Given a price system, each producer chooses a production plan so as to maximize his profit; the wealth of each consumer, equal to the sum of the value of his resources and of his share of profits, is therefore determined and he chooses his consumption plan so as to satisfy his preferences without his expenditure exceeding his wealth. Can we find a price system such that the sum of all the chosen consumptions equals the sum of all the chosen productions and of the resources of the economy? The available existence theorems give sufficient conditions on the consumption sets, the preferences and the resources of the consumers, and the production sets of the producers for this to be possible. The prices and the actions of the agents of a private ownership economy are thus explained.

The problem of optimality also presents itself in the usual form. For an economy satisfying certain weak conditions, if all the agents are adapted to a price system, that is to say, if each producer is maximizing his profit and if no consumer can better satisfy his preferences without spending more, the economy is at an optimum in the sense of Pareto. Conversely, for an economy satisfying slightly stronger conditions, with each optimal state is associated a price system to which all the agents are adapted. In this way, the role of prices in an economy is brought out.

To accept the preceding definition of an optimum amounts to accepting the different anticipations of the different consumers. This state of affairs is inevitable in an economic world where there is no valid objective concept of probability for a large class of exogenous events.

CHAPTER 9

Topological methods in cardinal
utility theory

In this paper we shall study the concept of cardinal utility in three different situations (stochastic objects of choice, stochastic act of choice; independent factors of the action set) by means of the same mathematical result that gives a topological characterization of three families of parallel straight lines in a plane. This result, proved first by G. Thomsen [24] under differentiability assumptions, and later by W. Blaschke [2] in its present general form (see also W. Blaschke and G. Bol [3]), can be briefly described as follows. Consider the topological image G of a two-dimensional convex set and three families of curves in that set such that (a) exactly one curve of each family goes through a point of G, and (b) two curves of different families have at most one common point. Is there a topological transformation carrying these three families of curves into three families of parallel straight lines? If the answer is affirmative, the hexagonal configuration of Figure 1(a) is observed. Let P be an arbitrary point of G, draw through it a curve of each family, and take an arbitrary point A on one of these curves; by drawing through A the curves of the other two families, we may obtain B and B', and from them C and C'. Clearly, if two of the curves marked by arrows intersect, the third must concur with them, since the same construction carried out for three families of parallel straight lines

This paper is a technical report of research undertaken by the Cowles Foundation for Research in Economics under contract with the Office of Naval Research. Reproduction in whole or in part is permitted for any purpose of the United States Government. I am very grateful to S. Kakutani, T. C. Koopmans, J. Marschak, and P. A. Samuelson for their comments on the various topics I shall discuss.

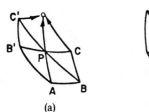

(a)   (b)   (c)

Figure 1

yields three concurrent lines. Thus a necessary condition for the existence of the desired topological transformation is that the hexagon of Figure 1(a) can be completed for every P and A such that the curves involved in the construction intersect. The Thomsen–Blaschke theorem asserts that this is also a sufficient condition if the three families of curves in G satisfy certain regularity requirements. Two equivalent forms of that condition are represented in Figures 1(b) and 1(c), which are self-explanatory. They are necessary for the reason given above. They are sufficient since they obviously imply the condition of Figure 1(a). Actually, a stronger theorem is true: if every point of G has a neighborhood in which one of the three configurations of Figure 1 holds, then there is on G a topological transformation of the desired type.

Of the three applications of this theorem to utility theory that will now be discussed, the first two have been presented in detail elsewhere [10], [9]. Only a brief account of them will be given here.

1   Stochastic objects of choice

Difficulties have been encountered in the testing of the axioms offered by J. von Neumann and O. Morgenstern [17] (or of axioms equivalent to them) for the existence of a cardinal utility in this situation. Some of these difficulties may be ascribed to the inability of subjects to grasp the meaning of complex prospects. This has led D. Davidson and P. Suppes [6][1] to suggest that the subjects be presented only with the simplest type of uncertain prospect, namely, even-chance mixtures of pairs of sure prospects. An axiomatization of this case will be given here. Let S be a set of sure prospects (e.g., commodity bundles). Given two elements a and b of S, the symbol ab denotes the prospect of having a with probability $\frac{1}{2}$ or b with probability $\frac{1}{2}$. The set $S \times S$ of prospects is completely preordered by the

[1] And not D. Davidson and J. Marschak [5], as I asserted in [10].

relation $\leqslant$, which is read "is not preferred to." As usual, $\sim$ is read "is indifferent to," and $\succ$ is read "is preferred to." In this context we make the following definition:

> *Definition 1.*   A utility function is a real-valued, order-preserving function u on $S \times S$ such that $u(ab) = \frac{1}{2}[u(aa) + u(bb)]$ for every a and b in S.

The problem of finding conditions on S and $\leqslant$ that guarantee the existence of a utility function defined in this fashion has been considered by F. P. Ramsey [19] and, more recently, by D. Davidson and P. Suppes [6], D. Davidson, P. Suppes, and S. Siegel [7], and P. Suppes [23]. The object of this section is to present a simple solution. The assumptions will be:

> *Assumption 1.1*
>
> S is connected and separable.

> *Assumption 1.2*
>
> $\leqslant$ is a complete preordering of $S \times S$ such that $\{ab \in S \times S \,|\, ab \succcurlyeq a'b'\}$ and $\{ab \in S \times S \,|\, ab \leqslant a'b'\}$ are closed for every $a'b'$ in $S \times S$.

> *Assumption 1.3*
>
> $[a_1b_2 \leqslant a_2b_1 \text{ and } a_2b_3 \leqslant a_3b_2] \Rightarrow [b_3a_1 \leqslant b_1a_3].$

The last assumption is clearly a necessary condition for the existence of a utility function. One can then prove the following theorem:

> *Theorem 1*
>
> Under Assumptions 1.1, 1.2, and 1.3 there is a continuous utility function determined up to an increasing linear transformation.

> *Proof.*   The proof uses a representation of $S \times S$ in R^3. According to [8], there is a continuous real-valued, order-preserving function f on $S \times S$. Let ab be a generic element of $S \times S$. Using the notation $\alpha = f(aa)$ and $\beta = f(bb)$, we define the representation by $ab \to (\alpha, \beta)$. Since S is connected, the range of α is a real interval Σ. The indifference classes of $S \times S$ are represented by

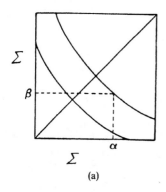

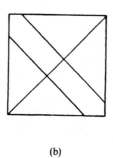

        (a)   (b)

Figure 2

curves in $\Sigma \times \Sigma$, two of which are drawn in Figure 2(a). These indifference curves have the marked diagonal as an axis of symmetry, and on any one of them one variable is a decreasing function of the other. If the function f happened to be a utility function, the indifference curves would satisfy the relation $\alpha + \beta = $ constant, and would thus be straight lines perpendicular to the diagonal, as in Figure 2(b). Since two real-valued, order-preserving functions on $S \times S$ are derived from one another by an increasing transformation, the proof amounts to showing that there is an increasing transformation on both coordinates carrying the indifference curves of Figure 2(a) into the straight lines perpendicular to the diagonal of Figure 2(b). Such a transformation carries the following three families of curves – the verticals, the horizontals, and the indifference curves – into the following three families of parallel straight lines – the verticals, the horizontals, and the perpendiculars to the diagonal. It exists if and only if the Thomsen–Blaschke condition is satisfied. And it is easy to check, using Assumption 1.3, that the hexagonal configuration of Figure 1(b) holds in Figure 2(a).

2   Stochastic act of choice[2]

Instead of introducing a stochastic element in the object of choice, we can introduce it in the act of choice. Let S be a set of actions. The subject is presented with a pair (a, b) of actions in S and asked to choose one. He is

---

[2] I wish to add to the bibliography of [9] the following items, which appeared too late to be included in it: J. S. Chipman [4], N. Georgescu-Roegen [12], R. D. Luce [16], and J. Pfanzagl [18].

assumed to choose a with probability $p(a, b)$ and to choose b with probability $p(b, a) = 1 - p(a, b)$. Formally:

Assumption 2.1

S is a set, and p is a function from $S \times S$ to $[0, 1]$ such that $p(a, b) + p(b, a) = 1$ for every (a, b) in $S \times S$.

It is natural to give the inequality $p(a, b) > p(c, d)$ the interpretation "*a* is preferred to *b* more than *c* is preferred to *d*," i.e., to make the following definition:

Definition 2.   A utility function for (S, p) is a real-valued function u on S such that $[p(a, b) \leqq p(c, d)] \Leftrightarrow [u(a) - u(b) \leqq u(c) - u(d)]$.

D. Davidson and J. Marschak [5], who have studied this aspect of cardinal utility, remark that $u(a) - u(b) \leqq u(c) - u(d)$ is equivalent to $u(a) - u(c) \leqq u(b) - u(d)$, hence that the existence of a utility function for (S, p) implies

Assumption 2.2

$[p(a, b) \leqq p(c, d)] \Leftrightarrow [p(a, c) \leqq p(b, d)]$.

The third assumption is a continuity condition:

Assumption 2.3

If $p(b, a) \leqq q \leqq p(c, a)$, then there is an action d in S such that $p(d, a) = q$.

Theorem 2

Under Assumptions 2.1, 2.2, and 2.3 there is for (S, p) a utility function determined up to an increasing linear transformation.

Proof.   The proof uses a representation of S in $[0, 1]$. Let k be an arbitrary element of S, which will be kept fixed. The generic element a of S is represented by the number $\alpha = p(a, k)$. According to Assumption 2.3, the range of α is an interval Σ in $[0, 1]$. The number $p(a, b)$ is readily seen from Assumption 2.2 to depend only on the images α, β of a, b in the representation. Let π be the function defined on $\Sigma \times \Sigma$ by $p(a, b) = \pi(\alpha, \beta)$.

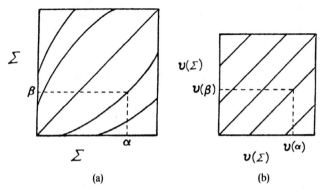

Figure 3

It is clear that finding a utility function u for (S, p) is equivalent to finding a utility function v for (Σ, π), the two utility functions being related by $u(a) = v(\alpha)$.

In Figure 3(a) five isoprobability curves have been drawn. The marked diagonal corresponds to the probability $\frac{1}{2}$; two curves corresponding to probabilities adding up to 1 are symmetric to each other with respect to the marked diagonal; and on any isoprobability curve one variable is an increasing function of the other. The proof of the theorem amounts to showing that there is an increasing transformation v on both coordinates carrying the isoprobability curves of Figure 3(a) into the straight lines $v(\beta) - v(\alpha) =$ constant of Figure 3(b). Such a transformation carries the following three families of curves – the verticals, the horizontals, and the isoprobability curves – into the following three families of parallel straight lines – the verticals, the horizontals, and the parallels to the diagonal. It exists if and only if the Thomsen–Blaschke condition is satisfied. And it is easy to check, using Assumption 2.2, that the hexagonal configuration of Figure 1(a) holds in Figure 3(a).

3 Independent factors of the action set

The last situation in which a cardinal utility will be defined is a generalization of the classical economic problem of independent commodities. A calculus solution and references to the literature will be found in P. A. Samuelson [20, Chap. 7]. (Other questions closely related to the present topic have been studied by W. Leontief in [14] and [15], also with a calculus technique.) Differentiability assumptions will be dropped here.

This will result, as usual, in an answer that is both more general and more natural.

Consider a consumer making a consumption plan represented by an m-tuple x of real numbers, where m is the number of commodities. If the class of commodities is partitioned into n subclasses indicated by an index i running from 1 to n, a consumption plan can also be represented by the n-tuple (x_i), where x_i is the tuple of real components of x corresponding to the ith subclass of commodities. For certain partitions of the class of commodities one is led to try to represent the preferences of the consumer for x by a real-valued function u of the form

$$u(x) = \sum_{i=1}^{n} u_i(x_i).$$

Two examples are the partition according to basic needs, such as food, housing, and clothing; the partition according to time-interval, when the consumption plan covers several consecutive time-intervals and the definition of a commodity includes the time-interval in which it is available (see, for instance, R. H. Strotz [21], [22], and W. M. Gorman [13]).

The main concepts of the analysis can now be formally introduced:

Assumption 3.1

Given n connected and separable spaces $S_1, \ldots, S_n$, $\leqslant$ is a complete preordering of their product

$$S = \prod_{i=1}^{n} S_i$$

such that $\{x \in S \,|\, x \succcurlyeq x'\}$ and $\{x \in S \,|\, x \leqslant x'\}$ are closed for every x' in S.

Definition 3.   A utility function is a real-valued, order-preserving function u on S such that for every $x = (x_i)$ in S

$$u(x) = \sum_{i=1}^{n} u_i(x_i),$$

where u_i is a real-valued function on S_i for every $i = 1, \ldots, n$.

The concept that is basic to this discussion is that of independence. Let N be the set of the first n integers, and let I be an arbitrary subset of N. Imagine that the x_i (where $i \in I$) are given; then the preordering $\leqslant$ on S induces on the product $\Pi_{i \notin I} S_i$ a preordering that will be called the *preordering given* $(x_i)_{i \in I}$. It is clear that this preordering is independent of the particular tuple $(x_i)_{i \in I}$ chosen if there is a utility function on S. Thus a necessary condition for the existence of a utility has been obtained; it will be shown to be sufficient provided that S has more than two essential factors. The factor S_i will be said to be *inessential* if for every $(x_j)_{j \neq i}$ all the elements of S_i are indifferent for the preordering given $(x_j)_{j \neq i}$; otherwise it will be said to be *essential*. Summing up, we have the following definitions:

> *Definitions 4.* Let I be a subset of $N = \{1, \ldots, n\}$, and for every $i \in I$ let x_i be an element of S_i. The preordering given $(x_i)_{i \in I}$ is the preordering induced by. $\preccurlyeq$ on $\Pi_{i \notin I} S_i$ when the element of S_i is equal to x_i for every $i \in I$. The n factors of S are independent if for every subset I of N the preordering given $(x_i)_{i \in I}$ is independent of $(x_i)_{i \in I}$. The factor S_i is essential if for some $(x_j)_{j \neq i}$ not all its elements are indifferent for the preordering given $(x_j)_{j \neq i}$.

Theorem 3

Under Assumption 3.1, if the n factors of S are independent, and if more than two of them are essential, there is a continuous utility function determined up to an increasing linear transformation.

The case of two essential factors of S, which has been discussed by E. Adams and R. Fagot [1] and W. Edwards [11], is an immediate generalization of the situation studied in Section 1, from which it differs only by the absence of the symmetry displayed by Figure 2(a). The solution of this case will appear here implicitly as a step in the following proof.

> *Proof.* Denote by $\preccurlyeq_i$ the preordering given $(x_j)_{j \neq i}$ (which is independent of $(x_j)_{j \neq i}$ by assumption). It is easily seen that
>
> $$\ll x_i \sim_i x_i' \text{ for every } i \gg \quad \text{implies} \quad \ll (x_i) \sim (x_i') \gg. \tag{1}$$

According to [8] there is on S a continuous real-valued, order-preserving function v, and similarly there is on each S_i a real-valued, order-preserving function v_i. By (1) the image y of x by v depends only on the images y_i of x_i by v_i; let f be the function defined in this fashion:

$$y = f(y_1, \ldots, y_n). \tag{2}$$

The image T_i of S_i by v_i is a real interval, since S_i is connected and v_i is continuous. This interval degenerates to a point if and only if S_i is inessential. The function f from

$$T = \prod_{i=1}^{n} T_i$$

to the reals is increasing in each variable; it is also continuous in each variable. It follows, without difficulty, that f is continuous.

The initial problem, which consists in finding the $n + 1$ real-valued functions $u_1, \ldots, u_n, u$, defined respectively on $S_1, \ldots, S_n, S$, is equivalent to the notably simpler one of finding $n + 1$ real-valued, increasing transformations $t_1, \ldots, t_n, t$, defined respectively on $T_1, \ldots, T_n, f(T)$, such that (2) becomes

$$t(y) = \sum_{i=1}^{n} t_i(y_i).$$

It is this second problem that we shall now solve. It will be assumed that there are no inessential sets S_i, i.e., no degenerate intervals T_i, since their role is trivial. The terminology and the notation adopted for the preordering of S will be freely used for the preordering obtained by carrying it over to T in the obvious fashion. The latter preordering naturally enjoys the independence property of the former.

By fixing the values of $y_3, \ldots, y_n$ in the *interiors* of $T_3, \ldots, T_n$ (the reason for this restriction to the interiors will appear later), we obtain a plane P of R^n and, in this plane, a preordering of the points (y_1, y_2) of $T_1 \times T_2$. We next prove that the indifference curves of this preordering and the parallels to the axes satisfy the condition of Figure 1(b) in the small. Given a point of $T_1 \times T_2$ in the plane P, we can always find in P a closed rectangular neighborhood U of that point, having its sides parallel to the axes and such that the indifference hypersurface going through the greatest (according to the preordering) vertex of U intersects the linear variety orthogonal to P through the least (according to the preordering) vertex of U. The above restriction to interiors was designed to ensure this possibility. Consider two indifferent points a and b of U, defined respectively by the pairs of their two first coordinates (y_1^2, y_2^1) and (y_1^1, y_2^2); consider similarly the two indifferent points c and d of U, defined respectively by (y_1^3, y_2^1) and (y_1^1, y_2^3) (the reasoning can be followed in Figure 4, drawn for the case $n = 3$). To prove that the condition of Figure 1(b) holds is to prove that the two points e and f of U, defined respectively by (y_1^3, y_2^3) and (y_1^2, y_2^3) are indifferent. The critérion according to which U was chosen implies immediately that the indifference hypersurface through a and b intersects the linear variety orthogonal to P through the point h of U defined by (y_1^1, y_2^1). Let p be a point in that intersection (in the case $n = 3$, p is unique). Then let q (resp. r) be the point derived from p by the translation hc (resp. hd). Since p and b are indifferent, so are q and e by the independence assumption. Similarly, the indifference of p and a implies that of r and f. Finally, the indifference of c and d implies that of q and r. Summing up, we have $e \sim q, q \sim r, r \sim f$; hence $e \sim f$.

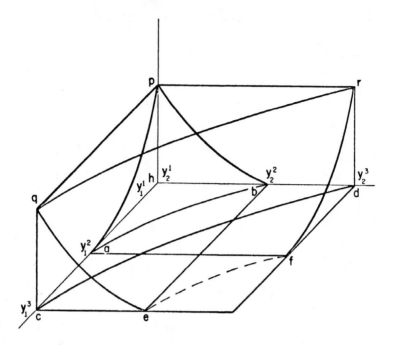

Figure 4

Thus there are two continuous increasing transformations t_1, t_2 defined on T_1, T_2, respectively, carrying the indifference curves in $T_1 \times T_2$ into the straight lines $t_1(y_1) + t_2(y_2) = $ constant.

A reasoning by induction will complete the proof. Assume that there are continuous increasing transformations $t_1, \ldots, t_{k-1}$ on $T_1, \ldots, T_{k-1}$ such that the indifference hypersurfaces in

$$\prod_{i=1}^{k-1} T_i$$

are represented by

$$\sum_{i=1}^{k-1} t_i(y_i) = \text{constant.}$$

This additive representation will be extended to

$$\prod_{i=1}^{k} T_i.$$

Denote $t_i(y_i)$ by z_i; the y indifference hypersurface in

$$\prod_{i=1}^{k} T_i$$

can be represented by

$$z_1 + \ldots + z_{k-1} = g_k(y_k, y), \tag{3}$$

where g_k is a continuous function of (y_k, y), decreasing in y_k and increasing in y. Consider a point (y_k^0, y^0) *interior* to the domain of g_k. It will be proved that this point has a neighborhood V in which g_k is the sum of a function of y_k and a function of y. For this, take $(z_1^0, \ldots, z_{k-1}^0)$ in R^{k-1} in the *interior* of the set of $(z_1, \ldots, z_{k-1})$ defined by $z_i \in t_i(T_i)$ for every $i = 1, \ldots, k-1$ and

$$\sum_{i=1}^{k-1} z_i = g_k(y_k^0, y^0).$$

Thus, in particular,

$$\sum_{i=1}^{k-2} z_i^0 + z_{k-1}^0 = g_k(y_k^0, y^0). \tag{4}$$

Then select a closed rectangular neighborhood V of (y_k^0, y^0) having its sides parallel to the axes and small enough for the operations connected with (5) and (6) to be possible, and let (y_k^1, y^1) be an arbitrary point of V.

Define z_{k-1}^1 in $t_{k-1}(T_{k-1})$ by

$$\sum_{i=1}^{k-2} z_i^0 + z_{k-1}^1 = g_k(y_k^1, y^0). \tag{5}$$

Choose $z_1^1, \ldots, z_{k-2}^1$ in $t_1(T_1), \ldots, t_{k-2}(T_{k-2})$ such that

$$\sum_{i=1}^{k-2} z_i^1 + z_{k-1}^0 = g_k(y_k^0, y^1). \tag{6}$$

The two points $(z_1^0, \ldots, z_{k-2}^0, z_{k-1}^0, y_k^0)$ and $(z_1^0, \ldots, z_{k-2}^0, z_{k-1}^1, y_k^1)$ are on the y^0 indifference hypersurface, according to (4) and (5). Hence, by the independence assumption, the two points $(z_1^1, \ldots, z_{k-2}^1, z_{k-1}^0, y_k^0)$ and $(z_1^1, \ldots, z_{k-2}^1, z_{k-1}^1, y_k^1)$ are indifferent. Since the first is on the y^1 indifference hypersurface according to (6), we have

$$\sum_{i=1}^{k-2} z_i^1 + z_{k-1}^1 = g_k(y_k^1, y^1). \tag{7}$$

Subtracting (6) from (7) and (4) from (5), we obtain

$$g_k(y_k^1, y^1) - g_k(y_k^0, y^1) = z_{k-1}^1 - z_{k-1}^0 = g_k(y_k^1, y^0) - g_k(y_k^0, y^0).$$

The relation

$$g_k(y_k^1, y^1) = g_k(y_k^1, y^0) + g_k(y_k^0, y^1) - g_k(y_k^0, y^0)$$

proves that g_k decomposes in V as desired.

The property in the large follows from the property in the small: throughout its domain, g_k is the sum of a decreasing function of y_k and an increasing function of y, and can therefore be written in the form

$$g_k(y_k, y) = -t_k(y_k) + h_k(y).$$

It suffices to substitute this for g_k in (3) to see that t_k is a transformation on T_k, allowing us to extend the additive representation to

$$\prod_{i=1}^{k} T_k.$$

References

[1] Adams, E., and R. Fagot. A Model of Riskless Choice, *Behavioral Science*, 4 (1959), 1–10.
[2] Blaschke, W. Topologische Fragen der Differentialgeometrie. I, *Mathematische Zeitschrift*, 28 (1928), 150–57.
[3] Blaschke, W., and G. Bol. *Geometrie der Gewebe*, Berlin: Springer, 1938.
[4] Chipman, J. S. Stochastic Choice and Subjective Probability (abstract), *Econometrica*, 26 (1958), 613.
[5] Davidson D., and J. Marschak. Experimental Tests of Stochastic Decision Theory, in C. W. Churchman and Ph. Ratoosh, eds., *Measurement: Definitions and Theories*, New York: Wiley, 1959.
[6] Davidson, D., and P. Suppes. A Finitistic Axiomatization of Subjective Probability and Utility, *Econometrica*, 24 (1956), 264–75.
[7] Davidson, D., P. Suppes, and S. Siegel. *Decision Making*, Stanford, Calif.: Stanford University Press, 1957.
[8] Debreu, G. Representation of a Preference Ordering by a Numerical Function, in R. M. Thrall, C. H. Coombs, and R. L. Davis, eds., *Decision Processes*, New York: Wiley, 1954, pp. 159–65.
[9] Debreu, G. Stochastic Choice and Cardinal Utility, *Econometrica*, 26 (1958), 440–44.
[10] Debreu, G. Cardinal Utility for Even-Chance Mixtures of Pairs of Sure Prospects, *Review of Economic Studies*, 26 (1959), 174–77.
[11] Edwards, W. Subjective Probability in Decision Theories, hectographed, Willow Run Laboratories, University of Michigan, 1959.
[12] Georgescu-Roegen, N. Threshold in Choice and the Theory of Demand, *Econometrica*, 26 (1958), 157–68.
[13] Gorman, W. M. Separable Utility and Aggregation, mimeographed, University of Birmingham, 1959.
[14] Leontief, W. A Note on the Interrelation of Subsets of Independent Variables of a Continuous Function with Continuous First Derivatives, *Bulletin of the American Mathematical Society*, 53 (1947), 343–50.

[15] Leontief, W. Introduction to a Theory of the Internal Structure of Functional Relationships, *Econometrica*, 15 (1947), 361–73.

[16] Luce, R. D. A Probabilistic Theory of Utility, *Econometrica*, 26 (1958), 193–224.

[17] von Neumann, J., and O. Morgenstern. *Theory of Games and Economic Behavior*, 2d. ed., Princeton, N.J.: Princeton University Press, 1947.

[18] Pfanzagl, J. *Die axiomatischen Grundlagen einer allgemeinen Theorie des Messens*, Würzburg: Physica, 1959.

[19] Ramsey, F. P. *The Foundations of Mathematics*, New York: Harcourt, Brace, 1931, pp. 156–98.

[20] Samuelson, P. A. *Foundations of Economic Analysis*, Cambridge, Mass.: Harvard University Press, 1947.

[21] Strotz, R. H. Myopia and Inconsistency in Dynamic Utility Maximization, *Review of Economic Studies*, 23 (1956), 165–80.

[22] Strotz, R. H. The Empirical Implications of a Utility Tree, *Econometrica*, 25 (1957), 269–80.

[23] Suppes, P. The Role of Subjective Probability and Utility in Decision-Making, in J. Neyman, ed., *Proceedings of the Third Berkeley Symposium on Mathematical Statistics and Probability*, Berkeley and Los Angeles: University of California Press, 1956, V, 61–73.

[24] Thomsen, G. Un teorema topologico sulle schiere di curve e una caratterizzazione geometrica delle superficie isotermo-asintotiche, *Bollettino della Unione Matematica Italiana*, 6 (1927), 80–85.

CHAPTER 10

New concepts and techniques for equilibrium analysis[1]

1 Introduction

In the study of the existence of an equilibrium for a private ownership economy, one meets with the basic mathematical difficulty that the demand correspondence of a consumer may not be upper semicontinuous when his wealth equals the minimum compatible with his consumption set.[2] One can prevent this minimum-wealth situation from ever arising by suitable assumptions on the economy; for example, in K. J. Arrow and G. Debreu [1], Theorem I, it is postulated that free disposal prevails and that every consumer can dispose of a positive quantity of every commodity from his resources and still have a possible consumption. However, assumptions of this type have not been readily accepted on account of their strength, and this in spite of the simplicity that they give to the analysis. Thus A. Wald [11,(Section II)]; K. J. Arrow and G. Debreu [1,(Theorem II or II')]; L. W. McKenzie [7], [8], [9]; D. Gale [4]; H. Nikaidô [10]; and W. Isard and D. J. Ostroff [5] permit the minimum-wealth situation to arise but introduce features of the economy that nevertheless insure the existence of an

[1] The research on which this paper reports was done partly at the Center for Advanced Study in the Behavioral Sciences and partly at the Cowles Foundation at Yale University under Task NR 047-006 with the Office of Naval Research.

I wish to acknowledge my debt to W. Isard for the stimulation I derived from the conversations I had with him on the possibility of weakening certain of the assumptions of W. Isard–D. J. Ostroff [5], to K. J. Arrow, D. Gale, L. Hurwicz, S. Kakutani, T. C. Koopmans, L. W. McKenzie and R. S. Phillips for their valuable comments and suggestions.
[2] Throughout this article I shall follow the notation and the terminology of [3].

equilibrium. The first purpose of the present article is to attempt to unify these various approaches. To this end, we use, for each consumer, a smoothed demand correspondence which coincides with the demand correspondence whenever the minimum-wealth situation does not arise and which is everywhere upper semicontinuous.[3] The existence proof is then carried out as before, but, because of the alteration of the demand correspondences, one obtains, instead of an equilibrium, a *quasi-equilibrium*, a formal definition of which follows.[4].

A quasi-equilibrium of the private ownership economy $\mathcal{E} = ((X_i, \preccurlyeq_i), (Y_j), (\omega_i), (\theta_{ij}))$ is an $(m + n + 1)$-tuple $((x_i^*), (y_j^*), p^*)$ of points of $((X_i), (Y_j), R^l)$, respectively, such that

(α) for every i, x_i^* is a greatest element of $\{x_i \in X_i | p^* \cdot x_i \leq p^* \cdot \omega_i + \sum_j \theta_{ij} p^* \cdot y_j^*\}$ for $\preccurlyeq_i$ and/or $p^* \cdot x_i^* = p^* \cdot \omega_i + \sum_j \theta_{ij} p^* \cdot y_j^* = \text{Min } p^* \cdot X_i$;

(β) for every j, $p^* \cdot y_j^* = \text{Max } p^* \cdot Y_j$;

(γ) $\sum_i x_i^* - \sum_j y_j^* = \sum_i \omega_i$;

(δ) $p^* \neq 0$.

There remains only to establish that, in the private ownership economies for which an equilibrium has been proved to exist, there is a quasi-equilibrium which is an equilibrium. We will show in Section 4 how this can be done.

The second purpose of this article is to deal with the fact, discovered by L. W. McKenzie [8], [9], that the irreversibility assumption on the total production set $(Y \cap (-Y) \subset \{0\})$ is superfluous, by means of new techniques. Instead of bounding the economy by a well-chosen cube, one uses an increasing sequence of cubes becoming indefinitely large. To each economy in this sequence, one seeks to apply the general market equilibrium theorem of [2]. But the asymptotic cone AY of the total production set may be a linear manifold. This difficulty is resolved by adding to Y a certain cone $-\Delta$ with vertex 0 which has the properties that $AY - \Delta$ is *not* a linear manifold and that the solution of the problem is not altered by this addition.

Thirdly, it will be proved that it suffices to assume, for every i, the insatiability of the ith consumer *in his attainable consumption set* $\hat{X}_i$. This

---

[3] Similar smoothing operations have already been used in this area by H. W. Kuhn [6] and H. Nikaidô [10].

[4] That definition is easily seen to imply $p^* \cdot x_i^* = p^* \cdot \omega_i + \sum_j \theta_{ij} p^* \cdot y_j^*$ for every i. From (α), $p^* \cdot x_i^* \leq p^* \cdot \omega_i + \sum_j \theta_{ij} p^* \cdot y_j^*$ for every i. If the strict inequality occurred for some consumer, then, summing over i and using the fact that $\sum_i \theta_{ij} = 1$ for every j, one would obtain $p^* \cdot \sum_i x_i^* < p^* \cdot \omega + p^* \cdot \sum_j y_j^*$, a contradiction of ($\gamma$).

fact appeared as a simple remark in K. J. Arrow and G. Debreu [1]. But, in the presence of all the weakened assumptions that we are listing, its proof is no longer immediate. We shall further exploit the concept of attainability for consumption sets to strengthen the theorem in another way. *Let D be the smallest cone with vertex 0 owning all the points of the form $\sum_i (x_i - \omega_i)$, where $x_i \succ_i \hat{X}_i$ for every i.*[5]

By adding $-D$ in (c.2) below, we obtain a notably weaker assumption. Let us also note the connection between this problem and that discussed at the end of the last paragraph. One can choose for Δ *any closed, convex cone with vertex 0, nondegenerate to {0}, contained in D and satisfying (c.2) when it is substituted for D.*

Fourthly, after having exploited the concept of attainability for consumption sets, we exploit it for the total production set.[6] The basic concept is presented in the following definition:

> An augmented total production set is a subset $\ddot{Y}$ of the commodity space containing Y and such that
>
> $$(\{\omega\} + \ddot{Y}) \cap X = (\{\omega\} + Y) \cap X,$$
>
> i.e., such that $\ddot{Y}$ and Y give rise to the same attainable consumptions.

The set $\ddot{Y}$ takes the place of the set Y in assumption (c.2) below. Here again there results a strengthening of the theorem, which is considerable for some economies.

Our fifth purpose will be to show that the weak-convexity assumption on preferences "for every x_i' in X_i, the set $\{x_i \in X_i | x_i \succcurlyeq_i x_i'\}$ is convex" suffices to establish the theorem. This can be done without great difficulty once the proper concept, namely the restricted demand correspondence φ_i of Lemma 1, has been introduced.

Finally, two trivial improvements will be made. The lower boundedness of the consumption sets and the impossibility of free production will be

---

[5] According to the assumptions of the theorem, every $\hat{X}_i$ is compact (see the beginning of (b) in Section 3, and the discussion in 5.4 of [3]). Thus if the economy has attainable states, i.e., if $\hat{X}_i$ is not empty, $\hat{X}_i$ has a greatest element $\bar{x}_i$ for $\leqslant_i$. Assumption (b.1) then implies that $\{x_i \in X_i | x_i \succ_i \bar{x}_i\}$, which is equal to $\{x_i \in X_i | x_i \succ_i \hat{X}_i\}$, is not empty.

Moreover, if $x_i \succ_i \hat{X}_i$ for every i, then $\sum_i (x_i - \omega_i) \neq 0$. Equality to 0, which belongs to Y, would mean that every x_i is attainable. Therefore D is nondegenerate to $\{0\}$.

Finally, by (b.3), the set $\{x_i \in X_i | x_i \succ_i \hat{X}_i\} - \{\omega_i\}$ is convex for every i. Hence, the sum over i of these sets is convex. And D, which is the smallest cone with vertex 0 containing that sum, is also convex.

[6] That a strengthening of the theorem in this direction should be possible was suggested to me by K. J. Arrow and L. W. McKenzie.

replaced respectively by $AX \cap (-AX) = \{0\}$ and $AX \cap AY = \{0\}$. This will have the advantage of yielding a coordinate-free theory.

In conclusion, we shall prove

Theorem[7]

The private ownership economy $\mathscr{E}$ has a quasi-equilibrium if

(a.1) $AX \cap (-AX) = \{0\}$;

for every i

(a.2) X_i is closed and convex,

(b.1) for every consumption x_i in $\hat{X}_i$ there is a consumption in X_i preferred to x_i,

(b.2) for every x_i' in X_i the sets $\{x_i \in X_i | x_i \succcurlyeq_i x_i'\}$ and $\{x_i \in X_i | x_i \preccurlyeq_i x_i'\}$ are closed in X_i,

(b.3) for every x_i' in X_i, the set $\{x_i \in X_i | x_i \succcurlyeq_i x_i'\}$ is convex;

(c.1) $(\{\omega\} + Y) \cap X \neq \varnothing$,

(c.2) there is a closed, convex augmented total production set $\ddot{Y}$ such that, for every i,

$(\{\omega_i\} + A\ddot{Y} - D) \cap X_i \neq \varnothing$;

for every j,

(d.1) $0 \in Y_j$;

(d.2) $AX \cap AY = \{0\}$.

Assumption (c.2) is now too weak to insure that $\mathscr{E}$ has attainable states. It was, therefore, necessary to add (c.1).

With the exception of (c.2) every assumption is so simple as not to require comments. Let us stress, however, that the case of bounded consumption sets and/or bounded production sets (and in particular the pure exchange case where $Y = \{0\}$) is covered by the theorem. As for (c.2), its complexity has seemed justified by the gain in generality that it permits.

2   Lemmata

In this section all the assumptions of the theorem hold. Moreover X is assumed to be bounded.

Since X_i is compact, the demand correspondence ξ_i of the ith consumer is defined for every pair of a price system p and a wealth w_i such that $w_i \geqq \text{Min } p \cdot X_i$. The elements of $\xi_i(p, w_i)$ are the consumptions in $\gamma_i(p, w_i) = \{x_i \in X_i | p \cdot x_i \leqq w_i\}$ to which no consumption in $\gamma_i(p, w_i)$ is preferred. However, instead of letting the ith consumer choose any con-

[7] In fact, as will be proved, $\mathscr{E}$ has a quasi-equilibrium $((x_i^*), (y_j^*), p^*)$ such that $p^* \cdot \sum_j y_j^* = \text{Max } p^* \cdot (\ddot{Y} - D)$.

sumption in $\xi_i(p, w_i)$, we restrict his choice to the most expensive ones, i.e., to the set

$$\varphi_i(p, w_i) = \{x_i \in \xi_i(p, w_i) \mid p \cdot x_i = \text{Max}\, p \cdot \xi_i(p, w_i)\}.$$

An essential property of φ_i will be its upper semicontinuity; therefore we state

Lemma 1

If $w_i^0 \geqq \text{Min}\, p^0 \cdot X_i$, then $\varphi_i(p^0, w_i^0)$ is nonempty, convex. If $w_i^0 > \text{Min}\, p^0 \cdot X_i$, then φ_i is upper semicontinuous at (p^0, w_i^0).

Proof. The first implication is immediate; let us therefore prove the second. That is, let us study two infinite sequences $(p^q, w_i^q) \to (p^0, w_i^0)$ and $x_i^q \to x_i^0$ such that $x_i^q \in \varphi_i(p^q, w_i^q)$ for every q. We must show that $x_i^0 \in \varphi_i(p^0, w_i^0)$.

By (1) of 4.8 and (1) of 4.10 in [3], ξ_i is upper semicontinuous at (p^0, w_i^0); hence $x_i^0 \in \xi_i(p^0, w_i^0)$. Therefore it suffices to show that

$$x_i \in \xi_i(p^0, w_i^0) \Rightarrow p^0 \cdot x_i \leqq p^0 \cdot x_i^0,$$

i.e., $(p^0 \cdot x_i \leqq w_i^0 \quad \text{and} \quad x_i \sim_i x_i^0) \Rightarrow p^0 \cdot x_i \leqq p^0 \cdot x_i^0$.

Since $p^q \cdot x_i^q \leqq w_i^q$ for every q, two cases will be distinguished:
   (i) $p^0 \cdot x_i^0 = w_i^0$.
Then, obviously, $p^0 \cdot x_i \leqq p^0 \cdot x_i^0$.
   (ii) $p^0 \cdot x_i^0 < w_i^0$.
Then, for q large enough, $p^0 \cdot x_i^q < w_i^0$. Hence $x_i^q \leqslant_i x_i^0$, for $x_i^0 \in \xi_i(p^0, w_i^0)$. Consider now a point x_i' different from x_i on the segment $[x_i^0, x_i]$. As $p^0 \cdot x_i \leqq w_i^0$ and $p^0 \cdot x_i^0 < w_i^0$, one has $p^0 \cdot x_i' < w_i^0$ and, for q large enough, $p^q \cdot x_i' < w_i^q$. Moreover, $x_i' \succ_i x_i^0 \succ_i x_i^q$, the first relation following from $x_i \sim_i x_i^0$ and (b.3). But $x_i' \succ_i x_i^q$ with $p^q \cdot x_i' < w_i^q$ and $x_i^q \in \varphi_i(p^q, w_i^q)$ implies $p^q \cdot x_i' \leqq p^q \cdot x_i^q$. In the limit, $p^0 \cdot x_i' \leqq p^0 \cdot x_i^0$. And, since x_i' is arbitrarily close to x_i, also $p^0 \cdot x_i \leqq p^0 \cdot x_i^0$.   Q.E.D.

To smooth the correspondence φ_i we define the correspondence ψ_i by:

if $w_i > \text{Min}\, p \cdot X_i$, then $\psi_i(p, w_i) = \varphi_i(p, w_i)$;
if $w_i = \text{Min}\, p \cdot X_i$, then $\psi_i(p, w_i) = \{x_i \in X_i \mid p \cdot x_i = w_i\}$.

Lemma 2

If $w_i^0 \geqq \text{Min}\, p^0 \cdot X_i$, then $\psi_i(p^0, w_i^0)$ is nonempty, convex and ψ_i is upper semicontinuous at (p^0, w_i^0).

Proof. If $w_i^0 > \mathrm{Min}\ p^0 \cdot X_i$, this is only a restatement of Lemma 1. If $w_i^0 = \mathrm{Min}\ p^0 \cdot X_i$, the proof is immediate.

The success of the technique that consists in bounding the economy by a sequence of cubes rests on the following simple remark.

Lemma 3

Let $\mathcal{Y}^q$ be a nondecreasing infinite sequence of subsets of the commodity space having $\mathcal{Y}$ as their union. Let p^q be an infinite sequence of price systems tending to p^*. Then $\underline{\lim}\ (\mathrm{Sup}\ p^q \cdot \mathcal{Y}^q) \geqq \mathrm{Sup}\ p^* \cdot \mathcal{Y}$.

Proof. Let y be a point in $\mathcal{Y}$. For q large enough, $y \in \mathcal{Y}^q$; therefore $p^q \cdot y \leqq \mathrm{Sup}\ p^q \cdot \mathcal{Y}^q$. In the limit, $p^* \cdot y \leqq \underline{\lim}\ (\mathrm{Sup}\ p^q \cdot \mathcal{Y}^q)$. Hence, the result follows.

The next four lemmata state fundamental properties of the sets $\ddot{Y}$ and D. It will be convenient to agree that

$E(Y)$ denotes the economy $((X_i, \preccurlyeq_i), Y, \omega)$.

Lemma 4

$A\ddot{Y} \cap D = \{0\}$.

Proof. Let y be a point in the intersection. $y \in A\ddot{Y}$, and there are an m-tuple (x_i) such that $x_i \succ_i \hat{X}_i$ for every i and a number $\lambda \geqq 0$ satisfying the equality $y = \lambda \sum_i (x_i - \omega_i)$. If $\lambda > 0$, we divide by λ and obtain $y/\lambda = \sum_i x_i - \omega$. The point y/λ is also in $A\ddot{Y}$, which is contained in $\ddot{Y}$ by (14) of 1.9 in [3]. Thus (x_i) is attainable for $E(\ddot{Y})$, hence for $E(Y)$, a contradiction. Therefore, $\lambda = 0$.

It follows immediately from Lemma 4 and $\Delta \subset D$ that $A\ddot{Y} - \Delta$ and $\ddot{Y} - \Delta$ are closed (by (9) of 1.9 in [3]). They are obviously convex.

Lemma 5

$D \cap (-D) = \{0\}$.

Proof. Let δ be a point in the intersection. $\delta \in D$ implies $\delta = \lambda^1 \sum_i (x_i^1 - \omega_i)$ with $\lambda^1 \geqq 0$ and $x_i^1 \succ_i \hat{X}_i$ for every i. Similarly,

$-\delta \in D$ implies $-\delta = \lambda^2 \sum_i (x_i^2 - \omega_i)$ with $\lambda^2 \geqq 0$ and $x_i^2 \succ_i \hat{X}_i$ for every i. Thus $\lambda^1 \sum_i x_i^1 + \lambda^2 \sum_i x_i^2 = (\lambda^1 + \lambda^2)\omega$. If $\lambda^1 + \lambda^2 > 0$, we divide by $\lambda^1 + \lambda^2$, putting $\lambda^1/(\lambda^1 + \lambda^2) = \alpha^1$, and $\lambda^2/(\lambda^1 + \lambda^2) = \alpha^2$, and we obtain $\sum_i(\alpha^1 x_i^1 + \alpha^2 x_i^2) = \omega$. The point $\alpha^1 x_i^1 + \alpha^2 x_i^2$ is in X_i and it is preferred to $\hat{X}_i$. Hence it cannot be attainable as the last equality implies. Therefore $\lambda^1 = 0 = \lambda^2$.

Lemma 6

$A\ddot{Y} - \Delta$ is not a linear manifold.

Proof. Assume the contrary. $A\ddot{Y} - \Delta$, which contains $-\Delta$, would also contain Δ. Thus, given δ_1 in Δ different from 0, there would be y in $A\ddot{Y}$ and δ_2 in Δ such that $y - \delta_2 = \delta_1$, i.e., $y = \delta_1 + \delta_2$. Since $\delta_1 + \delta_2 \in \Delta$, this implies, by Lemma 4, that $\delta_1 \dotplus \delta_2 = 0$. Hence, by Lemma 5, $\delta_1 = 0 = \delta_2$, a contradiction of $\delta_1 \neq 0$.

Lemma 7

If the consumption x_i is attainable for the economy $E(\ddot{Y} - D)$, then $x_i \succ_i \hat{X}_i$ does not hold.

Proof. Consider an attainable state of $E(\ddot{Y} - D)$. The sum of the consumptions in that state satisfies $\sum_i x_i - \omega = y - \delta$, where $y \in \ddot{Y}$ and $\delta \in D$. The last relation can also be written $\delta = \lambda \sum_i (x_i' - \omega_i)$ with $\lambda \geqq 0$ and $x_i' \succ_i \hat{X}_i$ for every i. Therefore

$$\sum_i x_i + \lambda \sum_i x_i' = \omega(1 + \lambda) + y.$$

Divide by $1 + \lambda$, putting $\alpha = 1/(1 + \lambda)$ and $\beta = \lambda/(1 + \lambda)$,

$$\sum_i (\alpha x_i + \beta x_i') = \omega + \alpha y.$$

Since $\alpha x_i + \beta x_i' \in X_i$ for every i and $\alpha y \in \ddot{Y}$, the consumption $\alpha x_i + \beta x_i'$ is attainable for $E(\ddot{Y})$, hence for $E(Y)$. If $x_i \succ_i \hat{X}_i$, then $\alpha x_i + \beta x_i' \succ_i \hat{X}_i$, a contradiction.

The last lemma concerns the approximation process by means of which the statement of footnote 7 will be proved.

Lemma 8

Let C be a convex cone with vertex 0 in the commodity space. There is a nondecreasing sequence (Γ^q) of closed, convex cones with vertex 0, contained in C and whose union contains the relative interior of C.

Proof. Since the problem can be treated in the smallest linear subspace containing C, there is no loss of generality in assuming that C has a nonempty interior. We shall also assume that C is nondegenerate to $\{0\}$; in that case the theorem is trivially true. Denote by $|z|$ the norm of the vector z, by S the set of vectors with unit norm, $\{z \in R'||z| = 1\}$, and, given z in R' and a positive real number r, by $s(z, r)$ the set of points whose distance to z is less than r, $\{z' \in R'||z' - z| < r\}$. Consider the set $\{z \in S | s(z, 1/q) \subset C\}$, which is not empty for q large enough. We will show that Γ^q, the smallest cone with vertex 0 containing that set, has all the required properties.

Γ^q *is closed.* To prove this, it suffices to study an infinite sequence (z^k) of points of $\Gamma^q \cap S$ tending to z^0. We wish to show that C contains $s(z^0, 1/q)$. Let z be a point of the latter set. One has $|z - z^0| < 1/q$. Hence, for k large enough, $|z - z^k| < 1/q$. Therefore z belongs to $s(z^k, 1/q)$, which is contained in C.

Γ^q *is convex.* To prove this, it suffices to study two points z^1, z^2 in $\Gamma^q \cap S$ and one of their convex combinations $z^0 = \alpha^1 z^1 + \alpha^2 z^2$, different from 0. We wish to show that C contains $s(z^0/|z^0|, 1/q)$. Let z be a point of the latter set. One has $|z - (z^0/|z^0|)| < 1/q$. However $|z^0| \leq 1$ by convexity of the norm. Hence $||z^0|z - z^0| < 1/q$. Therefore, the points $z^1 + (|z^0|z - z^0)$ and $z^2 + (|z^0|z - z^0)$ both belong to C. Thus, their convex combination with coefficients α^1, α^2, which is $|z^0|z$, also belongs to C. Hence z does.

It is clear that $q' > q$ implies $\Gamma^{q'} \supset \Gamma^q$, that the Γ^q are contained in C, and that their union contains the interior of C.

3   Proof of the theorem

The proof will be decomposed into two parts. Initially the total consumption set will be assumed to be bounded. Later the general case will be treated.

Let us remark at the outset that, according to (c.2), and because D is nondegenerate (see footnote 5), there is in D, for each i, a closed half-line L_i with origin 0 such that $\{\omega_i\} + A\ddot{Y} - L_i$ intersects X_i.

(a) Case of a bounded X

The cone Δ, which will remain fixed until the end of (a), is chosen to be a closed, convex cone with vertex 0, containing the m half-lines L_i and contained in D. Such a choice is possible because D is convex (see footnote 5). Clearly, Δ is nondegenerate and satisfies (c.2) when one substitutes it for D.

Let now K^q be an increasing sequence of closed cubes with center 0, becoming indefinitely large. Remembering that n is the number of producers, we introduce the notation

$$Y_j^q = Y_j \cap K^q, \qquad Y^q = (\ddot{Y} - \Delta) \cap (nK^q).$$

Given an arbitrary price system p, the supremum of profit on Y_j^q is finite (Y_j^q is bounded), and the maximum of profit on Y^q exists (Y^q is compact since $\ddot{Y} - \Delta$ is closed by Lemma 4). We introduce the further notation

$$\pi_j^q(p) = \text{Sup } p \cdot Y_j^q, \quad \pi^q(p) = \text{Max } p \cdot Y^q, \quad d^q(p) = \pi^q(p) - \sum_j \pi_j^q(p).$$

As $\sum_j Y_j^q \subset Y^q$, we have

$$d^q(p) \geqq 0 \qquad \text{for every } p.$$

Finally, we denote the set of y that maximize profit on Y^q by

$$\eta^q(p) = \{ y \in Y^q | p \cdot y = \pi^q(p) \}.$$

It follows immediately from (3) of 3.5 in [3] that the correspondence η^q is upper semicontinuous everywhere, and that the functions π_j^q, π^q, hence the functions d^q, are continuous everywhere.

We give to the ith consumer the wealth

$$w_i^q(p) = p \cdot \omega_i + \sum_j \theta_{ij} \pi_j^q(p) + \frac{1}{m} d^q(p),$$

m being the number of consumers. Notice that, for every p,

$$w_i^q(p) \geqq p \cdot \omega_i \quad \text{and} \quad \sum_i w_i^q(p) = p \cdot \omega + \pi^q(p). \tag{1}$$

The first assertion follows from $\pi_j^q(p) \geqq 0$ (since $0 \in Y_j^q$) and $d^q(p) \geqq 0$. The second follows from $\sum_i \theta_{ij} = 1$ for every j and from the definition of d^q. Notice also that w_i^q is clearly continuous everywhere.

The price system p will now be restricted to the set

$$P = (A\ddot{Y} - \Delta)^0 \cap S,$$

where $(A\ddot{Y} - \Delta)^0$ is the polar of $A\ddot{Y} - \Delta$, and S is the set of vectors with unit norm. Every x_i in $(\{\omega_i\} + A\ddot{Y} - \Delta) \cap X_i$ satisfies $p \cdot x_i \leqq p \cdot \omega_i$ for every p in P. Hence $w_i^q(p) \geqq \text{Min } p \cdot X_i$ for every p in P. Therefore, the correspondence ζ^q such that

$$\zeta^q(p) = \sum_i \psi_i(p, w_i^q(p)) - \eta^q(p) - \{\omega\}$$

is defined everywhere on P. According to Lemma 2, and on account of the continuity of w_i^q and of the upper semicontinuity of η^q, the correspondence ζ^q is upper semicontinuous on P. Moreover, for every p in P, the set $\zeta^q(p)$ is easily seen to be nonempty, convex and to satisfy $p \cdot \zeta^q(p) \leqq 0$, since any x_i in $\psi_i(p, w_i^q(p))$ satisfies $p \cdot x_i \leqq w_i^q(p)$, any y in $\eta^q(p)$ satisfies $p \cdot y = \pi^q(p)$, and $\sum_i w_i^q(p) = p \cdot \omega + \pi^q(p)$. Finally, by Lemmata 4 and 6, $A\ddot{Y} - \Delta$ is a closed, convex cone with vertex 0, which is not a linear manifold. Thus the theorem of [2] can be applied to the cone $(A\ddot{Y} - \Delta)^0$ and the correspondence ζ^q. There are

$$p^q \in P, \ z^q \in A\ddot{Y} - \Delta \quad \text{such that} \quad z^q \in \zeta^q(p^q).$$

In other words, there are $x_i^q \in \psi_i(p^q, w_i^q(p^q))$ and $\bar{y}^q \in \eta^q(p^q)$ such that

$$\sum_i x_i^q - \bar{y}^q - \omega = z^q.$$

Introducing $y^q = \bar{y}^q + z^q$, one obtains

$$\sum_i x_i^q - y^q - \omega = 0. \tag{2}$$

However, $\bar{y}^q \in \ddot{Y} - \Delta$ and $z^q \in A\ddot{Y} - \Delta$ imply

$$y^q \in \ddot{Y} - \Delta \tag{3}$$

because $\ddot{Y} + A\ddot{Y} \subset \ddot{Y}$ by (14) of 1.9 in [3]. Therefore, x_i^q is attainable for the economy $E(\ddot{Y} - \Delta)$. And, by Lemma 7, if $x_i \succ_i \hat{X}_i$, then $x_i \succ_i x_i^q$. This, jointly with $x_i^q \in \psi_i(p^q, w_i^q(p^q))$, will be shown to imply

$$p^q \cdot x_i^q = w_i^q(p^q). \tag{4}$$

If $w_i^q(p^q) = \text{Min } p^q \cdot X_i$, then the equality is obvious.

If $w_i^q(p^q) > \text{Min } p^q \cdot X_i$, then $x_i^q \in \varphi_i(p^q, w_i^q(p^q))$. Hence $p^q \cdot x_i > w_i^q(p^q)$. Therefore, if $p^q \cdot x_i^q < w_i^q(p^q)$, the points of the segment $[x_i^q, x_i]$ close enough to x_i^q would satisfy the wealth constraint defined by $(p^q, w_i^q(p^q))$, be at least as desired as x_i^q, *and be more expensive than* x_i^q. This would contradict the definition of φ_i.

Summing (4) over i, and using (1), one obtains $p^q \cdot \sum_i x_i^q = p^q \cdot \omega + \pi^q(p^q)$. According to (2), this proves that

$$p^q \cdot y^q = \pi^q(p^q).$$

Now, the p^q belong to the bounded set S; the m-tuples (x_i^q) belong to $\Pi_i X_i$, which is a product of bounded sets; therefore, by (2), the y^q are bounded, and the numbers $p^q \cdot y^q$ are also bounded. The $\pi_j^q(p^q)$ are nonnegative, and their sum over j is at most equal to $\pi^q(p^q)$, that is to $p^q \cdot y^q$. Hence the n-tuples $(\pi_j^q(p^q))$ are bounded. Let us therefore extract a subsequence of the $(p^q, (x_i^q), (\pi_j^q(p^q)))$ converging to $(p^*, (x_i^*), (\pi_j^*))$, still using the index q for the convergent subsequence since no ambiguity can arise. According to (2), y^q tends to y^*, which satisfies

$$\sum_i x_i^* - y^* - \omega = 0. \tag{5}$$

And, by (3) and the closedness of $\ddot{Y} - \Delta$,

$$y^* \in \ddot{Y} - \Delta. \tag{6}$$

Also $d^q(p^q)$ tends to $d^* = p^* \cdot y^* - \sum_j \pi_j^*$, and for every i,

$$w_i^q(p^q) \quad \text{tends to} \quad w_i^* = p^* \cdot \omega_i + \sum_j \theta_{ij}\pi_j^* + \frac{1}{m} d^*. \tag{7}$$

While, by upper semicontinuity of ψ_i, for every i,

$$x_i^* \in \psi_i(p^*, w_i^*). \tag{8}$$

By a first application of Lemma 3, $p^q \cdot y^q = \text{Max } p^q \cdot Y^q$ implies $p^* \cdot y^* \geqq$ Sup $p^* \cdot (\ddot{Y} - \Delta)$. But $y^* \in \ddot{Y} - \Delta$; therefore

$$p^* \cdot y^* = \text{Max } p^* \cdot (\ddot{Y} - \Delta). \tag{9}$$

By a second application of Lemma 3, $\pi_j^q(p^q) = \text{Sup } p^q \cdot Y_j^q$ for every j implies

$$\pi_j^* \geqq \text{Sup } p^* \cdot Y_j \quad \text{for every } j. \tag{10}$$

According to (6),

$$y^* = y' - \delta, \tag{11}$$

where $y' \in \ddot{Y}$ and $\delta \in \Delta$. Since, by (9), y^* maximizes profit relative to p^* on $\ddot{Y} - \Delta$, so do y' on $\ddot{Y}$ and $-\delta$ on $-\Delta$. The latter implies that

$$p^* \cdot \delta = 0.$$

As $\delta \in D$, it has the form $\delta = \lambda \sum_i(x_i - \omega_i)$, where $\lambda \geqq 0$ and $x_i \succ_i \hat{X}_i$ for every i. But (5) and (6) show that each x_i^* is attainable for the economy $E(\ddot{Y} - \Delta)$. Hence, by Lemma 7, $x_i^* \prec_i x_i$. This establishes

$$\text{if } w_i^* > \text{Min } p^* \cdot X_i, \quad \text{then} \quad p^* \cdot x_i > w_i^*, \tag{12}$$

for $w_i^* > \text{Min } p^* \cdot X_i$ implies, by (8), that $x_i^* \in \varphi_i(p^*, w_i^*)$. On the other hand, it is obvious that

$$\text{if } w_i^* = \text{Min } p^* \cdot X_i, \quad \text{then} \quad p^* \cdot x_i \geqq w_i^*. \tag{13}$$

To conclude the first part of the proof we distinguish two cases:

(a.a) $w_{i'}^* > \text{Min } p^* \cdot X_{i'}$ *for some i'*. Then, from (12) and (13), $p^* \cdot \sum_i x_i > \sum_i w_i^* = p^* \cdot \omega + p^* \cdot y^*$. Therefore, $p^* \cdot \sum_i (x_i - \omega_i) > p^* \cdot y^* \geqq 0$, the last inequality resulting from the fact that y^* maximizes profit relative to p^* on a set owning 0. However, $p^* \cdot \sum_i (x_i - \omega_i) > 0$ and $p^* \cdot \delta = 0$ yield $\lambda = 0$, i.e., $\delta = 0$. Thus, by (11), $y^* \in \ddot{Y}$ and, on account of (5), $y^* \in Y$. As $Y \subset Y - \Delta$, (9) implies $p^* \cdot y^* = \text{Max } p^* \cdot Y$. But summing (10) over j, one obtains $\sum_j \pi_j^* \geqq \text{Sup } p^* \cdot Y$. Consequently, $d^* = p^* \cdot y^* - \sum_j \pi_j^*$, which is nonnegative, is actually zero. And, for every j, $\pi_j^* = \text{Sup } p^* \cdot Y_j$. It now suffices to take in each Y_j, a y_j^* in such a way that $\sum_j y_j^* = y^*$ to obtain a quasi-equilibrium $((x_i^*), (y_j^*), p^*)$ of $\mathscr{E}$. Indeed (δ) of the definition of a quasi-equilibrium is satisfied because $p^* \in P$; (γ) is (5); (β) is fulfilled because $p^* \cdot y^* = \text{Max } p^* \cdot Y$ implies $p^* \cdot y_j^* = \text{Max } p^* \cdot Y_j$ for every j; (α) is satisfied because of (8) and because (7) has become $w_i^* = p^* \cdot \omega_i + \sum_j \theta_{ij} p^* \cdot y_j^*$.

(a.b) $w_i^* = \text{Min } p^* \cdot X_i$ *for every* i. By (8), $p^* \cdot x_i^* = \text{Min } p^* \cdot X_i$ for every i; therefore $p^* \cdot \sum_i x_i^* = \text{Min } p^* \cdot X$ while, by (9), $p^* \cdot y^* = \text{Max } p^* \cdot (\ddot{Y} - \Delta) \geqq \text{Sup } p^* \cdot Y$. Hence, the hyperplane H with normal p^* going through the point $\sum_i x_i^*$, which is also $\omega + y^*$ by (5), separates X and $\{\omega\} + Y$. But, by (c.1), the economy $E(Y)$ has attainable states. We now show that any one of them $((x_i'), (y_j'))$ forms with p^* a quasi-equilibrium of $\mathscr{E}$. Indeed the point $\sum_i x_i' = \omega + \sum_j y_j'$ is necessarily in the hyperplane H. Therefore $p^* \cdot \sum_i x_i' = \text{Min } p^* \cdot X$, and $p^* \cdot \sum_j y_j' = \text{Max } p^* \cdot Y$. These equalities respectively imply $p^* \cdot x_i' = \text{Min } p^* \cdot X_i$ for every i, and $p^* \cdot y_j' = \text{Max } p^* \cdot Y_j$ for every j. Finally, we recall that, by (10), $\pi_j^* \geqq \text{Max } p^* \cdot Y_j$ for every j, that $d^* \geqq 0$, and that $\sum_j \pi_j^* + d^* = p^* \cdot y^*$. As $\omega + y^*$ is in the hyperplane H, one has $p^* \cdot y^* = \text{Max } p^* \cdot Y = \sum_j \text{Max } p^* \cdot Y_j$, and all the inequalities above must be equalities. Therefore, (7) becomes $w_i^* = p^* \cdot \omega_i + \sum_j \theta_{ij} p^* \cdot y_j'$.

(b)   *General case*

An immediate transposition of the proof of (2) of 5.4 in [3] shows that the set of attainable states of the economy $E(Y)$ is bounded; it is also closed, for it coincides with the set of attainable states of the economy $E(\ddot{Y})$, to which one applies (1) of 5.4 in [3]. Hence $\hat{X}_i$ is compact for every i. Let then K^q be an increasing sequence of closed cubes with center 0, becoming indefinitely large, containing the $\hat{X}_i$ and owning, for each i, a consumption preferred to $\hat{X}_i$ and a consumption in the intersection of X_i and $\{\omega_i\} + A\ddot{Y} - L_i$, where the L_i are the half-lines described at the outset of this section. We introduce the notation

$$X_i^q = X_i \cap K^q.$$

Consider now a sequence (Γ^q) of cones with vertex 0 having all the properties listed in Lemma 8, with D substituted for C. We define Δ^q as

$\Gamma^q + \sum_i L_i$. This is a convex cone with vertex 0, nondegenerate, contained in D and satisfying (c.2) for the private ownership economy $\mathscr{E}^q = ((X_i^q, \preccurlyeq_i), (Y_j), (\omega_i), (\theta_{ij}))$. The cone Δ^q is also closed as a sum of closed cones with vertex 0, all contained in D which, by Lemma 5, satisfies $D \cap (-D) = \{0\}$ (see (9) of 1.9 in [3]). Moreover, the sequence of the Δ^q is nondecreasing, and their union contains the relative interior of D since the union of the Γ^q does.

According to part (a) of the proof (see (9) in particular), for every q, the economy $\mathscr{E}^q$ has a quasi-equilibrium $((x_i^q), (y_j^q), p^q)$ such that $p^q \in S$ and $p^q \cdot \sum_j y_j^q = \text{Max } p^q \cdot (\ddot{Y} - \Delta^q)$.

The m-tuples (x_i^q) are attainable for $E(Y)$, hence bounded; the total productions $\sum_j y_j^q$, which equal $\sum_i x_i^q - \omega$, are therefore bounded; and the p^q are bounded since they have a unit norm. Putting

$$\pi_j^q = p^q \cdot y_j^q = \text{Max } p^q \cdot Y_j, \tag{14}$$

and noting that $\pi_j^q \geq 0$ for every j and that $\sum_j \pi_j^q = p^q \cdot \sum_j y_j^q$, which is bounded, we establish that the n-tuples (π_j^q) are bounded.

Let us then extract a subsequence of the $((x_i^q), (\pi_j^q), p^q)$ converging to $((x_i^*), (\pi_j^*), p^*)$, still using the index q for the convergent subsequence. $\sum_j y_j^q$ tends to $y^* = \sum_i x_i^* - \omega$. Since the total production $\sum_j y_j^q$ is attainable for $E(Y)$, it belongs to $Y \cap (X - \{\omega\}) = \ddot{Y} \cap (X - \{\omega\})$. As the latter is closed, $y^* \in Y$. Thus we can choose, for every j, a y_j^* in Y_j in such a way that $\sum_j y_j^* = y^*$. We shall prove that $((x_i^*), (y_j^*), p^*)$ is a quasi-equilibrium of $\mathscr{E}$, and that $p^* \cdot y^* = \text{Max } p^* \cdot (\ddot{Y} - D)$.

We first deal with the last fact. Let z be an arbitrary point in $\ddot{Y}$ − relative interior of D, i.e., $z = y - \delta$, where y is in $\ddot{Y}$, and δ is in the relative interior of D. For q large enough, $\delta \in \Delta^q$. Therefore, $p^q \cdot (y - \delta) \leq p^q \cdot \sum_j y_j^q$. In the limit, $p^* \cdot (y - \delta) \leq p^* \cdot y^*$. Hence $p^* \cdot (\ddot{Y}$ − relative interior of $D) \leq p^* \cdot y^*$. Hence, also $p^* \cdot (\ddot{Y} - D) \leq p^* \cdot y^*$.

By Lemma 3, (14) implies $\pi_j^* \geq \text{Sup } p^* \cdot Y_j$. However, $\sum_j \pi_j^* = p^* \cdot y^*$, while $y^* \in Y$ implies $p^* \cdot y^* \leq \text{Sup } p^* \cdot Y$. Consequently, $p^* \cdot y^* = \text{Sup } p^* \cdot Y$, and $\pi_j^* = \text{Sup } p^* \cdot Y_j$, for every j. This means that y^* maximizes profit relative to p^* on Y; hence so does every y_j^* on Y_j. Therefore

$$\pi_j^* = p^* \cdot y_j^* = \text{Max } p^* \cdot Y_j \quad \text{for every } j.$$

There remains to check that (α) of the definition of a quasi-equilibrium is satisfied. Denote $p^q \cdot \omega_i + \sum_j \theta_{ij} \pi_j^q$ by w_i^q, and its limit, $p^* \cdot \omega_i + \sum_j \theta_{ij} \pi_j^*$, by w_i^*. According to footnote 4, $p^q \cdot x_i^q = w_i^q$ for every (i, q); hence, in the limit, $p^* \cdot x_i^* = w_i^*$ for every i. Let us, therefore, assume that $w_i^* = \text{Min } p^* \cdot X_i$ does not hold for the ith consumer.

Consider x_i' in X_i such that $p^* \cdot x_i' < w_i^*$. The existence of such points is insured by the assumption. For q large enough, $p^q \cdot x_i' < w_i^q$, and $x_i' \in X_i^q$;

hence $w_i^q > \text{Min } p^q \cdot X_i^q$ and, by definition of a quasi-equilibrium for $\mathscr{E}^q$, we have $x_i^q \succcurlyeq_i \{x_i \in X_i^q | p^q \cdot x_i \leqq w_i^q\}$. Therefore $x_i' \preccurlyeq_i x_i^q$. In the limit, $x_i' \preccurlyeq_i x_i^*$.

Consider now $\{x_i \in X_i | p^* \cdot x_i \leqq w_i^*\}$. Any point x_i of that set can be approximated by points x_i' of X_i for which $p^* \cdot x_i' < w_i^*$. Since every such x_i' satisfies $x_i' \preccurlyeq_i x_i^*$, one also has $x_i \preccurlyeq_i x_i^*$. And x_i^* is indeed a greatest element of $\{x_i \in X_i | p^* \cdot x_i \leqq w_i^*\}$ for $\preccurlyeq_i$.

4   Equilibrium and quasi-equilibrium

To prove that a certain private ownership economy $\mathscr{E}$ has an equilibrium, it suffices to prove that $\mathscr{E}$ has a quasi-equilibrium in which

$$p^* \cdot x_i^* = p^* \cdot \omega_i + \sum_j \theta_{ij} p^* \cdot y_j^* = \text{Min } p^* \cdot X_i \qquad (\alpha.2)$$

occurs for no consumer.

A simple way of obtaining such a quasi-equilibrium is to replace "$A\ddot{Y} - D$" by "interior of $A\ddot{Y} - D$" in assumption (c.2). According to footnote 7, $\mathscr{E}$ has a quasi-equilibrium whose price system p^* belongs to the polar of $A\ddot{Y} - D$. Therefore $p^* \cdot \omega_i > \text{Inf } p^* \cdot X_i$ for every i, and (α.2) cannot occur. Theorem I of K. J. Arrow, and G. Debreu [1] is of this type, since it assumes implicitly that Y contains $-\Omega$, the nonpositive orthant, and explicitly that

$$(\{\omega_i\} - \text{Interior of } \Omega) \cap X_i \neq \varnothing \quad \text{for every } i.$$

In W. Isard and D. J. Ostroff [5], the emphasis is on the location aspect of equilibrium. Let us suppose that their hypotheses on the technology are altered along the lines of the theorem of this article so as to insure that a quasi-equilibrium exists.[8] If free disposal prevails, the price system in this quasi-equilibrium is nonnegative. According to [5], in each region, each consumer can obtain a possible consumption by disposing of a positive amount of every commodity located in his region. Therefore, (α.2) occurs for him only if the prices of all the commodities in his region are zero. Assume that such is the case. If there were, in some other region, a commodity with a positive price, the economy of [5] is such that an exporter from the first region to the second could increase his profit indefinitely. This contradicts (β) of the definition of a quasi-equilibrium. Hence, all prices would be zero, a contradiction of (δ). Consequently, (α.2) occurs for no consumer.

---

[8] One can construct an economy with two regions, one good and one transportation service, and a constant returns to scale, free disposal technology satisfying all their assumptions and such that a total production, every coordinate of which is positive, is possible. That economy cannot have an equilibrium, since, for any price system different from 0, the total profit of producers can be indefinitely increased.

We now strengthen assumption (c.2) of the theorem, adding to it

> and that the relative interiors of $\{\omega\} + \ddot{Y}$ and of X have a nonempty intersection.

And we call (c) the result of this addition, which makes (c.1) redundant. This strengthening is a generalization of the second part of assumption 5 of L. W. McKenzie [8]. We also assume[9]

> (e) if, in a quasi-equilibrium, $p^* \cdot x_i^* = \text{Min } p^* \cdot X_i$ occurs for some consumer, then it occurs for every consumer.

We then prove

Proposition

The private ownership economy $\mathscr{E}$ has an equilibrium if it satisfies (e) and the assumptions of the theorem where (c.1) and (c.2) are replaced by (c).

Proof. Let $\mathscr{L}$ be the smallest linear manifold containing $X - \{\omega\} - \ddot{Y}$. According to (c), the origin belongs to $\mathscr{L}$, which is therefore a linear subspace of the commodity space. Since $0 \in \ddot{Y}$, the set $X - \{\omega\}$ is contained in $X - \{\omega\} - \ddot{Y}$, hence in $\mathscr{L}$. Moreover, $\ddot{Y} \subset (X - \{\omega\}) - (X - \{\omega\} - \ddot{Y})$. As both sets in this difference are contained in $\mathscr{L}$, so is $\ddot{Y}$. Consider now the set $\sum_i \{x_i \in X_i | x_i >_i \hat{X}_i\} - \{\omega\}$ at the end of footnote 5. It is contained in $X - \{\omega\}$, hence in $\mathscr{L}$, and so is the cone D. According to (c), the set $X_i - \{\omega_i\}$ intersects $A\ddot{Y} - D$. But both $A\ddot{Y}$ and D are contained in $\mathscr{L}$. Therefore, every set $X_i - \{\omega_i\}$ intersects $\mathscr{L}$, while their sum $X - \{\omega\}$ is contained in $\mathscr{L}$. To see that this implies "$X_i - \{\omega_i\} \subset \mathscr{L}$ for every i," take x_i in $(X_i - \{\omega_i\}) \cap \mathscr{L}$ for each i. The sets $X_i - \{\omega_i\} - \{x_i\}$ own 0; hence their sum $X - \{\omega\} - \{\sum_i x_i\}$ contains them all. However, this sum is contained in $\mathscr{L}$, since $\sum_i x_i$ belongs to $\mathscr{L}$. Finally, observe that $Y_j \subset \ddot{Y}$ for every j. In conclusion, $\mathscr{L}$ contains every $X_i - \{\omega_i\}$ and every Y_j, and, following L. W. McKenzie [8], we can treat the equilibrium problem in $\mathscr{L}$.

According to the theorem, there is a quasi-equilibrium $((x_i^*), (y_j^*), p^*)$ such that $p^* \cdot \sum_j y_j^* = \text{Max } p^* \cdot (\ddot{Y} - D)$. We will

---

[9] Notice, from the proof of the proposition, that it suffices to make this assumption for quasi-equilibria such that $p^* \cdot \sum_j y_j^* = \text{Max } p^* \cdot (\ddot{Y} - D)$.

show that (α.2) occurs for no consumer. Assume that it occurs for one of them; by (e), it occurs for all. Thus $p^* \cdot x_i^* = \text{Min } p^* \cdot X_i$ for every i; hence $p^* \cdot \sum_i x_i^* = \text{Min } p^* \cdot X$. Therefore, the hyperplane H with normal p^*, through $\sum_i x_i^*$, separates X and $\{\omega\} + \ddot{Y} - D$. A fortiori it separates X and $\{\omega\} + \ddot{Y}$. H cannot contain both sets, for $\mathscr{L}$ would not be the smallest linear manifold containing $X - \{\omega\} - \ddot{Y}$. Thus, one of them has points strictly on one side of H. Consequently, its relative interior is strictly on that side of H and cannot intersect the relative interior of the other set, a contradiction of (c).

The proposition that we have just established generalizes the results of A. Wald [11, (Section II)], K. J. Arrow and G. Debreu [1, (Theorem II or II′)], D. Gale [4], H. Nikaidô [10], and L. W. McKenzie [8], [9]. The only assumption which does not obviously hold in these various cases is (e). We will give two illustrations of the reasoning involved in checking this point.

In the economy of Theorem II′ of K. J. Arrow and G. Debreu [1], there is a (nonempty) set $\mathscr{D}'$ of always desired commodities such that, for every i, for every consumption x_i in $\hat{X}_i$, and for every h in $\mathscr{D}'$, the ith consumer can obtain a consumption in X_i preferred to x_i by increasing the hth coordinate of x_i. There is also a set $\mathscr{P}'$ of always productive commodities such that for every attainable total production y and for every h in $\mathscr{P}'$, one can obtain a production in Y whose output of every commodity different from h is at least as large as in y, and whose output of at least one commodity in $\mathscr{D}'$ is larger than in y. It is assumed that each consumer can dispose of a positive quantity of at least one commodity in $\mathscr{D}' \cup \mathscr{P}'$ from his resources and still have a possible consumption. The economy has a quasi-equilibrium $((x_i^*), (y_j^*), p^*)$, and p^* is nonnegative since free disposal prevails. Let us suppose that (α.2) occurs for the i'-th consumer. Thus, at least one commodity in $\mathscr{D}' \cup \mathscr{P}'$ has a zero price. If this commodity is in $\mathscr{P}'$, some commodity in $\mathscr{D}'$ has a zero price; otherwise there would be a total production in Y yielding a total profit larger than $p^* \cdot y^*$. Hence, there is a commodity h in $\mathscr{D}'$ with a zero price. Consider now an arbitrary consumer, say the ith one. By consuming more of the hth commodity, he can obtain a consumption preferred to x_i^* without spending more. Consequently, x_i^* does not satisfy the preferences of the ith consumer under the constraint $p^* \cdot x_i \leqq p^* \cdot x_i^*$, and, by ($\alpha$) of the definition of a quasi-equilibrium, $p^* \cdot x_i^* = \text{Min } p^* \cdot X_i$. Therefore, (e) is satisfied.

If I_k is a set of consumers, and if a_i is a real number, or a vector of the commodity space, or a subset of the commodity space associated with the ith consumer, we now denote by a_{I_k} the sum $\sum_{i \in I_k} a_i$. Generalizing a concept of D. Gale [4], L. W. McKenzie [8], [9] considers an economy that is *irreducible* in the following sense.[10] Let (I_1, I_2) be a partition of the set of consumers into two nonempty subsets. If $((x_i), y)$ is an attainable state of the economy, then there is z in $Y + \{\omega_{I_2}\} - X_{I_2}$ such that $x_{I_1} - y + z$ can be allocated to the consumers in I_1 so as to make all of them at least as well off, and at least one of them better off, than in the given state.

Let then $((x_i^*), (y_j^*), p^*)$ be a quasi-equilibrium of the economy, and let I_2 be the set of consumers for whom $(\alpha.2)$ occurs. To show that irreducibility implies (e), we have to show that if $I_2 \neq \varnothing$, then its complement $I_1 = \varnothing$. For this, we assume $I_1 \neq \varnothing \neq I_2$ and derive a contradiction. One has $p^* \cdot x_{I_2}^* = \text{Min } p^* \cdot X_{I_2}$ and $p^* \cdot y^* = \text{Max } p^* \cdot Y$. Hence $Y + \{\omega_{I_2}\} - X_{I_2}$ is below the hyperplane with normal p^*, through $y^* + \omega_{I_2} - x_{I_2}^*$, which is equal to $x_{I_1}^* - \omega_{I_1}$. By the definition of irreducibility, there is z in $Y + \{\omega_{I_2}\} - X_{I_2}$ (hence $p^* \cdot z \leq p^* \cdot (x_{I_1}^* - \omega_{I_1})$) such that $x_{I_1}^* - y^* + z$ is collectively preferred to $x_{I_1}^*$ by the consumers in I_1. Summing the wealth equations of these consumers, one obtains $p^* \cdot x_{I_1}^* = p^* \cdot \omega_{I_1} + \sum_j \theta_{I_1 j} p^* \cdot y_j^*$; hence $p^* \cdot (x_{I_1}^* - \omega_{I_1}) = \sum_j \theta_{I_1 j} p^* \cdot y_j^* \leq p^* \cdot y^*$. Therefore, $p^* \cdot z \leq p^* \cdot y^*$, and

$$p^* \cdot (x_{I_1}^* - y^* + z) \leq p^* \cdot x_{I_1}^*. \tag{15}$$

Since, for every i in I_1, the consumption x_i^* satisfies the preferences of the ith consumer under the constraint $p^* \cdot x_i \leq p^* \cdot x_i^*$, inequality (15) means that $x_{I_1}^* - y^* + z$ cannot be collectively preferred to $x_{I_1}^*$ by the consumers in I_1, if all the preferences satisfy the assumption "$x_i' \succ_i x_i$ implies $tx_i' + (1 - t)x_i \succ_i x_i$ if $0 < t < 1$," by the usual argument on Pareto optima.

References

[1] Arrow, K. J., and G. Debreu, Existence of an Equilibrium for a Competitive Economy, *Econometrica* XXII (July 1954), 265–90.
[2] Debreu, G., Market Equilibrium, *Proceedings of the National Academy of Sciences of the U.S.A.*, XLII (November 1956), 876–78.
[3] Debreu, G., *Theory of Value*, (New York; Wiley, 1959).
[4] Gale, D., General Equilibrium for Linear Models, hectographed, The RAND Corporation, 1957.
[5] Isard, W. and D. J. Ostroff, Existence of a Competitive Interregional Equilibrium, *Papers and Proceedings of the Regional Science Association*, IV (1958), 49–76.
[6] Kuhn, H. W., On a Theorem of Wald, *Linear Inequalities and Related Systems*, H. W. Kuhn and A. W. Tucker, eds. (Princeton: Princeton University Press, 1956), 265–73.
[7] McKenzie, L. W., Competitive Equilibrium with Dependent Consumer

---

[10] The economy of K. J. Arrow and G. Debreu [1, (Theorem II')] is irreducible. But in this case, as well as in the case of D. Gale [4], it seems easier to establish (e) directly then to establish irreducibility.

Preferences, *Proceedings of the Second Symposium in Linear Programming*, H. A. Antosiewicz, ed. (Washington: National Bureau of Standards, 1955), 277-94.

[8] McKenzie, L. W., On the Existence of General Equilibrium for a Competitive Market, *Econometrica*, XXVII (January 1959), 54-71.

[9] McKenzie, L. W., On the Existence of General Equilibrium: Some Corrections, *Econometrica*, XXIX (April 1961), 247-48.

[10] Nikaidô, H., A Supplementary Note to "On the Classical Multilateral Exchange Problem," *Metroeconomica*, IX (December 1957), 209-10.

[11] Wald, A., Über einige Gleichungssysteme der mathematischen Ökonomie, *Zeitschrift für Nationalökonomie*, VII (1936), 637-70. Translated as On Some Systems of Equations of Mathematical Economics, *Econometrica*, XIX (October 1951), 368-403.

CHAPTER 11

A limit theorem on the core of an economy

By Gerard Debreu and Herbert Scarf[1]

1   Introduction

In his *Mathematical Psychics* [5], Edgeworth presented a remarkable study of the exchanges of two commodities that might arise in an economy with two types of consumers. The first case that he considers concerns two individuals each of whom initially possesses certain quantities of each commodity. The result of trading consists of a reallocation of the total amounts of the two commodities and may, therefore, be described geometrically by a point in the Edgeworth box corresponding to that economy.

Edgeworth confines his attention to those exchanges which are Pareto optimal, i.e., those which cannot yield greater satisfaction for one consumer without impairing that of the other by means of additional trade. He further restricts the admissible final allocations to those which are at least as desired by *both* consumers as the allocation prevailing before trading. Those allocations which are not ruled out by either of these considerations constitute the "contract curve."

As Edgeworth remarks, a competitive allocation is on the contract curve (under assumptions listed in Section 2). But so are many other allocations,

[1] The work of Gerard Debreu was supported by the Office of Naval Research first under Task NR 047–006 with the Cowles Commission for Research in Economics, and then under Contract ONR 222 (77) with the University of California. The work of Herbert Scarf was supported by an Office of Naval Research Contract ONR–225 (28) with Stanford University. Reproduction in whole or in part is permitted for any purpose of the United States Government.

and nothing in the analysis of the case of two consumers indicates that the competitive solutions play a privileged role. In order to single out the competitive allocations Edgeworth introduces an expanded economy which consists of $2n$ consumers divided into two types; everyone of the same type having identical preferences and identical resources before trading takes place. The object is to demonstrate that as n becomes large, more and more allocations are ruled out, and eventually only the competitive allocations remain. This statement can be paraphrased by saying that the contract curve shrinks to the set of competitive equilibria as the number of consumers becomes infinite.

It is clear that the two principles mentioned above for ruling out allocations must be supplemented by some additional principles if this result is to be correct. The general principle which Edgeworth formulated is that of "recontracting." Consider an allocation of the total resources of the $2n$ consumers and consider any collection of consumers (which need not include the same number of each type). This collection "recontracts out," if it is possible for its members to redistribute their initial resources among themselves in such a way that some member of the collection prefers the new outcome to the allocation previously given while no member desires it less. The presumption is that an allocation is not made if it can be recontracted out by some group of consumers.

Edgeworth shows that the set of allocations which are not recontracted out decreases a n increases, and has the set of competitive equilibria as a limit. The proof given in *Mathematical Psychics* could easily be rewritten in the style of contemporary mathematical economics. It is, however, based on the geometrical picture of the Edgeworth box and does not seem to be applicable to the general case involving more than two commodities and more than two types of consumers.

As Martin Shubik pointed out, the question can be studied from the point of view of n-person game theory. In a very stimulating paper [12] he analyzed the Edgeworth problem, using the von Neumann–Morgenstern concept of a solution, and also Gillies' [6] concept of the "core." Other discussions of markets as n-person games may be found in von Neumann and Morgenstern [7] and in several papers by Shapley [9, 10].

In all these contributions, extensive use is made of a transferable utility. While this concept has been readily accepted in game theory, it has remained foreign to the mainstream of economic throught. Some recent work has been done, however, on a version of n-person game theory which avoids the assumption of transferable utility [1, 2] and which includes a definition of the core. It is this concept which corresponds to the Edgeworth notion of recontracting.

In [8] Scarf analyzed the core in the latter sense in an economy with an arbitrary number of types of consumers and an arbitrary number of commodities. Economies consisting of r consumers of each type were considered and it was proved that an allocation which assigns the same commodity bundle to all consumers of the same type and which is in the core for all r must be competitive. An economy consisting of an infinite sequence of consumers of each type was also studied and it was demonstrated that an allocation in the core of this economy is competitive. A suggestion for a simplication of the proofs of these theorems and for a weakening of their assumptions was given by Debreu [4].

Our main purpose is to show that the first of the two theorems mentioned in the last paragraph is very widely applicable and, thereby, to obtain a further considerable simplification of the study of the core and to discard an awkward assumption used in both papers [8, (Section 4, A.2)] and [4, (A.4)]. Our second purpose is to cover a case in which production is possible.

In the traditional Walrasian analysis of equilibrium the resources of the consumers and their shares in the producers' profits are specified. All the agents of the economy are assumed to adapt themselves to a price system which one then tries to choose so as to equate total demand and total supply. In the Paretian study of optimality, prices are seen from a second and very different point of view. The problem of efficient organization of an economy with an unspecified distribution of resources is considered, and it is essentially shown that a state of the economy is an optimum one if and only if there exists a price system to which every consumer and every producer is adapted. In Edgeworth's theorem, and in the generalization that we present here, prices appear in a third and again very different light. Given an economy with a specified distribution of resources composed of a certain number of types of consumers which is small relative to the numbers of consumers of each type, an outcome is viable, i.e., no coalition can block it, if and only if there exists a price system to which consumers and producers are adapted. That is to say, competitive equilibria, and only they, are viable. As in the study of Pareto optima, prices emerge from the analysis in a situation in which they were not introduced *a priori*.

2   The core in a pure exchange economy

At first we study an economy in which no production can take place. We consider m consumers each with specific preferences for commodity bundles consisting of nonnegative quantities of a finite number of commodities. Such a commodity bundle is represented by a vector in the nonnegative orthant of the commodity space, and the preferences of the ith consumer by a complete preordering, $\succcurlyeq_i$. The interpretation of $x' \succcurlyeq_i x$ is, of course, that the ith consumer either prefers x' to x or is indifferent between them. If x' is strictly preferred to x, then we write $x' \succ_i x$.

Three assumptions will be made on the preferences:

1   *Insatiability.* Let x be an arbitrary nonnegative commodity bundle. We assume that there is a commodity bundle x' such that $x' \succ_i x$.

2   *Strong-convexity.* Let x' and x be arbitrary different commodity bundles with $x' \succcurlyeq_i x$, and let α be an arbitrary number such that $0 < \alpha < 1$. We assume that $\alpha x' + (1 - \alpha)x \succ_i x$.

3   *Continuity.* We assume that for any nonnegative x', the two sets

$$\{x|x \succcurlyeq_i x'\} \quad \text{and} \quad \{x|x \preccurlyeq_i x'\}$$

are closed.

Each consumer owns a commodity bundle which he is interested in exchanging for preferred commodity bundles. The vector ω_i will represent the resources of the ith consumer. We find it convenient to make the following assumption:

4   *Strict positivity of the individual resources.* We assume that every consumer owns a strictly positive quantity of every commodity.

The core can now be defined. Since production is not considered in the present section, the result of trading consists of an allocation of the total supply $\sum_{i=1}^{m} \omega_i$, and is therefore described by a collection of m nonnegative commodity bundles $(x_1, \ldots, x_m)$ such that

$$\sum_{i=1}^{m} (x_i - \omega_i) = 0.$$

An allocation is in the core if it cannot be recontracted out by any set of consumers S, i.e., if no set of consumers S can redistribute their own initial supply among themselves so as to improve the position of any one member of S without deterioration of that of any other. We emphasize here that it is permissible for an arbitrary set of consumers to combine and reallocate their own assets independently of the remaining consumers in the economy.

To give a formal definition of the core we introduce the notion of set of consumers blocking an allocation. Let $(x_1, \ldots, x_m)$ with $\sum_{i=1}^{m} (x_i - \omega_i) = 0$ be an assignment of the total supply to the various consumers, and let S be an arbitrary set of consumers. We say that the allocation is blocked by S if it is possible to find commodity bundles x_i' for all i in S such that

$$\sum_{i \in S} (x_i' - \omega_i) = 0, \tag{1}$$

and

$$x_i' \succcurlyeq_i x_i, \tag{2}$$

for all i in S, with strict preference for at least one member of S.

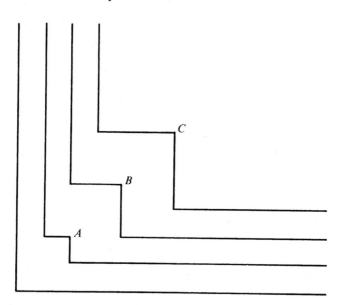

Figure 1

The core of the economy is defined as the collection of all allocations of the total supply which cannot be blocked by any set S. One immediate consequence of this definition is that an allocation in the core is Pareto optimal. We prove this by taking for the set S all consumers. On the other hand, if we take the possible blocking set to consist of the ith consumer himself, then we see that an allocation in the core must satisfy the condition $x_i \succcurlyeq_i \omega_i$; i.e., the ith consumer does not prefer his initial holding to the commodity bundle that he receives on the basis of an allocation in the core. Many other conditions will, of course, be obtained as more general sets S are considered.

It is not clear that there always will be some allocations in the core. One can easily construct examples in n-person game theory in which every imputation is blocked by some coalition so that the core is empty. Economies with an empty core may also be found if the usual assumptions on preferences are relaxed. The following example due to Scarf, Shapley, and Shubik is typical.

Consider an economy with two commodities and three consumers, each of whom has preferences described by the indifferences curves in Figure 1. It is shown in [11] that if the initial resources of each consumer consist of one unit of each commodity, then the core of the resulting economy is empty. This conclusion does not depend on the lack of smoothness of the indifference curves.

In this paper we make the customary assumptions listed above, in which case it may be shown that the core is not empty. The procedure for doing this is to observe that a competitive allocation exists, and then to demonstrate that every competitive allocation is in the core.

It is known that, given our four assumptions on preferences and initial holdings, there is a competitive equilibrium [3]. That is to say, there are nonnegative commodity bundles $x_1, \ldots, x_m$ with $\sum_{i=1}^{m}(x_i - \omega_i) = 0$ and a price vector p, such that x_i satisfies the preferences of the ith consumer subject to the budget constraint $p \cdot x_i \leq p \cdot \omega_i$. The familiar argument of welfare economics by which a competitive allocation is proved to be Pareto optimal has been extended, as follows, by Shapley to prove:

Theorem 1

A competitive allocation is in the core.

First notice that $x_i' \succ_i x_i$ obviously implies $p \cdot x_i' > p \cdot \omega_i$. For, otherwise, x_i does not satisfy the preferences of the ith consumer under his budget constraint. Notice also that $x_i' \succcurlyeq_i x_i$ implies $p \cdot x_i' \geq p \cdot \omega_i$. For, if $p \cdot x_i' < p \cdot \omega_i$, there is, according to our assumptions 1 and 2, a consumption vector in a neighborhood of x_i' that satisfies the budget constraint and that is preferred to x_i.

Let S be a possible blocking set, so that $\sum_{i \in S}(x_i' - \omega_i) = 0$ with $x_i' \succcurlyeq_i x_i$ for all i in S, and with strict preference for at least one i. From the two remarks we have just made, $p \cdot x_i' \geq p \cdot \omega_i$ for all i in S, with strict inequality for at least one i. Therefore

$$\sum_{i \in S} p \cdot x_i' > \sum_{i \in S} p \cdot \omega_i,$$

a contradiction of $\sum_{i \in S}(x_i' - \omega_i) = 0$.

3   The core as the number of consumers becomes infinite

We shall now follow the procedure first used by Edgeworth for enlarging the market. We imagine the economy to be composed of m types of consumers, with r consumers of each type. For two consumers to be of the same type, we require them to have precisely the same preferences and precisely the same vector of initial resources. The economy therefore consists of mr consumers, whom we index by the pair of numbers (i, q), with $i = 1, 2, \ldots, m$ and $q = 1, 2, \ldots, r$. The first index refers to the type of the individual and the second index distinguishes different individuals of the same type.

An allocation is described by a collection of mr nonnegative commodity bundles x_{iq} such that

$$\sum_{i=1}^{m} \sum_{q=1}^{r} x_{iq} - r \sum_{i=1}^{m} \omega_i = 0.$$

The following theorem makes for the simplicity of our study:

Theorem 2

An allocation in the core assigns the same consumption to all consumers of the same type.

For any particular type i, let x_i represent the least desired of the consumption vectors x_{iq} according to the common preferences for consumers of this type and assume that for some type i' two consumers have been assigned different commodity bundles. Then

$$\frac{1}{r} \sum_{q=1}^{r} x_{iq} \succcurlyeq_i x_i, \qquad \text{for all } i,$$

with strict preference holding for i'. However,

$$\sum_{i=1}^{m} \left(\frac{1}{r} \sum_{q=1}^{r} x_{iq} - \omega_i \right) = 0,$$

and therefore the set consisting of one consumer of each type, each of whom receives a least preferred consumption, would block.

The theorem we have just proved implies that an allocation in the core for the repeated economies considered here may be described by a collection of m nonnegative commodity bundles $(x_1, \ldots, x_m)$ with $\sum_{i=1}^{m} (x_i - \omega_i) = 0$. The particular collections of commodity bundles in the core will, of course, depend on r. It is easy to see that the core for $r + 1$ is contained in the core for r, for a coalition which blocks in the economy with r repetitions will certainly be available for blocking in the economy with $(r + 1)$ repetitions.

If we consider a competitive allocation in the economy consisting of one participant of each type and repeat the allocation when we enlarge the economy to r participants of each type, the resulting allocation is competitive for the larger economy and consequently is in the core. We see, therefore, that as a function of r, the cores form a nonincreasing sequence of sets, each of which contains the collection of competitive allocations for the economy consisting of one consumer of each type. Our main result is that no other allocation is in the core for all r.

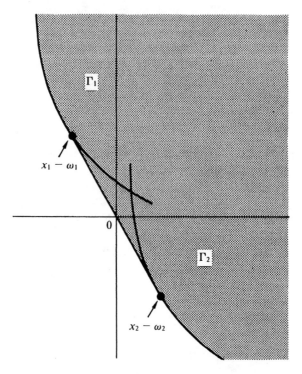

Figure 2

Theorem 3

If $(x_1, \ldots, x_m)$ is in the core for all r, then it is a competitive allocation.

Let Γ_i be the set of all z in the commodity space such that $z + \omega_i \succ_i x_i$, and let Γ be the convex hull of the union of the sets Γ_i. Since, for every i, Γ_i is convex (and nonempty), Γ consists of the set of all vectors z which may be written as $\sum_{i=1}^{m} \alpha_i z_i$, with $\alpha_i \geqq 0$, $\sum_i^m \alpha_i = 1$, and $z_i + \omega_i \succ_i x_i$. Figure 2 describes this set in the case of two commodities and two types of consumers.

We first form the set of commodity bundles which are preferred to x_1 and from each of these subtract the vector ω_1, obtaining the set Γ_1. We do the same with x_2 and ω_2 in order to obtain Γ_2. We then take the union of Γ_1 and Γ_2 and form the convex hull obtaining Γ. Verifying that the origin does not belong to the set Γ in the the general case of an arbitrary number of commodities and an arbitrary number of types of consumers is the key step in the proof of Theorem 3.

Let us suppose that the origin belongs to Γ. Then $\sum_{i=1}^{m} \alpha_i z_i = 0$ with $\alpha_i \geq 0$, $\sum_{i=1}^{m} \alpha_i = 1$ and $z_i + \omega_i \succ_i x_i$. Select an integer k, which will eventually tend to $+\infty$, and let a_i^k be the smallest integer greater than or equal to $k\alpha_i$. Also let I be the set of i for which $\alpha_i > 0$.

For each i in I we define z_i^k to be $[(k\alpha_i)/(a_i^k)]z_i$ and observe that $z_i^k + \omega_i$ belongs to the segment $[\omega_i, z_i + \omega_i]$ and tends to $z_i + \omega_i$ as k tends to infinity. The continuity assumption on preferences implies that $z_i^k + \omega_i \succ_i x_i$ for sufficiently large k. Moreover,

$$\sum_{i \in I} a_i^k z_i^k = k \sum_{i \in I} \alpha_i z_i = 0.$$

Consider the coalition composed of a_i^k members of type i to each one of whom we assign $\omega_i + z_i^k$, where i runs over the set I. Such a coalition blocks the allocation $(x_1, \ldots, x_m)$ repeated a number of times equal to $\max_{i \in I} a_i^k$. This contradicts the assumption that $(x_1, \ldots, x_m)$ is in the core for all r.

We have, therefore, established that the origin does not belong to the convex set Γ. Consequently, there is a hyperplane through it with normal p such that $p \cdot z \geq 0$ for all points z in Γ.

If $x' \succ_i x_i$, then $x' - \omega_i$ is in Γ_i, hence in Γ, and we obtain $p \cdot x' \geq p \cdot \omega_i$. Since in every neighborhood of x_i there are consumptions strictly preferred to x_i, we also obtain $p \cdot x_i \geq p \cdot \omega_i$. But

$$\sum_{i=1}^{m} (x_i - \omega_i) = 0.$$

Therefore $p \cdot x_i = p \cdot \omega_i$ for every i.

The argument is virtually complete at this stage. We have demonstrated the existence of prices p such that for every i, (1) $x' \succ_i x_i$ implies $p \cdot x' \geq p \cdot \omega_i$ and (2) $p \cdot x_i = p \cdot \omega_i$. As is customary in equilibrium analysis, there remains to show that x_i actually satisfies the preferences of the ith consumer subject to his budget constraint, i.e., that $x' \succ_i x_i$ actually implies $p \cdot x' > p \cdot \omega_i$. Since ω_i has all of its components strictly positive, there is a nonnegative x^0 strictly below the budget hyperplane. If for some x'', both $x'' \succ_i x_i$ and $p \cdot x'' = p \cdot \omega_i$, the points of the segment $[x^0, x'']$ close enough to x'' would be strictly preferred to x_i and strictly below the budget hyperplane, a contradiction of (1). This completes the demonstration of Theorem 3.

4 The core in a productive economy

An entirely straightforward extension of our results on the core to an economy in which production is possible can be given. We assume that all

coalitions of consumers have access to the same production possibilities
described by a subset Y of the commodity space. A point y in Y represents a
production plan which can be carried out. Inputs into production appear as
negative components of y and outputs as positive components. From now
on, in addition to the four conditions given in Section 2 (insatiability,
strong-convexity and continuity of preferences, and strict positivity of the
individual resources), we impose on the economy the following condition:

  5   *Y is a convex cone with vertex at the origin.*

Thus Sections 2 and 3 dealt with the particular case where the cone Y is
degenerate to the set having the origin as its only element.

  In the new context, an allocation for an economy with m consumers
is a collection of nonnegative commodity bundles $(x_1, \ldots, x_m)$ such that
there is in Y a production plan y satisfying the equality of demand and
supply $\sum_{i=1}^{m} x_i = y + \sum_{i=1}^{m} \omega_i$, i.e. such that $\sum_{i=1}^{m} (x_i - \omega_i)$ belongs to Y.
This allocation is blocked by the set S of consumers if it is possible to find
commodity bundles x_i' for all i in S such that (1) $\sum_{i \in S}(x_i' - \omega_i)$ belongs to Y,
and (2) $x_i' \succcurlyeq_i x_i$ for all i in S, with strict preference for at least one member of
S. The core of the economy is defined as the collection of all allocations
which cannot be blocked.

  An allocation is competitive if there exists a price system p such that the
profit is maximized on Y (since Y is a cone with vertex at the origin, the
maximum profit is zero) and that x_i satisfies the preferences of the ith
consumer under the constraint $p \cdot x \leqq p \cdot \omega_i$. Assumptions 1–5 are no
longer sufficient to insure the existence of a competitive allocation, but
Theorem 1 remains true: A competitive allocation is in the core.

  , The proof hardly differs from the one we have given. The two opening remarks are unchanged. Let S be a possible blocking set, so that
$\sum_{i \in S}(x_i' - \omega_i) = y$ in Y with $x_i' \succcurlyeq_i x_i$ for all i in S, with strict preference
for at least one i, and with $p \cdot y \leqq 0$. Since $p \cdot x_i' \geqq p \cdot \omega_i$ for all i in S, with
strict inequality for at least one i, we have $\sum_{i \in S} p \cdot x_i' > \sum_{i \in S} p \cdot \omega_i$, or
$p \cdot y > 0$, a contradiction.

  As before we consider an economy composed of m types of consumers
with r consumers of each type. An allocation is described by a collection of
mr commodity bundles x_{iq} such that $\sum_{i=1}^{m} \sum_{r=1}^{q} x_{iq} - r \sum_{i=1}^{m} \omega_i$ belongs to
Y. It is a simple matter to verify the analogue of Theorem 2: *An allocation in*
the core assigns the same consumption to all consumers of the same type. The
only modification in the previous proof involves the fact that $y \in Y$ implies
$(1/r)y \in Y$.

  The allocations in the cores may therefore be described by a collection of
m commodity bundles $(x_1, \ldots, x_m)$ with $\sum_{i=1}^{m} (x_i - \omega_i)$ in Y. Again it is clear
that the cores form a nonincreasing sequence of sets as r increases. We now
indicate the proof of the analogue of Theorem 3: *If $(x_1, \ldots, x_m)$ is in the core*

for all r, then it is a competitive allocation. The set Γ is defined, as before, to be the convex hull of the union of the m sets.

$$\Gamma_i = \{z | z + \omega_i \succ_i x_i\}.$$

We then show that Γ and Y are disjoint. Suppose, to the contrary, that $\sum_{i=1}^m \alpha_i z_i = y$ in Y with $\alpha_i \geq 0$, $\sum_{i=1}^m \alpha_i = 1$, and $z_i + \omega_i \succ_i x_i$. Using the same definitions of k, a_i^k, I and z_i^k as in the proof of Theorem 3, we see that $z_i^k + \omega_i \succ_i x_i$ for sufficiently large k. Moreover,

$$\sum_{i \in I} a_i^k z_i^k = k \sum_{i \in I} \alpha_i z_i = ky.$$

Since $ky \in Y$, the allocation is blocked by the coalition we have described in proving Theorem 3. Thus a contradiction has been obtained.

The two convex sets Γ and Y may, therefore, be separated by a hyperplane with normal p such that $p \cdot z \geq 0$ for all points z in Γ and $p \cdot y \leq 0$ for all points y in Y. The demonstration then proceeds as before to verify that we indeed have a competitive allocation.

5   Generalizations

Until now we have constrained the consumption bundles of consumers to belong to the nonnegative orthant of the commodity space. This restriction, which was made only to keep the exposition as simple as possible, is not essential. Instead we can require the consumptions of all the consumers of the ith type ($i = 1, \ldots, m$) to belong to a given subset X_i of the commodity space. We impose on these consumption sets the condition:

0   X_i is convex.

We make the appropriate modifications on Assumptions 1–4; in particular, in 3, the two sets $\{x | x \succcurlyeq_i x'\}$ and $\{x | x \preccurlyeq_i x'\}$ are now assumed to be closed in X_o, and in 4, ω_i is now assumed to be interior to X_i. Then the three theorems are established without alteration of their proofs.

A second generalization consists in replacing Assumption 2 (strong convexity of preferences) by

2′   *Convexity.* Let x' and x be arbitrary commodity bundles with $x' \succ_i x$, and let α be an arbitrary number such that $0 < \alpha < 1$. We assume that $\alpha x' + (1 - \alpha)x \succ_i x$.

This substitution affects neither the statement nor the proof of Theorem 1. In order to establish the analogue of Theorem 2, we consider an economy with r consumers of each one of m types. Given an allocation (x_{iq}) in its core, we define $\bar{x}_i$ to be $(1/r)\sum_{q=1}^r x_{iq}$ and, as before, we denote by x_i the least desired of the consumption bundles x_{iq} according to the common preferences for consumers of the ith type. Since $\sum_{i=1}^{m} (\bar{x}_i - \omega_i)$ belongs to Y, the coalition consisting of one consumer of each type who receives a least preferred consumption blocks, unless $\bar{x}_i \sim_i x_i$ for every i. Therefore, by 2', *an allocation in the core assigns to all consumers of the same type consumptions indifferent to the average of the consumptions for that type.* This suggests defining the *strict core* of the economy as the collection of all unblocked allocations with the same consumption bundles assigned to all consumers of the same type. As we have just seen, with any allocation in the core is associated an allocation (consisting of the m average consumptions repeated r times) in the strict core which is indifferent to the first allocation for every consumer. Thus the distinction between the core and the strict core is not essential. However, we can treat the strict core under 2' exactly as we treated the core under 2. As a function of r, the strict cores form a nonincreasing sequence of sets and *if $(x_1, \ldots, x_m)$ is in the strict core for all r, then it is a competitive allocation.*

References

[1] Aumann, R. J., The Core of a Cooperative Game without Side Payments, *Transactions of the American Mathematical Society*, XCVIII (March 1961), 539–52.

[2] Aumann, R. J. and B. Peleg, Von Neumann-Morgenstern Solutions to Cooperative Games without Side Payments, *Bulletin of the American Mathematical Society*, LXVI (May 1960), 173–79.

[3] Debreu, Gerard, New Concepts and Techniques for Equilibrium Analysis, *International Economic Review*, III (September 1962), 257–73.

[4] Debreu, Gerard, On a Theorem of Scarf, *The Review of Economic Studies*, XXX (1963).

[5] Edgeworth, F. Y., *Mathematical Psychics* (London: Kegan Paul, 1881).

[6] Gillies, D. B., *Some Theorems on n-Person Games*, Ph. D. Thesis (Princeton University, 1953).

[7] von Neumann, John and Oskar Morgenstern, *Theory of Games and Economic Behavior* (Princeton, Princeton, N. J.: Princeton University Press, 1947).

[8] Scarf, Herbert, An Analysis of Markets with a Large Number of Participants, *Recent Advances in Game Theory* (The Princeton University Conference, 1962).

[9] Shapley, L. S., *Markets as Cooperative Games* (The Rand Corporation, 1955), P. 629.

[10] Shapley, L. S., *The Solutions of a Symmetric Market Game* (The Rand Corporation, 1958), P. 1392.

[11] Shapley, L. S. and Martin Shubik, *Example of a Distribution Game Having No Core*, unpublished manuscript prepared at the Rand Corporation, July 1961.

[12] Shubik, Martin, Edgeworth Market Games, *Contributions to the Theory of Games IV*, ed. A. W. Tucker and R. D. Luce (Princeton, N. J.: Princeton University Press, 1959).

CHAPTER 12

Continuity properties of Paretian utility[1]

1   Introduction

In the study of real-valued representations (Paretian utility functions) of a completely preordered space (space of actions preordered by preferences), the continuity properties of the representation can be made to rest on the following result.

$\bar{R}$ will denote the *extended real line*, i.e., the real line with $-\infty$ and $+\infty$ adjoined. A *degenerate* set is a set having at most one element. Given a subset S of $\bar{R}$, a *lacuna* of S is a nondegenerate interval of $\bar{R}$ without points of S but having a lower bound and an upper bound in S; a *gap* of S is a maximal lacuna of S.

Theorem

If S is a subset of $\bar{R}$, there is an increasing function g from S to $\bar{R}$ such that all the gaps of $g(S)$ are open.

The proof will be given in Section 2.

When I introduced this result in the proof of Lemma I of [1], I also asserted that g could be given a certain specific form. In Section 4, I shall prove that this assertion is not correct, using a modification of the triadic set of Cantor due to David A. Freedman. This error does not affect the

[1] This work was supported by the Office of Naval Research under Contract ONR 222 (77) with the University of California. Reproduction in whole or in part is permitted for any purpose of the United States Government.

applications that were made of the result, for in these the specific form of the function g is irrelevant.

In Section 3 I shall discuss the use of the theorem in the proof of the continuity properties of Paretian utility functions and, in particular, the recent contribution of John T. Rader [5].

2   Proof of the theorem

An *extremal* element of a preordered set is a greatest or a least element of that set.

An *f*-set is a nondegenerate subset A of S such that $(a \in A, b \in A, a < b) \Rightarrow (\{c \in S | a \leqq c \leqq b\}$ is a *finite* subset of $A)$.

Consequently, an *f*-set necessarily has one of the four forms: finite; $a_0 < a_1 < a_2 < \cdots ; \cdots < a_{-2} < a_{-1} < a_0 ; \cdots < a_{-1} < a_0 < a_1 < \cdots$.

An *i*-set is a nondegenerate subset A of S without extremal points such that $(a \in A, b \in A, a < b) \Rightarrow (\{c \in S | a \leqq c \leqq b\}$ is an *infinite* subset of $A)$.

A *singular* point of S is a point that belongs to no *f*-set and to no *i*-set.

(1)   If A, B are two *f*-sets (resp. *i*-sets) and $A \cap B \neq \varnothing$, then $A \cup B$ is an *f*-set (resp. *i*-set).

$A \cup B$ is nondegenerate and has no extremal point if neither A nor B does. It is, therefore, sufficient to check that if $a \in A \cup B$, $b \in A \cup B$ and $a < b$, then $\{c \in S | a \leqq c \leqq b\}$ is a finite (resp. infinite) subset of $A \cup B$.

Select c in $A \cap B$ and consider a in A and b in B. If $c \leqq a < b$, then $a \in B$ and the proposition is proved. Similarly, the proposition holds if $a < b \leqq c$. Finally, if $a < c < b$, the proposition follows readily too.

(2)   If C is an *f*-set (resp. *i*-set), then there is a maximal *f*-set (resp. *i*-set) containing C.

Take the union of all the *f*-sets (resp. *i*-sets) containing C and apply (1).

Define an *F*-set (resp. *I*-set) as a maximal *f*-set (resp. *i*-set). Define also an *E*-set as an *F*-set or an *I*-set.

(3)   Two distinct *E*-sets are disjoint.

If they are both *F*-sets, or both *I*-sets, the assertion is obvious. If A is an *F*-set and B is an *I*-set, they have at most one point in common. Assume that c is such a common point. A has at least another point a. Now B cannot have points on the same side of c as a. Therefore c is an extremal point of B, a contradiction.

For two subsets A, B of S, the relation $A < B$ means that $(a \in A, b \in B) \Rightarrow (a < b)$.

(4)   If A and B are two distinct E-sets, then $A < B$ or $B < A$.

Assume that for $a \in A$ and $b \in B$ one has $a < b$ and that for $a' \in A$ and $b' \in B$ one has $b' < a'$. Since A and B are disjoint, two cases may occur: (1) $b' < a$, which with $a < b$ implies $a \in B$, a contradiction; or (2) $a < b'$, which with $b' < a'$ implies $b' \in A$, a contradiction.

(5)   If A is an E-set and a is a singular point, then $\{a\} < A$ or $A < \{a\}$.

Assume that for $b \in A$ and $c \in A$ one has $b < a < c$; then $a \in A$, a contradiction.

(6)   If S is nondegenerate, then it contains an E-set.

If there is a pair (a, b) of points in S such that $a < b$ and $\{c \in S | a \le c \le b\}$ is finite, then the latter set is an f-set. By (2) there is an F-set containing it.

If for every pair (a, b) of points in S such that $a < b$ the set $\{c \in S | a \le c \le b\}$ is infinite, then, by removing from S its extremal points if any, one obtains an I-set.   Q.E.D.

Therefore, a nondegenerate S can be partitioned into its E-sets and the (possibly empty) set of its singular points. The case of a degenerate S, for which the theorem is trivially true, will be excluded until the end of this section.

According to (4), if A, B are two distinct E-sets, the open intervals $]\text{Inf } A, \text{Sup } A[$ and $]\text{Inf } B, \text{Sup } B[$ are disjoint. Since the intervals associated with the E-sets in this fashion are nondegenerate, their class is countable (possibly finite), and so is the class of the E-sets. The latter can therefore be arranged in a sequence $E_1, E_2, \ldots$, all of whose elements are understood to be distinct.

(7)   If E_n is an F-set and α_n, β_n are two points of $\bar{R}$ such that $\alpha_n < \beta_n$, then there is an increasing function g_n from E_n to $\bar{R}$ such that all the gaps of $g_n(E_n)$ are open, $\alpha_n = \text{Inf } g_n(E_n)$ and $\beta_n = \text{Sup } g_n(E_n)$.

This is obvious if one recalls the four possible forms of an F-set.

(8)   If E_n is an I-set and α_n, β_n are two points of $\bar{R}$ such that $\alpha_n < \beta_n$, then there is an increasing function g_n from E_n to $\bar{R}$ such that $g_n(E_n)$ has no gap, $\alpha_n = \text{Inf } g_n(E_n)$ and $\beta_n = \text{Sup } g_n(E_n)$.

Let D_n be a countable dense subset of E_n. Following the procedure of [2, (Section 4.6)], one can first define an increasing function from D_n onto the rationals of the open interval $]\alpha_n, \beta_n[$. Then by extending that function from D_n to E_n, one obtains an increasing function g_n from E_n to the open interval $]\alpha_n, \beta_n[$. Since all the rationals of this interval belong to $g_n(E_n)$, the latter set has no gap.   Q.E.D.

The function g from S to $\bar{R}$ is now defined inductively. To this effect, we take for each E_n first a pair (α_n, β_n) of points of $\bar{R}$ such that $\alpha_n < \beta_n$ and then a function g_n satisfying the conditions of (7) if E_n is an F-set, of (8) if E_n is an I-set. Two E-sets are said to be *adjacent* if there is at most one point of S between them.

For E_1, take $\alpha_1 = 0, \beta_1 = 1$.

For E_n, consider the three cases that may arise.

(a) $E_m < E_n$ for every $m < n$. Let E_j be the greatest of these E_m. If E_j and E_n are adjacent, take $\alpha_n = \beta_j$ and $\beta_n = \beta_j + 1$. If E_j and E_n are not adjacent, take $\alpha_n = \beta_j + 1$ and $\beta_n = \beta_j + 2$.

(b) $E_m > E_n$ for every $m < n$. In this case replace in (1) j by k, "greatest" by "least", α by β, β by α and $+$ by $-$.

(c) There are some $E_m < E_n$ with $m < n$; let E_j be the greatest of these. There are also some $E_m > E_n$ with $m < n$; let E_k be the least of these.

If E_j, E_n are adjacent and E_n, E_k are too, take $\alpha_n = \beta_j$ and $\beta_n = \alpha_k$.

If E_j, E_n are adjacent but E_n, E_k are not, take $\alpha_n = \beta_j$ and $\beta_n = (\beta_j + 2\alpha_k)/3$.

If E_n, E_k are adjacent but E_j, E_n are not, take $\alpha_n = (2\beta_j + \alpha_k)/3$ and $\beta_n = \alpha_k$.

If neither E_j, E_n nor E_n, E_k are adjacent, take $\alpha_n = (2\beta_j + \alpha_k)/3$ and $\beta_n = (\beta_j + 2\alpha_k)/3$.

g coincides with g_n on E_n for every n. It remains to define g for the singular points of S. Let a be one of them. If $\{a\} < E_n$ for every n, define $g(a)$ as Inf α_n (which may be $-\infty$). If $E_n < \{a\}$ for every n, define $g(a)$ as Sup β_n (which may be $+\infty$). To dispose of the residual case for which there are E_m and E_n such that $E_m < \{a\} < E_n$, we prove

(9) If the class of the E-sets is partitioned into two nonempty classes $\mathcal{A}$ and $\mathcal{B}$ such that $(E_r \in \mathcal{A}$ and $E_s \in \mathcal{B}) \Rightarrow (E_r < E_s)$, then $\mathrm{Sup}_{E_r \in \mathcal{A}}\, \beta_r = \mathrm{Inf}_{E_s \in \mathcal{B}}\, \alpha_s$.

Given n large enough, let E_{p_n} be the greatest of the E_m in $\mathcal{A}$ such that $m < n$, and let E_{q_n} be the least of the E_m in $\mathcal{B}$ such that $m < n$. If, for some n, E_{p_n} and E_{q_n} are adjacent, then $\beta_{p_n} = \alpha_{q_n}$ and the proposition is proved. If E_{p_n} and E_{q_n} are adjacent for no n, then, for every n, the interval $[\beta_{p_{n+1}}, \alpha_{q_{n+1}}]$, which is contained in the interval $[\beta_{p_n}, \alpha_{q_n}]$, either has the same length or has a length three times smaller. Since the latter must occur for infinitely many n, the proposition is also proved in this situation.   Q.E.D.

Going back to the residual case described before the statement of (9), we define $\mathcal{A}$ as the class of all the $E_r < \{a\}$ and $\mathcal{B}$ as the class of all the $E_s > \{a\}$. These two classes satisfy the conditions of (9). Therefore $\mathrm{Sup}_{E_r < \{a\}}\, \beta_r = \mathrm{Inf}_{\{a\} < E_s}\, \alpha_s$. By definition, $g(a)$ is this common value.

To check that the function g from S to $\bar{R}$ is increasing, consider a and b in S such that $a < b$. If a and b belong to the same E_n, obviously $g(a) < g(b)$. If $a \in E_m$, $b \in E_n$ and E_m, E_n are not adjacent, then it is again clear that $g(a) < g(b)$. If $a \in E_m$, $b \in E_n$ and E_m, E_n are adjacent, then $\beta_m = \alpha_n$; one cannot have $g_m(a) = \beta_m$ and $g_n(b) = \alpha_n$, otherwise E_m would be an F-set finite on the right and E_n would be an F-set finite on the left; consequently, neither E_m nor E_n would be a maximal f-set; thus, $g(a) < g(b)$ in this case too. If a is singular, $b \in E_n$, and there is an E_m between $\{a\}$ and E_n, then clearly $g(a) < g(b)$. If a is singular, $b \in E_n$, and there is no E_m between $\{a\}$ and E_n, then $g(a) = \alpha_n$; one cannot have $g_n(b) = \alpha_n$, otherwise E_n would be an F-set finite on the left; consequently a would not be singular and E_n would not be a maximal f-set; thus, $g(a) < g(b)$. If b is singular and $a \in E_n$, the last two sentences are altered in an obvious way. Finally, if a and b are singular, there must be an E_n between them; therefore, $g(a) < g(b)$.

The last step in the proof consists in checking that all the gaps of $g(S)$ are open. Let then G be a gap of $g(S)$. We will prove by contradiction that G is a gap of some $g(E_n)$. Assume that such is not the case, and let $\mathcal{A}$ be the class of all the E_r such that $\beta_r \leq \mathrm{Inf}\, G$, let $\mathcal{B}$ be the class of all the E_s such that $\mathrm{Sup}\, G \leq \alpha_s$. Since $\mathcal{A}$ and $\mathcal{B}$ exhaust the class of the E-sets, and since $\mathrm{Inf}\, G < \mathrm{Sup}\, G$, it follows from (9) that either $\mathcal{A}$ or $\mathcal{B}$ is empty. If $\mathcal{A}$ is empty, there is exactly one point of $g(S)$ that is $\leq \mathrm{Inf}\, G$. This point must be $\mathrm{Inf}\, G$ and be the image of a singular point a. Thus $g(a) < \mathrm{Sup}\, G$, while $\mathrm{Sup}\, G \leq \mathrm{Inf}_{E_s \in \mathcal{B}}\, \alpha_s$. As $\mathcal{B}$ is the class of all the E_n, the inequality $g(a) < \mathrm{Inf}_{E_s \in \mathcal{B}}\, \alpha_s$ contradicts the definition of $g(a)$. If $\mathcal{B}$ is empty, one obtains a contradiction in the same way. Therefore, G is a gap of some $g(E_n)$. However, if E_n is an I-set, $g(E_n)$ has no gap; if E_n is an F-set, all the gaps of $g(E_n)$ are open.

3   Continuity properties of the representation

The reasoning of Lemma I of [1] can now be repeated. Consider a *pre-ordered* set X, i.e., a set X and a reflexive, transitive binary relation on X denoted $\leqslant$. For two elements y and z of X, we define "$y \prec z$" as "$y \leqslant z$ and not $z \leqslant y$." For two subsets Y and Z of X, we define "$Y \prec Z$" as "$y \prec z$ for every y in Y and z in Z." The *upper* (resp. *lower*) *preorder topology* on X is the weakest topology for which the set $\{x \in X | x \geqslant y\}$ (resp. $\{x \in X | x \leqslant y\}$) is closed for every y in X. The set X is said to be *completely preordered* by $\leqslant$ if $[y \in X \text{ and } z \in X] \Rightarrow [y \leqslant z \text{ and/or } z \leqslant y]$.

Corollary

Let X be a completely preordered set. If there is an increasing function v from X to $\bar{R}$, then there is an increasing function u from X to $\bar{R}$ that is upper semicontinuous in the upper preorder topology and lower semicontinuous in the lower preorder topology.

Proof. Apply the theorem to the subset $v(X)$ of $\bar{R}$. There is an increasing function g from $v(X)$ to $\bar{R}$ such that all the gaps of $g(v(X))$ are open. Define u by $u(x) = g(v(x))$. Thus u is an increasing function from X to $\bar{R}$ and all the gaps of $u(X)$ are open.
   We will only consider the upper preorder topology on X and establish the upper semicontinuity of u by proving that, for every γ in $\bar{R}$, the inverse image $u^{-1}([\gamma, +\infty])$ is closed. A similar proof can be given for lower semicontinuity in the lower preorder topology.
   If $\gamma \in u(X)$, i.e, if there is y in X such that $u(y) = \gamma$, then $u^{-1}([\gamma, +\infty]) = \{x \in X | x \geqslant y\}$, a closed set.
   If $\gamma \notin u(X)$ and γ is not in a gap of $u(X)$, either $\gamma \leqq \operatorname{Inf} u(X)$, in which case $u^{-1}([\gamma, +\infty]) = X$, a closed set; or $\operatorname{Sup} u(X) \leqq \gamma$, in which case $u^{-1}([\gamma, +\infty]) = \varnothing$, a closed set; or $[\gamma, +\infty] = \bigcap_{\alpha \in u(X), \alpha \leqq \gamma} [\alpha, +\infty]$, in which case $u^{-1}([\gamma, +\infty]) = \bigcap_{\alpha \in u(X), \alpha \leqq \gamma} u^{-1}([\alpha, +\infty])$, a closed set since it is an intersection of closed sets.
   If γ is in a gap of $u(X)$, this gap is an open interval $]\lambda, \mu[$, where λ and μ belong to $u(X)$. Therefore $u^{-1}([\gamma, +\infty]) = u^{-1}([\mu, +\infty])$, a closed set.   Q.E.D.

Proposition 1

Let X be a completely preordered topological space having a countable base of open sets. If the set $\{x \in X | x \succcurlyeq y\}$ is closed for every y in X, then there is an upper semicontinuous, increasing function u from X to $\bar{R}$. (Rader [5]).

Proof. We first construct an increasing function v from X to $\bar{R}$ following Rader. Let $O_1, O_2, \ldots$ be the open sets in the countable base. Given an element x of X, define

$$N(x) = \{n | O_n \prec \{x\}\} \quad \text{and} \quad v(x) = \sum_{n \in N(x)} \frac{1}{2^n},$$

adopting the convention that a sum over an empty set of indices is 0.

If $y \preccurlyeq z$, then $N(y)$ is a subset of $N(z)$ and $v(y) \leqq v(z)$. Thus v is nondecreasing. It is actually increasing, for if $y \prec z$, then y belongs to the open set $\{x \in X | x \prec z\}$. Consequently, for some n, one has $y \in O_n \prec \{z\}$. For that n, one does not have $O_n \prec \{y\}$; therefore $N(y)$ is a proper subset of $N(z)$ and $v(y) < v(z)$.

We now apply the corollary and obtain an increasing function u from X to $\bar{R}$ upper semicontinuous in the *upper preorder topology*. Since the given topology on X is stronger than or equal to the upper preorder topology, the proof is completed.

Proposition 2

Proposition 2 is derived from Proposition 1 by substituting $\preccurlyeq$ for $\succcurlyeq$ and "lower" for "upper", and does not require a new proof.

Theorem II of [1] states

Proposition 3

Let X be a completely preordered topological space having a countable base of open sets. If the sets $\{x \in X | x \succcurlyeq y\}$ and $\{x \in X | x \preccurlyeq y\}$ are closed for every y in X, then there is a continuous, increasing function u from X to $\bar{R}$.

Proof. According to Proposition 1, there is an increasing function v from X to $\bar{R}$. Therefore, according to the Corollary, there is an increasing function u from X to $\bar{R}$ upper semicontinuous in the upper preorder topology and lower semicontinuous in the lower preorder topology. Since the given topology on X is stronger than or equal to both these topologies, u is both upper and lower semicontinuous in the given topology.   Q.E.D.

As another consequence of the corollary we prove

Proposition 4

Let X be a completely preordered, connected, separable topological space. If the sets $\{x \in X | x \succcurlyeq y\}$ and $\{x \in X | x \preccurlyeq y\}$ are closed for every y in X, then there is a continuous, increasing function u from X to $\bar{R}$. (Eilenberg [3]).

Proof. Let $Z = \{z_1, z_2, \ldots\}$ be a countable dense subset of X. Consider y and y' in X such that $y \prec y'$. The two sets $\{x \in X | x \preccurlyeq y\}$ and $\{x \in X | y' \preccurlyeq x\}$ are closed, nonempty, and disjoint. Therefore, they do not exhaust X, which is connected. Since the open set $\{x \in X | y \prec x \prec y'\}$ is not empty, it owns some z_n in Z. We now construct an increasing function v from X to $\bar{R}$, following Milgram [4, (26–27)]. Given an element x of X, define

$$N(x) = \{n | z_n \prec x\} \quad \text{and} \quad v(x) = \sum_{n \in N(x)} \frac{1}{2^n}.$$

If $y \preccurlyeq y'$, then $N(y)$ is a subset of $N(y')$ and $v(y) \leq v(y')$. Thus v is nondecreasing. It is actually increasing, for if $y \prec y'$, then for some n, one has $y \prec z_n \prec y'$. Therefore $N(y)$ is a proper subset of $N(y')$ and $v(y) < v(y')$.

Applying the Corollary, one obtains, as in the proof of Proposition 3, a continuous increasing function u from X to $\bar{R}$.   Q.E.D.

Finally, we give a proposition that, in conjunction with the Corollary, slightly strengthens Lemma II of [1].

Proposition 5

Let X be a completely preordered set having a countable subset Z such that if x and y in X satisfy $x \prec y$, then there is z in Z satisfying $x \preccurlyeq z \preccurlyeq y$. Then there is an increasing function v from X to $\bar{R}$.

Proof. Let A be the set of the indifference classes of X, and let C be the set of the indifference classes of X having an element in Z.

The set A is completely ordered by the relation $\leqq$ induced by $\leqslant$, and it has a countable subset C playing for A the role that Z played for X. We now consider the pairs (b, b') of elements of A such that $b \prec b'$ and there is no a in A satisfying $b \prec a \prec b'$. Thus, b and/or b' must be in C. Consequently, these pairs form a countable class, since at most two of them have a given element of C as a component. We add the components of the pairs in that countable class to C and obtain a new countable set $C^* = \{c_1, c_2, \ldots\}$. Given an element x of X, we denote the indifference class of x by $a(x)$ and define, as in the proof of Proposition 4,

$$N(x) = \{n | c_n \prec a(x)\} \quad \text{and} \quad v(x) = \sum_{n \in N(x)} \frac{1}{2^n}.$$

4   An example

In this section, S denotes a bounded subset of the real line. Given a point x of S, let $f(x)$ be the sum of the lengths of the non-open gaps G of S such that Sup $G \leqq x$. The function g of the theorem could be given the specific form $g(x) = x - f(x)$ only if $[x \in S, x' \in S, x < x']$ implied $[f(x') - f(x) < x' - x]$. To prove that g cannot be so restricted it suffices to exhibit a subset S of $[0, 1]$ such that 0 and 1 belong to S, S has no open gap, and the sum of the lengths of the gaps of S is one. In other words, S should be such that $S \subset [0, 1]; 0 \in S; 1 \in S; [a \in S, b \in S, a < b] \Rightarrow$ [there is c in S satisfying $a < c < b$]; the measure of the closure of S is zero. The following set having all these properties has been communicated to me by David A. Freedman. The ternary number system is used. S is made up of 0, 1 and all the reals between 0 and 1 having ternary expansions 0. $p_1 p_2 \cdots$ where (i) for all n, $p_n \neq 1$, (ii) for infinitely many n, $p_n = 0$, (iii) for infinitely many n, $p_n = 2$. It is clear that $[a \in S, b \in S, a < b] \Rightarrow$ [there is c in S satisfying $a < c < b$] and that S is contained in the triadic set C of Cantor which is made up of all the reals in $[0, 1]$ whose ternary expansions satisfy (i). However C is closed and has measure zero.

References

[1] Debreu, G., Representation of a Preference Ordering by a Numerical Function, *Decision Processes*, ed. R. M. Thrall, C. H. Coombs, and R. L. Davis (New York: Wiley, 1954), 159–65.
[2] Debreu, G., *Theory of Value*, (New York: Wiley, 1959).
[3] Eilenberg, S., Ordered Topological Spaces, *American Journal of Mathematics*, LXIII (Part 1, 1941), 39–45.

[4] Milgram, A. N., Partially Ordered Sets, Separating Systems and Inductiveness, *Reports of a Mathematical Colloquium*, Second Series, 1 (University of Notre Dame, 1939), 18–30.

[5] Rader, J. T., The Existence of a Utility Function to Represent Preferences, *The Review of Economic Studies*, XXX (1963), 229–32.

CHAPTER 13

Neighboring economic agents[1]

The intuitive concept of similar economic agents lends itself to a natural mathematical formalization which will be introduced by means of the example of an exchange economy $\mathscr{E}$. The commodity space S of $\mathscr{E}$ is assumed to be a normed real vector space. An agent of $\mathscr{E}$ is characterized by his resources, his needs, and his preferences, three concepts which are given the following precise definitions. His resources are described by a point ω of S; his needs by a non-empty subset X of S; his preferences by a reflexive binary relation $\leqslant$ on X such that $P = \{(x, y) \in X \times X | x \leqslant y\}$ is closed. The characteristic properties of the preference set P are: (1) P is a non-empty closed subset of $T = S_1 \times S_2$, where $S_1 = S_2 = S$, and (2) $x \in \text{proj}_{S_i} P(i = 1 \text{ or } 2)$ implies $(x, x) \in P$. Thus an agent a of $\mathscr{E}$ is defined as a pair $(\omega, P) \in S \times \mathscr{P}$, where $\mathscr{P}$ denotes the set of the subsets P of T satisfying conditions (1) and (2). The set $S \times \mathscr{P}$ of agents will be denoted by A.

Since the concept of two neighboring points ω, ω' of S is clear, to define the concept of two neighboring agents, a, a' of A it suffices to make precise the notion of two neighboring preference sets P, P' of $\mathscr{P}$. Y. Kannai [4] has considered the case in which S is the Euclidean space R^l, the needs of every agent are described by the closed positive orthant Ω of R^l and his preferences by a complete, transitive, reflexive binary relation $\leqslant$ on Ω satisfying the condition $\{(x, y) \in \Omega \times \Omega | x \leqslant y\}$ is closed. Y. Kannai then endows the set Ξ of preference relations on Ω with the weakest topology making the set $\{(x, y, \leqslant) \in \Omega \times \Omega \times \Xi | x \leqslant y\}$ closed. Here we need a stronger structure and endow $\mathscr{P}$ with the Hausdorff distance ([3],

[1] I thank the National Science Foundation for its support of my work. I am also grateful to W. Hildenbrand, E. Malinvaud, and R. Radner for the valuable conversations I had with them.

pp. 166–168). Let t be a metric on the set T. For a point y of T and a non-empty subset Z of T, one defines $\tau^0(y, Z) = \inf_{z \in Z} t(y, z)$. For two non-empty subsets Y and Z of T, one defines $\tau^1(Y, Z) = \sup_{y \in Y} \tau^0(y, Z)$, and $\tau(Y, Z) = \text{Max}\{\tau^1(Y, Z), \tau^1(Z, Y)\}$. On the set of the non-empty closed subsets of T, τ has all the properties of a metric but that of being always finite. Now a metric t can be defined on T $= S_1 \times S_2$ in several ways which are equivalent for our purpose, for instance $t[(x, y), (x', y')] = |x' - x| + |y' - y|$. It seems natural to say, in an imprecise manner, that two preference sets P, P' are neighboring if their Hausdorff distance $\tau(P, P')$ is small. Therefore we define a distance α on the set A of the agents of $\mathscr{E}$ by $\alpha[(\omega, P), (\omega', P')] = |\omega' - \omega| + \tau(P, P')$. The Borel σ-field of A, generated by the open sets of A, is denoted by $\mathscr{A}$. To complete the description of the economy $\mathscr{E}$ there would only remain to introduce a positive real measure ν on $\mathscr{A}$, where for every $C \in \mathscr{A}$, $\nu(C)$ is interpreted as the fraction of the totality of agents in the set C.

Given an agent a in A, we now denote his resources by $\omega(a)$, his preference set by $P(a)$, his consumption set by $X(a)$, and his preference relation by $\leqslant_a$. We will need two basic properties of the relation $\leqslant$ and of the correspondence X.

(1) $\{(a, x, y) \in A \times S \times S \,|\, x \leqslant_a y\}$ is closed.

Proof.   This set is also

$$\{(a, x, y) \in A \times S \times S \,|\, (x, y) \in P(a)\} =$$
$$\{(a, x, y) \in A \times S \times S \,|\, \tau^0[(x, y), P(a)] = 0\}.$$

However, P is a continuous function from A to $\mathscr{P}$ and τ^0 is a continuous function from (S $\times$ S) $\times \mathscr{P}$ to R.   Q.E.D.

Before formulating the second property we recall several definitions about a correspondence φ from a set E to a set F. Given a subset Y of F,

$$\varphi^w(Y) = \{e \in E \,|\, \varphi(e) \cap Y \neq \varnothing\} \quad \text{and} \quad \varphi^s(Y) = \{e \in E \,|\, \varphi(e) \subset Y\}.$$

The *graph* of φ is $G(\varphi) = \{(e, f) \in E \times F \,|\, f \in \varphi(e)\}$.

Consider now a topological space E and a space F with a metric d and denote by δ^1 and δ the Hausdorff hemidistance and the Hausdorff distance on the set of the non-empty subsets of F derived from d as τ^1 and τ were derived from t above. Let φ be a correspondence from E to F and let e_0 be a point of E. The correspondence φ is *lower hemi-continuous at e_0* if for every real $\varepsilon > 0$, there is a neighborhood U of e_0 such that $e \in$ U implies $\delta^1[\varphi(e_0), \varphi(e)] < \varepsilon$; the correspondence φ is *upper hemi-continuous at e_0* if for every real $\varepsilon > 0$, there is a neighborhood U of e_0 such that $e \in$ U implies $\delta^1[\varphi(e), \varphi(e_0)] < \varepsilon$; the correspondence φ is *continuous at e_0* if it is lower hemi-continuous and upper hemi-continuous at e_0. It is immediately seen that if φ is lower hemi-continuous on E, then for every open set Y in F, the set $\varphi^w(Y)$ is open and that if for every open set Y in F, the set $\varphi^s(Y)$ is open, then φ is upper hemi-continuous on E. For a *closed-valued* φ if φ is upper hemi-continuous, then $G(\varphi)$ is closed. For a *compact-valued* φ, if for every open set Y in F, the set $\varphi^w(Y)$ is open, then φ is lower hemi-continuous on E and if φ is upper hemi-continuous on E, then for every open set Y in F, $\varphi^s(Y)$ is open.

Finally, let E be a set, $\mathscr{C}$ be a σ-field of subsets of E, F be a topological space. A compact-valued correspondence φ from E to F is *measurable* if for every open set Y in F, $\varphi^s(Y)$ belongs to $\mathscr{C}$.

(2) The correspondence X from A to S is continuous.

Proof. Let σ be the Hausdorff distance defined on the set of the non-empty closed subsets of S. Clearly $\sigma[X(a), X(a')] \leqq \tau(P(a), P(a')) \leqq \alpha(a, a')$.   Q.E.D.

Let now v be a value function on S, i.e., a continuous linear form on S, and, given a point x of S denote by $v \cdot x$ the image of x by v. The dual S' of S is endowed with the usual norm $|v| = \sup_{|x| \leqq 1} |v \cdot x|$. Once v is given, the agent a is restricted to choose his consumption-vector in the set

$$\gamma(a, v) = \{x \in X(a) | v \cdot x \leqq v \cdot \omega(a)\}.$$

We now give a straightforward generalization of a standard result about the continuity of the correspondence γ.

(3) If B is a subset of $A \times S'$ such that for every $(a, v) \in B$, $\gamma(a, v)$ is compact, convex and $\text{Inf } v \cdot X(a) < v \cdot \omega(a)$, then the correspondence γ from B to S has a closed graph and is lower hemi-continuous.

Proof. In B, $\gamma(a, v)$ is clearly non-empty.

Let $\beta(a, v) = \{x \in S | v \cdot x \leqq v \cdot \omega(a)\}$. From the continuity of ω on A and the continuity of the function: $(x, v) \to v \cdot x$ on $S \times S'$ follows immediately that the graph of the correspondence β from B to S is closed. Since $G(\gamma) = G(\beta) \cap G(X)$ and $G(X)$ is closed in $B \times S$, the graph of γ is closed.

To prove that the correspondence γ is lower hemi-continuous on B, consider an open subset Y of S and a point (a_0, v_0) of B in $\gamma^w(Y)$, i.e., such that $\gamma(a_0, v_0) \cap Y \neq \varnothing$. We want to show that (a_0, v_0) is interior to $\gamma^w(Y)$ relative to B. There is $x_1 \in X(a_0) \cap Y$

such that $v_0 \cdot x_1 \leqq v \cdot \omega(a_0)$. However, there is also $x_2 \in X(a_0)$ such that

$$v_0 \cdot x_2 < v_0 \cdot \omega(a_0).$$

Since $\gamma(a_0, v_0)$ is convex and Y is open, there is x_0 on the segment $[x_1, x_2]$ such that $x_0 \in X(a_0) \cap Y$ and $v_0 \cdot x_0 < v_0 \cdot \omega(a_0)$. Therefore, there are open neighborhoods U' of a_0 in A, V of v_0 in S' and W' of x_0 in S such that $[a \in U', v \in V, x \in W']$ implies $[v \cdot x < v \cdot \omega(a)]$. Let $W = W' \cap Y$. By lower hemi-continuity of the correspondence X on A, since $X(a_0) \cap W \neq \emptyset$, there is a neighborhood U'' of a_0 in A such that $a \in U''$ implies $X(a) \cap W \neq \emptyset$. Let $U = U' \cap U''$. For every $(a, v) \in (U \times V) \cap B$, one has $\gamma(a, v) \cap W \neq \emptyset$.   Q.E.D.

Remark: If the dimension of S is finite, a straightforward compactness argument shows that under the assumptions of (3), the correspondence γ from B to S is continuous.

The agent a who can choose any consumption-vector in $\gamma(a, v)$, will actually choose an element of $\gamma(a, v)$ that is maximal for $\leqslant_a$, i.e., an element of

$$\gamma^0(a, v) = \{x \in \gamma(a, v) | x <_a y \text{ for no } y \text{ in } \gamma(a, v)\}.$$

Since given v, one wishes to integrate the correspondence $\gamma^0(. , v)$ on a subset Â of A, one is led to ask

(I)   given v, under what conditions is the correspondence $\gamma^0(. , v)$ measurable?

And since one wishes the integral $\int_{\hat{A}} \gamma^0(a, v) dv(a)$ to be an upper hemi-continuous correspondence on a subset of S, one is led to ask

(II)   given a, under what conditions is the correspondence $\gamma^0(a, .)$ upper hemi-continuous?

When A is an abstract measure space these two questions must be answered by different techniques. In particular, for the first appeal has to be made to the possibility of choosing a measurable function from A to S whose graph is contained in the graph of a measurable correspondence from A to S. When A is endowed with a distance, both questions are simultaneously answered by the following result, particular cases of which have been repeatedly used in the theory of economic equilibrium and in game theory.

(4) Let M be a topological space, H be a metric space, φ be a compact-valued continuous correspondence from M to H, and for every $e \in M$, $\preccurlyeq_e$ be a complete preordering on $\varphi(e)$ such that

$$\{(e, x, y) \in M \times H \times H | x \preccurlyeq_e y\}$$

is closed. If $\varphi^0(e)$ is the set of greatest elements of $\varphi(e)$ for $\preccurlyeq_e$, then the correspondence φ^0 from M to H is compact-valued and upper hemi-continuous,

Proof. Given $e \in M$, for every $x \in \varphi(e)$, the set $\{y \in \varphi(e) | x \preccurlyeq_e y\}$ *is* compact, non-empty. Since these sets are nested, their intersection $\varphi^0(e)$ is non-empty and compact.

For every $e \in M$, $\varphi^0(e) \subset \varphi(e)$. Moreover, φ is an upper hemi-continuous compact-valued correspondence. Therefore, by [1], p. 117, theorem 7, it suffices to prove that the graph $G(\varphi^0)$ of φ^0 is closed. Consider a point (e_0, y_0) of $M \times H$ adherent to $G(\varphi^0)$. This point is also adherent to $G(\varphi)$, which is closed by [1], p. 117, theorem 6. Hence $y_0 \in \varphi(e_0)$.

There remains to establish that y_0 is a greatest element of $\varphi(e_0)$ for $\preccurlyeq_{e_0}$. Consider an arbitrary point $x_0 \in \varphi(e_0)$, and arbitrary open neighborhoods V of x_0 and W of y_0 in H. By lower hemi-continuity of φ, since $V \cap \varphi(e_0) \neq \varnothing$, there is a neighborhood U of e_0 in M such that $e \in U$ implies $V \cap \varphi(e) \neq \varnothing$. The neighborhood $U \times W$ of (e_0, y_0) intersects $G(\varphi^0)$. Let (e, y) be a point in $(U \times W) \cap G(\varphi^0)$. The element y is greatest in $\varphi(e)$ for $\preccurlyeq_e$. Therefore for every $x \in V \cap \varphi(e)$, one has $x \preccurlyeq_e y$. In conclusion (e_0, x_0, y_0) is adherent to $\{(e, x, y) \in M \times H \times H | x \preccurlyeq_e y\}$ which is closed. Hence $x_0 \preccurlyeq_{e_0} y_0$.   Q.E.D.

Let then $\hat{A}$ be a subset of A and B be a subset of S' such that γ is a compact valued continuous correspondence on $\hat{A} \times B$ and assume that for every $a \in \hat{A}$, $\preccurlyeq_a$ is a complete preordering. By propositions (1) and (4), the correspondence γ^0 from $\hat{A} \times B$ to S is upper hemi-continuous. Therefore given a, $\gamma^0(a, .)$ is upper hemi-continuous on B, which answers question (II), and, given v, $\gamma^0(., v)$ is upper hemi-continuous on $\hat{A}$, hence $\mathscr{A}$-measurable, which answers question (I). Aside from the simplification that it permits, the use of the distance α on A enables one to establish the measurability of $\gamma^0(. , v)$ without making on S assumptions of separability (or even of metrizability as we will emphasize at the end of this paper), a result that has not been possible to obtain so far with the abstract measure space approach. Still another reason for introducing the distance α on A is that it allows one to dispense with measurability assumptions on ω, on X, and on $\preccurlyeq$.

The preceding discussion has been carried out in terms of spaces endowed with a distance. This framework, which was chosen because of its conceptual simplicity, is not entirely satisfactory. The assumption that S has a metric is unnecessarily restrictive and the various distances that we have considered are to some extent arbitrary. Indeed, given a distance d on a set E, the concept of interest in this paper is the class of subsets of $E \times E$ containing sets of the form $\{(x, y) \in E \times E \mid d(x, y) \leq \varepsilon\}$ where ε is strictly positive. In other words, the proper concept for the present analysis is that of a uniform structure (N. Bourbaki [2], Chap. 2). Now given a uniform structure on a set E, one can define a uniform structure on the set of subsets of E (N. Bourbaki [2], Ex. 5, p. 227) which coincides with the uniform structure generated by the Hausdorff distance in the case of a metric space E. The principle which was applied earlier to the case of an exchange economy is therefore very general. In an economy where an agent can be characterized by a family of points or of subsets of a family of uniform spaces, a natural uniform structure can be defined on the set of agents.

References

[1] Berge, C. *Espaces Topologiques*, 2d ed., Paris, Dunod, 1966.
[2] Bourbaki, N. *Eléments de Mathématique, Topologie Générale*, Chaps. 1–2, 4th ed., Paris, Hermann, 1965.
[3] Hausdorff, F. *Set Theory*, New York, Chelsea, 1962.
[4] Kannai, Y. *Continuity Properties of the Core of a Market*, hectographed, Department of Mathematics, The Hebrew University of Jerusalem, July 1964.

CHAPTER 14

Economies with a finite set of equilibria[1]

A mathematical model which attempts to explain economic equilibrium must have a nonempty set of solutions. One would also wish the solution to be unique. This uniqueness property, however, has been obtained only under strong assumptions,[2] and, as we will emphasize below, economies with multiple equilibria must be allowed for. Such economies still seem to provide a satisfactory explanation of equilibrium as well as a satisfactory foundation for the study of stability provided that all the equilibria of the economy are locally unique. But if the set of equilibria is compact (a common situation), local uniqueness is equivalent to finiteness. One is thus led to investigate conditions under which an economy has a finite set of equilibria.

Now nonpathological examples of economies with infinitely many equilibria can easily be constructed in the case of pure exchange of two commodities between two consumers. Therefore one can at best prove that outside a small subset of the space of economies, every economy has a finite set of equilibria. For the precise definition of "small" in this context, one

[1] This paper was presented as the Irving Fisher lecture at the Brussels meeting of the Econometric Society, September 1969.

My work was done partly at the University of California, Berkeley, under a research grant of the National Science Foundation, partly while I was visiting the Center for Operations Research and Econometrics of the Catholic University of Louvain as a Guggenheim Fellow, and partly while I was an Erskine Fellow at the University of Canterbury. The support of all these institutions is gratefully acknowledged.

I also wish to thank Y. Kannai, S. Smale, and R. Thom for the extremely valuable conversations I had with them.

[2] An excellent survey of the work done on this uniqueness problem will be found in K. J. Arrow and F. H. Hahn [2, Chapter 9].

179

might think of "null" with respect to an appropriate measure on the space of economies. Such a null set, however, could be dense in the space and a stricter definition is required. Our main result asserts that, under assumptions we will shortly make explicit, outside a null closed subset of the space of economies, every economy has a finite set of equilibria.

The key mathematical tool in the proof is Sard's theorem [**12, 1**, pp. 37–41, **13**, pp. 45–55], which we now state. Let U be an open subset of R^a and let F be a continuously differentiable function from U to R^b. A point $x \in U$ is *a critical point of* F if the Jacobian matrix of F at x has a rank smaller than b. A point $y \in R^b$ is *a critical value of* F if there is a critical point $x \in U$ with $y = F(x)$. A point of R^b is *a regular value of* F if it is not a critical value.

Sard's theorem

If all the partial derivatives of F to the cth order included, where $c > \max(0, a - b)$, exist and are continuous, then the set of critical values of F has Lebesgue measure zero in R^b.

The economies we consider are pure exchange economies with l commodities and m consumers whose needs and preferences are fixed and whose resources vary. Let L be the set of strictly positive real numbers, P be the set of strictly positive vectors in R^l (i.e., the set of vectors in R^l having all their components strictly positive), and S be the set of vectors in P for which the sum of the components is unity. It is convenient to specify the preferences of the ith consumer by means of his *demand function* f_i, a function from $S \times L$ to $\bar{P}$ such that for every $(p, w_i) \in S \times L$, one has $p \cdot f_i(p, w_i) = w_i$, where the dot denotes inner product in R^l. Given the price vector p in S and his wealth w_i in L, the ith consumer demands the commodity vector $f_i(p, w_i)$ in the closed positive cone $\bar{P}$ of R^l. Having chosen a norm in R^l, we introduce an assumption which will be made for some consumer in the theorem, for every consumer in the proposition:

> *Assumption* (A): If the sequence (p^q, w_i^q) in $S \times L$ converges to (p^0, w_i^0) in $(\bar{S} \backslash S) \times L$, then $|f_i(p^q, w_i^q)|$ converges to $+\infty$.

Assumption (A) expresses the idea that every commodity is desired by the ith consumer.

An *economy* is defined by $(f_1, \ldots, f_m, \omega_1, \ldots, \omega_m)$ an m-tuple of demand functions, and an m-tuple $\omega = (\omega_1, \ldots, \omega_m)$ of vectors in P. Since the demand functions remain fixed, an economy is actually defined by $\omega \in P^m$.

Given $\omega \in P^m$, an element p of S is an *equilibrium price vector* of the economy ω if

$$\sum_{i=1}^{m} f_i(p, p \cdot \omega_i) \stackrel{.}{=} \sum_{i=1}^{m} \omega_i.$$

We denote by $W(\omega)$ the set of p satisfying this equality.

Finally, we say that subset of R^{lm} is *null* if it has Lebesgue measure zero in R^{lm}.

Theorem: Given m continuously differentiable demand functions $(f_1, \ldots, f_m)$, if some f_i satisfies (A), then the set of $\omega \in P^m$ for which $W(\omega)$ is inifinite has a null closure.

Proof: We assume, without loss of generality, that the first consumer satisfies (A). Let $U = S \times L \times P^{m-1}$, an open set in R^{lm}. We define the function F from U to R^{lm} by associating with the generic element $e = (p, w_1, \omega_2, \ldots, \omega_m)$ of U the value $F(e) = (\omega_1, \omega_2, \ldots, \omega_m)$ where

$$\omega_1 = f_1(p, w_1) + \sum_{i=2}^{m} f_i(p, p \cdot \omega_i) - \sum_{i=2}^{m} \omega_i.$$

We immediately notice that for every $e \in U$, one has $p \cdot \omega_1 = w_1$. We also notice that, given $\omega \in P^m$, the price vector p belongs to $W(\omega)$ if and only if $F(p, p \cdot \omega_1, \omega_2, \ldots, \omega_m) = \omega$ and that the points of $W(\omega)$ are in one-to-one correspondence with the points of $F^{-1}(\omega)$.

Since F is continuously differentiable, by Sard's theorem,

(1) the set C of critical values of F is null.

We now want to prove that $C \cap P^m$ is closed relative to P^m. To this end, we first establish that, although the function F may not be proper [**13**, p. 43], it has the closely related property:

(2) if K is a compact subset of P^m, then $F^{-1}(K)$ is compact.

Consider a sequence with generic term $e^q = (p^q, w_1^q, \omega_2^q, \ldots, \omega_m^q)$ in $F^{-1}(K)$. We must show that it has a subsequence converging to a point of $F^{-1}(K)$. Let $\omega^q = F(e^q)$ and form the sequence $s^q = (p^q, w_1^q, \omega^q)$. As we noticed earlier, for every q, $p^q \cdot \omega_1^q = w_1^q$. Since ω^q belongs to K, w_1^q is bounded and s^q has a subsequence $\dot{s}^q$ converging to $(p^0, w_1^0, \omega^0) \in \bar{S} \times \bar{L} \times K$. We claim that $p^0 \in S$ and $w_1^0 \in L$. The second relation is a consequence of the equality

$p^0 \cdot \omega_1^0 = w_1^0$ obtained in the limit and of the fact that $p^0 \in \bar{S}$ and $\omega_1^0 \in P$. As for the first relation, assume that $p^0 \in \bar{S} \setminus S$. By (A), $|f_1(\dot{p}^q, \dot{w}_1^q)|$ would tend to $+\infty$, a contradiction of the fact that for every q, $f_1(p^q, w_1^q) \leq \sum_{i=1}^{m} \omega_i^q$ where the right-hand side is bounded. Summing up, $\dot{e}^q$ converges to $e^0 = (p^0, w_1^0, \omega_2^0, \ldots, \omega_m^0)$ which belongs to U. By continuity of F, one has $F(e^0) = \omega^0$. Therefore $e^0 \in F^{-1}(K)$.

Assertion (2) readily implies

(3) if E contained in U is closed relative to U, then $F(E) \cap P^m$ is closed relative to P^m.

Consider a sequence with genetic term ω^q in $F(E) \cap P^m$ converging to ω^0 in P^m. The set K consisting of all the ω^q and ω^0 is a compact subset of P^m. For every q, select $e^q \in E$ such that $F(e^q) = \omega^q$. The element e^q belongs to $F^{-1}(K)$ which is compact by (2). Therefore there is a subsequence $\{\dot{e}^q\}$ of $\{e^q\}$ converging to $e^0 \in F^{-1}(K)$. Since every $\dot{e}^q$ belongs to E which is closed relative to U, e^0 belongs to E. By continuity of F, $\omega^0 = F(e^0)$. Thus $\omega^0 \in F(E) \cap P^m$.

As a corollary of (3) we obtain

(4) $C \cap P^m$ is closed relative to P^m.

A critical point of F is a point of U at which the Jacobian of F vanishes. Since the Jacobian of F at e is a continuous function of e, the set E of critical points of F is closed relative to U. However, $C = F(E)$.

To complete the proof of the theorem, we remark (see for instance [10, p. 8])

(5) if $\omega \in P^m$ is a regular value of F, then $F^{-1}(\omega)$ is finite.

Notice first that by (2), $F^{-1}(\omega)$ is compact. Consider an element e of $F^{-1}(\omega)$. At e the Jacobian of F does not vanish. Therefore by the inverse function theorem [7, pp. 268–269], there are open neighborhoods U_e of e and V_e of ω homeomorphic under the restriction of F to U_e. In particular e is the only element of $F^{-1}(\omega)$ in U_e. Since $F^{-1}(\omega)$ can be covered by a finite set of open neighborhoods U_e, $F^{-1}(\omega)$ is finite.

In conclusion, if $\omega \in P^m$ is such that $W(\omega)$ is infinite, then $\omega \in C$. By (1), $C \cap P^m$ is null. By (4), so is its closure.   Q.E.D.

We add a remark to the preceding proof which describes how the set $W(\omega)$ depends on ω.

Remark: Under the assumptions of the theorem, if $\omega^0 \in P^m$ is a regular value of F, there are an open neighborhood V of ω^0 and k continuously differentiable functions $g_1, \ldots, g_k$ from V to S such that for every ω in V, the set $W(\omega)$ consists of the k distinct elements $g_1(\omega), \ldots, g_k(\omega)$.

Proof: The proof is a variant of the reasoning of [10, p. 8]. Let $e_1, \ldots, e_k$ be the elements of $F^{-1}(\omega^0)$. They have pairwise disjoint open neighborhoods $U_1, \ldots, U_k$ homeomorphic, under the restrictions $\gamma_1, \ldots, \gamma_k$ of F to these neighborhoods, to open neighborhoods $V_1, \ldots, V_k$ of ω^0 contained in P^m. Consider $V = \bigcap_{i=1}^k V_i \backslash F(U \backslash \bigcup_{i=1}^k U_i)$.

Since $U \backslash \bigcup_{i=1}^k U_i$ is closed relative to U, the intersection of its image by F and P^m is closed relative P^m by (3). Since ω^0 does not belong to that image, V is indeed an open neighborhood of ω^0. Let g_j' be the restriction to V of γ_j^{-1}. For every $\omega \in V$, the set $F^{-1}(\omega)$ consists of the k distinct elements $g_1'(\omega), \ldots, g_k'(\omega)$. It now suffices to define $g_j(\omega)$ as $\text{proj}_S g_j'(\omega)$ and to recall that the elements of $W(\omega)$ are in one-to-one correspondence with the elements of $F^{-1}(\omega)$.   Q.E.D.

In particular if $\omega \in P^m$ is a regular value of F and $r(\omega)$ denotes the number of elements of $W(\omega)$, the function r from $P^m \backslash C$ to the set of nonnegative integers is *locally constant*. It is easy therefore to obtain examples of nonempty open sets of economies having multiple equilibria. It suffices to construct an F-regular economy with two commodities and two consumers satisfying the assumptions of the theorem and having several equilibria. There is a neighborhood of that economy in which every economy has the same number of equilibria.

The theorem asserts that excluding a null closed set, every economy in P^m has a finite set of equilibria. Since this set might be empty, this result must be supplemented by the following proposition.

Proposition

Given m continuous demand functions $(f_1, \ldots, f_m)$, if every f_i satisfies (A), then for every $\omega \in P^m$, the set $W(\omega)$ is not empty.

Since this proposition does not seem to be covered by any of the theorems about the existence of an equilibrium, we give a short proof.

Proof: Given $\omega \in P^m$, choose a real number t greater than the sum of the components of $\sum_{i=1}^{m} \omega_i$. Let T be the set of vectors x in $\bar{P}$ for which the sum of the components of x is smaller than or equal to t, and let $\hat{T}$ be the set of the vectors x in $\bar{P}$ for which the sum of the components of x equals t. For $i = 1, \ldots, m$ we define the correspondence ϕ_i from $\bar{S} \times L$ to T as follows: if $(p, w_i) \in S \times L$ and $f_i(p, w_i) \in T$, then $\phi_i(p, w_i) = \{f_i(p, w_i)\}$; if $(p, w_i) \in S \times L$ and $f_i(p, w_i) \notin T$, then $\phi_i(p, w_i) = \{x\}$ where x is the intersection point of $\hat{T}$ and the segment $[0, f_i(p, w_i)]$; if $(p, w_i) \in (\bar{S} \backslash S) \times L$, then $\phi_i(p, w_i) = \{x \in \hat{T} | p \cdot x \le w_i\}$.

Next we check the correspondence ϕ_i is upper hemicontinuous in $\bar{S} \times L$. Consider a sequence $(p^q, w_i^q) \in \bar{S} \times L$ converging to $(p^0, w_i^0) \in \bar{S} \times L$ and a sequence x^q in T converging to x^0 and such that for every q, $x^q \in \phi_i(p^q, w_i^q)$. We wish to show that $x^0 \in \phi_i(p^0, w_i^0)$. If $p^0 \in S$, the continuity of f_i clearly implies $x^0 \in \phi_i(p^0, w_i^0)$. If $p^0 \in \bar{S} \backslash S$, then *either* for infinitely many q, $p^q \in \bar{S} \backslash S$, in which case $[x^q \in \hat{T}$ and $p^q \cdot x^q \le w_i^q]$, *or* for infinitely many q, $p^q \in S$, which implies by (A) that for infinitely many q, $[p^q \in S$ and $f_i(p^q, w_i^q) \notin T]$, in which case also $[x^q \in \hat{T}$ and $p^q \cdot x^q \le w_i^q]$. Therefore in the limit, $x^0 \in \hat{T}$ and $p^0 \cdot x^0 \le w_i^0$.

Now for every $p \in \bar{S}$ define $\psi_i(p) = \phi_i(p, p \cdot \omega_i) - \{\omega_i\}$ and $\psi(p) = \sum_{i=1}^{m} \psi_i(p)$. The correspondence ψ is defined on $\bar{S}$ and takes its values in a compact subset of R^l; it is upper hemicontinuous; for every $p \in \bar{S}$, $\psi(p)$ is convex; for every $p \in \bar{S}$ and every $z \in \psi(p)$, one has $p \cdot z \le 0$. Therefore by [**8, 11, 4**, or **5**, 5.6] there are $p^* \in \bar{S}$ and $z^* \le 0$ such that $z^* \in \psi(p^*)$. Consequently for every i, there is $x_i^* \in \phi_i(p^*, p^* \cdot \omega_i)$ such that $\sum_{i=1}^{m} x_i^* \le \sum_{i=1}^{m} \omega_i$. This inequality excludes that for some i, $x_i^* \in \hat{T}$. Thus $p^* \in S$ and for every i, $x_i^* = f_i(p^*, p^* \cdot \omega_i)$. This equality in turn implies $p^* \cdot x_i^* = p^* \cdot \omega_i$ and, since $p^* \in S$, $\sum_{i=1}^{m} x_i^* = \sum_{i=1}^{m} \omega_i$.   Q.E.D.

We have assumed that the consumption set X_i of the ith consumer is $\bar{P}$ only to keep the exposition as simple as possible. For instance, the theorem and the proposition extend in a straightforward manner to the case in which X_i is a nonempty, closed, convex subset of R^l bounded below and containing the translate of $\bar{P}$ to each one of the points of X_i.

Differentiability of the demand function has been related to differentiability properties of the utility function in recent studies by Katzner [**9**], Dhrymes [**6**], and Barten, Kloek, and Lempers [**3**]. In particular Katzner makes the following assumptions on the utility function u from $\bar{P}$ to the real line: (i) u is continuous in $\bar{P}$ and twice continuously differentiable in P; (ii) the derivative Du is strictly positive in P; (iii) $[x' \in P, x'' \in P, x' \ne x''$,

$u(x') = u(x'')$, and $0 < t < 1$] implies $[u(tx'' + (1 - t)x') > u(x')]$;
(iv) $u(x) > u(0)$ implies $x \in P$.

Under these assumptions, given $p \in S$ and $w \in L$, there is a unique maximizer $f(p, w)$ of u in the set $\{x \in \bar{P} | p \cdot x \le w\}$. The function f is a homeomorphism of $S \times L$ onto P. Its inverse g transforms $x \in P$ into $(p, w) \in S \times L$ where p is the point where the ray from the origin determined by $Du(x)$ intersects S, and $w = p \cdot x$. Katzner observes that the demand function f is continuously differentiable on a dense, open subset of $S \times L$. By another application of Sard's theorem one can actually prove the stronger result—f *is continuously differentiable outside a subset of $S \times L$ which is closed relative to $S \times L$ and has Lebesgue measure zero in R^l.* Since g is continuously differentiable, the set Γ of its critical values has Lebesgue measure zero in R^l. The set of its critical points is clearly closed relative to P. Therefore its image Γ by the homeomorphism g is closed relative to $S \times L$. At every point of $S \times L \backslash \Gamma$, f is continuously differentiable by the inverse function theorem.

References

[1] Abraham, R., and J. Robbin, *Transversal Mappings and Flows*, New York, Benjamin, 1967.

[2] Arrow, K. J., and F. H. Hahn, *Competitive Equilibrium Analysis*, San Francisco, Holden-Day, forthcoming.

[3] Barten, A. P., T. Kloek, and F. B. Lempers, A Note on a Class of Utility and Production Functions Yielding Everywhere Differentiable Demand Functions, *Review of Economic Studies*, **36** (1969), 109–111.

[4] Debreu, G., Market Equilibrium, *Proceedings of the National Academy of Sciences, U.S.A.*, **42** (1956), 876–878.

[5] Debreu, G., *Theory of Value*, New York, Wiley, 1959.

[6] Dhrymes, P. J., On a Class of Utility and Production Functions Yielding Everywhere Differentiable Demand Functions, *Review of Economic Studies*, **34** (1967), 399–408.

[7] Dieudonné, J., *Foundations of Modern Analysis*, New York, Academic Press, 1960.

[8] Gale, D., The Law of Supply and Demand, *Mathematica Scandinavica*, **3** (1955), 155–169.

[9] Katzner, D. W., A Note on the Differentiability of Consumer Demand Functions, *Econometrica*, **36** (1968), 415–418.

[10] Milnor, J. W., *Topology from the Differentiable Viewpoint*, The University Press of Virginia. Charlottesville, Va., 1965.

[11] Nikaido, H., On the Classical Multilateral Exchange Problem, *Metroeconomica*, **8** (1956), 135–145.

[12] Sard, A., The Measure of the Critical Points of Differentiable Maps, *Bulletin of the America Mathematical Society*, **48** (1942), 883–890.

[13] Sternberg, S., *Lectures on Differential Geomeotry*, Englewood Cliffs, N.J., Prentice-Hall, 1964.

CHAPTER 15

Smooth preferences[1,2]

In an attempt to explain the observed state of an economy as an equilibrium resulting from the interaction of agents with partially conflicting aims, a mathematical model $\mathscr{E}$ of that economy is constructed. We will denote the set of equilibria of $\mathscr{E}$ by $E(\mathscr{E})$. Three basic questions must then be asked about the adequacy of the model $\mathscr{E}$. Before formulating them, however, I ought to stress their generality. Although in the following discussion, reference will be made only to the concept of Walrasian equilibrium of an exchange economy with a finite set of private commodities, these questions apply to any equilibrium concept introduced in the mathematical study of social systems.

1   Non-emptiness of $E(\mathscr{E})$

Since the purpose of the model $\mathscr{E}$ is to explain economic equilibrium, it is adequate only if $E(\mathscr{E})$ is not empty. This is the existence problem to which A. Wald [39] addressed himself in 1935–1936, and to which numerous contributions were made during the last twenty years. The main tools for its solution were provided by algebraic topology in the form of fixed point theorems. Rather than lingering on this first question, which is accessory to my main object, I refer to the recent extensive account by K. J. Arrow and

[1] Presidential Address given at the September 1971 meeting of the Econometric Society in Barcelona.
[2] My research work on the problem of smooth preferences was made possible by the support of the National Science Foundation which is gratefully acknowledged. I also wish to thank S. S. Chern, M. Hirsch, H. Rosenberg, and especially S. Smale for conversations of great value to me.

F. H. Hahn [2], to which may be added the articles by R. J. Aumann [4], D. Schmeidler [35], and W. Hildenbrand [23] about economies with a measure space of agents, and the monograph by H. Scarf and T. Hansen [34] about the computation of economic equilibria.

2   Discreteness of $E(\mathscr{E})$

Ideally the set $E(\mathscr{E})$ would have exactly one element. A significant amount of work has also been done on the problem of uniqueness of equilibrium (K. J. Arrow and F. H. Hahn [2, Ch. 9] give a comprehensive survey of this question), but no very satisfactory solution has been offered up to now. The assumptions made on $\mathscr{E}$ in order to obtain a unique equlibrium are exceedingly strong. Indeed it suffices to look into Edgeworth's box to find economies with two commodities and two consumers having no pathologies, exhibiting several equilibria, even a continuum of equilibria.

An alternative approach is to introduce an appropriate topology on the set of states of $\mathscr{E}$ and to make the weaker requirement of *local* uniqueness. A state of $\mathscr{E}$ having a neighborhood in which it is the unique element of $E(\mathscr{E})$ provides a determinate explanation of equilibrium insofar as only small changes in that state can take place. Conversely if an equilibrium e is not locally unique, there are arbitrarily small perturbations of the state of the economy from e giving rise to no tendency for the economy to return to e. Thus one is led to search for assumptions on $\mathscr{E}$ insuring that all the elements of $E(\mathscr{E})$ are locally unique, i.e., that the set $E(\mathscr{E})$ is discrete. Actually this second adequacy requirement will usually appear in a stronger form, for in almost every case (possibly in every case) in which an equilibrium existence theorem has been proved for the economy $\mathscr{E}$, the set of equilibrium price vectors of $\mathscr{E}$ was compact. But for a compact set, discreteness is equivalent to finiteness.

Instead of requiring that all the elements of $E(\mathscr{E})$ be locally unique, one might be satisfied with a model $\mathscr{E}$ for which there is at least one locally unique equilibrium, but the conditions one is led to impose on $\mathscr{E}$ in order to obtain the latter imply the former. These conditions are differentiability assumptions (for instance on individual demand functions), and here the main mathematical tools for the solution of the problem of discreteness of the set of equilibria have been provided by differential topology. The results obtained in the last two years, G. Debreu [11], F. Delbaen [14], E. Dierker [15], E. and H. Dierker [16], K. Hildenbrand [21, 24, Sec. 2.5], T. Rader [30, 31], and S. Smale [37] are of the following nature. A precise definition of a well-behaved or *regular* economy is given such that every regular economy has a discrete set of equilibria; *critical* means non-regular. An appropriate topology is introduced on the set $\mathscr{S}$ of economies and the set $\mathscr{C}$

of critical economies is shown to be "negligible." If $\mathscr{S}$ is finite-dimensional (e.g., the set of economies with a finite set of agents, fixed preferences, and variable endowments), "negligible" means closed and of Lebesgue measure zero. When $\mathscr{S}$ is infinite-dimensional (which is the case in the above example as soon as preferences vary in an infinite-dimensional space, or the set of agents is infinite), in the situations studied so far the critical set $\mathscr{C}$ was shown to be "negligible" in the sense that it is closed and has an empty interior or, in the situation investigated by S. Smale [37], in the sense that it is contained in a countable union of closed sets with empty interiors.

The comments made earlier on the problem of global uniqueness of equilibrium call for a digression. Consider economies with l commodities. The characteristics of an agent a are his demand function f_a and his endowment ω_a. Denoting by P the set of strictly positive vectors in R^l, by S the set of vectors in P whose lth coordinate is unity, and by L the set of strictly positive reals, we assume that f_a establishes a one-to-one correspondence between $S \times L$ and P, that $p \cdot f_a(p, w) = w$ for every pair of a price vector p in S, and of a wealth w in L, and that f_a is continuously differentiable. The set of demand functions satisfying these conditions is denoted by $\mathscr{D}$. We assume that ω_a belongs to P. Thus a is an element of $A = \mathscr{D} \times P$ which we endow with a suitable topology. An economy $\mathscr{E}$ is identified with a positive measure v on A such that $v(A) = 1$. The set of these economies (measures) is also endowed with a suitable topology. Now if all the agents of the economy are identical, i.e., if the measure v is concentrated on one point $(\bar{f}, \bar{\omega})$ of A, a trivial case of global uniqueness of equilibrium obtains. Every agent consumes the commodity vector $\bar{\omega}$, and the unique equilibrium price vector is $\bar{p}$ such that $\bar{f}(\bar{p}, \bar{w}) = \bar{\omega}$. Assume in addition that the Jacobian determinant of $\bar{f}$ is different from zero at $(\bar{p}, \bar{w})$, a condition we will discuss in detail below. Finally let $p \mapsto F(p)$ be the function from S to R^{l-1} defined by $F_i(p) = \bar{f}_i(p, p \cdot \bar{\omega})$ for $i = 1, \ldots, l - 1$. It is not difficult to prove that the Jacobian determinant of F at $\bar{p}$ equals the Jacobian determinant of $\bar{f}$ at $(\bar{p}, \bar{w})$. Therefore the economy with identical agents described above satisfies the definition of regularity of F. Delbaen [**14**, 4.12] and K. Hildenbrand [**24**, Sec. 2.5]. Consequently it has a neighborhood of economies also possessing a unique equilibrium. In other words, economies with sufficiently similar agents, in the precise sense we have given, have exactly one equilibrium. One may hope to go beyond this general assertion about global uniqueness by studying specific classes of economies (measures on A) exhibiting concentration around a central point. Indeed the possibility of deriving strong conclusions from the investigation of specific classes of measures on A seems to be a, so far largely unfulfilled, promise of the measure-theoretical approach in equilibrium and analysis.

3   Continuity of *E*

The data of the model $\mathscr{E}$ (endowments, preference relations, or demand functions) cannot be exactly observed. If the correspondence *E* is not continuous at $\mathscr{E}$, an arbitrarily small error of observation on $\mathscr{E}$ yields an essentially different set of predicted equilibria. In such a situation the explanatory value of the model $\mathscr{E}$ seems to be limited. Therefore, the third adequacy requirement is that the correspondence *E* be continuous. The preceding considerations, which are common in the study of physical systems, apply with even greater force to social systems.

Actually this third requirement is closely related to the second, for in the papers listed in Section 2 that investigate this problem, it is shown that *E* is continuous on the set of regular economies. It is also related to studies of limit theorems and of hemi-continuity properties for various economic equilibrium concepts. References for the two concepts of the core and of Walrasian equilibrium are F. Y. Edgeworth [18], M. Shubik [36], H. Scarf [33], G. Debreu and H. Scarf [12,13], Y. Kannai [26], W. Hildenbrand [22,24], W. Hildenbrand and J. F. Mertens [25], K. J. Arrow and F. H. Hahn [2], B. Grodal [19], T. Bewley [6], and D. J. Brown and A. Robinson [7,8].[3]

With the motivation of the last two adequacy requirements, I now propose to study from the differentiable viewpoint the three main concepts of the theory of consumer behavior: (i) preference relations, (ii) demand functions, and (iii) utility functions. The third is unsatisfactory as a primitive concept, for the axioms of the theory must be formulated in terms of observable choices made by a consumer among commodity vectors, and the existence of a utility function with specified properties (e.g., a twice continuously differentiable utility function) must be derived from these behavior axioms. Revealed preference theory chooses the second as a primitive concept. We will choose the first.

The study of differentiable preference relations, which goes back to G. B. Antonelli's article [1] of 1886, has given rise to an extensive literature, completely surveyed by L. Hurwicz [9, Ch. 9]. Before presenting the approach to differentiable preferences in Antonelli's tradition, let us note that *henceforth consumption vectors will belong to P, the interior of the positive cone of* R^l. A description of the preferences of a consumer can be given by specifying for every *x* in *P*, a non-zero vector $g(x)$ in R^l, the intended interpretation for which is that the hyperplane $H(x)$ through *x* orthogonal to $g(x)$ is tangent at *x* to the indifference hypersurface of *x*, and $g(x)$ indicates a direction of preference. We normalize $g(x)$ by requiring that $\|g(x)\| = 1$, where the vertical bars denote Euclidean norm, and we assume

---

[3] A more complete bibliography will be found in W. Hildenbrand [24].

that the function g from P to the unit sphere of R^l is of class C^1 (continuously differentiable). A basic problem is then the existence of a utility function u from P to R, of class C^2 (twice continuously differentiable), and such that its derivative Du is everywhere a strictly positive multiple of g, i.e., such that everywhere in P,

$$Du = \lambda g, \tag{1}$$

where λ is a function from P to the set of strictly positive real numbers. By equating the partial derivatives $\partial_i \partial_j u$ and $\partial_j \partial_i u$, by writing similar equalities for the pairs (j, k) and (k, i) of indices, and by eliminating λ and its first partial derivatives, one obtains the following necessary conditions on g for the existence of functions u and λ respectively of class C^2 and C^1 satisfying (1) on P:

$$\forall(i, j, k), g_i(\partial_j g_k - \partial_k g_j) + g_j(\partial_k g_i - \partial_i g_k) + g_k(\partial_i g_j - \partial_j g_i) = 0. \tag{2}$$

However the question of the sufficiency of these conditions (which are clearly not independent) is a less trivial matter. It is possible to prove that (2) implies for every point x^0 of P, the existence of an open neighborhood V of x^0, and of a utility function u of class C^2 defined and satisfying (1) on V. This result, whose long history in economic theory is told in detail in L. Hurwicz [9, Ch. 9], can be established as an application of a standard theorem of differential topology (N. J. Hicks [20, Sec. 9.1]), intimately related to the theorem of Frobenius on total differential equations (J. Dieudonné [17, Sec. 10.9]). The function H introduced earlier, associating with every x in P, the hyperplane $H(x)$ in R^l, is an $(l - 1)$-dimensional distribution of class C^1. Consider now two vector fields X and Y of class C^1 defined on an open subset U of P and lying in H, i.e., for every x in U, $X(x) \in H(x)$ and $Y(x) \in H(x)$, and check that the Lie bracket of X and Y, i.e., the vector $[X, Y]$ of R^l whose ith coordinate is $X \cdot DY_i - Y \cdot DX_i$, also lies in H. Thus the distribution H is involutive, and the first theorem of [20, Sec. 9.1] applies (the proof given in [20] is written for a C^∞ distribution but can be transposed for a C^1 distribution). Given a point x^0 of P, there is an open neighborhood V of x^0 and a C^2 coordinate system $y_1, \ldots, y_l$ defined on V such that the subsets of V on which y_l is constant are integral manifolds of H. The function y_l is a utility function V.

But conditions (2) do *not* imply the existence of a utility function u of class C^2 defined and satisfying (1) everywhere on P. As P. A. Samuelson [32] used spirals around a point in his discussion of local integrability, we will use spirals around a circle to show that global integrability is not a consequence of local integrability. Consider in R^2 the circles C_r with center 0 and radius r such that $0 < r \leq 1$, and the spirals S_k with equations $\rho(\theta) = ke^{-\theta} + 1$ in polar coordinates, where the angle θ is measured in ra-

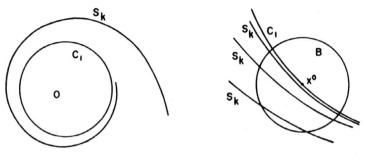

Figure 1   Figure 2

dians and $e^{-2\pi} < k \cdot \leq 1$. For every such k, the spiral S_k winds around,
and approaches, C_1 as θ increases indefinitely (see Figure 1). Through
every point x of R^2 different from 0, there is a unique curve of the above
family. Let $g(x)$ be its unit normal pointing toward 0. Clearly g satisfies (2).
However there can be no C^2 real-valued function $\bar{u}$ satisfying (1) on $R^2 \backslash \{0\}$.
Assume that there is such a function $\bar{u}$, and examine a point x^0 of the circle
C_1, a small open ball B with center x^0, and a spiral S_k(see Figure 2). The
function $\bar{u}$ has the same constant value on every arc of S_k in B, while (1)
implies that the value of $\bar{u}$ increases as one moves toward 0 in B, a
contradiction. Since this example does not satisfy the condition imposed
earlier that consumption vectors belong to the open positive cone P of R^2,
we translate Figure 1 from 0 to a point $0'$ with both coordinates strictly
greater than 1, and restrict our attention to those parts of the spirals lying in
P.

The preceding example is still not fully satisfactory, for the vector field g
cannot be extended continuously to $0'$; in economic terms, $0'$ is a satiation
point. To overcome this difficulty, consider the equilateral triangle with
vertices a_1, a_2, a_3 on the coordinate axes of R^3 at distance 3 from the origin,
$T = \{x \in R^3 | x \gg 0, x_1 + x_2 + x_3 = 3\}$, where $x \gg 0$ means that all the
coordinates of x are strictly positive; let Δ be the straight line in R^3 defined
by the equations $x_1 = x_2 = x_3$; and let e be the point $(1, 1, 1)$ where Δ
intersects T (see Figure 3). We now place Figure 1 in the plane of T with the
center of the concentric circles at e, choose a point q of Δ with strictly
negative coordinates, and construct for every spiral S_k, the cone $\sum_k$ with
vertex q generated by S_k. Figure 4 is drawn in the plane Q_1 containing Δ and
the first coordinate axis. The segment a_1, a, with end points excluded, is the
intersection of T with the plane Q_1. The points c, c' of the segment a_1, a at
distance 1 from e are the intersection of the circle C_1 in T with the plane Q_1.
The point b is the intersection of the two straight lines q, c and $0, a_1$. Next we
draw a smooth convex curve γ symmetric around Δ, coinciding with the

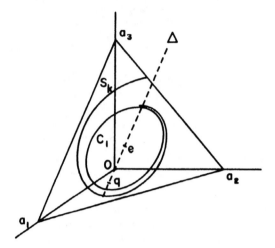

Figure 3

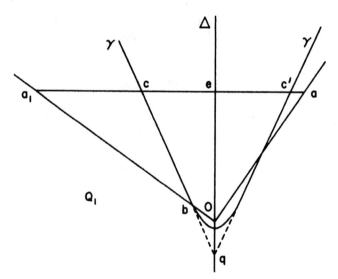

Figure 4

straight line q, c above b, and intersecting Δ below 0. Denote by Γ_0 the revolution surface generated by rotating γ around Δ, and by Γ_k the surface obtained from Γ_0 by an upward translation parallel to Δ by a distance $k \geqq 0$. A point x of P, the open positive cone of R^3, belongs to exactly one surface of either the family $\{\sum_k\}$, or the family $\{\Gamma_k\}$. The unit normal $g(x)$ to that surface at the point x, pointing toward Δ satisfies conditions (2)

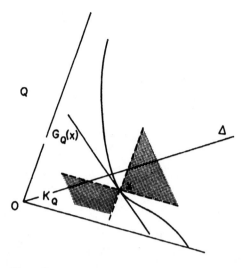

Figure 5

everywhere on P. As before, by considering a point x^0 of C_1, we show that there cannot be a C^2 real-valued function $\bar{u}$ satisfying (1) on P.

It is possible however to prove that if for every x in P, the open positive cone of R^l, one has $g(x) > 0$, then local integrability implies global integrability. The inequality $g(x) > 0$ means that the vector $g(x)$ has all its coordinates non-negative, and is different from 0; in economic terms, preferences are locally monotone. As a consequence of (2), there is through every point of P, a maximal connected integral manifold of the distribution H (L. Auslander and R. E. MacKenzie [5, Sec. 8.8] or S. Sternberg [38, Sec. 3.5]). To study the structure of these manifolds, we examine their intersections with two-dimensional planes containing Δ, the straight line in R^l with equations $x_1 = x_2 = \ldots = x_l$. Let Q be such a plane, and let K_Q be the intersection of Q and P. Given a point x of K_Q, the hyperplane $H(x)$ supports the translate of P from 0 to x, since $g(x) > 0$. Therefore the straight line $G_Q(x)$, intersection of $H(x)$ and Q, supports the translate of K_Q from 0 to x. Now the intersection of Q and an integral manifold of the distribution H is an integral curve of the distribution G_Q. Clearly a connected integral curve of G_Q through x cannot intersect the translates of K_Q and $-K_Q$ from 0 to x (represented by the shaded angles of Figure 5); if it did, there would be a point on this curve at which the tangent would not support the translate of K_Q from 0 to that point. Consequently the maximal connected integral (MCI) curve of G_Q through x intersects any ray from 0 in K_Q in exactly one point; and either it tends to a straight line parallel to an edge of K_Q or its closure intersects the boundary of K_Q. Given two MCI

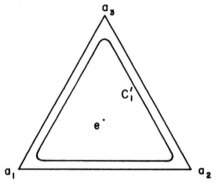

Figure 6

curves of G_Q, one is above the other in the sense that all the rays from 0 in K_Q intersect these two curves in the same order. Consider now a point y of Δ. As Q ranges over the set of planes containing Δ, the MCI curves of G_Q through y generate the MCI manifold of H through y. Given x in P, the MCI manifold of H through x intersects Δ in a unique point $U(x)$ with equal coordinates $u(x)$. The function u is of class C^2 and satisfies (1) everywhere on P (in particular, $Du(x) > 0$ for every x in P).

The preceding reasoning fails in the example illustrated by Figures 3 and 4 because for any plane Q containing Δ, there are MCI curves of G_Q which do not intersect Δ. A slight modification of that example also shows that local monotony of preferences is somehow required for local integrability to imply global integrability. To see this, it suffices to replace the circle C_1 by a smooth curve C_1' close to the boundary of the equilateral triangle T, to insert a suitable family of spirals between C_1' and the boundary of T, and a suitable family of closed curves inside C_1', and to choose q close to 0. (See Figure 6.) In this manner one can approximate local monotony as closely as one wishes, and still not global integrability.

Thus, following Antonelli's approach, we have been led to preferences characterized by a *function $g > 0$ of class C^1 from P, the open positive cone of R^l, to the unit sphere of R^l, satisfying* (2) on P. Let $\mathscr{G}$ be the set of functions g fulfilling all these conditions. A natural topology can be defined on this set $\mathscr{G}$ of preference relations, for instance, as the topology of uniform convergence (or of uniform convergence on compact subsets of P) of g and of its l partial derivatives $\partial_i g$.

An alternative approach to smooth preference relations consists of making differentiability assumptions on their graphs. Given two open sets X and Y in R^n, a function h from X onto Y is a C^k-*diffeomorphism* if h is one-to-one, and both h and h^{-1} are of class C^k. A set M of points in R^n is a

C^k-*hypersurface* if for every $z \in M$, there is an open neighborhood U of z, a C^k-diffeomorphism h of U onto an open set V in R^n, and a hyperplane H in R^n such that $M \cap U$ is carried by h into $H \cap V$. In other words, M is locally a hyperplane, up to a C^k-diffeomorphism. Let now $\leqslant$ be a complete preference preordering on P, i.e., a complete, transitive, and reflexive binary relation on the open positive cone of R^l. Define the relation of strict preference $[x < y]$ by $[x \leqslant y$ and not $y \leqslant x]$, and the relation of indifference $[x \sim y]$ by $[x \leqslant y$ and $y \leqslant x]$. Let us also say that the preference relation is *continuous* if the set $\mathscr{P} = \{(x, y) \in P \times P | x \leqslant y\}$ is closed in $P \times P$, and that it is *monotone* if $x \ll y$ implies $x < y$. *Henceforth we will assume that $\leqslant$ is a monotone, continuous, complete preordering on P.* In these conditions, the boundary of $\mathscr{P}$ in $P \times P$ is the set $\mathscr{I} = \{(x, y) \in P \times P | x \sim y\}$. We will say that $\leqslant$ *is a preference relation of class C^k* if $\mathscr{I}$ is a C^k-hypersurface in R^{2l}.

At this point, three ways of approaching the question of smooth preferences have been, explicitly or implicitly, mentioned. One can postulate (i) a monotone, continuous, complete preference preordering $\leqslant$ on P of class C^2, (ii) a function $g > 0$ from P to the unit sphere of R^l of class C^1 satisfying (2) on P, or (iii) a real-valued utility function u on P of class C^2, satisfying $Du(x) > 0$ for every x in P. We will prove that these three postulates are equivalent.

It has been established above that (ii) implies (iii).

Next observe that (iii) implies (i). The only property of the preference preordering $\leqslant$ which is not obvious is that it is of class C^2. Letting $v(x, y) = u(x) - u(y)$, we obtain $\mathscr{I} = \{(x, y) \in P \times P | u(x) - u(y) = 0\} = \{z \in P \times P | v(z) = 0\}$. Since Du is different from 0 on P, so is Dv on $P \times P$. Consequently at every point z of $\mathscr{I}$, there is a local C^2-diffeomorphism h of the desired type.

Finally to see that (i) implies (ii), consider a point x^0 in P, and let $z^0 = (x^0, x^0)$, which is a point of $\mathscr{I}$ by reflexivity of $\leqslant$. As a consequence of (i), there is an open neighborhood V of z^0 in $P \times P$, and a C^2 real-valued function v on V such that $v(z) = 0$ is equivalent to $z \in \mathscr{I} \cap V$, $v(z) \leqq 0$ is equivalent to $z \in \mathscr{P} \cap V$, and $Dv \neq 0$ in V. Symmetry of the relation $\sim$ and monotony of the relation $\leqslant$ imply that for every (x, x) in V, $Dv(x, x)$ has the form $(q(x), - q(x))$ where $q(x) > 0$. Given any x^1 in P, the indifference class of x^1 is $\{x \in P | (x, x^1) \in \mathscr{I}\}$. It is obtained by taking the intersection of $\mathscr{I}$ and the linear manifold $\{(x, y) \in R^l \times R^l | y = x^1\}$, and projecting into the first factor space R^l. Since for every x in an open neighborhood U of x^0 such that $U \times U \subset V$, the normal $Dv(x, x)$ to $\mathscr{I}$ at (x, x) projects into the first factor space R^l as $q(x) > 0$, one obtains the unit normal $g(x)$ at x to the indifference hypersurface through x by dividing $q(x)$ by its Euclidean norm. Clearly g has all the properties listed in (ii).

One of the three preceding equivalent postulates, namely, (i), will be made from now on. We will also assume that $\leqslant$ is strongly convex, i.e., $[x \sim y, x \neq y,$ and $0 < t < 1]$ implies $[x \prec tx + (1 - t)y]$, and that the closures of the indifference hypersurfaces of $\leqslant$ do not intersect the boundary of P. Thus, in addition to the conditions already imposed, *henceforth we assume that $\leqslant$ is a strongly convex preference relation of class C^2, and that the closures of its indifference hypersurfaces are contained in P.* It follows that given a price vector p in R^l such that $p \gg 0$ and $\|p\| = 1$, and a wealth w in R such that $w > 0$, there is a unique commodity vector $f(p, w)$ satisfying optimally the preferences $\leqslant$ in the set $\{x \in P \mid p \cdot x \leqq w\}$.

Studies of the discreteness of $E(\mathscr{E})$, the set of equilibria of the economy $\mathscr{E}$, and of the continuity of the correspondence E mentioned earlier emphasize the desirability of obtaining by the procedure of the last paragraph a continuously differentiable demand function f. The derivation of a C^1 demand function from a C^2 preference relation is also part of the general program of investigating the equivalence of the two approaches to the theory of consumer behavior from preference relations or from demand functions. Digressing on the importance of this program, let us note that the introduction of an infinite set A of agents to analyze the connection between the core of an economy and the set of its equilibria has led to a search for richer and richer mathematical structures on A. Thus in R. J. Aumann [3], A is a measurable space. In Y. Kannai [26], G. Debreu [10], and W. Hildenbrand [22], A becomes a metric measurable space. The natural next step is to endow A with an algebraic structure. Such a structure should help in the study of the specific classes of measures on A to which an allusion was made at the end of Section 2, as well as in the study of the smoothing effect of the aggregation of individual demands to which an allusion will be made later. Now although a satisfactory metric could be defined on A by taking preference relations as a primitive concept, there seems to be more hope of finding an economically meaningful algebraic structure on A by taking demand functions as primitive.

The assumptions made so far on the preference relation $\leqslant$ do not imply the differentiability of the demand function f associated with $\leqslant$, as an example of D. W. Katzner [27] shows. Our purpose now is to give an additional, necessary and sufficient, condition for f to be of class C^1. The discussion will be centered on a standard concept of differential geometry, the Gaussian curvature of a hypersurface in R^l, which can be defined as follows (N. J. Hicks [20, Sec. 2.2]). Let M be a C^2 hypersurface in R^l, let x^0 be a point of M, and denote that unit normal to M at a point x of M in a neighborhood of x^0 by $g(x)$. To define the Gaussian curvature of M at x^0, consider a parametrized curve γ in M through x^0 with tangent vector t at x^0. Associate with each point x of γ, the point $g(x)$ in the unit sphere M' of

R^l. We obtain in this manner a parametrized curve γ' in M' through $g(x^0)$ with tangent vector t' at $g(x^0)$. The vector t' depends only on the vector t (and not on the parametrized curve γ). It is parallel to the hyperplane $H(x^0)$ tangent to M at x^0. The function $t \mapsto t'$ (the Weingarten map) is linear. By definition, its determinant is the Gaussian curvature of M at x^0.

To calculate the curvature $c(x^0)$ at a point x^0 of P of the indifference hypersurface through x^0, notice first that monotony and strong convexity of the relation $\leqslant$ imply strong monotony, i.e., $g(x) \gg 0$ on P (or $x \prec y \Rightarrow x \prec y$). Next choose the first $l - 1$ coordinates in R^l of a point of M, resp. of M', as a coordinate system in a neighborhood of x^0, resp. of $g(x^0)$. Thus $c(x^0)$ is the Jacobian determinant of the transformation $(x_1, \ldots, x_{l-1}) \mapsto (g_1(x), \ldots, g_{l-1}(x))$ where $x_l = \xi(x_1, \ldots, x_{l-1})$ is determined implicitly by $u(x_1, \ldots, x_l) = u(x^0)$. Therefore $c = |\partial_j g_i + \partial_l g_i \partial_j \xi|$ where $i, j = 1, \ldots, l - 1$. Substituting $-g_j/g_l$ for $\partial_j \xi$, and performing straightforward determinant manipulations, we obtain

$$c = - \begin{vmatrix} \partial_j g_i & g_i \\ g_j & 0 \end{vmatrix}, \qquad (i, j = 1, \ldots, l). \tag{3}$$

In this formula, the square $l \cdot l$ matrix $[\partial_j g_i]$ is bordered by a column of g_i, a row of g_j, and the number 0.

Given a unit vector p in P, denote by $\hat{p}$ the $(l - 1)$-vector $(p_1, \ldots, p_{l-1})$. The demand function f corresponding to this particular representation of the price system is the inverse of the function $x \mapsto (\hat{g}(x), v(x))$ where x is a commodity vector in P and $v(x)$ is the inner product $g(x) \cdot x$. The function f^{-1} will be studied as the composition of the two functions $\alpha\colon x \mapsto (\hat{g}(x), u(x))$ and $\beta\colon (\hat{p}, y) \mapsto (\hat{p}, m(y))$ where p is a strictly positive unit vector in R^l, y is a real number in the range of u, and $m(y) = \min_{u(z) \geq y} p \cdot z$. The Jacobian determinant of α is

$$J(\alpha) = \begin{vmatrix} \partial_j g_i \\ \partial_j u \end{vmatrix},$$

where $i = 1, \ldots, l - 1$, and $j = 1, \ldots, l$. By a simple manipulation of this determinant, we obtain $J(\alpha) = g_l \cdot c \cdot \|Du\|$. As for the Jacobian of β, it is $J(\beta) = Dm$. However the function m is the inverse of the function $w \mapsto \max_{p \cdot z \leq w} u(z)$ where w is a strictly positive real number. By a simple and classical calculation, $Dm^{-1} = \|Du\|$. Therefore $J(\beta) = \|Du\|^{-1}$. Summing up, $J(f^{-1}) = J(\beta \circ \alpha) = g_l c$. Since α and β are of class C^1, if $J(\beta \circ \alpha) \neq 0$ at the point x^0, then the demand function f is of class C^1 at the point $f^{-1}(x^0)$. Conversely if f is of class C^1, then $\beta \circ \alpha$ is a C^1 diffeomorphism and, consequently, its Jacobian is nonsingular (see J. Milnor [29, p. 4]). In conclusion, the demand function f is of class C^1 at the point $f^{-1}(x^0)$ if and only if the Gaussian curvature at x^0 of the indifference hypersurface through x^0 is different from zero. Since c can be expressed in terms of the classical determinant

$$\delta = \begin{vmatrix} \partial_i \partial_j u & \partial_i u \\ \partial_j u & 0 \end{vmatrix}$$

according to the formula $c = -\delta/\|Du\|^{l+1}$, which is easily derived from (3), the preceding intuitive condition of non-zero curvature is directly related to the condition $\delta \neq 0$ given by D. W. Katzner [27] for the differentiability of demand. It is also equivalent to the "strong convexity hypothesis" of E. Malinvaud [28], to which I refer for a proof of this assertion.

At this point, we consider a preference relation $\preccurlyeq$ on P as well behaved if it is a monotone, convex, continuous, complete preordering of class C^2, if its indifference hypersurfaces have everywhere a non-zero curvature, and if their closures are contained in P. By definition, a preference preordering on P is convex if for every x in P, the set of commodity vectors at least as desired as x is convex. The conditions listed above clearly imply that $\preccurlyeq$ is strongly convex. To appraise the strength of these conditions, let us endow the set of continuous, complete preference relations on P with one of the metrics proposed so far (Y. Kannai [26], G. Debreu [10], and W. Hildenbrand [22]). As an extension of unpublished results of B. Grodal on the approximation of a convex preference relation by a sequence of strongly convex preference relations, one may conjecture that in this framework, a monotone, convex, continuous, complete preference relation on P can be approximated on compact subsets of P by a sequence of preference relations satisfying all the conditions listed at the beginning of this paragraph.[4]

Going further in this direction, one might search for a topology on the set $\mathscr{K}$ of preference relations satisfying all the conditions listed at the beginning of the last paragraph, with the exception of non-zero curvature of indifference hypersurfaces, such that the subset $\mathscr{K}^0$ of preference relations satisfying all those conditions is open and dense in $\mathscr{K}$. Since $\mathscr{K}$ can be identified with a subset of the set $\mathscr{G}$ defined at the end of the discussion of global integrability, the topology sought should be closely related to the topologies suggested for $\mathscr{G}$. In light of the results of F. Delbaen [14] and E. and H. Dierker [16] on the open density of the set of regular economies with a finite set of consumers, variable endowments, and variable C^1 demand functions, such a topology on $\mathscr{K}$ might easily yield a theorem of S. Smale's [37] type in which the set of regular economies is open dense in the

---

[4] Added in proof: This conjecture was proved independently by F. Delbaen and by A. Mas-Colell (who has also answered the question raised in the next two sentences).

space of economies although the demand functions may not be continuously differentiable everywhere, and in fact may not even be defined everywhere.

Still another way to approach the study of regular differentiable economies is to postulate an atomless measure v on the space A of economic agents defined as the Cartesian product $P \times \mathscr{F}$, where the first factor is interpreted as the set of endowments, and $\mathscr{F}$ is the set of monotone, convex, continuous, complete preference relations on P, endowed with one of the metrics of Y. Kannai [26], G. Debreu [10], and W. Hildenbrand [22]. One expects[5] that if the measure v is suitably diffused over the space A, integration over A of the demand *correspondences* of the agents will yield a total demand *function*, possibly even a total demand function of class C^1.

References

[1] Antonelli, G. B., *Sulla Teoria Matematica Della Economia Politica*. Pisa, 1886. Reprinted in *Giornale degli Economisti e Annali di Economia*, Nuova Serie, 10 (1951), 233–263. Translated as Chapter 16 in [9].

[2] Arrow, K. J., and F. H. Hahn, *General Competitive Analysis*. San Francisco: Holden-Day, 1971.

[3] Aumann, R. J., Markets with a Continuum of Traders, *Econometrica*, 32 (1964), 39–50.

[4] Aumann, R. J., Existence of Competitive Equilibria in Markets with a Continuum of Traders, *Econometrica*, 34 (1966), 1–17.

[5] Auslander, L., and R. E. MacKenzie: *Introduction to Differentiable Manifolds*. New York: McGraw-Hill, 1963.

[6] Bewley, T., Edgeworth's Conjecture, forthcoming in *Econometrica*.

[7] Brown, D. J., and A. Robinson, Nonstandard Exchange Economies, Cowles Foundation Discussion Paper No. 308, May 1971.

[8] Brown, D. J., and A. Robinson, The Cores of Large Standard Exchange Economies, Cowles Foundation Discussion Paper No. 326, January 1972.

[9] Chipman, J. S., L. Hurwicz, M. K. Richter, and H. F. Sonnenschein, *Preferences, Utility, and Demand*. New York: Harcourt Brace Jovanovich, 1971.

[10] Debreu, G., Neighboring Economic Agents, in *La Décision*, Colloques Internationaux du C.N.R.S. No. 171, Paris, 1969.

[11] Debreu, G., Economies with a Finite Set of Equilibria, *Econometrica*, 38 (1970), 387–392.

[12] Debreu, G., and H. Scarf, A Limit Theorem on the Core of an Economy, *International Economic Review*, 4 (1963), 235–246.

[13] Debreu, G. and Scarf, The Limit of the Core of an Economy, in *Decision and Organization*, C. B. McGuire and R. Radner, eds. Amsterdam: North Holland, 1972, 283–295.

---

[5] Added in proof: As R. J. Aumann and W. Hildenbrand pointed out to me, the formulation of this problem I gave in Barcelona was not satisfactory. I hope that the present one, in all its vagueness, will contribute to stimulation of interest in an important and difficult question.

[14] Delbaen, F., Lower and Upper Hemi-Continuity of the Walras Correspondence, Doctoral Dissertation, Free University of Brussels, 1971.

[15] Dierker, E., Two Remarks on the Number of Equilibria of an Economy, forthcoming in *Econometrica*.

[16] Dierker, E., and H. Dierker, On the Local Uniqueness of Equilibria, forthcoming in *Econometrica*.

[17] Dieudonné, J., *Foundation of Modern Analysis*. New York: Academic Press, 1960.

[18] Edgeworth, F. Y., *Mathematical Psychics*. London: Paul Kegan, 1881.

[19] Grodal, B., A Theorem on Correspondences and Continuity of the Core, in *Differential Games and Related Topics*. H. W. Kuhn and G. P. Szegö, eds. Amsterdam: North Holland, 1971, 221–233.

[20] Hicks, N. J., *Notes on Differential Geometry*. New York: Van Nostrand Reinhold, 1965.

[21] Hildenbrand, K., Continuity of the Equilibrium-Set Correspondence, forthcoming in *Journal of Economic Theory*.

[22] Hildenbrand, W., On Economies with Many Agents, *Journal of Economic Theory*, 2 (1970), 161–188.

[23] Hildenbrand, W., Existence of Equilibria for Economies with Production and a Measure Space of Consumers, *Econometrica*, 38 (1970), 608–623.

[24] Hildenbrand, W., *Core and Equilibria of a Large Economy*. Forthcoming.

[25] Hildenbrand, W., and J. F. Mertens, Upper Hemi-Continuity of the Equilibrium-Set Correspondence for Pure Exchange Economies, *Econometrica*, 40 (1972), 99–108.

[26] Kannai, Y., Continuity Properties of the Core of a Market, *Econometrica*, 38 (1970), 791–815.

[27] Katzner, D. W.: A Note on the Differentiability of Consumer Demand Functions, *Econometrica*, 36 (1968), 415–418.

[28] Malinvaud, E., Prices for Individual Consumption, Quantity Indicators for Collective Consumption, forthcoming in *Review of Economic Studies*.

[29] Milnor, J. W., *Topology from the Differentiable Viewpoint*. Charlottesville: University Press of Virginia, 1965.

[30] Rader, T., Nice Demand Functions, forthcoming in *Econometrica*.

[31] Rader, T., Absolutely Continuous Constrained Maximizers, forthcoming in *Journal of Optimization Theory and Applications*.

[32] Samuelson, P. A., The Problem of Integrability in Utility Theory, *Economica*, 17 (1950), 355–385.

[33] Scarf, H., An Analysis of Markets with a Large Number of Participants, in *Recent Advances in Game Theory*. Princeton, N.J.: The Princeton University Conference, 1962, 127–155.

[34] Scarf, H., with the collaboration of T. Hansen, *The Computation of Economic Equilibria*. Forthcoming.

[35] Schmeidler, D., Competitive Equilibria in Markets with a Continuum of Traders and Incomplete Preferences, *Econometrica*, 37 (1969), 578–585.

[36] Shubik, M., Edgeworth Market Games, in *Contributions to the Theory of Games IV*. A. W. Tucker and R. D. Luce, eds. Princeton, N.J.: Princeton University Press, 1959, 267–278.

[37] Smale, S., Global Analysis and Economics II, mimeographed, Department of Mathematics, University of California, Berkeley, 1972.

[38] Sternberg, S., *Lectures on Differential Geometry*. Englewood Cliffs, N.J.: Prentice-Hall, 1964.

[39] Wald, A., "Über einige Gleichungssysteme der mathematischen Ökonomie," *Zeitschrift für Nationalökonomie*, 7 (1936), 637–670. Translated as On Some Systems of Equations of Mathematical Economics, *Econometrica*, 19 (1951), 368–403.

Smooth preferences: a corrigendum

Marcel K. Richter[1] recently informed me of conversations that he had with Andreu Mas-Colell and Leonard Shapiro about one aspect of the problem of local integrability in the theory of differentiable preferences, and mentioned the following example given, in a different context, by Alan Weinstein in a mathematics course at the University of California, Berkeley.

Using the notation of [1], consider in a neighborhood of 0 in R^2 the problem of integrability of the unit vector field g defined by:

$$g_1(x, y) = \frac{y^2}{\sqrt{1 + y^4}}, \qquad g_2(x, y) = \frac{1}{\sqrt{1 + y^4}}, \qquad \text{for } y \geq 0,$$

and

$$g_1(x, y) = 0, \qquad g_2(x, y) = 1, \qquad \text{for } y \leq 0.$$

g is C^1 (and, of course, locally integrable), but not C^2. Associated with it is a utility function u defined by $u(x, y) = y/(1 - xy)$, for $y \geq 0$, and $u(x, y) = y$, for $y \leq 0$.

u is C^1 and $Du(0) \neq 0$, but, as A. Mas-Colell noted, there is no utility function v associated with the vector field g that is C^2, and for which $Dv(0) \neq 0$. Thus, the assertion I made on this point in [1, p. 606, lines 26–28] is incorrect. On line 28, "C^2" must be replaced by "C^1." By the same token, in [1, p. 610, lines 40–44] (ii) does not imply (iii).

However, the assertion of the equivalence of (i) and (iii) is valid (for a proof see [4, footnote 1]), and (iii) trivially implies (ii).

It must also be observed that C^1-differentiability of the demand function [1, pp. 612–613] can be obtained even though there is no C^2 utility function without critical point. Assume that g is C^1 and locally integrable. Then every indifference hypersurface is C^1 and has a C^1 normal, which readily implies that it is actually a C^2-hypersurface. Assume, in addition, that g is positive; that it satisfies the condition of convexity and nonzero Gaussian curvature "for every x in $P = \text{Int } R_+^l$, for every y in R^l, $y \neq 0$, such that $y \cdot g(x) = 0$, one has $y \cdot J(g, x) y < 0$" where $J(g, x)$ is the Jacobian of g at x;

[1] I am very grateful to M. K. Richter for having noticed the error I made in [1], and to him, A. Mas-Colell, and L. Shapiro for their comments.

and that for every x in P, the closure relative to R^l of the indifference hypersurface of x is contained in P. Let $S = \{p \in P | \|p\| = 1\}$ and $L = \text{Int } R_+$. The preceding conditions imply that there is a well defined demand function from $S \times L$ to P. Now consider the C^1 function $\phi: P \to P$ defined by $\phi(x) = (g_1(x), \ldots, g_{l-1}(x), x \cdot g(x))$. The Jacobian determinant of ϕ at x can directly be shown to equal

$$\begin{vmatrix} \partial_j g_i \\ g_j \end{vmatrix} \qquad (i = 1, \ldots, l-1; j = 1, \ldots, l)$$

which, in turn, equals $c g_l$, where c denotes Gaussian curvature. Since $c g_l$ is different from zero, the demand function ϕ^{-1} is C^1.

Finally, it may be worth noting that all the assertions made in [1] would be correct if it were written in the context of C^∞ functions and hypersurfaces. A justification for working in that context is provided by the approximation results of [2 and 3].

References

[1] Debreu, G., Smooth Preferences, *Econometrica*, 40 (1972), 603–615.
[2] Kannai, Y., Approximation of Convex Preferences, *Journal of Mathematical Economics*, 1 (1974), 101–106.
[3] Mas-Colell, A., Continuous and Smooth Consumers: Approximation Theorems, *Journal of Economic Theory*, 8 (1974), 305–336.
[4] Mas-Colell, Regular, Nonconvex Economies, Working Paper IP-223. Center for Research in Management Science, University of California, Berkeley, July 1975. Forthcoming in *Econometrica*.

CHAPTER 16

Excess demand functions

The problem of characterizing the excess demand function of an l-commodity exchange economy may be formulated in the following terms.

Let $S = \{p \in R^l | p \gg 0, \|p\| = 1\}$, the set of strictly positive price-vectors with unit Euclidean norm.

> *Definition.* A consumer is a pair $(\preccurlyeq, e)$ where $\preccurlyeq$ is a strictly convex, monotone, continuous, complete preference preorder on R^l_+, and e is an endowment-vector in R^l_+.
>
> A function $f: S \to R^l$ is the individual excess demand function of the consumer $(\preccurlyeq, e)$ if for every p in S, $e + f(p)$ is the greatest element for $\preccurlyeq$ of $\{x \in R^l_+ | px \leqq pe\}$.

(In this context, a preference preorder is said to be strictly convex if the convex combination, with weights different from 0 and 1, of two distinct, indifferent consumption-vectors is strictly preferred to both.)

It is easy to show that an individual excess demand function $f(1)$ is continuous, and (2) satisfies $pf(p) = 0$ for every p in S. Consequently the excess demand function of an exchange economy with a finite number of consumers enjoys these two properties, since it is a finite sum of individual excess demand functions. This remark prompts the

> *Definition.* A continuous function $f: S \to R^l$ is an excess demand function if for every p in S, $pf(p) = 0$,

I am grateful to Roy Radner for his objection to an inesthetic feature of the first version of this paper, and to the National Science Foundation for its support.

203

and the question: given an excess demand function f, is there a finite number of consumers whose individual excess demand functions sum to f?

The first attack on this problem was made by Hugo Sonnenschein (1973) who conjectured (pp. 345 and 353) that the answer to this question is affirmative (with the ε-qualification introduced below), and who obtained the solutions presented in H. Sonnenschein (1972 and 1973). The main result of these two articles was extended, in a simple and ingenious manner, by Rolf Mantel (1974) who showed that if f is continuously differentiable, and satisfies a certain additional condition, then for every $\varepsilon > 0$, f can be expressed as the sum of $2l$ individual excess demand functions on $S_\varepsilon = \{p \in S | \text{for every } i, p_i \geq \varepsilon\}$. Another extension is provided by the

Theorem

Let f be an excess demand function. For every $\varepsilon > 0$, there are l consumers whose individual excess demand functions sum to f on S_ε.

Thus, differentiability assumptions can be dispensed with, and, as Rolf Mantel conjectured (1974), the additive decomposition that he performed with $2l$ consumers can be performed with only l consumers. Moreover, it is generally impossible to perform the additive decomposition of the theorem with fewer than l consumers.

Proposition

There are an excess demand function f and an $\varepsilon > 0$, such that f cannot be expressed as a sum of fewer than l individual excess demand functions on S_ε.

1   Proof of the theorem

Given p in R^l different from 0, we denote by $T(p)$ the hyperplane through 0 orthogonal to p. We also denote by a^i the positive unit vector on the ith coordinate axis of R^l, and by $b^i(p)$ the orthogonal projection of a^i into $T(p)$.

For every p in S, let $\theta^0(p)$ be the least real t such that $f(p) + tp \geq 0$. The function θ^0 is clearly continuous on S. Let θ be a continuous function: $S \to R$ such that for every p in S, $\theta(p) > \theta^0(p)$. Thus

$$f(p) + \theta(p)p = \sum_{i=1}^{l} \beta_i(p)a^i,$$

where every β_i is continuous and strictly positive.

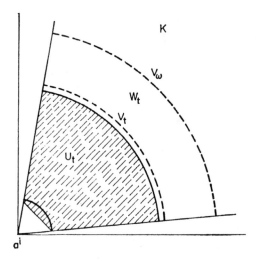

Figure 1

Projecting orthogonally into $T(p)$ we obtain

$$f(p) = \sum_{i=1}^{l} \beta_i(p)b^i(p).$$

For every i, we define the function $f^i: S \to R^l$ by

$$f^i(p) = \beta_i(p)b^i(p),$$

and we prove that for every $\varepsilon > 0$, f^i is an individual excess demand function on S_ε. (The indirect utility function v_i of the ith consumer on S_ε is $p \mapsto v_i(p) = -p_i$.) Until the end of the proof we consider only one consumer, namely, the ith, and we construct his preference relation $\preccurlyeq_i$, and his endowment e^i.

Let $P = \{p \in R^l | p_i = 1$, and for every $j \neq i$, $p_j > 0\}$ be the (relative) in-terior of the positive orthant of the hyperplane $\{p \in R^l | p_i = 1\}$. Define the set P_ε as the projection of the set S_ε from 0 into P, and define the function $\bar{f}^i$: $P \to R^l$ by $\bar{f}^i(p) = f^i(p/\|p\|)$. Consider now a closed, convex cone K with vertex a^i, containing the compact set P_ε, and such that $K \setminus \{a^i\}$ is contained in P. Let α' (resp. ω) be the Minimum (resp. Maximum) of $\|p - a^i\|$ for $p \in P_\varepsilon$. Choose a real α such that $0 < \alpha < \alpha'$. In the sequel, the real t is always understood to be in $[\alpha, \omega]$. Let σ be the Minimum of $\sum_{j \neq i} p_j$ for p in the set $\{p \in K | \|p - a^i\| = \alpha\}$, and for every t, define $U_t = \{p \in K | \sum_{j \neq i} p_j \geq \sigma,$ and $\|p - a^i\| \leq t\}$. The set U_t (which is shaded on Fig. 1) is compact and convex. Denote now by $\hat{B}(r)$ the closed ball in the hyperplane $\{p \in R^l | p_i = 0\}$ with center 0, and radius $r \geq 0$, and choose a function $g: [\alpha, \omega] \to R$

that is continuous, strictly positive, strictly increasing, and such that $g(\alpha)$ $< \alpha' - \alpha$, and $U_\omega + \hat{B}(g(\omega))$ is contained in P.

For every t, let $L_t = U_t + \hat{B}(g(t))$. This set is compact, and convex. Actually, at every point of its (relative) boundary, L_t has a unique supporting (relative) hyperplane. Moreover, if $t < t'$, then L_t is contained in the (relative) interior of $L_{t'}$. As we have already noted, $L_\omega \subset P$. Also, $P_\varepsilon \subset K \cap (L_\omega \backslash L_\alpha)$.

Denote by V_t the set $\{p \in K \,|\, \|p - a^i\| = t + g(t)\}$ [V_t, which is contained in the (relative) boundary of L_t, is an indirect indifference class in K]. Let, also, W_t be the set $\{p \in K \,|\, t + g(t) \leq \|p - a^i\| \leq \omega + g(\omega)\}$ (W_t is an indirect preference-or-indifference class in $K \cap L_\omega$).

Given a set A in R^l we denote by ∂A its boundary, and by A^* the set $\{x \in R^l \,|\, \text{for every } p \in A, px \geq 0\}$. Thus A^* is a closed, convex cone with vertex 0 We also denote a single element set $\{p\}$ by p.

The·cone L_t^* is strictly convex (i.e., a straight line segment contained in ∂L_t^* is necessarily contained in a ray), $R_+^l \backslash 0$ is contained in Int L_t^*, and for every p in V_t, the hyperplane $T(p)$ supports L_t^* along the ray $[b^i(p)]$. This ray is orthogonal to p in the plane (p, a^i), and makes a constant acute angle with a^i when p varies in V_t. Moreover, if $t < t'$, then $(L_{t'}^* \backslash 0) \subset$ Int L_t^*.

We endow the set $\mathscr{S}$ of non-empty, closed subsets of R^l with the topology of closed convergence of Hausdorff (1962, pp. 168–170) and, in the sequel, continuity of a function from $[\alpha, \omega]$ to $\mathscr{S}$ is always understood with respect to that topology. The three functions, $t \mapsto L_t$, $t \mapsto L_t^*$, and $t \mapsto \partial L_t^*$ are clearly continuous.

The (direct) preference-or-indifference set Q_t that we seek to construct must be such that for every p in V_t, the set $Q_t - e^i$ is weakly above the hyperplane $T(p)$, and intersects it only at $\bar{f}^i(p)$. We will construct Q_t in such a way that $Q_t - e^i \subset L_t^*$, and $(Q_t - e^i) \cap \partial L_t^* = C_t$, where $C_t = \bar{f}^i(V_t)$ (see Figure 2).

The germ from which $Q_t - e^i$ will grow is the set $D_t = \bar{f}^i(W_t)$. This set is compact, contained in L_t^*, and $D_t \cap \partial L_t^* = C_t$. Moreover, the function $t \mapsto D_t$ is continuous. For every x in D_t, let $d(x, t)$ be the distance from x to ∂L_t^*, and let $B(x, r)$ denote the closed ball with center x, and radius $r \geq 0$. Define $E_t = \bigcup_{x \in D_t} B(x, \frac{1}{2}d(x, t))$. The set E_t is compact, contained in L_t^*, and $E_t \cap \partial L_t^* = C_t$. In addition, $t < t'$ implies $E_{t'} \subset$ Int E_t; and the function $t \mapsto E$ is continuous.

Since E_t may not be convex, we form F_t, the convex hull of E_t. Again F_t is compact, contained in L_t^*, and $F_t \cap \partial L_t^* = C_t$. Also, $t < t'$ implies $F_{t'} \subset$ Int F_t; and the function $t \mapsto F_t$ is continuous.

To insure the monotony property of the preference relation, recall that $(R_+^l \backslash 0) \subset$ Int L_t^*, and define $G_t = F_t + R_+^l$. The set G_t is closed, convex, contained in L_t^*, and $G_t \cap \partial L_t^* = C_t$. Moreover, $t < t'$ implies $G_{t'} \subset$ Int G_t; and the function $t \mapsto G_t$ is continuous.

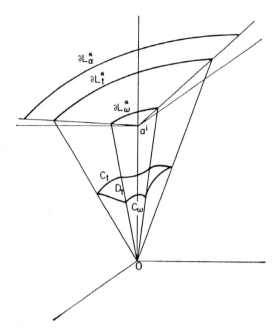

Figure 2

Since the set G_t may not be strictly convex (i.e., its boundary may contain straight line segments), we alter it in the following manner. Let π be a point of P in the (relative) interior of L_α. Therefore, the hyperplane $H = \partial \pi^*$ is supporting for L_α^*, and $H \cap L_\alpha^* = 0$. Let δ be the vector $(1, \ldots, 1)$ in R^l. For every $q \in H$, define $\lambda_t(q)$ as the least s such that $q + s\delta \in L_t^*$, and $\gamma_t(q)$ as the least s such that $q + s\delta \in G_t$. The functions λ_t and γ_t are convex; $\lambda_t \leq \gamma_t$; and $\lambda_t(q) = \gamma_t(q)$ is equivalent to $q + \lambda_t(q)\delta \in C_t$. Also, the functions $(t, q) \mapsto \lambda_t(q)$ and $(t, q) \mapsto \gamma_t(q)$ are continuous.

Let, now, ρ be a continuous convex function defined on $\Delta = \{(x, y) \in R_+^2 \mid x \leq y\}$ such that ρ is strictly increasing in each variable; for every $x \in R_+$, $\rho(x, x) = x$; if $x \neq y$ and/or $x' \neq y'$, then ρ is strictly convex on the segment $[(x, y), (x', y')]$. (An example of such a function ρ is given in the Appendix.)

As a consequence of the preceding properties, $[0 \leq x < y]$ implies $[x < \rho(x, y) < y]$, since $\rho(x, x) = x$, $\rho(y, y) = y$, and ρ is increasing.

Next define $\mu_t(q) = \rho[\lambda_t(q), \gamma_t(q)]$ for every $q \in H$. The function μ_t is convex, and $\lambda_t \leq \mu_t \leq \gamma_t$. Moreover, the function $(t, q) \mapsto \mu_t(q)$ is continuous. Let M_t be the set of $q + s\delta$ where $q \in H$, and $s \geq \mu_t(q)$. Clearly the set M_t is closed, convex, and

$$G_t \subset M_t \subset L_t^*.$$

Also, $M_t \cap \partial L_t^* = C_t$, because $\mu_t(q) = \lambda_t(q)$ is equivalent to $\lambda_t(q) = \gamma_t(q)$, hence to $q + \lambda_t(q)\delta \in C_t$. Moreover, if $t < t'$, then $M_{t'} \subset \mathrm{Int}\ M_t$, because $\lambda_t(q) \leqq \lambda_{t'}(q)$, and $\gamma_t(q) < \gamma_{t'}(q)$; hence, $\mu_t(q) < \mu_{t'}(q)$. Also, the function $t \mapsto M_t$ is continuous.

Finally, μ_t is strictly convex. To prove this, consider two distinct points q, q' in H and a real s, $0 < s < 1$. One has $\mu_t[sq + (1 - s)q'] = \rho[\lambda_t(sq + (1 - s)q'), \gamma_t(sq + (1 - s)q')]$.

However,

$$\lambda_t(sq + (1 - s)q') \leqq s\lambda_t(q) + (1 - s)\lambda_t(q'), \tag{1}$$

and

$$\gamma_t(sq + (1 - s)q') \leqq s\gamma_t(q) + (1 - s)\gamma_t(q').$$

Moreover,

$$\rho[s\lambda_t(q) + (1 - s)\lambda_t(q'), s\gamma_t(q) + (1 - s)\gamma_t(q')] \tag{2}$$
$$\leqq s\rho[\lambda_t(q), \gamma_t(q)] + (1 - s)\rho[\lambda_t(q'), \gamma_t(q')]$$
$$= s\mu_t(q) + (1 - s)\mu_t(q').$$

If $\lambda_t(q) = \gamma_t(q)$, and $\lambda_t(q') = \gamma_t(q')$, then $q + \lambda_t(q)\delta \in C_t$, and $q' + \lambda_t(q')\delta \in C_t$. The segment connecting these two points of C_t cannot have other points in ∂L_t^*. Therefore, inequality (1) is strict. Since ρ is strictly increasing, $\mu_t(sq + (1 - s)q') < s\mu_t(q) + (1 - s)\mu_t(q')$.

If $\lambda_t(q) = \lambda_t(q')$, the segment $[q + \lambda_t(q)\delta, q' + \lambda_t(q')\delta]$, which is parallel to H, cannot have points in ∂L_t^* other than its end points, because L_t^* is a strictly convex cone, and H is strictly supporting for L_t^*. Therefore, inequality (1) is strict as before.

If the two points $(\lambda_t(q), \gamma_t(q))$ and $(\lambda_t(q'), \gamma_t(q'))$ of Δ are distinct, and if $\lambda_t(q) \neq \gamma_t(q)$ and/or $\lambda_t(q') \neq \gamma_t(q')$, then inequality (2) is strict, and again $\mu_t(sq + (1 - s)q') < s\mu_t(q) + (1 - s)\mu_t(q')$.

The endowment-vector e^i of the ith consumer is now chosen in R_+^l in such a way that $-e^i$ is a lower bound for D_α.

For every t in $[\alpha, \omega]$, the preference-or-indifference set Q_t of the ith consumer is defined by $Q_t = (M_t + e^i) \cap R_+^l$. For $\tau \in]0, \alpha]$, define $Q_\tau = (\tau/\alpha)Q_\alpha$. For $\tau \geqq \omega$, define $Q_\tau = (\tau/\omega)Q_\omega$. Finally, define $Q_0 = R_+^l$.

2   Appendix: Construction of a function ρ having the required properties

For $(x, y) \in \Delta$, let $\phi(x, y) = \sqrt{(x^2 + y^2)/2}$. In R^3, the graph of ϕ is a cone with vertex 0 containing the ray $\Gamma = \{(x, y, z) \in R_+^3 \mid x = y = z\}$. The function ϕ is *continuous, convex, strictly increasing in each variable; for every x in* $R_+, \phi(x,x) = x$; and if $xy' \neq yx'$, then ϕ is strictly convex on the segment $[(x,y),(x',y')]$.

For $(x,y) \in \Delta$, let $\psi(x,y) = \sqrt{[(y-x)^2 + 1]} + x - 1$. In R^3, the graph of ψ is a cylinder obtained by adding the ray Γ to the curve $\{(x, y, z) \in R_+^3 \mid x = 0, z = \sqrt{(y^2 + 1)} - 1\}$. The function ψ enjoys the properties italicized above; and if $y - x \neq y' - x'$, then ψ is strictly convex on the segment $[(x,y),(x',y')]$.

Now let $\rho = \frac{1}{2}\phi + \frac{1}{2}\psi$. The function ρ also enjoys the italicized properties. Consider a segment $[(x,y),(x',y')]$ with distinct end points. If $x \neq y$ and/or $x' \neq y'$, then $xy' \neq yx'$ and/or $y - x \neq y' - x'$. Therefore, on that segment, one of the functions ϕ, ψ is strictly convex, and so is ρ.

3   Proof of the proposition

Given p in R^l different from 0, we denote by $T(p)$ the hyperplane through 0 orthogonal to p. Select a point p^0 in S, and for every $p \in S$, let $f(p)$ be the orthogonal projection of $p - p^0$ into $T(p)$. The function f is an excess demand function on S, and for every $p \neq p^0$, one has $(p - p^0)f(p) > 0$.

Now choose $\varepsilon > 0$ such that for every $i, p_i^0 > \varepsilon$, and assume that on S_ε, f is the sum of k individual excess demand functions, $f^1,\ldots,f^k$, where $k < l$. Since $\sum_{i=1}^k f^i(p^0) = f(p^0) = 0$, the vectors $f^i(p^0)$ in $T(p^0)$ are *not* linearly independent. Let Λ be the linear subspace that they generate. One has dim $\Lambda < $ dim $T(p^0)$. Therefore there is p^1 in S_ε, $p^1 \neq p^0$ such that the orthogonal projection of $p^1 - p^0$ into $T(p^0)$ is orthogonal to Λ. Consider the ith consumer. For him $(p^1 - p^0)f^i(p^0) = 0$. We now use a revealed preference theory argument. $p^0 f^i(p^0) = 0$ yields $p^1 f^i(p^0) = 0$. Therefore, $e^i + f^i(p^1) \succcurlyeq_i e^i + f^i(p^0)$. Hence $p^0 f^i(p^1) \geq p^0 f^i(p^0) = 0$. However, $p^1 f^i(p^1) = 0$. Thus, for every $i = 1,\ldots,k$, one has $(p^1 - p^0)f^i(p^1) \leq 0$. Consequently, $(p^1 - p^0)f(p^1) \leq 0$, a contradiction.

References

Hausdorff, F., 1962, *Set theory* (New York, Chelsea).
Mantel, R., 1974, On the characterization of aggregate excess demand, *Journal of Economic Theory* 7, 348–353.
Sonnenschein, H., 1972, Market excess demand functions, *Econometrica* 40, 549–563.
Sonnenschein, H., 1973, Do Walras' identity and continuity characterize the class of community excess demand functions?, *Journal of Economic Theory* 6, 345–354.
Sonnenschein, H., 1974, The utility hypothesis and market demand theory, *Western Economic Journal*, 11, 404–410.

CHAPTER 17

The rate of convergence of the core of
an economy

The core of a finite economy has been shown to converge, as the number of
its agents tends to infinity, under conditions of increasing generality in a
series of contributions, of which the first, by Edgeworth (1881), studied
replicated exchange economies with two commodities and two types of
agents, and the latest, by Hildenbrand (1974), considers sequences of finite
exchange economies (with a given finite number of commodities) whose
distributions on the space of agents' characteristics converge weakly.
However, information on the *rate* of convergence of the core seems to be
contained in only two articles. In Shapley and Shubik (1969, section 5) an
example is given of an Edgeworth replicated economy whose core
converges like the inverse of the number of agents. Recently, Shapley (1975)
provided examples of Edgeworth replicated economies whose cores
converge arbitrarily slowly, but concluded with the conjecture that for any
fixed concave utility functions only a set of initial allocations of measure
zero will yield cores that converge more slowly than the inverse of the
number of agents. The theorem stated below for replicated economies with
arbitrary numbers of commodities, and of types, asserts that such is indeed
the case provided that *preference relations are of class C^2*, and satisfy the
conditions listed in the definition of the economy. At the same time, the
theorem implies that the set of exceptional allocations is *closed* as well as of
measure zero.

I wish to thank the Miller Institute of the University of California, Berkeley, for its support
of my research, and Shiing-Shen Chern and Stephen Smale for the very valuable conversations
I had with them.

In order to state the definition of an economy, we introduce the notation

$$P = \text{Int } \mathbf{R}^l_+; \quad S = \{p \in P \,|\, \|p\| = 1\}$$

where $\|p\|$ denotes the Euclidean norm of p; and $L = \text{Int } \mathbf{R}_+$.

> *Definition.* The economy $\mathscr{E}$ is a list of m preference preorders $\preccurlyeq_i$ on P, and m endowment-vectors e_i in P such that for every $i(= 1,\ldots,m)$, $\preccurlyeq_i$ is monotone, convex, complete, and of class C^2; every indifference hypersurface has everywhere a non-zero Gaussian curvature, and its closure is contained in P.[1]

Given a pair (p, w) of a price-vector p in S, and a wealth w in L, we denote by $f_i(p, w)$ the consumption-vector demanded by the ith consumer. The preceding properties imply that the demand function f_i is of class C^1 on $S \times L$ [Katzner (1968)].

With an initial allocation $e = (e_1,\ldots,e_m)$ in P^m is associated the excess demand function F_e defined on S by

$$p \mapsto F_e(p) = \sum_i [f_i(p, p \cdot e_i) - e_i].$$

This function obeys Walras' law, i.e., for every p in S, one has $p \cdot F_e(p) = 0$. An equilibrium price-vector is, by definition, a p in S for which $F_e(p) = 0$. Given a vector z in $\mathbf{R}^l$, denote by $\hat{z}$ the vector in $\mathbf{R}^{l-1}$ whose coordinates are the first $l - 1$ coordinates of z, Because of Walras' law it is equivalent to define an equilibrium price-vector as a p in S for which $\hat{F}_e(p) = 0$.

> *Definition.* The economy $\mathscr{E}$ is regular if 0 is a regular value of $\hat{F}_e$.

This definition, due to E. and H. Dierker (1972), is equivalent to that of Debreu (1970), as a calculation on Jacobian determinants of Balasko (1975) shows [still other definitions of a regular economy were given by Smale (1974) and Balasko (1975)]. Thus, given the m preference preorders of the economy, the set of e for which $\mathscr{E}$ is not regular is a subset of P^m of Lebesgue measure zero, and closed relative to P^m.

Now consider $\mathscr{E}_n$, the n-replica of $\mathscr{E}$. The following results are taken from Debreu and Scarf (1963). Any allocation in the core of $\mathscr{E}_n$ gives identical consumption-vectors to all the agents of the same type. It can therefore be represented by a point x in P^m. In this manner the core of $\mathscr{E}_n$ is represented by a subset C_n of P^m. Let W be the set of Walras allocations of $\mathscr{E}$, and therefore of $\mathscr{E}_n$. The sets W and C_n are non-empty, and compact. They

---

[1] A study of preference relations enjoying these properties will be found in Debreu (1972).

satisfy the relations $W \subset C_{n+1} \subset C_n$. Moreover, as n tends to infinity, the Hausdorff distance $\delta(C_n, W)$ of C_n and W tends to zero. In the regular case this last assertion can be strengthened as follows.

Theorem

For a regular economy $\mathscr{E}$, as n tends to infinity, $\delta(C_n, W) = 0(1/n)$.

That is to say, $n \, \delta(C_n, W)$ is bounded. In other words, the distance between the core of $\mathscr{E}_n$ and its set of Walras allocations converges to zero at least as fast as the inverse of the number of agents.

It would be very desirable to extend this result to the general framework of Hildenbrand (1974, chs. 2 and 3). There is little doubt that such an extension is possible.

Before proving the theorem we note the following lemma:

Lemma

The function F_e is proper.

Proof. We must check [Dieudonné (1972, p. 243)] that if K is a compact subset of $\mathbf{R}^l$, then $H = F_e^{-1}(K)$ is compact. Let (p^q) be a sequence in H. Since $\bar{S}$ is compact, there is a subsequence $(\bar{p}^q)$ converging to p^0 in $\bar{S}$. Assume that $p^0 \notin S$. In this case our assumptions on preferences and on initial endowments imply that $\|F_e(\bar{p}^q)\|$ tends to $+\infty$, a contradiction of $F_e(\bar{p}^q) \in K$. Thus $p^0 \in S$, which implies $F_e(p^0) \in K$. Therefore $p^0 \in H$. Q.E.D.

Proof of the theorem

Let

$$X_i = \left\{ z \in P \,\middle|\, z \succcurlyeq_i e_i \quad \text{and} \quad z \leqq \sum_j e_j \right\}.$$

For every n, and for every allocation x in C_n, x_i belongs to X_i. The subset X_i of P is compact. Therefore so is $\bigcup_i X_i$. Select a compact subset X of P containing $\bigcup_i X_i$ in its interior. Thus there is an open ball V in $\mathbf{R}^l$ with center 0 and radius $v > 0$ such that for every n, for every i, and for every allocation x in C_n, the open ball $x_i + V$ is contained in X.

Given a point z in P, denote by $I_i(z)$ the indifference hypersurface of the ith type through z, and by $g_i(z)$ the unit normal to $I_i(z)$ at z oriented in the direction of preference. Our assumptions imply strong monotony of preferences. Consequently, for every i, and for every pair (z, z') of points in P, the angle of $g_i(z)$ and $g_i(z')$ is strictly smaller than $(\pi/2)$. Since this angle depends continuously on (z, z'), its maximum $\bar\theta$ over all i, and over all pairs (z, z') in $X \times X$ is also strictly smaller than $(\pi/2)$.

We now investigate curvature properties of the indifference hypersurfaces, the importance of which for this analysis was anticipated by Nishino (1971) and Shapley (1975). For a type i, and a point z in P, consider the $l - 1$ principal curvatures at z of $I_i(z)$. By convexity, all these principal curvatures have the same sign; none of them vanish since the Gaussian curvature is everywhere different from zero. Denote by $\gamma_i(z)$ the largest of their absolute values. The function γ_i is continuous; let $\bar\gamma$ be its maximum over all i, and over all z in X.

Consider a unit vector t tangent to $I_i(z)$ at z in $\bigcup_i X_i$, and the curve Γ intersection of $I_i(z)$ and of the plane Π generated by $g_i(z)$ and t. At a point z' of $\Gamma \cap X$, let t' be a unit vector tangent to Γ, and let u be the unit normal to Γ contained in Π and oriented in the direction of preference. Also, let θ be the angle of u and $g_i(z')$, the unit normal to $I_i(z)$ at z'. Clearly θ is at most equal to the angle of $g_i(z)$ and $g_i(z')$. Hence $\theta \leq \bar\theta$. Now by Meusnier's theorem [Laugwitz (1965, p. 53)], at z' the curvature of Γ equals the normal curvature of $I_i(z)$ determined by t' divided by $\cos\theta$. Moreover, by Euler's theorem [Laugwitz (1965, p. 55) states the theorem in R^3; Eisenhart[2] (1926, p. 154) states it in $\mathbf{R}^l$], at z' the normal curvature of $I_i(z)$ determined by t' is at most equal to $\gamma_i(z')$. Summing up, the curvature of Γ at z' is at most equal to $(\gamma_i(z'))/\cos\theta$. Consequently the curvature of Γ at z' is at most equal to $\bar\gamma/\cos\bar\theta$; which we denote by $1/\rho$.

Next we study the intersection $\hat\Gamma$ of Γ and of the ball $z + V$. Taking t and $g_i(z)$ as unit coordinate-vectors in the plane Π, we look at $\hat\Gamma$ as the graph of a C^2 convex function. Since $\hat\Gamma$ has everywhere a curvature at most equal to $1/\rho$, it is not difficult to show that $\hat\Gamma$ does not intersect the open ball in Π with center $z + \rho g_i(z)$ and radius ρ. Since this assertion holds for any unit vector t tangent to $I_i(z)$ at z, the set $I_i(z) \cap (z + V)$ does not intersect the open ball $B_i(z)$ in $\mathbf{R}^l$ with center $z + \rho g_i(z)$ and radius ρ. Thus $z' \in (z + V) \cap B_i(z)$ implies $z' \succ_i z$ for every i, for every z in $\bigcup_i X_i$.[3]

We now examine an allocation x in C_n. Let A_n be the set of agents of $\mathscr{E}_n$. Denote by a a generic element of A_n, and by $T(a)$ its type. Write, also, by an abuse of notation, $\preccurlyeq_a, e_a, \ldots$ for $\preccurlyeq_{T(a)}, e_{T(a)}, \ldots$. Consider a non-empty coalition E, writing $\#E$ for the number of its elements. Since E does not block x, one has

[2] A reference I owe to S. S. Chern.
[3] This assertion is easily seen to imply the assumption of "uniform smoothness" of Nishino (1971, p. 41).

$$\sum_{a \in E} e_a \notin \sum_{a \in E} \{z \in P | z \succ_a x_a\},$$

or

$$\frac{1}{\#E} \sum_{a \in E} (e_a - x_a) \notin \frac{1}{\#E} \sum_{a \in E} [\{z \in P | z \succ_a x_a\} - x_a]. \qquad (1)$$

In particular, select an agent $\bar{a}$ of the ith type and let $E = A_n \backslash \bar{a}$ [a type of coalition considered by Edgeworth (1881), Hansen (1969), and Nishino (1971)]. Since

$$\sum_{a \in A_n} (e_a - x_a) = 0,$$

one has

$$\sum_{a \in E} (e_a - x_a) = x_{\bar{a}} - e_{\bar{a}}.$$

Thus from (1),

$$\frac{1}{\#E} (x_{\bar{a}} - e_{\bar{a}}) \notin \frac{1}{\#E} \sum_{a \in E} [\{z \in P | z \succ_a x_a\} - x_a].$$

Letting $y_i = x_i - e_i$, and $q_n = \#A_n$, one obtains

$$\frac{1}{q_n - 1} y_i \notin \frac{1}{\#E} \sum_{a \in E} [\{z \in P | z \succ_a x_a\} - x_a]. \qquad (2)$$

Since $\|y_i\| \leq \|\sum_{j=1}^m e_j\|$, the norm of $[1/(q_n - 1)]y_i$ is bounded by $\alpha_n = [1/(q_n - 1)] \|\sum_j e_j\|$. From now on, we choose n large enough to satisfy the inequality $\alpha_n < \min \{v, 2\rho\}$. Therefore $[1/(q_n - 1)]y_i \in V$. Since x is a Pareto optimum, all the $g_i(x_i)$ have a common value p. Denote by B the open ball in $\mathbf{R}^l$ with center ρp and radius ρ. As we have shown earlier, for every $a \in A_n$, $B \cap V$ is contained in $\{z \in P | z \succ_a x_a\} - x_a$. From (2), we conclude that $[1/(q_n - 1)]y_i \notin B \cap V$. Therefore $[1/(q_n - 1)]y_i \notin B$.[4]

The maximum of $p \cdot z$ for $\|z\| \leq \alpha_n$ and $z \notin B$ is easily found to be $\alpha_n^2/2\rho$. Thus for every i,

$$\frac{p \cdot y_i}{q_n - 1} \leq \frac{\alpha_n^2}{2\rho}.$$

Hence,

$$p \cdot y_i \leq \frac{1}{2\rho(q_n - 1)} \left\| \sum_j e_j \right\|^2$$

---

[4] Some of the ideas of this paragraph, and of the next one are related to Nishino (1971, especially to Lemma 4, pp. 44–45).

However, $\sum_{i=1}^{m} p \cdot y_i = 0$. Consequently, for every i,

$$p \cdot y_i \geqq -\frac{m-1}{2\rho(q_n-1)} \left\| \sum_j e_j \right\|^2$$

Summing up,

$$|p \cdot y_i| \leqq \frac{m-1}{2\rho(nm-1)} \left\| \sum_j e_j \right\|^2,$$

or for every i,

$$p \cdot e_i - p \cdot x_i = 0(1/n). \tag{3}$$

As x_i belongs to X, and $p = g_i(x_i)$, the vector p belongs to the set $g_i(X)$, a compact subset of S. Similarly, $p \cdot x_i$ and $p \cdot e_i$ belong to $X \cdot g_i(X)$, a compact subset of L. Thus by using the mean-value theorem of the calculus, we obtain from (3)

$$f_i(p, p \cdot e_i) - f_i(p, p \cdot x_i) = 0(1/n),$$

which yields successively:

$$f_i(p, p \cdot e_i) - x_i = 0(1/n),$$

$$\sum_{i=1}^{m} [f_i(p, p \cdot e_i) - x_i] = 0(1/n),$$

$$\sum_{i=1}^{m} [f_i(p, p \cdot e_i) - e_i] = 0(1/n).$$

Hence,

$$F_e(p) = 0(1/n). \tag{4}$$

Since 0 is a regular value of $\hat{F}_e$, the set $\hat{F}_e^{-1}(0)$ is discrete. But W is compact and non-empty. Therefore $\hat{F}_e^{-1}(0)$ is finite and non-empty. Let $p^1, \ldots, p^r, \ldots, p^s$ be its elements. For each r, there is in S an open neighborhood U^r of p^r, and there is in $\mathbf{R}^{l-1}$ a non-empty open ball U with center 0 such that the U^r are pairwise disjoint, and for every r, U^r and U are C^1-diffeomorphic under the restriction of $\hat{F}_e$ to U^r. Consider now the set $S \backslash \bigcup_r U^r$, which is closed relative to S. Since F_e is proper by the lemma, the set $Q = F_e(S \backslash \bigcup_r U^r)$ is closed [Dieudonné (1972, p. 243)]. The origin 0 of $\mathbf{R}^l$ does not belong to Q. Consequently from (4), for n large enough, $F_e(p) \notin Q$; hence $p \in \bigcup_r U^r$. Thus p belongs to some U^k, and from (4), by another application of the mean-value theorem, one obtains

$$p - p^k = 0(1/n). \tag{5}$$

This relation and (3) yield

$$p \cdot x_i - p^k \cdot e_i = p \cdot (x_i - e_i) + (p - p^k) \cdot e_i$$
$$= 0(1/n).$$

Hence by a last application of the mean-value theorem, for every i,

$$f_i(p, p \cdot x_i) - f_i(p^k, p^k \cdot e_i) = 0(1/n).$$

Thus, denoting by x_i^k the equilibrium consumption-vector of the ith type associated with p^k, for every i,

$$x_i - x_i^k = 0(1/n) \qquad \text{Q.E.D.}$$

References

Balasko, Y., 1975, Some results on uniqueness and stability of equilibrium in general equilibrium theory, *Journal of Mathematical Economics*, **2**, forthcoming.

Debreu, G., 1970, Economies with a finite set of equilibria, *Econometrica*, **38**, 387–392.

Debreu, G., 1972, Smooth preferences, *Econometrica*, **40**, 603–615.

Debreu, G. and H. Scarf, 1963, A limit theorem on the core of an economy, *International Economic Review*, **4**, 235–246.

Dierker, E. and H. Dierker, 1972, The local uniqueness of equilibria, *Econometrica*, **40**, 867–881.

Dieudonné, J., 1972, *Treatise on analysis III* (Academic Press, New York).

Edgeworth, F. Y., 1881, *Mathematical psychics* (Paul Kegan, London).

Eisenhart, L. P., 1926, *Riemannian geometry* (Princeton University Press, Princeton, N.J.).

Hansen, T., 1969, A note on the limit of the core of an exchange economy, *International Economic Review*, **10**, 479–483.

Hildenbrand, W., 1974, *Core and equilibria of a large economy* (Princeton University Press, Princeton, N.J.).

Katzner, D. W., 1968, A note on the differentiability of consumer demand functions, *Econometrica*, **36**, 415–418.

Laugwitz, D., 1965, *Differential and Riemannian geometry* (Academic Press, New York).

Nishino, H., 1971, On the occurrence and the existence of competitive equilibria, *Keio Economic Studies*, **8**, 33–67.

Shapley, L. S., 1975, An example of a slow-converging core, *International Economic Review*, **16**, 345–351.

Shapley, L. S. and M. Shubik, 1969, Pure competition, coalitional power, and fair division, *International Economic Review*, **10**, 337–362.

Smale, S., 1974, Global analysis and economics IIA, *Journal of Mathematical Economics*, **1**, 1–14.

CHAPTER 18

Four aspects of the mathematical theory of economic equilibrium

The observed state of an economy can be viewed as an equilibrium resulting from the interaction of a large number of agents with partially conflicting interests. Taking this viewpoint, exactly one hundred years ago, Léon Walras presented in his *Eléments d'Economie Politique Pure* the first general mathematical analysis of this equilibrium problem. During the last four decades, Walrasian theory has given rise to several developments that required the use of basic concepts and results borrowed from diverse branches of mathematics. In this article, I propose to review four of them.

1   The existence of economic equilibria

As soon as an equilibrium state is defined for a model of an economy, the fundamental question of its existence is raised. The first solution of this problem was provided by A. Wald (**1935–1936**), and after a twenty-year interruption, research by a large number of authors has steadily extended the framework in which the existence of an equilibrium can be established. Although no work was done on the problem of existence of a Walrasian equilibrium from the early thirties to the early fifties, several contributions, which, later on, were to play a major role in the study of that problem, were made in related areas during that period. One of them was a lemma proved

The author gratefully acknowledges the support of the Miller Institute of the University of California, Berkeley, and of the National Science Foundation, and the comments of Birgit Grodal, Werner Hildenbrand, Andreu Mas-Colell, and Herbert Scarf.

by J. von Neumann (**1937**) in connection with his model of economic growth. This lemma was reformulated by S. Kakutani (**1941**) as a fixed-point theorem which became the most powerful tool for proofs of existence in economics. Another contribution, due to J. Nash (**1950**), was the first use of that tool in the solution of a problem of social equilibrium. For later reference we state Kakutani's theorem. Given two sets U and V, a *correspondence* ρ from U to V associates with every element $u \in U$, a nonempty subset $\rho(u)$ of V.

Theorem

If D is a nonempty, compact, convex subset of a Euclidean space, and ρ is a convex-valued, closed-graph correspondence from D to D, then there is d^* such that $d^* \in \rho(d^*)$.

As a simple prototype of a Walrasian equilibrium problem, we now consider an exchange economy with l commodities, and a finite set A of consumers. The consumption of consumer $a \in A$ is described by a point x_a in R^l_+; the ith coordinate x^i_a of x_a being the quantity of the ith commodity that he consumes. A price system p is an l-list of strictly positive numbers, i.e., a point in $P = \mathrm{Int}\, R^l_+$; the ith coordinate of p being the amount to be paid for one unit of the ith commodity. Thus the value of x_a relative to p is the inner product $p \cdot x_a$. Given the price vector $p \in P$, and his wealth $w \in L$, the set of strictly positive numbers, consumer a is constrained to satisfy the budget inequality $p \cdot x_a \leqq w$. Since multiplication of p and w by a strictly positive number has no effect on the behavior of consumers, we can normalize p, restricting it to the strictly positive part of the unit sphere $S = \{p \in P \,|\, \|p\| = 1\}$. We postulate that, presented with the pair $(p, w) \in S \times L$, consumer a demands the consumption vector $f_a(p, w)$ in R^l_+, and that the demand function f_a is continuous. If that consumer is insatiable, f_a also satisfies

$$\text{for every } (p, w) \in S \times L, \quad p \cdot f_a(p, w) = w. \tag{1}$$

To complete the description of the economy $\mathscr{E}$, we specify for consumer a an initial endowment vector $e_a \in P$. Thus the characteristics of consumer a are the pair (f_a, e_a) and $\mathscr{E}$ is the list $((f_a, e_a))_{a \in A}$ of those pairs for $a \in A$. Consider now a price vector $p \in S$. The corresponding wealth of consumer a is $p \cdot e_a$; his demand is $f_a(p, p \cdot e_a)$. Therefore the excess demand of the economy is

$$F(p) = \sum_{a \in A} [f_a(p, p \cdot e_a) - e_a].$$

And p is an equilibrium price vector if and only if $F(p) = 0$. Because of (1), the function F from S to R^l satisfies

Walras' law: $p \cdot F(p) = 0$.

Consequently, F is a continuous vector field on S, all of whose coordinates are bounded below. Finally, we make an assumption about the behavior of F near ∂S.

> *Boundary condition:* If p_n in S tends to p_0 in ∂S, then $\{F(p_n)\}$ is unbounded.

This condition expresses that every commodity is collectively desired. Here and below I freely make unnecessarily strong assumptions when they facilitate the exposition. Of the many variants of the existence theorem that have been proposed, I select the following statements by E. Dierker (**1974,** Sec. 8), some of whose antecedents were L. McKenzie (**1954**), D. Gale (**1955**), H. Nikaidô (**1956**), and K. Arrow and F. Hahn (**1971**).

Theorem

> If F is continuous, bounded below, and satisfies Walras' law and the boundary condition, then there is an equilibrium.

We indicate the main ideas of a proof because they will recur in this section and in the next. Here it is most convenient to normalize the price vector so that it belongs to the simplex $\Pi = \{p \in R^l_+ \,|\, \sum_{i=1}^l p^i = 1\}$.

Consider a price vector $p \notin \partial \Pi$ yielding an excess demand $F(p) \neq 0$. According to a commonly held view of the role of prices, a natural reaction of a price-setting agency to this disequilibrium situation would be to select a new price vector so as to make the excess demand $F(p)$ as expensive as possible, i.e., to select [K. Arrow and G. Debreu (**1954**)] a price vector in the set

$$\mu(p) = \left\{\pi \in \Pi \,\Big|\, \pi \cdot F(p) = \underset{q \in \pi}{\text{Max}}\, q \cdot F(p)\right\}.$$

When $p \in \partial \Pi$, the excess demand is not defined. In this case, we let $\mu(p) = \{\pi \in \Pi \,|\, \pi \cdot p = 0\}$.

By Kakutani's theorem, the correspondence μ from Π to Π has a fixed point p^*. Obviously, $p^* \notin \partial \Pi$. But then $p^* \in \mu(p^*)$ implies $F(p^*) = 0$.

From the fact that $\mu(p)$ is always a face of Π one suspects (rightly as we will see in the next section) that Kakutani's theorem is too powerful a tool for this result. But such is not the case in the general situation to which we will turn after having pointed out the broad interpretation that the concept of commodity must be given. In contemporary Walrasian theory, a commodity is defined as a good or a service with specified physical characteristics, to be delivered at a specified date, at a specified location, if [K. Arrow (**1953**)] a specified event occurs. Aside from this mere question of interpretation of a concept, the model can be expanded so as to include a finite set B of producers. Producer $b \in B$ chooses a production vectory y_b (whose positive coordinates correspond to outputs, and negative coordinates to inputs) in his production set Y_b, a nonempty subset of R^l, interpreted as the set of feasible production vectors. When the price vector p is given, producer b actually chooses his production vector in a nonempty subset $\psi_b(p)$ of Y_b. It is essential here, as it was not in the case of consumers, to provide for situations in which p does not uniquely determine the reaction of every producer, which may arise for instance if producer b maximizes his profit $p \cdot y_b$ in a cone Y_b with vertex 0 (constant returns to scale technology). In an economy with production, consumer a not only demands goods and services, but also supplies certain quantities of certain types of labor, which will appear as negative coordinates of his consumption vector x_a; this vector x_a is constrained to belong to his consumption set X_a, a given nonempty subset of R^l. A suitable extension of the concept of demand function covers this case. However, the wealth of a consumer is now the sum of the value of his endowment vector and of his shares of the profits of producers. In this manner, an integrated model of consumption and production is obtained, in which a state of the economy is a list $((x_a)_{a \in A}, (y_b)_{b \in B}, p)$ of vectors of R^l, where, for every $a \in A$, $x_a \in X_a$; for every $b \in B$, $y_b \in Y_b$; and $p \in \Pi$. The problem of existence of an equilibrium for such an economy has often been reduced to a situation similar to that of the last theorem, the continuous excess demand function being replaced by an excess demand correspondence with a closed graph. Alternatively, it can be formulated in the following general terms, in the spirit of J. Nash (**1950**). The social system is composed of a finite set C of agents. For each $c \in C$, a set D_c of possible actions is given. Consequently, a state of the system is an element d of the product $D = X_{c \in C} D_c$. We denote by $d_{C \backslash c}$ the list of actions obtained by deleting d_c from d. Given $d_{C \backslash c}$, i.e., the actions chosen by all the other agents, agent c reacts by choosing his own action in the set $\rho_c(d_{C \backslash c})$. The state d^* is an equilibrium if and only if, for every $c \in C$, $d_c^* \in \rho_c(d_{C \backslash c}^*)$. Thus, the reaction correspondence ρ from D to D being defined by $\rho(d) = X_{c \in C} \rho_c(d_{C \backslash c})$, the state d^* is an equilibrium if and only if it is a fixed point of ρ (see Figure 1). In the integrated economic model of consumption and production that we discussed, one of the agents is the impersonal market to which we assign the reaction correspondence μ introduced in the proof of the existence theorem.

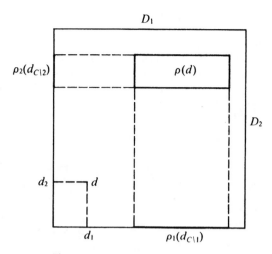

D_1

$\rho_2(d_{C\backslash2})$

$\rho(d)$

D_2

d_2 d

d_1 $\rho_1(d_{C\backslash1})$

Figure 1

Still broader interpretations and further extensions of the preceding model have been proposed. They include negative or zero prices, preference relations with weak properties instead of demand functions for consumers, measure spaces of agents, infinite-dimensional commodity spaces, monopolistic competition, public goods, redistribution of income, indivisible commodities, transaction costs, money, the use of nonstandard analysis, ... Since this extensive, and still rapidly growing, literature cannot be surveyed in detail here, I refer to the excellent account by K. Arrow and F. Hahn (1971), to the books mentioned in the next sections, and to recent volumes of *Econometrica*, *Journal of Economic Theory*, and *Journal of Mathematical Economics*.

2   The computation of economic equilibria

While the first proof of existence is forty years old, decisive steps towards an efficient algorithm for the computation of Walras equilibria were taken only during the last decade. In **1964**, C. Lemke and J. Howson gave an effective procedure for the computation of an equilibrium of a non-zero-sum two-person game. H. Scarf (**1967, 1973**) then showed how a technique similar to that of C. Lemke and J. Howson could be used to compute an approximate Walras equilibrium, and proposed a general algorithm for the calculation of an approximate fixed point of a correspondence. This algorithm, which has revealed itself to be surprisingly efficient, had the drawback of not permitting a gradual improvement of the degree of approximation of the solution. An essential extension due to C. Eaves

(1972, 1974), stimulated by a fixed-point theorem of F. Browder **(1960)**, overcame this difficulty.

Before presenting a version of the algorithm based on H. Scarf **(1973)**, and C. Eaves **(1974)**, we note that in the preceding proof of existence, we have actually associated with every point $p \in \Pi$ a set $\Lambda(p)$ of integers in $I = \{1, \ldots, l\}$, as follows.

$$\Lambda(p) = \{i \,|\, F^i(p) = \underset{j}{\text{Max}}\, F^j(p)\} \qquad \text{if } p \notin \partial\Pi,$$

$$= \{i | p^i = 0\} \qquad \text{if } p \in \partial\Pi.$$

The point p^* is an equilibrium if and only if $\Lambda(p)^* = I$, in other words, if and only if it is in the intersection of the closed sets $E_i = \{p | i \in \Lambda(p)\}$. Showing that this intersection is not empty would yield an existence proof in the manner of D. Gale **(1955)**.

We specify our terminology. By a simplex, we always means a closed simplex, and, of course, similarly for a face a simplex. A *facet* of an n-simplex is an $(n - 1)$- face. For each $p \in \Pi$, select now a label $\lambda(p)$ in $\Lambda(p)$. A set M of point is said to be *completely labeled*, abbreviated to *c.l.*, if the set $\lambda(M)$ of its labels is I. The labeling λ is chosen so as to satisfy the following restrictions on $\partial\Pi$:

(α) the set of vertices of Π is c.l.,
(β) no facet of Π is c.l.[1]

The algorithm will yield a c.l. set of l points of Π whose diameter can be made arbitrarily small, and consequently a point of Π at which the value of F can be made arbitrarily small.

Let T be the part of R^l_+ that is above Π, and $\mathcal{T}$ be a standard regular triangulation of T having for vertices the points of T with integral coordinates, used by H. Kuhn **(1960, 1968)**, T. Hansen **(1968)**, and C. Eaves **(1972)**, and illustrated by the figure (Figure 2). (Other considerably more efficient triangulations of, or more appropriately pseudomanifold structures on, T have been used, C. Eaves **(1972, 1974)**. Give any point in T the same label as its projection from 0 into Π; and say that two $(l - 1)$-simplexes of $\mathcal{T}$ are *adjacent* if there is an l-simplex of $\mathcal{T}$ of which they are facets. Consider now an $(l - 1)$-simplex s of $\mathcal{T}$ with c.l. vertices.

(i)   If $s = \Pi$, s is a facet of exactly one l-simplex of $\mathcal{T}$: hence there is exactly one $(l - 1)$-simplex of $\mathcal{T}$ with c.l. vertices adjacent to s.

(ii)   If $s \neq \Pi$, because of (β), s is not in the boundary of T; therefore s is a facet of exactly two l-simplexes of $\mathcal{T}$; hence there are exactly two $(l - 1)$-simplexes of $\mathcal{T}$ with c.l. vertices adjacent to s.

---

[1] Here is a simple example of a labeling of $\partial\Pi$ satisfying those restrictions. Given $p \in \partial\Pi$, select any $\lambda(p)$ in $\Lambda(p)$ such that $\lambda(p) - 1$ (mod l) is not in $\Lambda(p)$.

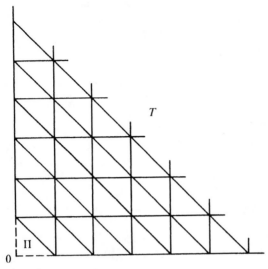

Figure 2

The algorithm starts from $s^0 = \Pi$. Take s^1 to be the unique $(l - 1)$-simplex of $\mathscr{T}$ with c.l. vertices adjacent to s^0. For $k > 0$, take s^{k+1} to be the unique $(l - 1)$-simplex of $\mathscr{T}$ with c.l. vertices adjacent to s^k, and other than s^{k-1}. Clearly this algorithm never returns to a previously used $(l - 1)$-simplex and never terminates. Given any integer n, after a finite number of steps, one obtains an $(l - 1)$-simplex with c.l. vertices above the hyperplane $\{p \in R \mid \sum_{i \in 1}^{l} p^i = n\}$. Projecting from 0 to Π, one obtains a sequence of c.l. sets of l points of Π whose diameter tends to 0 as n tends to $+\infty$.

An approximate fixed point (i.e., a point close to its image) of a continuous function from a finite-dimensional, nonempty, compact, convex set to itself can be obtained by a direct application of this algorithm. But in order to solve the analogous problem for a fixed point of a correspondence, and consequently, for a Walras equilibrium of an economy with production, H. Scarf and C. Eaves have used vector labels rather than the preceding integer labels. With every point p of Π, one now associates a suitably chosen vector $\lambda(p)$ in R^{l-1}, and one says that a set M of points of Π is c.l. if the origin of R^{l-1} belongs to the convex hull of $\lambda(M)$. As before, the labeling λ of Π is restricted to satisfy (α) and (β). The last two paragraphs can then be repeated word for word with the following single exception. Let σ be an l-simplex of $\mathscr{T}$, and s be a facet of σ with c.l. vertices. Denote by V_σ (resp. V_s) the set of vertices of σ (resp. of s). If $\lambda(V_\sigma)$ is in general position in R^{l-1}, then 0 is interior to the convex hull of $\lambda(V_s)$, and there is exactly one other facet of σ with c.l. vertices. However, if $\lambda(V_\sigma)$ is not in general position, a degenerate case where there are several other facets of σ with c.l.

vertices may arise. An appropriate use of the lexic refinement of linear programming resolves this degeneracy. In this general form, the algorithm can indeed be directly applied to the computation of approximate Kakutani fixed points.

The simplicity of this algorithm is very appealing, but its most remarkable feature is its efficiency. Experience with several thousand examples has been reported, in particular in H. Scarf (**1973**) and R. Wilmuth (**1973**). As a typical case of the version of the integer-labeling algorithm presented above (which uses an inefficient triangulation of T), let $l = 10$. To reach an elevation $n = 100$ in T, i.e., a triangulation of Π for which every edge is divided into 100 equal intervals, the number of iterations required rarely exceeds 2,000, and the computing time on an IBM 370 is usually less than 15 seconds. The number of vertices that are examined in the computation is therefore a small fraction of the number of vertices of the triangulation of Π at elevation 100.

The best general reference on the problem discussed in this section is H. Scarf (**1973**). *Mathematical Programming* is a good bibliographical source for more recent developments.

3   Regular differentiable economies

The model $\mathscr{E} = ((f_a, e_a))_{a \in A}$ of an exchange economy presented at the beginning of Section 1 would provide a complete explanation of the observed state of that economy in the Walrasian framework if the set $E(\mathscr{E})$ of its equilibrium price vectors had exactly one element. However, this global uniqueness requirement has revealed itself to be excessively strong, and was replaced, in the last five years, by that of local uniqueness. Not only does one wish $E(\mathscr{E})$ to be discrete, one would also like the correspondence E to be continuous. Otherwise, the slightest error of observation on the data of the economy might lead to an entirely different set of predicted equilibria. This consideration, which is common in the study of physical systems, applies with even greater force to the study of social systems. Basic differential topology has provided simple and satisfactory answers to the two questions of discreteness of $E(\mathscr{E})$, and of continuity of E.

At first, we keep the list $f = (f_a)_{a \in A}$ of demand functions fixed, and we assume that each one of them is of class C^r ($r \geq 1$). Thus an economy is identified with the point $e = (e_a)_{a \in A}$ in P^A. We denote by E the set of $(e, p) \in P^A \times S$ such that p is an equilibrium price vector for the economy e, and by $E(e)$ the set of equilibrium price vectors associated with a given e_ϵ (see Figure 3). The central importance of the manifold E, or of a related manifold of S. Smale (**1974**), has been recognized by S. Smale (**1974**) and

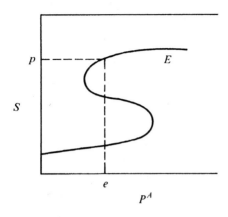

Figure 3

Y. Balasko (**1975a**). Recently, Y. Balasko (**1975b**) has noticed the property of C^r-isomorphism to P^A.

Theorem

E is a C^r-submanifold of $P^A \times S$ of the same dimension as P^A. If for every $a \in A$ the range of f_a is contained in P, then E is C^r-isomorphic to P^A.

Now let π be the projection $P^A \times S \to P^A$, and $\tilde{\pi}$ be its restriction to the manifold E.

Definition. The economy $\mathscr{E} = (f, e)$ is *regular* if e is a regular value of $\tilde{\pi}$. It is *critical* if it is not regular.

By Sard's theorem, the set of critical e has Lebesgue measure zero. Suppose in addition we assume that every demand function f_a satisfies the

Strong boundary condition. If (p_n, w_n) in $S \times L$ tends to (p_0, w_0) in $\partial S \times L$, then $\{f_a(p_n, w_n)\}$ is unbounded.

Then we readily obtain that $\tilde{\pi}$ is proper [Y. Balasko (**1975b**)]. In this case the critical set is closed (relative to P^A). It is therefore negligible in a strong sense. As for economies in the regular set $\mathscr{R}$, the complement of the critical set, they are well behaved in the following sense. At $e \in \mathscr{R}$, the compact set $E(e) = \tilde{\pi}^{-1}(e)$ is discrete, therefore finite, and $\tilde{\pi}^{-1}$ is locally a C^r-diffeomorphism.

In order to prepare for the discussion of regular economies in the context of the next section, we note an equivalent definition [E. and H. Dierker (**1972**)] of a critical point of the manifold E for $\tilde{\pi}$. Given e, let $F(p)$ be the excess demand associated with p, and denote by $\hat{F}(p)$ the projection of $F(p)$ into some fixed $(l - 1)$-dimensional coordinate subspace of R^l. Because of Walras' law, and because p is strictly positive, $F(p) = 0$ is equivalent to $\hat{F}(p) = 0$. Let then $J[\hat{F}(p)]$ be the Jacobian determinant of $\hat{F}$ at p. As Y. Balasko (**1975b**) shows, (e, p) is a critical point of $\tilde{\pi}$ if and only if $J[\hat{F}(p)] = 0$.

Since it is desirable to let demand functions vary as well as initial endowments [F. Delbaen (**1971**), E. and H. Dierker (**1972**)], we endow the set D of C^r demand functions $(r \geq 1)$ satisfying the strong boundary condition with the topology of uniform C^r-convergence.

An economy $\mathscr{E}$ is now defined as an element of $(D \times P)^A$, regular element of the latter space being a pair (f, e) for which the Jacobian determinant introduced in the last paragraph is different from zero for every equilibrium price vector associated with (f, e). The regular set is then shown to be open and dense in $(D \times P)^A$. Another extension, by S. Smale (**1974**), established the same two properties of the regular set in the context of utility functions with weak properties, rather than in the context of demand functions.

Still further generalizations, for instance, to cases where production is possible, have been obtained. E. Dierker (**1974**) surveys a large part of the area covered in this section more leisurely than I did. Recent volumes of the three journals listed at the end of Section 1 are also relevant here.

4   The core of a large economy

So far the discussion of consumer behavior has been in terms of demand functions. We now introduce for consumer a the more basic concept of a binary preference relation $\preccurlyeq_a$ on R^l_+, for which we read "$x \preccurlyeq_a y$" as "for agent a, commodity vector y is at least as desired as commodity vector x." The relation of strict preference "$x \prec_a y$" is defined by "$x \preccurlyeq_a y$ and not $y \preccurlyeq_a x$," and of indifference "$x \sim_a y$" by "$x \preccurlyeq_a y$ and $y \preccurlyeq_a x$." Similarly, for two vectors x, y in R^l we denote by "$x \leq y$" the relation "$y - x \in R^l_+$," by "$x < y$" the relation "$x \leq y$ and not $y \leq x$," and by "$x \ll y$" the relation "$y - x \in P$."

We assume that $\preccurlyeq_a$ is a complete preorder with a closed graph, and that it satisfies the monotony condition, $x < y$ implies $x \prec_a y$, expressing the desirability of all commodities for consumer a. The set of preference relations satisfying these assumptions is denoted by $\mathscr{P}$, and viewing an element of $\mathscr{P}$ as a closed subset of R^{2l}, we endow $\mathscr{P}$ with Hausdorff's (**1957**) topology of closed convergence [Y. Kannai (**1970**)].

The characteristics of consumer $a \in A$ are now a pair $(\preccurlyeq_a, e_a)$ of a preference relation in $\mathscr{P}$, and an endowment vector in R^l_+. Thus an exchange *economy* $\mathscr{E}$ is a function from A to $\mathscr{P} \times R^l_+$. The result of any exchange process in this economy is an *allocation*, i.e., a function x from A to R^l_+, that is *attainable* in the sense that $\sum_{a \in A} x_a = \sum_{a \in A} e_a$.

A proposed allocation x is *blocked* by a coalition E of consumers if

(i) $E \neq \varnothing$,

and the members of E can reallocate their own endowments among themselves to as to make every member of E better off, i.e., if

(ii)   there is an allocation y such that $\sum_{a \in E} y_a = \sum_{a \in E} e_a$ and, for every $a \in E, x_a \prec_a y_a$.

From this viewpoint, first taken by F. Edgeworth (**1881**), only the unblocked attainable allocations are viable. The set of those allocations is the *core* $C(\mathscr{E})$ of the economy. The goal of this section is to relate the core to the equilibrium concept that underlies the analysis of the first three sections. Formally, we define a *Walras allocation* as an attainable allocation x for which there is a price system $p \in \Pi$ such that, for every $a \in A$, x_a is a greatest element for $\preccurlyeq_a$ of the budget set $\{z \in R^l_+ \mid p \cdot z \leqq p \cdot e_a\}$.

The set of Walras allocations of $\mathscr{E}$ is denoted by $W(\mathscr{E})$. It satisfies the mathematically trivial but economically important relation $W(\mathscr{E}) \subset C(\mathscr{E})$.

Simple examples shown that for small economies the second set is much larger than the first. However, F. Edgeworth (**1881**) perceived that as the number of agents tends to $+\infty$ in such a way that each one of them becomes insignificant relative to their totality, the two sets tend to coincide. The conditions under which F. Edgeworth proved his limit theorem were very special. The first generalization was obtained by H. Scarf (**1962**), after M. Shubik (**1959**) had called attention to the connection between F. Edgeworth's "contract curve" and the game-theoretical concept of the core. The problem was then placed in its natural setting by R. Aumann (**1964**). The agents now form a positive measure space $(A, \mathscr{A}, \nu)$ such that $\nu(A) = 1$. The elements of $\mathscr{A}$ are the *coalitions*, and for $E \in \mathscr{A}$, $\nu(E)$ is interpreted as the fraction of the totality of agents in coalition E. Since the characteristics of an agent $a \in A$ are the pair $(\preccurlyeq_a, e_a)$, an *economy* $\mathscr{E}$ is defined [W. Hildenbrand (**1974**)], as a measurable function from A *to* $\mathscr{P} \times R^l_+$ such that e is integrable. The definitions of an unblocked attainable allocation and of a Walras allocation are extended in an obvious fashion. As trivially as before $W(\mathscr{E}) \subset C(\mathscr{E})$. But in the case in which the space of agents is atomless, i.e., in which every agent is negligible, R. Aumann (**1964**) has proved the following theorem:

Theorem

If the economy $\mathscr{E}$ is atomless and $\int_A e \, dv \gg 0$, then $W(\mathscr{E}) = C(\mathscr{E})$.

This remarkable result reconciles two fundamental and a priori very different equilibrium concepts. Its proof can be based [K. Vind (**1964**)] on Lyapunov's theorem on the convexity of the range of an atomless finite-dimensional vector measure.

There remains to determine the extent to which the equality of the core and of the set of Walras allocations holds approximately for a finite economy with a large number of nearly insignificant agents. This program is the object of W. Hildenbrand (**1974**), one of whose main results we now present.

Letting $K = \mathscr{P} \times R_+^l$ be the set of agents' characteristics, we introduce the basic concepts associated with the economy $\mathscr{E}$ that we need. The image measure $\mu = v \circ \mathscr{E}^{-1}$ of v via $\mathscr{E}$ is a probability on K called the *characteristic distribution* of $\mathscr{E}$. Given an allocation x for $\mathscr{E}$ (i.e., an integrable function from A to R_+^l), consider the function γ_x from A to $K \times R_+^l$ defined by $\gamma_x(a) = (\mathscr{E}(a), x(a))$. The image measure $v \circ \gamma_x^{-1}$ of v via γ_x is a probability on $K \times R_+^l$ called the *characteristic-consumption distribution* of x. We denote by $\mathscr{D}_W(\mathscr{E})$ the set of characteristic-consumption distributions of the Walras allocations of $\mathscr{E}$, and similarly by $\mathscr{D}_C(\mathscr{E})$ the set of characteristic-consumption distributions of the core allocations of $\mathscr{E}$. Finally, we formalize the idea of a competitive sequence of finite economies. $\# A_n$ will denote the number of agents of $\mathscr{E}_n$, μ_n the characteristic distribution of $\mathscr{E}_n$, and pr_2 the projection from K into R_+^l. The sequence $(\mathscr{E}_n)$ is *competitive* if

(i) $\# A_n \to +\infty$,
(ii) μ_n converges weakly to a limit μ,
(iii) $\int_K pr_2 \, d\mu_n \to \int_K pr_2 \, d\mu \gg 0$.

We denote by $\mathscr{E}^\mu$ the economy defined as the identity map from K, endowed with its Borel σ-field $\mathscr{B}(K)$, and the measure μ, to K. Then, endowing the set of probability measures on $K \times R_+^l$ with the topology of weak convergence, we obtain the theorem of W. Hildenbrand (**1974**, Chapter 3).

Theorem

If the sequence $(\mathscr{E}_n)$ is competitive, and U is a neighborhood of $\mathscr{D}_W(\mathscr{E}^\mu)$, then, for n large enough, $\mathscr{D}_C(\mathscr{E}_n) \subset U$.

To go further, and to obtain full continuity results, as well as results on the rate of convergence of the core of $\mathscr{E}_n$, we need an extension [F. Delbaen (1971), K. Hildenbrand (1974), and H. Dierker (1975)] of the concepts and of the propositions of Section 3 to present context of a measure space of agents. Specifically, we place ourselves in the framework of H. Dierker (1975). In addition to being in $\mathscr{P}$, the preference relations of consumers are now assumed to satisfy the following conditions. For every point $x \in P$, the preference-or-indifference set $\{y \in P | x \preccurlyeq y\}$ is convex, and the indifference set $I(x) = \{y \in P | y \sim x\}$ is a C^2-hypersurface of P whose Gaussian curvature is everywhere nonzero, and whose closure relative to R^l is contained in P. Finally denoting by $g(x)$ the positive unit normal of $I(x)$ at the point x, we assume that g is C^1 on P. These conditions make it possible to identify the preference relation $\preccurlyeq$ with the C^1 vector field g on P. The set G of these vector fields is endowed with the topology of uniform C^1 convergence on compact subsets. $\mathscr{M}$ then denotes the set of characteristic distributions on $G \times P$ with compact support. The assumptions that we have made imply that every agent has a C^1 demand function. Therefore it is possible to define a *regular* element μ of $\mathscr{M}$ as a characteristic distribution μ in $\mathscr{M}$ such that the Jacobian determinant introduced in Section 3 is different from zero for every equilibrium price vector associated with μ. Having suitably topologized the set $\mathscr{M}$, one can give, in the manner of H. Dierker (1975), general conditions under which the regular set is open and dense in $\mathscr{M}$.

In this framework, the following result on the rate of convergence of the core of an economy has recently been obtained [B. Grodal (1975)] for the case in which the agents' characteristics belong to a compact subset Q of $G \times P$. For a finite set A, d^A denotes the metric defined on the set of functions from A to R^l by $d^A(x, y) = \text{Max}_{a \in A} \|x(a) - y(a)\|$, and $\delta^A(X, Y)$ denotes the associated Hausdorff distance of two compact sets X, Y of functions from A to R^l. In the statement of the theorem, $\mathscr{M}_Q$ denotes the set of characteristic distributions on Q with the topology of weak convergence.

Theorem

If Q is a compact subset of $G \times P$ and μ is a regular characteristic distribution on Q, then there are a neighborhood V of μ in $\mathscr{M}_Q$, and a real number k such that for every economy $\mathscr{E}$ with a finite set A of agents, and whose characteristic distribution belongs to V,

$$\delta^A[C(\mathscr{E}), W(\mathscr{E})] \leq k/\#A.$$

Thus if $(\mathscr{E}_n)$ is a competitive sequence of economies on Q, and if the limit characteristic distribution is regular, then $\delta^{A_n}[C(\mathscr{E}_n), W(\mathscr{E}_n)]$ tends to 0 at least as fast as the inverse of the number of agents.

The basic reference for this section is W. Hildenbrand (**1974**). The analysis of Walras equilibria, of the core, and of their relationship has yielded valuable insights into the role of prices in an economy. But possibly of greater importance has been the recognition that the techniques used in that analysis are indispensable for the mathematical study of social systems: algebraic topology for the test of existence that mathematical models of social equilibrium must pass; differential topology for the more demanding tests of discreteness, and of continuity for the set of equilibria; combinatorial techniques for the computation of equilibria; and measure theory for the study of large sets of small agents.

References

K. J. Arrow (1953), Le rôle des valeurs boursières pour la répartition la meilleure des risques, *Econométrie*, pp. 41–47; discussion, pp. 47–48, *Colloq. Internat. Centre National de la Recherche Scientifique*, no. 40 (Paris, 1952), Centre de la Recherche Scientifique, Paris, 1953; translated in *Review of Economic Studies*, **31** (1964), 91–96. MR **16**, 943.

K. J. Arrow and G. Debreu (1954), Existence of an equilibrium for a competitive economy, *Econometrica*, **22**, 265–290. MR **17**, 985.

K. J. Arrow and F. H. Hahn (1971), *General competitive analysis*, Holden-Day, San Francisco, Calif.

R. J. Aumann (1964), Markets with a continuum of traders, *Econometrica*, **32**, 39–50. MR **30** No. 2908.

Y. Balasko (1975a), On the graph of the Walras correspondence, *Econometrica* (to appear).

Y. Balasko (1975b), Some results on uniqueness and on stability of equilibrium in general equilibrium theory, *J. Math. Economics* (to appear).

F. E. Browder (1960), On continuity of fixed points under deformations of continuous mappings, *Summa Brãsil. Mat.*, **4**, 183–191. MR **24** No. A543.

F. Delbaen (1971), Lower and upper semi-continuity of the Walras correspondence, Doctoral Dissertation, Free University of Brussels.

E. Dierker (1974), Topological methods in Walrasian economics, Lecture Notes in Economics and Mathematical Systems, **92**, Springer-Verlag, Berlin.

E. and H. Dierker (1972), On the local uniqueness of equilibria, *Econometrica*, **40**, 867–881.

H. Dierker (1975), Smooth preferences and the regularity of equilibria, *J. Math. Economics* (to appear).

B. C. Eaves (1972), Homotopies for computation of fixed points, *Math. Programming*, **3**, 1–22. MR **46** No. 3089.

B. C. Eaves (1974), Properly labeled simplexes, Studies in Optimization, MAA Studies in Mathematics, 10, G. B. Dantzig and B. C. Eaves, eds., Mathematical Association of America.

F. Y. Edgeworth (1881), *Mathematical Psychics*, Paul Kegan, London.

D. Gale (1955), The law of supply and demand, *Math. Scand.* **3**, 155–169. MR **17**, No. 985.

B. Grodal (1975), The rate of convergence of the core for a purely competitive sequence of economies, *J. Math. Economics* (to appear).

T. Hansen (1968), On the approximation of a competitive equilibrium, Ph.D. Dissertation, Yale University, New Haven, Conn.

F. Hausdorff (1957), *Set theory*, Chelsea, New York. MR **19**, No. 111.

K. Hildenbrand (1974), Finiteness of $\Pi(\mathscr{E})$ and continuity of Π, Appendix to Chapter 2 in W. Hildenbrand (1974).

W. Hildenbrand (1974), *Core and equilibria of a large economy*, Princeton University Press, Princeton, N.J.

S. Kakutani (1941), A generalization of Brouwer's fixed point theorem, *Duke Math. J.*, **8**, 457–459. MR **3**, No. 60.

Y. Kannai (1970), Continuity properties of the core of a market, *Econometrica*, **38**, 791–815.

H. W. Kuhn (1960), Some combinatorial lemmas in topology, *IBM J. Res. Develop.*, **4**, 518–524. MR **23** No. A1358.

H. W. Kuhn, (1968), Simplical approximation of fixed points, *Proc. Nat. Acad. Sci. U.S.A.*, **61**, 1238–1242.

C. E. Lemke and J. T. Howson, Jr. (1964), Equilibrium points of bimatrix games, *J. Soc. Indust. Appl. Math.*, **12**, 413–423. MR **30** No. 3769.

L. W. McKenzie (1954), On equilibrium in Graham's model of world trade and other competitive systems, *Econometrica*, **22**, 147–161.

J. Nash (1950), Equilibrium points in n-person games, *Proc. Nat. Acad. Sci. U.S.A.*, **36**, 48–49. MR **11**, 192.

J. von Neumann (1937), Über ein ökonomisches Gleichungssystem und eine Verallgemeinerung des Brouwerschen Fixpunktsatzes, Ergebnisse eines mathematischen Kolloquiums, no. 8, 83–73; Translated in *Review of Economic Studies*, **13** (1945), 1–9.

H. Nikaidô (1956), On the classical multilateral exchange problem, *Metroecon.*, **8**, 135–145. MR **18**, 266.

H. Scarf (1962), *An analysis of markets with a large number of participants*, Recent Advances in Game Theory, Princeton University Conference Report.

H. Scarf (1967), The approximation of fixed points of a continuous mapping, *SIAM J. Appl. Math.*, **15**, 1328–1343. MR **39** No. 3814.

H. Scarf (1973) (with the collaboration of T. Hansen) *The computation of economic equilibria*, Yale University Press, New Haven, Conn.

M. Shubik (1959), Edgeworth market games, Contributions to the Theory of Games, vol. IV, *Ann. of Math. Studies*, no. 40, Princeton University Press, Princeton, N. J. MR **21** No. 2538.

S. Smale (1974), Global analysis and economics, *IIA, J. Math. Economics*, **1**, 1–14.

K. Vind (1964), Edgeworth-allocations in an exchange economy with many traders, *Internat. Economic Rev.* **5**, 165–177.

A. Wald (1935), Über die eindeutige positive Lösbarkeit der neuen Produktionsgleichungen, *Ergebnisse eines mathematischen Kolloquiums*, no. 6, 12–20.

A. Wald (1936a), Über die Produktionsgleichungen der ökonomischen Wertlehre, *Ergebnisse eines mathematischen Kolloquiums*, no. 7, 1–6.

A. Wald (1936b), Über einige Gleichungssysteme der mathematischen Ökonomie, Z. *Nationalökonomie*, **7**, 637–670; translated as On some systems of equations of mathematical economics, *Econometrica*, **19** (1951), 368–503. MR **13**, No. 370.

L. Walras (1874–1877), *Eléments d'économie politique pure*, Lausanne, Corbaz; translated as *Elements of pure economics*, Irwin, Homewood, Ill., 1954.

R. J. Wilmuth (1973), The computation of fixed points, Ph.D. Dissertation, Stanford University, Stanford, Calif.

CHAPTER 19

The application to economics of differential topology and global analysis: regular differentiable economies

The recent introduction of differential topology into economics was brought about by the study of several basic questions that arise in any mathematical theory of a social system centered on a concept of equilibrium. The purpose of this paper is to present a detailed discussion of two of those questions, and then to make a rapid survey of some related developments of the last five years.

Let e be a complete mathematical description of the economy to be studied (e.g., for an exchange economy, e might be a list of the demand functions and of the initial endowments of the consumers). Assumptions made a priori about e (e.g., assumptions of continuity on the demand functions) define the space $\mathscr{E}$ of economies to which the study is restricted. By a state of an economy we mean a list of specific values of all the relevant endogenous variables (e.g., prices and quantities of all the commodities consumed by the various consumers). We denote by S the set of conceivable states. Now a given equilibrium theory associates with each economy e in $\mathscr{E}$, the set $E(e)$ of equilibrium states of e, a subset of S (see Figure 1).

As a first test of the adequacy of this mathematical model, it must be possible to prove that for every element e of a sufficiently broad class $\mathscr{E}$, the set $E(e)$ is not empty. This is the existence problem that has been extensively studied during the last decades. Mentioning only the early contributions of John von Neumann and Abraham Wald, I refer to the comprehensive

I gratefully acknowledge the support of the National Science Foundation in the preparation of this article.

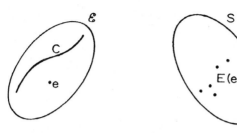

Figure 1

survey of the literature by Kenneth Arrow and F. H. Hahn. The mathematical tools for the solution were provided by algebraic topology in the form of fixed point theorems, or directly related results. An alternative approach of the last ten years, associated mainly with the name of Herbert Scarf, has consisted of developing efficient algorithms for the computation of an approximate equilibrium. The mathematical techniques used here were those of combinatorial topology.

Having obtained a general solution to the existence problem, one must investigate the structure of the set $E(e)$ of equilibria of the economy e. Consider an economy that has an equilibrium x such that in any neighborhood of x, there are infinitely many other equilibria. In this situation the explanation of equilibrium is essentially indeterminate, at least near x. Moreover the economic system e is unstable in the sense that arbitrarily small perturbations from x to a neighboring equilibrium induce no tendency for the state of the economy to return to x. It is therefore highly desirable to have an economy e for which the set of equilibria is *discrete*, i.e., such that for every equilibrium x in $E(e)$, there is a neighborhood of x in which x is the unique equilibrium of e. Unfortunately, even if every agent in the economy e is mathematically very well-behaved, one may obtain a set $E(e)$ that is not discrete (in the simplest case of an exchange economy with two consumers and two commodities, one can easily find in the associated Edgeworth box a set $E(e)$ made up of a continuum of points.) The pathology is due to the manner in which the agents are matched, a situation entirely different from that of existence theory where it was possible to give general conditions on the behavior of each agent separately ensuring that the set $E(e)$ would not be empty.

The way out of this difficulty is provided by differential topology. It consists of making suitable differentiability assumptions on the functions entering the description of e (e.g., demand functions are assumed to be continuously differentiable), and to define a concept of *regular* economy such that (a) the critical set C of nonregular economies is a negligible subset of $\mathscr{E}$, and (b) every regular economy has a discrete set of equilibria.

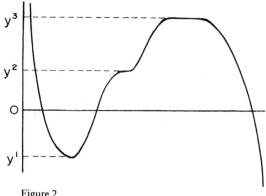

Figure 2

Actually an adequate model e of the economy must have still another property. Specifically if e' is close to e, then one would like the set of equilibria $E(e')$ to be close to $E(e)$. Otherwise an arbitrarily small error in the determination of the characteristics of e would yield an entirely different set of equilibria, thus depriving the theory of much of its explanatory power. Therefore it is also desirable for the definition of regularity to be such that (c) in a neighborhood of a regular economy, the set of equilibria depends continuously on the economy. The questions of discreteness of the set of equilibria and of continuous dependence of the set of equilibria on the economy, or closely related questions, have a long history in the study of physical systems. The recent work of R. Thom has considerably extended the range of their applications, in particular to biological systems. These questions clearly have no less relevance for social systems.

The solution of the problem that has just been outlined rests on A. Sard's theorem which Thom once characterized as one of the three main results of mathematical analysis. Consider a continuously differentiable function f from the real line R to R, and define a *critical point* as a point x where the derivative of f vanishes. The set of critical points of f can obviously be large. In the extreme case of a constant function it is the whole of R. Define now a *critical value* of f as the image of a critical point. In Figure 2 three critical values y^1, y^2, y^3 are displayed.

One feels that the set of those critical values is necessarily small, and indeed Sard's theorem asserts that it is negligible. To be precise, it has (Lebesgue) *measure zero*. In other words, given an arbitrarily small positive number ε, one can find a countable collection of intervals such that their union covers the critical set, and that the sum of the lengths of these

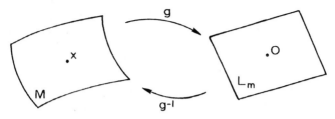

Figure 3

intervals is smaller than ε. Sard's theorem holds as well for a continuously differentiable function f from an m-dimensional Euclidean space to an m-dimensional Euclidean space. Here a *critical point of f* is a point where the determinant of the Jacobian of f vanishes. As before, a *critical value* of f is the image of a critical point, and the set of critical values has measure zero, i.e., it can be covered by a countable collection of m-dimensional cubes of arbitrarily small total volume. A *regular value* of f is, by definition, a noncritical value.

Sard's theorem is valid in still more general conditions. In order to present a stronger version that we will use later on, we need the concept of a (differentiable) manifold. A function g from an n-dimensional Euclidean space to an n-dimensional Euclidean space is said to be a *differentiable isomorphism* if it is one-to-one, and if g, as well as its inverse g^{-1} are continuously differentiable. Differential topology studies properties that are invariant under differentiable isomorphisms, a principle that leads to the following definition. A subset M of a Euclidean space L is an m-dimensional (differentiable) *manifold* if for each point x of M there is an m-dimensional linear subspace L_m of L such that a neighborhood in L of x and the part of M that it contains are differentiably isomorphic to a neighborhood in L of O and the part of L_m that it contains (see Figure 3). In other words, at every one of its points, M is locally an m-dimensional Euclidean space up to a differentiable isomorphism. Clearly one can do differential calculus on manifolds exactly as on Euclidean spaces; one can also easily define a subset of measure zero of a manifold M. Then the statement of Sard's theorem becomes: if f is a continuously differentiable function from an m-dimensional manifold M_1 to an m-dimensional manifold M_2, the set of critical values of f has measure zero in M_2.

To illustrate these general principles, assume that the economy e can be characterized by finitely many real parameters, or more precisely, that $\mathscr{E}$ is a finite-dimensional manifold. A simple strategy for showing that almost every economy in $\mathscr{E}$ is well-behaved consists of introducing a manifold M of the same dimension as $\mathscr{E}$, and a continuously differentiable function T from M to $\mathscr{E}$ such that a *regular* economy, defined as a regular value of T,

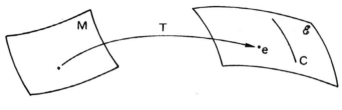

Figure 4

actually has properties (b) and (c) (see Figure 4). Sard's theorem implies that the set C of critical economies has measure zero.

To give an even more specific illustration, we consider an exchange economy with l commodities, m consumers, and fixed demand functions. Therefore the parameters of the economy are the initial holdings of each commodity by each consumer, a list e of lm positive numbers. We denote by $\mathscr{E}$ the set of those lm lists, and we observe for later use that the dimension of $\mathscr{E}$ is lm. The state of the economy is taken to be the price-system, i.e., a list p of l positive numbers. Since multiplying all prices by the same positive number does not affect the behavior of the agents, we can normalize the price-system and restrict it to belong to a manifold S, such that dim $S = l - 1$, for instance S may be the positive part of the unit sphere in the l-dimensional Euclidean space. Given the economy e and the price-system p, we write the l-list of the excesses of demand over supply on every market as $F(e, p)$, a vector in the l-dimensional space R^l. The price-system p is an equilibrium state if and only if

$$F(e, p) = 0. \tag{1}$$

Given e, the set of p satisfying (1) is $E(e)$. However, the excess demand function F obeys Walras' law. Namely for every e and p, the value of the excess demand equals 0; i.e., $p \cdot F(e, p) = 0$. Consequently the equilibrium condition (1) is equivalent to equating to O the list $\hat{F}$ of the first $l - 1$ components of F,

$$\hat{F}(e, p) = 0. \tag{2}$$

Now if the individual demand functions are continuously differentiable, we can follow the strategy we have outlined above in several ways. An elementary treatment that does not use the concept of a manifold can be given as in Debreu (1970, pp. 387–392). An alternative, and more satisfactory, solution takes as a central concept the set M of pairs (e, p) in the Cartesian product $\mathscr{E} \times S$ satisfying (2) [Stephen Smale (1974, pp. 1–14), Y. Balasko (1975, pp. 95–118)]. The space $\mathscr{E} \times S$ is of dimension $lm +$

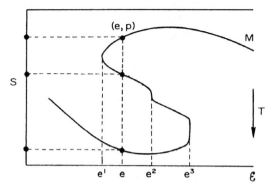

Figure 5

$l - 1$, and the equilibrium condition (2) imposes $(l - 1)$ restrictions on the pair (e, p). Therefore one may expect M to be a manifold of dimension lm, i.e., of the same dimension as $\mathscr{E}$. Indeed this is easily shown to be the case The function T from the *equilibrium manifold* M to $\mathscr{E}$ could hardly be simpler; it is the transformation $(e, p) \mapsto e$, i.e., the projection from M into $\mathscr{E}$. A regular economy is then defined as a regular value of T. Equivalently e is a regular economy if for every (e, p) in M projecting into e, the projection of the tangent space of M at (e, p) covers $\mathscr{E}$. Three critical economies e^1, e^2, e^3 are displayed on Figure 5. Sard's theorem yields the conclusion that (a) the set C of critical economies has measure zero.

Given a regular economy e in $\mathscr{E}$ (as on Figure 5), one obtains the set $E(e)$ of equilibrium price-systems p by taking in M the set $T^{-1}(e)$ of inverse images of e by the projection T, and by projecting $T^{-1}(e)$ into S. At every point of $T^{-1}(e)$, the determinant of the Jacobian of T is different from 0, and a direct application of the inverse function theorem yields that $T^{-1}(e)$ is a discrete subset of M. The pathologies associated with critical economies are made clear by Figure 5. For instance, the economy e^1 has a discrete set of (two) equilibria, but a continuous displacement of the economy in a neighborhood of e^1 produces at e^1 a sudden change in the set of equilibria. In particular, consider e on the right of e^1 and the associated equilibrium p on the upper branch of M (as on Figure 5). When e moves left, follow p by continuity. As e crosses e^1, the equilibrium state of the system jumps to the lower branch of M. The economy e^3 has a continuum of equilibria and an isolated equilibrium. At the point e^3 one also observes a sudden change in the set of equilibria for a continuous displacement of the economy in a neighborhood of e^3. Although the economy e^2 is critical, it has a discrete set of (three) equilibria, and in a neighborhood of e^3, the set of equilibria depends continuously on the economy.

One can obtain considerably stronger conclusions by making suitable assumptions on the behavior of the excess demand function F near the boundary of S. For instance, assume that given e, the excess demand $F(e, p)$ is unbounded when the price of a commodity tends to zero. In this case the set C of critical economies is *closed* in addition to being of measure zero, and is therefore negligible in a strong sense. Moreover (b') every regular economy has a *finite* set of equilibria, and (c') in a neighborhood of a regular economy, the set of equilibria depends in a *continuously differentiable* manner on the economy.

Property (c'), which strengthens property (c) of continuous dependence of the set of equilibria $E(e)$ on the economy e, has made it possible to answer the question of the rate of convergence of the core of an economy. Many authors from Edgeworth to W. Hildenbrand have shown with increasing generality that the core and the set of Walras equilibria of an economy tend toward each other as the number of agents increases in such a way that every one of them becomes insignificant. This precise formulation of the idea that an economy tends to become more competitive under these conditions raises the question of the rate of that convergence. A conjecture of Shapley (1975, pp. 345–351) has led to the proof (Debreu, 1975, pp. 1–7; B. Grodal, 1975, pp. 171–186) that outside the negligible critical set, the core and the set of Walras equilibria converge to each other at least as fast as the reciprocal of the number of agents converges to zero.

The results on negligible sets of critical economies that we have presented have been considerably extended by Balasko, Chichilnisky, Delbaen, E. and H. Dierker, Fuchs, K. Hildenbrand, Ichiishi, Kalman, Laroque, Mas-Colell, Mitiagin, Rader, Schecter, Smale, and Varian. In particular, the demand functions of the consumers, which we assumed to be fixed, have been treated as variables; economies with many agents, or with many commodities have been taken into account; production has been introduced into the model; demand functions have been replaced as primitive concepts by utility functions or by preference relations, neither of which are restricted to satisfy convexity assumptions. However in most of these extensions the description of the economy requires infinitely many real parameters, i.e., the dimension of the space $\mathscr{E}$ of economies is infinite, and it is no longer possible to use the previous measure theoretical definition of a negligible set. One can now prove only that in the space $\mathscr{E}$, the critical economies form a *closed subset C whose interior is empty*.

The introduction of differential topology into economic theory has made necessary a reexamination of several classical problems, for instance, that of differentiable preference relations. In particular, Smale has played a leading role in extending, simplifying, and making more rigorous the study of the set of Pareto optima, and of dynamic processes converging to that set, a program of research in which de Melo, Ong, Simon, Titus, and Y. H. Wan have participated. But of special importance among the applications of Global Analysis to economics has been Smale's recent work on Global Newton Methods where he gives a differential analog of the Scarf–Eaves algorithm for the computation of an economic equilibrium, unifying their approach with the traditional dynamic economic processes of Samuelson, and of Arrow, Block, and Hurwicz.

References

Note: These references include a bibliograhy of published work on the applications of differential topology to economics that is intended to be complete.

K. J. Arrow and L. Hurwicz, On the Stability of the Competitive Equilibrium, I, *Econometrica*, 1958, **26**, 522–52.

K. J. Arrow, H. D. Block and L. Hurwicz, On the Stability of the Competitive Equilibrium, II, *Econometrica*, 1959, **27**, 82–109.

K. J. Arrow and F. H. Hahn, *General Competitive Analysis*, San Francisco 1971.

Y. Balasko, Some Results on Uniqueness and on Stability of Equilibrium in General Equilibrium Theory, *J. Math. Econ.*, 1975, **2**, 95–118.

Y. Balasko, The Graph of the Walras Correspondence, *Econometrica*, 1975, **43**, 907–12.

G. Debreu, Economies with a Finite Set of Equilibria, *Econometrica*, 1970, **38**, 387–92.

G. Debreu, Smooth Preferences, *Econometrica*, 1972, **40**, 603–15.

G. Debreu, Four Aspects of the Mathematical Theory of Economic Equilibrium, *Proceedings of the International Congress of Mathematicians, Vancouver*, 1974, 65–77.

G. Debreu, The Rate of Convergence of the Core of an Economy, *J. Math. Econ.*, 1975, **2**, 1–7.

E. Dierker, Two Remarks on the Number of Equilibria of an Economy, *Econometrica*, 1972, **40**, 951–53.

E. Dierker, *Topological Methods in Walrasian Economics*, Lecture Notes in Economics and Mathematical Systems, **92,** Berlin, 1974.

E. Dierker and H. Dierker, The Local Uniqueness of Equilibria, *Econometrica*, 1972, **40**, 867–81.

H. Dierker, Smooth Preferences and the Regularity of Equilibria, *J. Math. Econ.*, 1975, **2**, 43–62.

H. Dierker, Equilibria and Core of Large Economies, *J. Math. Econ.*, 1975, **2**, 155–69.

I. Ekeland, Topologie Différentielle et Théorie des Jeux, *Topology*, 1974, **13**, 375–88.

G. Fuchs, Private Ownership Economies with a Finite Number of Equilibria, *J. Math. Econ.*, 1974, **1**, 141–58.

G. Fuchs, Structural Stability for Dynamical Economic Systems, *J. Math. Econ.*, 1975, **2**, 139–54.

G. Fuchs and G. Laroque, Continuity of Equilibria for Economies with Vanishing External Effects, *J. Econ. Theory*, 1974, **9**, 1–22.

B. Grodal, The Rate of Convergence of the Core for a Purely Competitive Sequence of Economies, *J. Math. Econ.*, 1975, **2**, 171–86.

J. Grote, A Global Theory of Games 1, *J. Math. Econ.*, 1974, **1**, 223–35.

J. Harsanyi, Games with Randomly Disturbed Payoffs: A New Rationale for Mixed-Strategy Equilibrium Points, *Int. J. Game Theory*, 1973, **2**, 1–23.

J. Harsanyi, Oddness of the Number of Equilibrium Points: A New Proof, *Int. J. Game Theory*, 1973, **2**, 235–50.

K. Hildenbrand, Continuity of the Equilibrium-Set Correspondence, *J. Econ. Theory*, 1972, **5**, 152–62.

K. Hildenbrand, Finiteness of II (𝓔) and Continuity of II, Appendix to Ch. 2 in W. Hildenbrand, *Core and Equilibria of a Large Economy*, Princeton, 1974.

A. Mas-Colell, A Note on a Theorem of F. Browder, *Math. Programming*, 1974, **6**, 229–33.

A. Mas-Colell, On the Continuity of Equilibrium Prices in Constant-Returns Production Economies, *J. Math. Econ.*, 1975, **2**, 21–33.

W. de Melo, Optimization of Several Functions, in *Dynamical Systems–Warwick 1974*, Lecture Notes in Mathematics, 468, A. Dold and B. Eckmann, eds., Springer-Verlag, Berlin, 1975.

B. Mitiagin, Notes on Mathematical Economics, *Uspehi Matematičeskih Nauk*, 1972, **27**, 3–19, translated in *Russian Mathematical Surveys*.

J. von Neumann, Zur Theorie der Gesellschaftsspiele, *Mathematische Annalen*, 1928, **100**, 295–320, translated in *Contributions to the Theory of Games IV*, A. W. Tucker and R. D. Luce, eds., Princeton, 1959.

J. von Neumann, Über ein ökonomisches Gleichungs-system und eine Verall-gemeinerung des Brouwerschen Fixpunktsatzes, *Ergebnisse eines mathematischen Kolloquiums*, 1937, No. 8, 73–83, translated in *Rev. Econ. Studies*, 1945, **13**, 1–9.

J. T. Rader, *Theory of General Economic Equilibrium*, New York, 1972, 182–201.

J. T. Rader, Absolutely Continuous Constrained Maximizers, *J. Optimization Theory and Applications*, 1973, **12**, 107–28.

J. T. Rader, Nice Demand Functions, *Econometrica*, 1973, **41**, 913–35.

R. Saigal and C. Simon, Generic Properties of the Complementarity Problem, *Math. Programming*, 1973, **4**, 324–35.

P. A. Samuelson, The Stability of Equilibrium: Comparative Statics and Dynamics, *Econometrica*, 1941, **9**, 97–120.

P. A. Samuelson, *Foundations of Economic Analysis*, Harvard University Press, Cambridge, Mass, 1947.

A. Sard, The Measure of the Critical Points of Differentiable Maps, *Bull. of the Amer. Math. Soc.*, 1942, **48**, 883–90.

H. Scarf, *The Computation of Economic Equilibria*, Yale University Press, New Haven, 1973.

L. S. Shapley, An Example of a Slow-Converging Core, *Int. Econ. Rev.*, 1975, **16**, 345–51.

C. P. Simon and C. Titus, Characterization of Optima in Smooth Pareto Economic Systems, *J. Math. Econ.*, 1975, **2**, 297–330.

S. Smale, Global Analysis and Economics I, in *Dynamical Systems*, M. Peixoto, ed., Academic Press, New York, 1973.

S. Smale, Global Analysis and Economics IIA, *J. Math. Econ.*, 1974, **1**, 1–14.

S. Smale, Global Analysis and Economics III, *J. Math. Econ.*, 1974, **1**, 107–17.

S. Smale, Global Analysis and Economics IV, *J. Math. Econ.*, 1974, **1**, 119–27.

S. Smale, Global Analysis and Economics V, *J. Math. Econ.*, 1974, **1**, 213–21.

S. Smale, Optimizing Several Functions, in *Manifolds-Tokyo, 1973*, Akio Hattori, ed., Tokyo, 1975.

S. Smale, Sufficient Conditions for an Optimum, in *Dynamical Systems-Warwick 1974*, Lecture Notes in Mathematics, **468**, A. Dold and B. Eckmann, eds., Springer-Verlag, Berlin, 1975.

S. Smale, An approach to the Analysis of Dynamic Processes in Economic Systems, in *Equilibrium and Disequilibrium in Economic Theory*, G. Schwödiauer, ed., Reidel, Boston, 1975.

D. Sondermann, Smoothing Demand by Aggregation, *J. Math. Econ.*, 1975, **2**, 201–23.

R. Thom, *Stabilité Structurelle et Morphogénèse*, Reading 1972, translated as *Structural Stability and Morphogenesis*, Benjamin, Reading, 1975.

H. R. Varian, On Persistent Disequilibrium, *J. Econ. Theory*, 1975, **10**, 218–28.

H. R. Varian, A Third Remark on the Number of Equilibria of an Economy, *Econometrica*, 1975, **43**, 985–86.

A. Wald, Über einige Gleichungssyteme der mathematischen Ökonomie, *Zeitschrift für National Ökonomie*, 1936, **7**, 637–70, translated in *Econometrica*, 1951, **19**, 368–403.

Y. H. Wan, On Local Pareto Optima, *J. Math. Econ.*, 1975, **2**, 35–42.

E. C. Zeeman, On the Unstable Behavior of Stock Exchanges, *J. Math. Econ.*, 1974, **1**, 39–49.

CHAPTER 20

Least concave utility functions

1   Introduction

The question of the representation of a convex preference preorder by a concave utility function was first raised and answered by de Finetti (1949), and further studied by Fenchel (1953, 1956), Moulin (1974), and by Kannai in the forthcoming article "Concavifiability and constructions of concave utility functions" which also discusses the problem of least concave utility functions. To illustrate the value of such a concave representation by one example, we consider an exchange economy $\mathscr{E}$ whose consumers have convex preferences, and, following Scarf (1967), we associate with the economy $\mathscr{E}$ a game without side payments in coalition form. If the preferences of each consumer are represented by a concave utility function, then the characteristic set of utility vectors of each coalition is convex, as in the original definition of Aumann–Peleg (1960). The convexity of these characteristic sets permits, for instance, a simplification [Scarf (1965) and Ekeland (1974); see also the related article of Shapley (1969)] of the proof of the non-emptiness of the core of Scarf (1967).

Recently, Kannai (1974) and Mas-Colell (1974) have taken an alternative approach to the preceding representation problem, and given conditions under which a convex preorder can be approximated by convex preorders representable by concave functions. Whatever the approach, as soon as one has a concave representation of a convex preorder, one is led to ask, as de Finetti (1949) does, whether there is a least concave representation. This is

The research on which this note reports was made possible by a grant of the National Science Foundation, whose support is gratefully acknowledged.

242

the question to which the present note is addressed. Its viewpoint differs from de Finetti's in that he obtains a least concave utility in the process of deriving conditions ensuring the existence of a concave utility, whereas we assume that a concave representation of the preorder is known to exist, and we show that there is least concave representation. We also dispense with the hypothesis that the preorder has a least and a greatest element.

2 Existence of a least concave representation

Let X be a convex set in a real topological vector space E, and $\leqslant$ be a complete preorder on X. We say that a real-valued function u on X represents $\leqslant$ if $[x \leqslant y]$ is equivalent to $[u(x) \leq u(y)]$, and we denote by U *the set of continuous, concave, real-valued functions on X representing $\leqslant$.* The set U is preordered by the relation "*v is more concave than u*" defined by "there is a real-valued, concave function f on $u(X)$ such that $v = f \circ u$." This definition is meaningful since $u(X)$ is an interval. The function f is strictly increasing; it is also continuous since it maps the interval $u(X)$ onto the interval $v(X)$. Finally, the relation "is more concave than" is indeed a preorder (reflexivity is obvious; transitivity nearly obvious). The main result of this note is the following

Theorem

If U is not empty, then U has a least element.

We observe that if u is more concave than v, and v is more concave than u, then u is derived from v by an increasing linear transformation from R to R (henceforth abbreviated as i.l.t.). The proof is trivial. $u = f \circ v$ and $v = f^{-1} \circ u$, where both f and f^{-1} are concave. Consequently, f is linear.

As a consequence of this observation, we note that if u and v are two least elements of U, then one is derived from the other by an i.l.t. Thus if a preference preorder is representable by a continuous, concave, real-valued utility function, then a least concave utility representing the preorder (whose existence is asserted by the theorem) is yet another instance of a cardinal utility.

The cardinal utility so obtained has an interpretation in the context of decision-making under uncertainty. Let X be an open convex set of commodity vectors in E, and let $\mathscr{P}$ be the set of probabilities on X. We identify each element x of X with the probability having $\{x\}$ as support. Now consider a risk-averse agent who preorders $\mathscr{P}$ by his preferences, and who satisfies the axioms of Blackwell–Girshick (1954, ch. 4).[1] This agent has a bounded von Neumann–Morgenstern utility v whose restriction v to X is a concave, real-valued function representing the restriction $\preccurlyeq$ to X of his preferences on $\mathscr{P}$. Since v is bounded, v is continuous [Bourbaki (1966, ch. 2, sect. 2.10)]. Therefore there is, by the theorem, a least concave, continuous, real-valued utility u on X representing $\preccurlyeq$, and one has $v = f \circ u$, where f is concave. Thus, in this situation, one can separate the preferences of the decision-maker for the commodity vectors in X represented by u, from his attitude toward risk described by the strictly increasing, continuous, concave function f from $u(X)$ to R.[2]

Returning to the statement of the theorem, and assuming in the remainder of this section that E *is a Banach space*, we ask whether the presence of a differentiable function in U implies that a least element of U is differentiable. An answer is given by the following proposition which is closely related to Lemma 1 in the forthcoming article "Differentiable value functions in concave dynamic optimization problems" by L. M. Benveniste and J. A. Scheinkman:

Proposition

Let x be an interior point of X that is not a greatest element of X. If there is an element of U that is C^1 at x, then a least element of U is C^1 at x.

Proof. Let v be an element of U that is C^1 at x, and u be a least element of U. By the theorem, $v = f \circ u$ where f is continuous, concave, and strictly increasing. Thus $u = f^{-1} \circ v$, where f^{-1} is continuous, convex, and strictly increasing. It suffices to prove that f^{-1} is C^1 at $v(x)$.

By assumption there is z in X such that $v(x) < v(z)$. Select y in X different from x, such that x belongs to the straight line segment $\overline{y, z}$ connecting y and z, and close enough to x for $v(y) < v(z)$ to hold. By concavity of v, one has $v(y) < v(x)$. Now on $[0, 1]$ define the function $\bar{v}$ by $\bar{v}(t) = v[(1 - t)y + tz]$, and similarly the

---

[1] The importance of the assumption of risk-aversion in the analysis of equilibrium with exogenous uncertain events was first noted by Arrow (1953). As Shubik (1975) remarked, that assumption is no less important in the analysis of equilibrium without exogenous uncertainty since, given a Walras allocation obtained in this framework in the absence of all uncertainty, risk-loving agents "would create markets for lotteries," and thereby attain a Pareto-superior state.

[2] In the context of this paragraph, the relation "more concave than" was interpreted as "more risk-averse than" by Pratt (1964) [resp. Kihlstrom–Mirman (1974)] in the case of utility functions defined on a convex subset of R [resp. R^n].

function $\bar{u}$ by $\bar{u}(t) = u[(1 - t)y + tz]$. Let also ξ be such that $x = (1 - \xi)y + \xi z$, and denote by g the restriction of f^{-1} to $v(\overline{y, z})$. One has $\bar{u} = g \circ \bar{v}$. Moreover, $\bar{v}(\xi) < \bar{v}(1)$ implies $\bar{v}'(\xi) > 0$ by concavity of $\bar{v}$. As we noted, $v(x)$ is interior to the interval $v(\overline{y, z})$. Denote by d_+ (resp. d_-) the right (resp. left) derivative of g at $\bar{v}(\xi)$. One has $\bar{u}'_+(\xi) = d_+\bar{v}'(\xi)$, and $\bar{u}'_-(\xi) = d_-\bar{v}'(\xi)$. However, by concavity of $\bar{u}$, $\bar{u}'_+(\xi) \leq \bar{u}'_-(\xi)$. Hence $d_+ \leq d_-$. But g is convex. Therefore $d_+ = d_-$, and g is C^1 at $\bar{v}(\xi)$.

3   Proof of the theorem

We assume that U is not empty, and exclude the trivial case in which all the elements of X are equivalent to each other.

Given an element y of X, we denote by $[y, \rightarrow[$ the set $\{x \in X | y \preceq x\}$; and given two elements y, z of X such that $y \preceq z$, we denote by $[y, z]$ the set $\{x \in X | y \preceq x \preceq z\}$.

Consider now two elements y, z of X such that $y \prec z$, and let $V(y, z)$ be the set of continuous, concave, real-valued functions v on $[y, \rightarrow[$ representing $\preceq$ on $[y, z]$, and such that $v(y) = 0$; $v(z) = 1$; $v(x) \geq 1$ for x in $[z, \rightarrow[$. This definition is meaningful since the set $[y, \rightarrow[$ is convex. Note also that if w is an element of U, then one easily obtains an element of $V(y, z)$ by making an i.l.t. T on w such that $\hat{w} = T \circ w$ satisfies $\hat{w}(y) = 0$, and $\hat{w}(z) = 1$, and by taking the restriction of $\hat{w}$ to $[y, \rightarrow[$. Thus $V(y, z)$ is not empty.

The initial step in the construction of a least element of U consists of defining for every x in $[y, \rightarrow[$,

$$u_{y,z}(x) = \inf_{v \in V(y,z)} v(x).$$

We prove that:

(1) $u_{y,z}$ is an element of $V(y, z)$.

Clearly, $u_{y,z}$ is a concave, real-valued function on $[y, \rightarrow[$ satisfying $u_{y,z}(y) = 0$, and $u_{y,z}(z) = 1$. Actually, $u_{y,z}(x) = 1$ for every x in $[z, \rightarrow[$. To see this, observe that if v is an element of $V(y, z)$, then the function $\hat{v}$ defined by "for x in $[y, z]$, $\hat{v}(x) = v(x)$; for x in $[z, \rightarrow[$, $\hat{v}(x) = 1$" also is. Thus there remains to show (a) that $u_{y,z}$ represents $\preceq$ on $[y, z]$ and (b) that $u_{y,z}$ is continuous.

(a) $u_{y,z}$ represents $\preceq$ on $[y, z]$. Let p, q be two points of $[y, z]$. Clearly, $p \sim q$ implies $u_{y,z}(p) = u_{yz}(q)$. We must prove that $y \preceq p \prec q \preceq z$ implies $u_{y,z}(p) < u_{y,z}(q)$. Note first that for any v in $V(y, z)$, one has $u_{y,z}(p) \leq v(p) < 1$. Since $\preceq$ is representable by a continuous real-valued function on

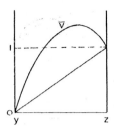

Figure 1

X, there is q' in the segment $\overline{p,z}$ such that $q' \sim q$. Concavity of $u_{y,z}$, $u_{y,z}(p) < 1$, and $u_{y,z}(z) = 1$ imply $u_{y,z}(p) < u_{y,z}(q')$ (see Figure 1).

(b) $u_{y,z}$ *is continuous.* The range of $u_{y,z}$, which is contained in $[0, 1]$, is actually equal to $[0, 1]$. To see this, it suffices to show that the range of $\bar{u}_{y,z}$, the restriction of $u_{y,z}$ to segment $\overline{y,z}$ is $[0, 1]$. Let v be an element of $V(y, z)$, and $\bar{v}$ be its restriction to $\overline{y,z}$. In the Cartesian product $\overline{y,z} \times R$ the graph of $\bar{u}_{y,z}$ is between the graph of $\bar{v}$ and the straight line segment connecting $(y, 0)$ and $(z, 1)$. Thus concavity of $\bar{u}_{y,z}$ and continuity of $\bar{v}$ imply that $\bar{u}_{y,z}$ is continuous on $\overline{y,z}$. Therefore its range is $[0, 1]$. Now let c be an element of $[0, 1]$. There is an element x of $[y, z]$ such that $u_{y,z}(x) = c$. By (a), the inverse image of the closed half-line $[c, +\infty[$ by $u_{y,z}$ is the set $[x, \rightarrow[$, which is closed in X since $\leqslant$ is representable by a continuous real-valued function on X. Similarly, the inversely image of $]-\infty, c]$ by $u_{y,z}$ is closed in X. This establishes the continuity of $u_{y,z}$.

The next step in the construction is the proof that:

(2) If $y \leqslant y' < z' \leqslant z$, then on $[y', z']$, $u_{y',z'}$ is derived from $u_{y,z}$ by an i.l.t.

(a) *The case in which* $z' = z$. Let T be the i.l.t. such that $\hat{v} = T \circ u_{y',z'}$ satisfies $\hat{v}(y') = u_{y,z}(y')$ and $\hat{v}(z') = u_{y,z}(z')$. Thus $T(1) = 1$. Clearly, the restriction of $T^{-1} \circ u_{y,z}$ to $[y', \rightarrow[$ belongs to $V(y', z')$. Therefore, because of the minimality of $u_{y',z'}$ one has $u_{y',z'}(x) \leqq T^{-1} \circ u_{y,z}(x)$ for x in $[y', \rightarrow[$. Hence,

$$\hat{v}(x) \leqq u_{y,z}(x), \qquad \text{for } x \text{ in } [y', \rightarrow[.$$

Now define the real-valued function v on $[y, \rightarrow[$ as follows:

$$v(x) = \hat{v}(x), \qquad \text{for } x \text{ in } [y', \rightarrow[,$$
$$v(x) = u_{y,z}(x), \qquad \text{for } x \text{ in } [y, y'].$$

We claim that v belongs to $V(y, z)$. Clearly, v is a real-valued function representing $\leqslant$ on $[y, z]$, satisfying $v(y) = 0$, and $v(x) = 1$ for x in $[z, \rightarrow[$.

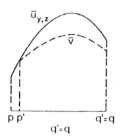

Figure 2

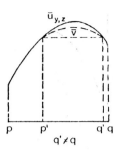

Figure 3

Moreover, the range of v is $[0, 1]$. Hence, by the argument used above, v is continuous. There remains to prove that v is concave, or equivalently, that for any pair (p, q) of points of X such that $y \leqslant p \leqslant q$ and $p \neq q$, the restriction $\bar{v}$ of v to the segment $\overline{p, q}$ is concave.

To this end, consider the set $\{x \in \overline{p,q} \mid y' \leqslant x\}$. If not empty, this set is a segment $\overline{p',q'}$ where the two extremities are named in such a way that p' is between p and q. Denote also by $\bar{u}_{y,z}$ the restriction of $u_{y,z}$ to $\overline{p,q}$. Aside from the two trivial cases

   (i) $p' = q'$,

and

   (ii) $p' = p$

(which implies $q' = q$), one has two possible situations which are presented in Figures 2 and 3. In either situation, the conclusion follows from:

> *Remark.* Given three numbers $a < b < c$, f a concave, real-valued function on $[a,b]$, g a concave, real-valued function on $[b,c]$ such that $f(b) = g(b)$. Then the real-valued function h on $[a,c]$ that coincides with f on $[a,b]$, and with g on $[b,c]$, is concave if and only if $g'_+(b) \leq f'_-(b)$.

This last condition is obviously satisfied at p' in Figure 2 and at p' and q' in Figure 3, since for every x in $\overline{p', q'}$, one has $\bar{v}(x) \leq \bar{u}_{y,z}(x)$.

Summing up, v belongs to $V(y, z)$. However, the minimality of $u_{y,z}$ implies that for every x in $[y, \rightarrow[$, one has $u_{y,z}(x) \leq v(x)$. Thus $u_{y,z}$ and $\hat{v}$ coincide in $[y', z']$.

(b) *The case in which* $y' = y$. The proof is entirely similar to that for case (a). Let again T be the i.l.t. such that $\hat{v} = T \circ u_{y',z'}$ satisfies $\hat{v}(y') = u_{y,z}(y')$ and $\hat{v}(z') = u_{y,z}(z')$. Thus $T(0) = 0$. Clearly, $T^{-1} \circ u_{y,z}$ belongs to $V(y',z')$.

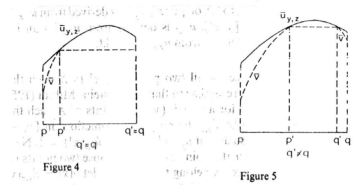

Figure 4

Figure 5

Therefore, because of the minimality of $u_{y',z'}$, one has $u_{y',z'}(x) \leq T^{-1} \circ u_{y,z}(x)$ for x in $[y, \rightarrow[$. Hence,

$$\hat{v}(x) \leq u_{y,z}(x), \qquad \text{for } x \text{ in } [y, \rightarrow[.$$

Now define the real-valued function v on $[y, \rightarrow[$ as follows:

$$v(x) = \hat{v}(x), \qquad \text{for } x \text{ in } [y, z'],$$
$$v(x) = u_{y,z}(x), \qquad \text{for } x \text{ in } [z', \rightarrow[.$$

We claim that v belongs to $V(y, z)$. Clearly, v is a real-valued function representing $\leqslant$ on $[y, z]$, satisfying $v(y) = 0$, and $v(x) = 1$ for x in $[z, \rightarrow[$. Moreover, the range of v is $[0, 1]$. Hence, by a now familiar argument, v is continuous. There remains to prove that v is concave, or equivalently, that for any pair (p, q) of points of X such that $y \leqslant p \leqslant q$ and $p \neq q$, the restriction $\bar{v}$ of v to the segment $\overline{p, q}$ is concave.

To this end, consider the set $\{x \in \overline{p, q} \mid z' \leqslant x\}$. If not empty, this set is a segment $\overline{p', q'}$ where the two extremities are named in such a way that p' is between p and q'. Denote also by $\bar{u}_{y,z}$ the restriction of $u_{y,z}$ to $\overline{p, q}$. Aside from the two trivial cases

(i) $p' = q'$,

and

(ii) $p' = p$

(which implies $q' = q$), one has the two possible situations presented in Figures 4 and 5.

In either situation, the conclusion follows from the preceding *Remark* whose last condition is obviously satisfied at p' in Figure 4 and at p' and q' in Figure 5, since for every x outside of $\overline{p', q'}$, one has $\bar{v}(x) \leq \bar{u}_{y,z}(x)$.

Summing up, v belongs to $V(y, z)$. However, the minimality of $u_{y,z}$ implies that for every x in $[y, \rightarrow[$, one has $u_{y,z}(x) \leq v(x)$.

Thus $u_{y,z}$ and $\hat{v}$ coincide in $[y', z']$.

(c) *The general case.* According to (a), on $[y', z']$, $u_{y',z'}$ is derived from $u_{y,z'}$ by an i.l.t. According to (b), on $[y, z']$, $u_{y,z'}$ is derived from $u_{y,z}$ by an i.l.t. Therefore, on $[y', z']$, $u_{y',z'}$ is derived from $u_{y,z}$ by an i.l.t.

Construction of u. Select once for all two points x^0, x^1 in X such that $x^0 \prec x^1$. Following a procedure similar to that of Herstein–Milnor (1953) or Blackwell–Girshick (1954), for any pair (y, z) of points of X such that $y \preccurlyeq x^0 \prec x^1 \preccurlyeq z$, we denote by $\hat{u}_{y,z}$ the real-valued function on $[y, \to[$ obtained from $u_{y,z}$ by an i.l.t. such that $\hat{u}_{y,z}(x^0) = 0$ and $\hat{u}_{y,z}(x^1) = 1$. Next, in order to define the value of u at a point x of X, we choose two points y, z of X such that $y \preccurlyeq z$, and x^0, x^1, x belong to $[y, z]$. We let $u(x) = \hat{u}_{y,z}(x)$. This definition is independent of (y, z), for if (y', z') is another pair with the same properties, and $I = [y, z] \cap [y', z']$, then by (2), $\hat{u}_{y,z}$ and $\hat{u}_{y',z'}$ coincide on I. Clearly, u is a continuous, concave, real-valued function representing $\preccurlyeq$. We note for later reference:

(3)   If $y \prec z$, then on $[y, z]$, $u_{y,z}$ is derived from u by an i.l.t.

Select y', z' in X such that $y' \prec z'$, and y, z, x^0, x^1 belong to $[y', z']$. By (2), on $[y, z]$, $u_{y,z}$ is derived from $u_{y',z'}$ by an i.l.t. By the definition of u, on $[y', z']$, $u_{y',z'}$ is derived from u by an i.l.t.

u is a least element of U.

Let v be an arbitrary element of U. Since u and v both represent $\preccurlyeq$, there is a strictly increasing real-valued function f on $u(X)$ such that $v = f \circ u$. We must prove that f is concave.

If it were not, there would be t_1, t_2, t_3 in $u(X)$ such that $t_1 < t_2 < t_3$, and

$$f(t_2) < \frac{t_3 - t_2}{t_3 - t_1} f(t_1) + \frac{t_2 - t_1}{t_3 - t_1} f(t_3),$$

which is equivalent to

$$\frac{f(t_2) - f(t_1)}{f(t_3) - f(t_1)} < \frac{t_2 - t_1}{t_3 - t_1}.$$

Select y^i in X such that $u(y^i) = t_i (i = 1, 2, 3)$, and let $\hat{v}$ be derived from v by an i.l.t. such that $\hat{v}(y^1) = 0$, and $\hat{v}(y^3) = 1$.
  Thus

$$\hat{v}(y^2) = \frac{\hat{v}(y^2) - \hat{v}(y^1)}{\hat{v}(y^3) - \hat{v}(y^1)} = \frac{v(y^2) - v(y^1)}{v(y^3) - v(y^1)} = \frac{f(t^2) - f(t^1)}{f(t^3) - f(t^1)}.$$

On the other hand,

$$u_{y_1,y_3}(y^2) = \frac{u_{y^1,y^3}(y^2) - u_{y^1,y^3}(y^1)}{u_{y^1,y^3}(y^3) - u_{y^1,y^3}(y^1)} = \frac{u(y^2) - u(y^1)}{u(y^3) - u(y^1)} = \frac{t_2 - t_1}{t_3 - t_1},$$

where the second equility follows from (3). Hence, $\hat{v}(y^2) < u_{y_1,y_3}(y^2)$, a contradiction of the minimality of u_{y_1,y_3}.

References

Arrow, K. J., 1953, Le rôle des valeurs boursières pour la rèpartition la meilleure des risques, *Econométrie, Colloques Internationaux du Centre National de la Recherche Scientifique, Paris*, no. 40, 41–48. Translated in: 1964, The role of securities in the optimal allocation of risk-bearing, *Review of Economic Studies*, **31**, 91–96.

Aumann, R. J. and B. Peleg, 1960, Von Neumann–Morgenstern solutions to cooperative games without side payments, *Bulletin of the American Mathematical Society*, **66**, 173–179.

Blackwell, D. and M. A. Girshick, 1954, *Theory of games and statistical decisions* (Wiley, New York).

Bourbaki, N., 1966, *Espaces vectoriels topologiques*, 2d ed. (Hermann, Paris) chs. I and II.

Ekeland, I., 1974, *La théorie des jeux* (Presses Universitaires de France, Paris).

Fenchel, W., 1953, Convex cones, sets, and functions, mimeo. (Department of Mathematics, Princeton University, Princeton, N. J.).

Fenchel, W., 1956, Über konvexe Funktionen mit vorgeschriebenen Niveaumannigfaltigkeiten, *Mathematische Zeitschrift*, **63**, 496–506.

Finetti, B. de. 1949, Sulle stratificazioni convesse, *Annali di Matematica Pura ed Applicata*, **30**, Serie 4, 173–183.

Herstein, I. N. and J. Milnor, 1953, An axiomatic approach to measurable utility, *Econometrica*, 21, 291–297.

Kannai, Y., 1974, Approximation of convex preferences, *Journal of Mathematical Economics*, **1**, 101–106.

Kihlstrom, R. E. and L. J. Mirman, 1974, Risk aversion with many commodities, *Journal of Economic Theory*, 8, 361–388.

Mas-Colell, A., 1974, Continuous and smooth consumers: Approximation theorems, *Journal of Economic Theory*, **8**, 305–336.

Moulin, H., 1974, Representation d'un préordre convexe par une fonction d'utilité concave ou différentiable, *Comptes Rendus de l'Académie des Sciences, Paris*, Série A. 278, 483–485.

Pratt, J. W., 1964, Risk aversion in the small and in the large, *Econometrica*, **32**, 122–136.

Scarf, H., 1965, The core of an *N* person game, *Cowles Foundation Discussion Paper* no. 182.

Scarf, H., 1967, The core of an *N* person game, *Econometrica*, **35**, 50–69.

Shapley, L. S., 1969, Utility comparison and the theory of games, *La Décision, Colloques Internationaux du Centre National de la Recherche Scientifique, Paris*, no. 171, 251–263.

Shubik, M., 1975, Competitive equilibrium, the core, preferences for risk and insurance markets, *Economic Record* 51, 73–83.